DOMESTIC VIOLENCE SOURCE BOOK

A REFERENCE BOOK FOR VICTIMS, LAWYERS & THE COURTS OF NEW JERSEY

HOW TO PROTECT A VICTIM FROM DOMESTIC ABUSE

WHAT ARE THE DOMESTIC VIOLENCE LAWS AND WHO ARE PROTECTED BY THEM?

HOW, WHEN & WHERE TO FILE DOMESTIC VIOLENCE COMPLAINTS

EVERY CASE & STATUTE ON DOMESTIC VIOLENCE

ELLIOT H. GOURVITZ
ARI H. GOURVITZ
MELISSA GOURVITZ

Published by Gourvitz & Gourvitz, LLC
ISBN-13:
978-0692275511 (Gourvitz)
ISBN-10:
0692275517

TABLE OF CONTENTS

i

INTRODUCTION

Every day, 3 women die in the U.S., due to domestic violence, committed by a current or former male partner.[1] The number of women who have experienced physical violence, at the hands of a intimate partner in their lifetimes, is 38,028,000. The number of women in the U.S. who experience physical violence by an intimate partner ever year is 4,774,000.[2]

Women with disabilities are 40 percent more likely to experience intimate partner violence, especially severe violence, than women without disabilities.[3]

Each minute in the U.S., 20 people are victims of intimate partner violence.[4] In 2011, 1,509 women were murdered males they knew, 264 of these occurred during an argument. [5]

Black women are 35% more likely to experience intimate partner violence than a white woman.[6]

1 in 4 women (24.3%) and 1 in 7 men (13.8%) in the United States have been the victim of severe physical violence by an intimate partner in their lifetime.[7] Men who were victims of child maltreatment are three to four times more likely to perpetrate intimate partner violence.[8]

Women lose 8,000,000 days worth of paid work each year as a result of the abuse perpetrated against them by a current or former male partner. This is equivalent to the amount of days in 32,000 full time jobs.[9]

In addition, the number of mental health care visits attributable to domestic violence

---

[1] "Each day, 3 women die because of domestic violence." National Network to End Domestic Violence. (2014).

[2] "Prevalence and Characteristics of Sexual Violence, Stalking, and Intimate Partner Violence Victimization — National Intimate Partner and Sexual Violence Survey, United States, 2011." Center for Disease Control and Prevention. Matthew J. Breiding, PhD, Sharon G. Smith, PhD, Kathleen C. Basile, PhD, Mikel L. Walters, PhD, Jieru Chen, MS, Melissa T. Merrick, PhD. Center for Disease Control and Prevention. September 5, 2014.

[3] Intimate Partner Violence Facts and Resources. American Psychological Association, 2013.

[4] Center for Disease Control and Prevention. National Intimate Partner and Sexual Violence Survey (NISVS), NISVS Infographic, September 2014.

[5] "When Men Murder Women: An Analysis of 2011 Homicide Data. Females Murdered by Males in Single Victim/Single Offender Incidents." Violence Policy Center. September 2013.

[6] Bureau of Justice Statistics. 2001.

[7] http://www.cdc.gov/violenceprevention/pdf/cdc_nisvs_overview_insert_final-a.pdf

[8] "16 facts on violence against women," World Health Organization: Violence and Injury Prevention. WHO 2014.

[9] National Center for Injury Prevention and Control. *Costs of Intimate Partner Violence Against Women in the United States.* Atlanta (GA): Centers for Disease Control and Prevention; 2003.

each year is 18,500,000.[10] The average health care costs associated with each incident of domestic violence are estimated at $948 in cases where women were the victims and $387 in cases where men were the victims.[11]

Sexual assault or forced sex occurs in approximately 40-45% of battering relationships.[12] Every 9 seconds in the U.S., a woman is beaten or assaulted.[13]

2 out of 5 gay or bisexual men will experience domestic partner violence during their lifetime. Conversely, 50 percent of lesbian women will experience domestic violence (not necessarily intimate partner violence) in their lifetime.[14] 81% of women stalked by a current or former intimate partner are also physically assaulted by that partner.[15]

According to a recent study, access to firearms yields a more than five-fold increase in risk of intimate partner homicide when considering other factors of abuse, which suggests that abusers who possess guns tend to inflict the most severe abuse on their partners.[16]

98 percent of women in the U.S. experience financial abuse that occurs in domestic violence cases. The number one reason domestic violence survivors stay or return to the abusive relationship is because the abuser controls their money supply, leaving them with no financial resources to break free.[17]

Domestic Violence is the third leading cause of homelessness among families.[18]

A woman is 70 times more likely to be killed in the few weeks after leaving her abusive partner than at any other time in the relationship.[19]

10,000,000 children are exposed to domestic violence each year.[20]

---

[10] *Ibid.*

[11] http://www.cdc.gov/media/pressrel/r051025.htm

[12] *Campbell*, et al. (2003). "Assessing Risk Factors for Intimate Partner Homicide." Intimate Partner Homicide NIJ Journal, 250, 14-19. Washington, D.C.: National Institute of Justice, U.S. Department of Justice.

[13] http://domesticviolencestatistics.org/domestic-violence-statistics/.

[14] http://www.hope-eci.org/_documents/lgbt.pdf.

[15] http://www.americanbar.org/groups/domestic_violence/resources/statistics.html.

[16] Jacquelyn C. Campbell et al., *Risk Factors For Femicide in Abusive Relationships: Results From A Multi-Site Case Control Study, 93 Am. J. of Public Health 1089, 1092 (2003)*, abstract available at http://www.ajph.org/cgi/content/abstract/93/7/1089.

[17] http://money.usnews.com/money/blogs/my-money/2011/04/26/how-to-stop-domestic-financial-abuse.

[18] http://www.safehorizon.org/page/domestic-violence-statistics--facts-52.html.

[19] Domestic Violence Intervention Program. Myths & Facts about Domestic Violence. 2014.

See Appendix A: Shelters and Help for Battered Women

See Appendix B: Needs of the Battered Woman

See Appendix C: Continuum of Family Violence

ACTS OF DOMESTIC VIOLENCE

Domestic Violence encompasses many actions, including:

Sexual abuse: Compelling a partner to do, or participate in sexual acts, which they only consent to out of fear of displeasing their abuser, rather than a desire to participate.

Economic abuse: The abuser maintains complete control over money, and distributes it as they see fit, so the partner cannot manage finances or be financially independent. Another means of accomplishing this may be sabotaging the partners at work. This might entail disrupting the victim constantly in an effort to make them lose their job.

Psychological abuse (verbal battering): Telling a partner they are worthless and that they would have no social or economic status, if not for the abuser. In this situation the abuser tries to make the victim come to believe they are lucky to have the abuser as a mate.

Quizzically, a sexually abused child is not a "victim" under the Domestic Violence Act because they are not emancipated minors nor victims under the statute.[21] In addition, a mother cannot bring a domestic violence action on behalf of the child. One way around this type of prohibition would be to allege and prove that the sexual abuse, though itself not covered by the statute, was perpetrated by the abuser with the intent (of husband), to harm the mother, knowing it would greatly disturb her. In this situation the victim covered under the Act would be the mother.

Domestic Violence oftentimes does not consist of just one isolated incident, it involves a pattern of interactions, consisting of one or more of the above listed acts, over a period of time.

Victims and abusers of domestic violence are not limited to any race, gender, sexual orientation, religion, social-economic status, nationality, or culture. Doctors, lawyers, rich men, poor men, beggars and thieves cannot escape being either the abused or the abuser. Domestic violence is also not limited to relationships between married husbands and wives, or intimate partners. People living together, homosexual partners, and other non-traditional partners are now included in the definition of domestic victim and abusers.

---

[20] http://www.thecenteronline.org/learn-more/did-you-know.
[21] *M.A. v. E.A.,* 388 *N.J. Super.* 612, 909 *A.2d* 1168 (App. Div. 2006); *N.J.S.A.* 2C:25-19(d).

Domestic violence also encompasses acts against the elderly by family members, friends, or by care givers. Elder abuse takes many forms including physical abuse, emotional abuse, financial exploitation, neglect, abandonment and even sexual abuse. In 1997 there were 897 domestic violence assaults reported in New Jersey against elderly individuals 60 years of age or older. 264 of these victims were assaulted by their spouses, and in 72% of these assaults the wife was the victim.[22]

ABUSER

Individuals who abuse and batter their victims will often rationalize their behavior. They reason that they have no choice but to act as they do toward the partner, their partner "made them do it", or that they are acting to protect their partner's. Trivial occurrences such as burning supper, failing to balance the checkbook, not being home when required and spending "too much money," are all triggering devices, which can precipitate the abusers rage. The abuser projects their own frustration, and physically takes it out against their partner.

Oftentimes, the abuser is under the influence of drugs or alcohol. The abuser will frequently blame their behavior on drugs and alcohol, forgetting that they voluntarily took these substances, knowing how they cause them to act. While alcohol is not the cause of violence against women, there is a significant relationship between male perpetrator problem drinking and violence against intimate female partners. Studies suggest that severe alcohol problems increase the risk for lethal and violent victimization of women in violent intimate partner relationships. More than two-thirds of the homicide and attempted homicide offenders used alcohol, drugs, or both during the incident. [23]

When the victim shows they have had enough, abusers will discourage their partner from seeking legal counsel, stating that they can "work it out between themselves,' and that spending money on attorney is wasteful and would be better used for the children. The abuser also promises to "change."

This book is meant to aid the victims of domestic violence, as well as those that are wrongfully accused. This is a source book for individuals, the attorneys who represent the parties, and the Courts. This book includes all of the existing statutes, and relevant laws in the State of New Jersey on domestic violence. More importantly this is a step by step guide on how to seek relief under the Act, how to protect oneself, how to apply the law to their particular situation, and where to find professional help. See Appendix E Help for Abusers.

---

[22] New Jersey Department of Law and Public Safety, fifteenth annual domestic violence official report 11 (1997).

[23] Sharps, P., Campbell, J.C., Campbell, D., Gary, F., & Webster, D. (2003). Risky Mix: Drinking, Drug Use, and Homicide. In Intimate Partner Homicide, NIJ Journal, 250, 8-13. Washington, D.C.: National Institute of Justice, U.S. Dept. of Justice.)

As the law changes and develops on domestic violence, this book will adapt to those changes. As more resources become available, said sources will also be included.

ELLIOT H. GOURVITZ
ARI H. GOURVITZ
MELISSA GOURVITZ

CHAPTER ONE

JURISDICTION AND DEFINITION OF DOMESTIC VIOLENCE

1.1   JURISDICTION

New Jersey Superior Courts have jurisdiction over civil issues under the Domestic Violence Act, when both parties are residents of the Township or county, so long as the parties involved and the actions committed meet the requisites specified in the Domestic Violence Act. This is so even when the act of domestic violence has occurred outside the state of New Jersey. [24] The Courts have also extended protection to those non-residents of New Jersey, asserting personal jurisdiction over a defendant who committed an act of domestic violence in another State (New York/Mississippi), when the victim came to New Jersey for refuge. [25]

The statute does not expressly mandate that the act of domestic violence take place in the State of New Jersey; or "foreclose" the victim from proving at final hearing that the act of domestic violence was committed in another state, where the victim has not sought or obtained an order of protection from another state. [26]

As stated in *State v. Reyes*:

> Under *N.J.S.A.* 2C:25-28(a), a victim alleging the commission of an act of domestic violence can file a complaint and seek emergency *ex parte* relief. A plaintiff may apply for such relief in a court having jurisdiction over the place where the alleged act of domestic violence occurred, where the defendant resides, *or where the plaintiff resides or is sheltered,* and the court shall follow the same procedures applicable to other emergency applications. [27]

The questions of who is considered a victim and jurisdiction are intricately related.

---

[24] *Sperling v. Teplitsky*, 294 *N.J. Super.* 312, 683 *A.2d* 244 (Ch. Div. 1996).

[25] *A.R. v. M.R.*, 351 *N.J. Super.* 512, 799 *A.2d* 27 (App. Div. 2002); *State v. Reyes*, 172 *N.J.* 154, 796 *A.2d* 879 (2002)(Court has both personal and subject matter jurisdiction. In these cases, the courts asserted personal jurisdiction because although the initial act of domestic violence occurred out of state, the Defendants were trying to contact or harass the victims who were seeking refuge in New Jersey).

[26] *J.N. v. D.S.*, 300 *N.J. Super.* 647, 693 *A.2d* 571 (Ch. Div. 1996).

[27] *State v. Reyes*, 172 *N.J.* 154,160-161, 796 *A.2d* 879 (2002).

1.2   WHO QUALIFIES AS A VICTIM OF DOMESTIC VIOLENCE

The former Domestic Violence Statute[28] required that in order to qualify as a victim and have the protection of the statute, the "victim" would have had to "cohabit" with the defendant within the definition of the Act.

A "cohabitant" referred to emancipated minors, or persons 18 years of age or older, of the opposite sex, who reside together or who currently are residing in the same living quarters; persons who together are the parents of one or more children, regardless of their marital status or whether they have lived together at any time; or persons 18 years of age or older who are related by blood and who currently are residing in the same living quarters.[29]

An amendment to the Act deleted this definition of a victim and adopted the more general term "present or former household member." "Household" is not a word of art, and is a word of uncertain meaning, utilized in place of cohabitants.[30]

Under the Act a Victim can be:

Any person who is 18 years of age or older; an emancipated minor; or a person of any age who has had or expects to have a child in common with the actor; or a person of any age who is or was in a dating relationship with the actor.

And the actor is:

A.   A spouse or former spouse

B.   A person who is a present or former household member

C.   A person with whom the victim has a child in common (or is expecting child in common)

D.   A person with whom the victim has a dating relationship. If the actor is under 18, juvenile law applies.

---

[28] *N.J.S.A.* 2C:25-3 to 16 *L.* 1981 *c.* 426.

[29] *Hamilton v. Ali*, 350 *N.J. Super.* 479, 795 *A.2d* 929 (Ch. Div. 2001).

[30] *Desiato v. Abbott*, 261 *N.J. Super.* 30, 617 *A.2d* 678 (Ch. Div. 1992)(Residency and cohabitation are not a prerequisite); *Arents v. General Accidents Ins.*, 280 *N.J. Super.* 423, 655 *A.2d* 936 (App. Div. 1995)(noting person may be resident of more than one household for insurance purposes and different than domicile);*See also Senate Judiciary Committee, Statement to Senate No.* 2230 at 1 (Feb. 21, 1992).

E.   Someone under 18 years of age is considered an emancipated minor under the following conditions:

  i.   Marries
  ii.   Enters military service
  iii. Is pregnant with or has a child in common with the defendant/victim
  iv.   Is so declared by a court of law

The New Act contains no requirement that a household member be of the opposite sex, or related to the victim, as did the former Act. This amendment recognizes non-traditional relationships, where parties are living together and are unmarried, or are in same sex relationships. The amendment acknowledges that in these changing times, people whom are not related to each other, share apartments and houses for a variety of reasons including economic reasons.[31] "Household member" is a more comprehensive term than family, and most courts acknowledge that the term "family to itself is a variable and capable of different definitions depending on the context in which it is used."[32]

Another amendment to this part to the Act recognized that parties who did not share households together, but have or had a "dating relationship," might be victims and or perpetrators of domestic violence and included them within the Act. *(Note: Before the amendment to the Act, to qualify as a victim, those involved in a dating relationship were required to have more than a casual dating relationship, but less than the parties residing together to qualify under the Act.)*

Before the amendment to the Act, to qualify as a victim, those involved in a dating relationship were required to have more than a casual dating relationship, but less than the parties residing together to qualify under the Act.[33]

In the case of unemancipated minors and the Domestic Violence Act, if an unemancipated minor commits domestic violence, the remedy is to file a juvenile petition against them. If a minor has a domestic violence act committed against them, and does not qualify under the act, i.e. not pregnant with a child in common; not married; not involved in a dating relationship with a covered abuser; or is not in the military service, they do not have the protection of the Act.

---

[31] *See Maura Beth Johnson, Note, Home Sweet Home?: New Jersey's Prevention of Domestic Violence Act of 1991 "17 Seton Hall Legis. J.* 234 (1993).

[32] *Brokenbaugh v. N.J. Mfrs. Ins. Co.,* 158 *N.J. Super.* 424, 386 A.2d 433 (App. Div. 1978).

[33] *Desiato v. Abbott,* 261 *N.J. Super.* 30, 34, 617 A.2d 678 (Ch. Div. 1992).

A. A SPOUSE OR FORMER SPOUSE

Those currently or formerly married to each other are covered under the statute.

B. HOUSEHOLD MEMBER

1. Cases Where The Court Found The Victim Was Household Member

In *Desiato,* the court analyzed who is a "household member," and concluded that people who did not even live together in the household, but had a dating relationship, qualified for protection. The Court noted that the definition of a household member required, more than a casual dating relationship but less than the parties residing together. The Court stressed that the <u>decision of who is a household member has to be made on a case-by-case determination</u>, which is to be measured by the frequency of time the parties spent together and the context of one or more of the following criteria, which it gave by way of example and not limitation, in order to establish a "family-like setting" consistent with the Legislative declaration:

1. Consistency of the relationship;

2. Over-night stays at each other's residence;

3. Personal items such as jewelry, clothing and personal grooming effects stored at each other's residences;

4. Shared property arrangements, such as automobile usage, access to each other's bank accounts and one mailing address for billings or other legalese;

5. Familiarity with each other's siblings and parents socially in dining and/or entertainment activities together, and/or attendance together at extended family functions such as weddings.

While not every family dispute gives rise to abuse for the exercise of jurisdiction under the Act, it is the very nature of the party's former domestic relationship, which has creates the present *de facto* household relationship. Courts have stated that a determination as to a party's status as a "household member" must be based upon the qualities and characteristics of the particular relationship and not upon a mechanistic formula in a definition. The parties share, whether by choice or circumstance, a substantial integrated family relationship "where each house has a separate sleeping quarters but must interact on a frequent basis.

Courts have even found that where the defendant's living arrangement with plaintiff

4

was for a "temporary" three month period, the intention of the Act was not abrogated, and Plaintiff was in fact a member of the household at the time the violence. The court also stated it was not necessary to prove circumstances of the invitation to live together, or what the agreement to live together was; these factors are irrelevant to have protection under the Act.[34]

In 2006, the question arose as to whether a mother and a daughter that previously lived in the same house for almost 30 years, but no longer did, were subject to the Act. The Court answered in the affirmative, finding that the parties involved were both "present" and "former" "household members" that had to interact on a frequent basis. The court also found their relationship gave rise to a "special opportunity for abuse." Moreover, the Court set forth factors to consider whether jurisdiction lies in a former relationship case, which are as follows:[35]

(1)   The nature and duration of the prior relationship;

(2)   Whether the past domestic relationship provides a special opportunity for abuse and controlling behavior;

(3)   The passage of time since the end of the relationship;

(4)   The extent and nature of any intervening contacts;

(5)   The nature of the precipitating incident; and

(6)   The likelihood of ongoing contact or relationship.

In another similar case, the Court exercised jurisdiction for domestic violence involving former household members (adult siblings), even though the parties had not resided together for over 50 years. The court found that the harassment of plaintiff by defendant over the intervening decades, albeit sporadic, conferred jurisdiction to issue the FRO, considering the fact that the present incidents arose directly from the parties' acrimonious family relationship and their status as former household members.[36]

The defendant was a "household member" where he lived in the same household for a period of seven months with the plaintiff's family, although the adult male defendant was not in a traditional familial, romantic or sexual relationship with the adult male plaintiff.[37]

---

[34] *Bryant v. Burnett*, 264 *N.J. Super.* 222, 624 *A.2d* 584 (App. Div. 1993), *certif. den.*, 134 *N.J.* 478, 634 *A.2d* 525 (1993).

[35] *Coleman v. Romano*, 388 *N.J. Super.* 342, 908 *A.2d* 254 (Ch. Div. 2006).

[36] *N.G. v. J.P.*, 426 *N.J. Super.* 398, 45 *A.3d* 371 (App. Div. 2012).

[37] *S.Z. v. M.C.*, 417 *N.J. Super.* 622, 11 *A.3d* 404 (App. Div. 2011).

Boarders in a rooming house were also considered "household members," even though they had separate bedrooms and shared a bathroom and a kitchen. Their housing arrangement with shared common areas placed the victim in a more "susceptible position for abusive and controlling behavior in the hands of the perpetrator."[38] The court reviewed the five criteria that establish a family-like setting under the PDVA, and adopted the language and reasoning of *Desiato*, discussed *infra*.

The court has interpreted other non-traditional family situations as coming within the Act. In one instance, where the parties lived within the same apartment complex, defendant, father of victim's grandson, was in the victim's apartment visiting with the child at least three days a week. He was engaged to the victim's daughter, was included in the family functions, stayed overnight in the apartment when the victim was not home, and qualified as a member of the household.[39]

2. Cases Where The Court Found The Victim Was Not A Household Member, Or Where The Court Declined Jurisdiction

In *Jutchenko*[40], plaintiff and defendant were two adult brothers who did not live in the same household for 20 years. While rejecting jurisdiction in this case, the court did leave open the possibility of jurisdiction under the Act, if there could be a showing that the relationship had promised a "specific opportunity" for "abusive and controlling behavior," and that the domestic violence was something more than an isolated abhorrent event.

In another case, Defendant, the victim's ex-boyfriend, damaged a car owned by victim's current boyfriend, while the victim was in the car. The Defendant and the victim had dated approximately four to five years prior to the incident. While they dated, the two lived together. The Court found the two were not household members covered under the Act as there was no pattern of abuse, no threat of continuous violence, or evidence of controlling behavior, which is injurious to the victim.[41]

Similarly, the court declined jurisdiction for a domestic violence action by a daughter against her father, with whom she hadn't resided for the last 15 years, relying upon the rationale of Jutchenko. The court found that the Plaintiff's action against her father for physically assaulting her and fracturing her nose was better suited for a criminal complaint for assault and a separate civil action for personal injuries in the Superior Court, Law Division.[42]

---

[38] *S.P. v. Newark Police Dept*, 428 *N.J. Super.* 210, 52 *A.3d* 178 (App. Div. 2012).
[39] *South v. North*, 304 *N.J. Super.* 104, 698 *A.2d* 553 (Ch. Div. 1997). *Jutchenko v.*
[40] *Jutchenko*, 283 *N.J. Super.* 17, 660 *A.2d* 1267 (App. Div. 1995). *Sperling v.*
[41] *Teplitsky.*, 294 *N.J. Super.* 312, 683 *A.2d* 244 (Ch. Div. 1996). *Sisco v. Sisco,*
[42] 296 *N.J. Super.* 245, 686 *A.2d* 792 (Ch. Div. 1996).

Remedial measures under the act cannot be sought against a mother and father living in the same household as a Defendant, where they have not committed any covered wrongdoing. While the Court recognized that defendant's parents have become embroiled in the dispute between the two parties, the fact remains that no Complaint was ever filed against them and they are not victims or perpetrators under the Act. As a result the court modified a restraining order, which directly prohibited defendant's parents from having any contact with the plaintiff and her family.[43]

In another 2006 case, the court rejected a domestic violence claim brought by a mother on behalf of her unemancipated minor. The Appellate Division decided that a sexually abused minor stepchild was not "a victim" or a "protected person" under the Act. They noted in this instance the abused child was not over the age of 18, nor previously emancipated. Additionally, the mother had no standing to file a domestic violence complaint for her child. The court also held that the abuse of the child could not be shown to be perpetuated with the intent to harm plaintiff i.e. warranting her own standing under the Act.[44] What if the abuse occurred in front of the mother and she objected or tried to stop the abuse each time? In such an instance, the perpetration with the knowledge this would disturb the mother would amount to harassment. *(Note: a criminal case is not precluded from being filed in a case where the victim is an unemancipated minor.)*

C. PERSON WITH WHOM THE VICTIM HAS A CHILD IN COMMON

The Domestic Violence Act also protects any person, regardless of age, who has been subjected to violence by a person with whom the victim has or a child in common, or expects to have a child in common.

Although at first glance it may look as though only emancipated parties may take advantage of the Act, the Act also protects individuals no matter what age, if they have a child, or are pregnant with a child of the abuser, regardless of having never lived with the abuser.

The term "child in common" is not specifically defined in *N.J.S.A.* 2C:25-19(d). However, courts have concluded that the intent of the Legislature was to protect victims of violence that occurred within family type relationships.

A women whom is pregnant with the abusers child, has a child in common with that abuser and qualifies for the protection of the act.[45]

---

[43] *D.C. v. F.R.*, 286 *N.J. Super.* 589, 670 *A.2d* 51 (App. Div. 1996).
[44] *M.A. v. E.A.*, 388 *N.J. Super.* 612, 909 *A.2d* 1168 (App. Div. 2006).
[45] *B.C. v. T.G.*, 430 *N.J. Super.* 455, 65 *A.3d* 281 (Ch. Div. 2013).

Where the plaintiff was the legal and physical custodian of defendant's child, the parties' relationship was properly characterized as having "a child in common."[46]

In a 2007 case, the court found that an act of domestic violence committed by a biological parent against the legal custodian of his child is covered by the Act. The Court quoted the Act's provision which stated that a person who has "a child in common" is subject to the Act, and that this term was not specifically defined. Further, the Court determined that it was within the intent of the Legislature to include this kind of family type relationship.

D. A PERSON WHO RESIDES OR IS SHELTERED IN THIS STATE (SANCTUARY)

The court can assert jurisdiction when the alleged act of domestic violence occurs out of the state and the alleged victim seeks sanctuary in this state. Courts have jurisdiction to issue a Final Restraining Order to an individual who seeks sanctuary in this state, when abuser enters the state from a foreign state. The alleged act of domestic violence does not have to occur in this state. In one particular case, Plaintiff was slapped in the face by defendant in their Bronx home. Plaintiff's sister picked up plaintiff and the child, which she brought to her home in Somerville, New Jersey. Defendant came to Plaintiff's sister's house and demanded to speak with her while banging vigorously on the door. A Temporary Restraining Order was subsequently issued in New Jersey and the court stated the Domestic Violence Act "was designed to provide the maximum protection to victims of domestic violence that the law can provide."[47]

In a case where the defendant slapped the victim, spat beer in her face, pushed and shoved her, yelled at her, called her obscene names and threatened that he was going to make her life a living hell, she sought protection.[48] Unable to get any assistance in Nebraska, the victim/Plaintiff became frightened and came home to New Jersey where 9 days later she filed a domestic violence complaint and obtained a temporary restraining order. Defendant was served by mail in Nebraska. The Court granted jurisdiction, stating:

> Were the court to deny jurisdiction in this case, the victim who seeks shelter in this state would be unprotected, unable to use the procedures established in this state which permit law enforcement officers and the courts to respond, promptly and effectively, to domestic violence cases. The victim would have to wait, in fear, for the alleged abuser to commit an additional act of

---

[46] *D.V. v. A.H.*, 394 *N.J. Super.* 388, 926 *A.2d* 887 (Ch. Div. 2007).
[47] *State v. Reyes*, 172 *N.J.* 154, 162, 796 *A.2d* 879 (2002).
[48] *J.N. v. D.S.*, 300 *N.J. Super* 647, 649, 693 *A.2d* 571 (Ch. Div. 1996).

domestic violence, this time in New Jersey, before having recourse to the law and to the courts of this state.

Considering the jurisdictional issue the Court continued:

> Were the court to find jurisdiction because the victim is here and has sought shelter within the borders of this State, what harm would the alleged abuser suffer? On a temporary basis, the abuser would be prohibited from having any contact with the victim or going to the victim's home or place of employment. Should the abuser choose to submit to the jurisdiction of the State of New Jersey, he/she would be entitled to a hearing where the victim and the alleged abuser would be afforded the opportunity to testify, present witnesses and cross examine those testifying against them before a final order would be entered. Should the abuser choose not to have the matter adjudicated in the courts of the State of New Jersey, there would be no final restraining order entered on the merits, but the victim would have the protection needed so long as the victim remains in the State of New Jersey. Nothing compels the abuser to answer the complaint in New Jersey and no penalties can be entered or imposed against the abuser by default. The notions of in persona jurisdiction are not thereby violated or placed in jeopardy. By its very nature, a temporary restraining order grants emergent, *ex-parte* relief only upon good cause shown, where there is a showing that restraints are necessary to protect the life, health or well-being of a victim.

> Balancing this state's broad policy against domestic violence and our Legislature's detailed statutory scheme for protecting victims against some limited interference with the alleged abuser's movements in the State of New Jersey, this court finds that it has jurisdiction to conduct a hearing and to decide whether or not a final restraining order should issue where there is an allegation that an act of domestic violence has been committed in another state, but where the victim, a New Jersey resident, flees from the abuser to New Jersey for shelter.

In a similar situation, the Court held it had jurisdiction to issue a restraining order against an alleged abuser who lived in Mississippi, but never lived in New Jersey. The court found it had personal jurisdiction over the Defendant because he threatened to track down victim and kill her in New Jersey.[49]

In the case of *Shah v. Shah*, the New Jersey Supreme Court first addressed the issue of what happens when a victim seeks shelter in the State under *N.J.S.A.* 2C:25-28(a), where the defendant had absolutely no contacts with the State. The court concluded that courts have the authority to issue ex-parte relief, in the form of a Temporary Restraining Order, upon a showing that the plaintiff is in danger of domestic violence, and that a Temporary Restraining Order is "necessary to protect the life, health and well-being of a victim on whose behalf the relief is sought."[50]

Acknowledging the lack of personal jurisdiction over the defendant, the Court found no problem with issuing the temporary relief, which it stated would remain in effect until the defendant came to Court in order to challenge it; but, also declared that it was unconstitutional to put a permanent order in place, or to order any affirmative relief, since the defendant never personally appeared in New Jersey, and only did so through his attorney. [51] Any affirmative relief requiring defendant to perform acts, may only be ordered by a court that has personal jurisdiction over him. *(Note: the affirmative relief originally ordered by the Appellate panel included that defendant turn over plaintiff's permit, social security card, immigration documents and mail.)*

A court has a right to protect its victims. It may issue a temporary domestic protection order in actions that constitute domestic violence exclusively outside of the state, but the only relief that can be granted are restraints, which can remain as temporary until the alleged abuser appears in this state and challenges same.

E. DATING RELATIONSHIPS, AND INDIVIDUALS WHO ARE UNDER 18 YEARS OF AGE

What is a dating relationship? The Act does not define it and the determination of what it is, and whether it exists, is up to the Judge.

1. Cases Where The Court Found A Dating Relationship

The next amendment to the Domestic Violence Act was made, cognizant of the fact that parties who do not share households, but have a "dating relationship," can be victims of domestic violence and included them in the Act. Those involved in a dating relationship were covered under the Act, pre-amendment as well, however the court required a showing that

---

[49] *A.R. v. M.R.,* 351 *N.J. Super.* 512, 514, 799 *A.2d* 27 (App. Div. 1995).
[50] *Shah v. Shah,* 184 *N.J.* 125, 875 *A.2d* 931 (2005).
[51] *Ibid.*

10

there is "more than a casual dating relationship between the parties, but less than the parties residing together."[52]

Subsequent to the advent of the amendment to this section, the types of dating relationships covered under the Act have changed to reflect the times. "Dating is a loose concept undoubtedly defined differently by members of different socio-economic groups and from one generation to the next, and courts should vigilantly guard against a slavish adherence to any formula that does not consider the parties' own understanding of their relationship as colored by socio economic and generational influences."[53] At the same time courts are conscious of the burgeoning domestic violence case load in the Superior Court, and jurisdictional scrutiny is necessary to ensure that the Act is not trivialized and the Superior Court is not overrun with disorderly person cases properly before municipal courts.

In 2009, the Appellant Division examined the relevant factors in determining whether a "dating relationship" exists. Defendant's relationship with the victim consisted of paying her for sex at local clubs, where she danced. The defendant argued that since he periodically gave the plaintiff money and that their interactions primarily occurred at the plaintiff's place of employment as a dancer, that their relationship was professional. Adversely, the plaintiff described the parties' relationship as a dating relationship, relaying instances where the parties were together outside of her place of employment, and money was not involved, including Thanksgiving dinner at the defendant's parents' home. In light of the facts of the case, the court held the parties were involved in a "dating relationship" covered under the Act and that monetary consideration is only one of the factors to consider when determining whether a dating relationship exist. In its decision, the court noted that the Act defines a victim of domestic violence as "any person who has been subjected to domestic violence by a person with whom the victim has had a dating relationship." Since the Act does not define the term "dating relationship," determining what constitutes a dating relationship has been left to the courts as the trier of fact.[54]

2. <u>Cases Where The Court Found There Was No Dating Relationship</u>

Another case raised the question of whether a single date, consisting of dinner, drinks, and dancing constituted a "dating relationship," and was answered by the trial court in the affirmative. The plaintiff obtained a Final Restraining Order against the defendant based upon an incident that occurred while the parties, along with dozens of others, vacationed in Israel. During the trip, the defendant violently assaulted the plaintiff during one particular evening when the parties were a night club. Plaintiff suffered several bruises, a broken orbit, jaw

---

[52] *Desiato v. Abbott*, 261 *N.J. Super.* 30, 34, 617 *A.2d* 678, 680 (Ch. Div. 1992).

[53] *J.S. v. J.F.*, 410 *N.J. Super.* 611, 983 *A.2d* 1151 (App. Div. 2009).

[54] *J.S. v. J.F.*, 410 *N.J. Super.* 611, 613, 983 *A.2d* 1151 (App. Div. 2009).

fractures, broken teeth, cuts that required stitches, and damage to her lungs. Defendant appealed the decision on the basis that the Plaintiff did not qualify as a "victim" under the statute. The Appellate Division reversed the trial court's decision and found a dating relationship did not exist in light of the "frequency and duration" of the parties relationship. The Court held that in ascertaining whether or not a dating relationship exists, courts should apply a six-question test articulated in *Andrews v. Rutherford* in addition to other relevant factors "unique to the parties."[55] The *Andrews* factors are as follows:

1. Was there a minimal social interpersonal bonding of the parties over and above a mere casual fraternization?

2. How long did the alleged dating activities continue prior to the acts of domestic violence alleged?

3. What were the nature and frequency of the parties' interactions?

4. What were the parties' ongoing expectations with respect to the relationship, either individually or jointly?

5. Did the parties demonstrate an affirmation of their relationship before others by statement or conduct?

6. Are there any other reasons unique to the case that support or detract from a finding that a "dating relationship exists? [56]

A case alleging domestic violence, involving a Plaintiff and Defendant, who had previously been involved in a dating relationship and had lived together, did not fall within the jurisdiction of the Act. In this case, the evidence revealed a significant time gap (4-5 years) separated the alleged act of violence and the conclusion of the dating relationship. Moreover, there was no evidence of continuation of violence or any ongoing controlling behavior on the part of defendant towards plaintiff prior to the incident.[57]

In a pre-Amendment case, where those involved in "dating relationships" were not covered under the act, the court addressed whether an unmarried plaintiff who had never lived with Defendant, qualified as a victim under the "child in common" section. Defendant contended he was the father of the fetus plaintiff terminated, but denied being the father of an alleged child born of the relationship. The Court here refused to recognize a fetus as a "child in

---

[55] *S.K. v. J.H.*, 426 *N.J. Super.* 230, 43 *A.3d.* 1248 (App. Div. 2012).
[56] *Andrews v. Rutherford*, 363 *N.J. Super.* 252, 832 *A.2d* 379 (Ch. Div. 2003).
[57] *Sperling v. Teplitsky*, 294 *N.J. Super.* 312, 683 *A.2d* 244 (Ch. Div. 1996).

common" under the previous Act. They reasoned had the legislature wanted to include fetus in its definition of "child in common" they would have. As to the other child, the court afforded Plaintiff a temporary restraining order prior to an evidentiary hearing, and genetic testing to determine whether Defendant was the father of Plaintiff's child, establishing a "child in common," warranting coverage under the Act. This case is relevant to this section, insofar as a terminated pregnancy may indicate the existence of a "dating relationship" under the current Act.[58]

F. EMANCIPATED AND UNEMANCIPATED MINOR(S)

1. Emancipated Minor

Someone under 18 years of age is considered an emancipated minor under the following conditions:

He or she-

*   Marries

*   Enters military service

*   Is pregnant with or has a child in common with the defendant/victim

*   Is so declared by a court of law [59]

2. Unemancipated Minors Involved in Dating Relationships with Adult Abusers

The Domestic Violence Act *N.J.S.A.* 2C:25-19(d), was amended in 1994 to permit a person of any age, even a minor, to seek a protective order from ongoing abuse by an adult dating partner. The New Jersey Legislature expanded the definition of victim of domestic violence to include any person, regardless of age, who has been subjected to domestic violence by a person with whom the victim has had a dating relationship. "The bill broadens the definition of persons protected by the act to include persons 18 years of age and under who are involved in teen date abuse situations, in order to extend the provisions for the imposition of court sanctions and professional interventions in that population." Where the victim of domestic violence is a minor, the minor is entitled to appointment of a guardian ad litem, to provide her with an adult voice and assistance at the domestic violence hearing; the minor's

---

[58] *Crosswell v. Shenouda*, 275 *N.J. Super.* 614, 646 *A.2d* 1140 (Ch. Div. 1994).
[59] *N.J.S.A.* 2C:25-19(e).

guardian ad litem can be, but does not have to be, her parent.[60]

---

[60] *J.L. v. G.D.*, 422 *N.J. Super.* 487, 29 *A.3d* 752 (Ch. Div. 2010).

CHAPTER TWO

PREPARATION OF DOMESTIC VIOLENCE CASES

2.1   PRE-INCIDENT CHECKLIST:

A. PREPARATION FOR A DOMESTIC VIOLENCE INCIDENT

[ ]   Cash--Store cash out of the house, preferably at a friend's or relative's home. Do not keep cash in your glove compartment or in the trunk of your car. There is nothing wrong with taking money from joint bank accounts or savings accounts, for expenses/ attorneys fees and placing it with someone you trust.

[ ]   Bank books, Savings Pass Books, and Check Books.

[ ]   Keys (House, Car)—have an extra set and keep hidden.

[ ]   Voice activated tape recorder and/or video tape.

[ ]   Preserve text messages and e-mails.

[ ]   Police call access--panic button, cellular phone, and friend.

[ ]   Clothes--Extra for self and children (out of home).

[ ]   Prescription drugs or medical insurance cards – store away.

[ ]   Lawyer's telephone number.

[ ]   Weapons--Dispose of or hide.

[ ]   Passports--get children's and yours and put in a safe place out of the house.

B. SAFETY PLANNING

[ ]   Get a cellular phone, change phone numbers, and get Caller I.D.

[ ]   Record your phone calls – See above.

[ ]   Change locks and if possible do not give your young children the keys.

[ ]   Install burglar alarms

[ ]   Prepare financial information

[ ]   Instruct your children not to let abuser in - no matter what!

[ ]   Remove sharp object such as knives from sight and if possible put locks on interior doors

[ ]   Prepare financial information

2.2   GUIDE FOR PREPARING CLIENT

Domestic violence can occur in a variety of situations, as illustrated in the previous chapter. Most instances our lawyers have personally have dealt with involve incidents throughout a marriage, predominately during divorce proceedings, where the parties emotions are heightened.

The first instance a lawyer usually learns a domestic violence case exists is upon communication from a victim, after an act of domestic violence has occurred. In rare instances, a potential victim will contact the lawyer prior to an incident, as the victim is aware of the fact that their partner has exhibited abusive tendencies, has threatened them, and feels that they have the propensity to do harm to them. At other times, a person will feel that the other party is trying to precipitate an action, falsely accusing them of domestic violence, and therefore look for guidance in protecting themselves.

Once domestic violence occurs or where the threat exists, our firm always gives the client advice on how to prepare for the aftermath of a domestic violence incident. The first principal, as basic as it may seem, is that no one should to be subjected to domestic violence, and has a right to be left alone. The victims or the persons who are being set up are not powerless, and there are remedies available.

If the form of domestic violence alleged is harassment, we always instruct our clients to have a voice activated tape recorder handy, which can be purchased for under $80.00. This is a tool which aids in substantiating their case, or alternatively to prove they did not commit any alleged acts of Domestic Violence. We also inform them that if they are one of the parties to a telephone conversation/conference, it is alright to tape the telephone conversations between themselves and the other party or parties on the phone, and the potential abuser. This is not contrary to the laws.

Example: Our firm represented a client who suspected his partner was going to set him up for a domestic violence matter in order to oust him from the marital home. His partner hoped to get a "leg up" on the matrimonial case by provoking an incident to "push his buttons." She wanted to make the client volatile in some manner. As a precaution, the client was instructed to tape conversations, and/or try to have witnesses with them at all times.

FOREWARNED IS FOREARMED.

We stress to our clients that in order to protect themselves, it is of utmost importance to be the first one to call the police immediately upon an act of violence. Alternatively, if the police are called on them, it is prudent to stay and explain the situation to the police; they are warned not to take off to another ensuing residence or avoid cooperating with the police.

As a side note on the police, it is important to note the following. The calling of the police is not all it is set out to be, and can sometimes back fire, being detrimental to one, or both of the parties. Due to the widespread occurrence of domestic incidents, the police are at times loathed to get involved in what are called "marital contretemps." Depending upon their attitude, the police can take a laissez-faire attitude and do nothing, or on the other hand, can be overzealous, looking for some excuse either to throw one of the parties out of the house, or arrest them under the Domestic Violence Act. The police are likely to do the latter where one party has a scratch, a wound, or some kind of indication of the battering. It is the police's obligation to arrest a person or persons if there is a visible sign of the battering. Too often our lawyers have experienced that the person who calls the police, later regrets it because their actions backfire, and they are also arrested. The police should not be the end all of everything, and you should be cautious of their involvement, especially if they have been called more than once before.

Clients are always reminded that they have ready access to the police. If their house has an alarm system with a panic button, that is available as well. Having a cellular phone handy, or a friend available to check on them periodically at the anticipated height of the problems are also well advised.

As additional preparation, I instruct clients to keep some cash stored outside of the house and readily available for them. I also suggest they have an extra set of keys to the house and car, making sure when they park the car it cannot be easily blocked in, i.e., in a garage or in a driveway. This is necessary to facilitate an easy escape if need be. Clients are instructed to have extra clothes for themselves in a separate place, as well as clothes for the children if applicable. Prescription drugs, medical insurance cards, and their attorney's telephone number, should also be readily stored in a safe place in the event they have to leave the house quickly. Lastly, if the victim knows of any weapons that are in the house, dispose of them before the incident occurs, or if the police inquire, during or following an indecent, turn them over to the police.

These few simple steps can be a lifesaver in more ways than one.

2.3   POST INCIDENT CHECKLIST

[ ]   Compose exact Narrative of the predicate event (the event that caused the filing of the action in the first place, which in itself must be substantial in nature).

[ ]   Summarize any previous history of domestic violence.

[ ]   State the exact nature of the predicate event.

[ ]   Compile testimonial evidence - subpoena and/or interview fact witnesses, but if you are the defendant, you cannot question the victim.

[ ]   Interview expert witnesses, including police and doctors.

[ ]   Collect physical evidence - torn clothing, broken dishes, photos and/or videos of injury and scene of incident.

[ ]   If you are the Defendant, get a copy of the tape of the Plaintiff's interview with the intake officer.

[ ]   Compile documentary evidence - former complaints, police reports, hospital and doctors' reports, bills for treatment, estimates for future treatments, 911 tapes, transcripts of initial proceedings for temporary restraining order before Judge.

[ ]   If client is using drugs or alcohol, have them stop in case tests are ordered.

[ ]   Prepare financial information - tax returns, case information statements, budget lists.

[ ]   Calculate and prove loss of earnings due to injury.

[ ]   Prepare Child Support Guidelines (have this filled out and available in the event the client is seeking interim relief).

[ ]   Gather checks, financial information; as well as life, medical and car insurance policies.

[ ]   Prepare estimates or provide actual bills for repair or replacement of

damaged or destroyed personal property.

[ ]   Gauge cost of counseling for victim, children and/or defendant.

[ ]   Consider the necessity for abuser to be counseled - anger management and psychiatric expenses.

[ ]   Estimate cost of past or future moving cost and if applicable travel expenses.

[ ]   Prepare an Attorney Certification of Services (legal fees).

[ ]   Set up further restraints (if necessary)- ie, at school, employment, homes of family members and friends, etc.

[ ]   Compose proof of occupancy of residence or a plan of alternate residence that your client needs.

[ ]   Set up payment of rent/mortgage.

[ ]   Schedule return of personal items: check books, keys, health and insurance documents.

[ ]   Arrange for seizure of weapons.

[ ]   Prepare parenting time schedule.

2.4   GUIDE FOR PREPARING A CASE

Assuming that the client came to you before they filed a Domestic Violence Complaint, you can prepare them for what they can expect, how the process works, and how to most effectively get the results they want.   If they have already filed the Complaint, and it has become a Temporary Restraining Order, it can always be amended, or if denied, resubmitted.

The lawyer's <u>initial objective</u> in their interview with the client is to have them describe the incident which gave rise to the domestic violence, the predicate event. The clients account of what occurred that constituted domestic violence is to be transcribed in an exact narrative, which should be as detailed as possible. Eventually you are going to check this against the statement that they gave the police or hearing officer, to ensure accuracy and consistency. These qualities, along with thoroughness are important because the issuance of a restraining order is limited to the facts contained in the complaint, although, under some circumstances it can be amended. The lawyer should then prepare the victim to file same, following the procedures in Section 2.3 infra, called "Filing the Complaint." [61]

Where the victim has already filed a complaint, the lawyer should also review the complaint and the certification, as well as the temporary restraining order with the victim to make sure that it is accurate and to determine whether there are any omissions or inconsistencies with what the victim is telling the lawyer.

Based upon the facts, the lawyer should determine what, if any, kind of domestic violence was committed, whether there was physical violence, any threats of physical violence, or any acts of harassment. Pulling telephones out of the walls, punching hands through walls, throwing objects (even if they didn't hit the victim,) are all acts of physical violence or harassment.

Secondly, the lawyer should find out if the parties have a history of domestic violence. This includes questioning whether there have been any previous domestic violence incidents, if any domestic violence complaints were filed, and whether the complaints were acted upon or dismissed. If acted upon, what became of them, how were they decided by the Court and are the restraints still in place? If the restraints were removed, or the temporary restraining order never converted into a final restraining order, find out why. Were promises made by the abuser for counseling, anger management, alcohol or drug therapy, which were not complied with nor had little use?

The forms the court gives you do not provide enough room for all of the information if there is a whole series of domestic violence that has occurred, especially in harassment cases.

---

[61] *J.F. v. B.K.*, 308 *N.J. Super.* 387, 706 *A.2d* 203 (App. Div. 1998).

You might have to put supplements on to the papers, and insist that you be permitted to do so, because while each incident itself may not be enough, the Courts have held that collectively they can constitute harassment or another act of domestic violence. If you do not include all of the acts, they may be precluded from being raised at trial, or the trial can be delayed to give the defendant an opportunity to answer the unspecified complaints.

The lawyer should also inquire if there were any witnesses present at the domestic incident aside from the parties, whether any of these witnesses were present at previous events and/or heard any promises that were made to reform. Generally, small children or any children of the marriage are not good witnesses and should be avoided if possible. Most courts will not even allow them to testify. Many witnesses only see the aftermath of the domestic violence incident rather than being eye witnesses to the events. These witnesses can still be valuable in order to report on the state of mind of the victim, the state of mind of the abuser, to testify as to what was told to them immediately before or after the incident, as well as to describe the physical condition of the location the act of domestic violence took place. If the witnesses are unfriendly, subpoena them or have them interviewed through third parties.

There is no real discovery allowed in domestic violence cases. Cases involving Domestic Violence are considered summary actions, and thus discovery is minimally if at all permitted. *N.J. Ct. R.* 5:5-1 provides: Except for summary actions discovery in civil family actions shall be permitted. Furthermore, *N.J. Ct. R.* 5:5-1(d) states: "All other discovery in family actions shall be permitted only by leave of court for good cause shown ..." This is applicable to all forms of discovery including the taking of depositions. If proceedings under the Prevention of Domestic Violence Act are deemed to be summary actions, then defendant may not take the deposition of plaintiff as of right.[62]

Expert witnesses and professionals, such as police and doctors, can be interviewed prior to trial, and if necessary, subpoenaed to appear at trial. Reports of the witnesses are not admissible in and of themselves; the party making the report must be present at the trial.[63] You should give your witnesses an approximate date and time for them to appear, and that they are to be "on call" to come and testify within an hour's notice. You must remember this is a summary proceeding, not a full trial, so if you have the evidence, keep it down to a minimum.

Interviews of the victim are not permitted, but it is possible to obtain a copy of their statements to the intake officer. In order to do so, permission must be requested from the court. If permission is granted, i.e. in the form of an Order, the Order can then be submitted to receive a copy of the intake statements.

---

[62] *Depos v. Depos*, 307 N.J. Super. 396, 704 A.2d 1049 (Ch. Div. 1997).

[63] *Peterson v. Peterson*, 374 N.J. Super. 116, 863 A.2d 1059 (App. Div. 2005).

Physical evidence, such as torn clothing, broken dishes and weapons used, should be preserved. Photos should be taken of the injuries and the scene of the incident with as much accuracy as possible, stating by whom the photograph was taken and the date on which it was taken. Police reports, both old and new, should be secured, and cannot be presented in Court without the police officer present, but they can be used effectively in other manners to be described later.

Collect all documentary evidence, former complaints and/or dismissals, police reports, hospital and doctors' reports of this incident and previous incidents, bills for treatment, etc. If possible, video tape both the injuries and the scene.

It is important to obtain any tapes/CD's, or transcripts, relating to the domestic violence case, as this will reveal any inconsistencies.

Compensatory damages resulting from the domestic violence, such as damage to automobile, etc., are recoverable. Any claims for such damages must be put in the Complaint, or you will not be able to present said damage claims any place else, even in a new matrimonial action for the restraint against other parties and places.

If the victim is using drugs or alcohol to excess, have them stop in case tests are ordered at time of trial.

In the event there was a tape of the proceedings between your client and the judge when the original Temporary Restraining Order was signed, secure a copy of it, or get or the transcript. If there was a 911 call or other phone calls with the police, get copies of those as well.

Get copies of the medical bills. Pay special attention to uncovered medical bills which can be reimbursed.

In order to prepare for court and secure support for your client, you should gather limited but essential financial information. Secure your clients income tax returns and last three pay statements, if they work. If you are able to get the defendants information, provide that also. Review this documentation and prepare requests for alimony and child support according to the Child Support Guidelines. The Child Support Guidelines both sole and shared parenting are in the Appendix F. See also Appendix H Evaluation of Interview.

Note that the award of support in domestic violence cases is temporary, to take care of immediate problems, and should not be misconstrued as a final determination of support. Such awards have been referred to as having the "Band-Aid Effect," in that they supply a limited amount of money, until another action is undertaken. Where there is no divorce action taking

23

place, this may be the only remedy available.

If time permits, prepare a Case Information Statement, setting forth all of their expenses. If not, obtain at least the financial statement or a budget sheet that is provided by the court.

If the defendant has been the one responsible for payment of the rent or mortgage payments in the past and has a legal duty to do so, and the issue has not been previously resolved in any other matrimonial action or pending in a matrimonial action, obtain the amount of the monthly mortgage or rent payments so that you can be prepared to ask the court for payment.

Be prepared to calculate and prove out of pocket expenses caused by the domestic violence, such as loss of earnings due to the injury, medical expenses, or damages to property. Estimate future medical bills which will be necessitated by the act of domestic violence, and prepare calculations of same. If personal property has been damaged or destroyed, take pictures of it as well as getting estimates for the repair/replacement of these items. In addition to obtaining the bills etc, also have witnesses either on call or subpoenaed to testify as to the bill, the necessity of same, and the appropriateness of the charge.

Assuming your client will obtain custody, determine what visitation if any the defendant will have with the child/children. Ask whether the victim and the defendant have any other children from previous marriages or relationships, and the support arrangements in place for them.

The New Jersey Child Support Guidelines can be either programmed by the attorney or the court. See Appendix F.

Question your client regarding whether or not they believe the abuser needs professional counseling. Also determine whether the victim or the children need counseling as a result of the incident, or from previous abuse. If so, select a psychologist, psychiatrist, or a health center, and find out the cost. The Court can order the abuser to pay for same.

Inquire as to whether the victim believes that the defendant has a substance abuse problem (alcohol or drug problem), or that they would benefit from anger management or other psychological help. (It should be determined through the help of the court or probation department, what programs are available in the county, preferably free of charge, to aid the defendant.) It may also be wise to request that the defendant undergo a psychiatric evaluation.

Additional expenses to consider are moving costs, and attorney's fees. If the victim is moving out of the house into another home, get moving expenses, and travel expenses (if distant). As to attorney's fees, the attorney should prepare a certification of services for legal fees, which will be submitted to the court. This should include legal fees incurred, as well as estimated amount for time they are going to be on trial.

In the event you are dealing with an extreme injury case, or a horrific domestic violence situation, be prepared to make an application for punitive damages. This may involve using experts in order to establish the level of damages incurred.

If further restraints are needed, which the victim wishes the abuser to stay away from, aside from the residence, such as the children's school, their place of employment, family members or friends, etc., be prepared to explain who they are, why the restraints are necessary, and to give their names and addresses. The form for a search warrant and affidavit are in Appendix O and P. You should also inquire whether or not the victim wants to stop the defendant from contacting not only herself or himself, but other people, i.e. parents, friends, co-workers, either by phone or any other means of communication, which prohibition can be specified in the order.

Be prepared to show that the victim has occupied the household since the domestic incident, to ensure they are given exclusive occupancy if a TRO is granted. If you are representing the defendant, have an alternate housing plan available in the event that the domestic violence order is granted, i.e., mother, father, friend, brother, etc. Remember, it is not necessary that the house be in the plaintiff's name, or the apartment be leased to the plaintiff, for them to secure sole possession. Also remember that there are no longer any in-house restraining orders, so once the order is entered, the defendant will not be permitted to remain in the house with the plaintiff. If it is impractical for the plaintiff to remain in the household, have another apartment available for them to move, with or without the children. It is essential to secure the costs of same when asking for relief, so the defendant can be made to pay for the victim's rent, where the defendant had a duty to support the victim.

If the defendant has taken any necessary personal items, belonging to the Plaintiff, such as an automobile, checkbook, health identification documents, keys to cars, keys to the house, or any other personal effects, get a list of the items so you are prepared to ask the court to issue an order to have them returned.

In the event the Defendant asks to come back to the residence to remove their belongings, or the victim believes they will do so, you should suggest that they pack their personal belongings and any necessary business records that the Defendant might need (after making copies of same for yourself), neatly. Make sure said things are readily available, to expedite matters and hopefully obviate the necessity of the defendant coming back to the home at all.

Be sure to ask your client whether there are any weapons in the home. Where there are weapons in the house, i.e., hunting knives or guns, they should be taken out of the house and given to the police. Where weapons are not easily accessible, secure a court order, so that they may be taken from the inaccessible place and given to the police.

A. VISITATION

In the event you believe that visitation is inimical to the child, you must express this concern during the interview process.

Some factors to consider when determining visitation are as follows:

- Whether the children have any physical or mental special needs, which would disrupt visitation.
- If there is a real risk that the children would be taken out of the state or the country.
- How do you want to arrange visitation: how long; where; where will be the pickup and drop off points; who will do the transportation of the child?
- Was there any child abuse? Was the domestic violence done in front of the child or children? Was there any damage done to the children's belongings?
- Does the defendant have the capability to take care of the child, or do they need help? If the child is very young-can they do feedings, bathing, diaper changing and other care? Have they done it before?
- Is there an adequate visitation facility: a crib, a car seat. Is the house or apartment is "child proof." The following pages contain a visitation risk assessment interview sheet.

Prepare a visitation schedule for the non-custodial parent, whether it is the victim or the abuser. If the victim is the person who does not have residential custody, and is perhaps a working parent, have their schedule available, specifying who in their absence will care for the children, their availability in cases of emergencies, and any substitutes they have available to babysit or take care of the children. If the non custodial parent is the abuser, prepare a parenting time schedule, especially if the abuser is not a danger to the children. If they are, it is prudent to ask for a "risk assessment", to be discussed later. In addition, secure the names of overseers, mediators, or supervisors, along with costs and times that they are available.

The visitation plan should minimize any contact between the parties during pick up and drop off. Some alternatives to facilitate the transfer of the children include curb side pickup, intermediary third parties, and worst case scenario, at a police station.[64-65]

---

[64] The Act provides that "orders for parenting time" may include a designation of a place of

B. PRESUMPTION OF CUSTODY TO NON-ABUSIVE PARENT

There is a presumption in the Domestic Violence Act that when custody is in dispute, custody should be given to the non abusive parent. The Legislature stated specifically within the Act that they believe the best interests of the child(ren) are served by an award of custody to the non-abusive parent.[66] The presumption arose after the Legislature found that there exists "a positive correlation between spousal abuse and child abuse, and that children, even when they are not themselves physically assaulted, suffer deep and lasting emotional effects from exposure to domestic violence."[67] As stated by the Court:

> Moreover, the presumption under *N.J.S.A.* 2C:25-29(b)(11) fulfills its function by influencing the determination of custody in the initial FRO proceeding. As set forth above, any subsequent change in custody requires a prima facie showing of "a change in circumstances warranting revision of custody or parenting time in the best interests of the child as defined in *N.J.S.A.* 9:2-4," and then proof at a hearing that the child's "best interests are served by modification of the existing custody order." If those showings are made, even after consideration of "the history of domestic violence," *N.J.S.A.* 9:2-4, re-application of the presumption to change the result would dictate a decision that is not in the best interest of the child.

> We recognize the DV Act is intended "'to assure the victims of domestic violence the *maximum protection* from abuse the law can provide.'" However, the Supreme Court has long emphasized that "the child's best interests are paramount in child custody matters." Though "'there is no such thing as an act of domestic violence that is not serious,'" some acts of domestic violence are more serious than others.

> Allowing our family courts to weigh the seriousness of the history of domestic violence against the other *N.J.S.A.* 9:2-4 factors, rather than binding them with a mechanical presumption, better

---

parenting time away from the plaintiff, the participation of a third party, or supervised parenting time.

[65] *N.J.S.A.* 2C:25-20(b)(3).

[66] *N.J.S.A.* 2C:25-29(b)(11); *R.K. v. F.K.*, 437 *N.J. Super.* 58, 96 *A.3d* 291 (App. Div. 2014); *Grover v. Terlaje*, 379 *N.J. Super.* 400, 879 *A.2d* 138 (App. Div 2005).

[67] *J.D. v. M.A.D.*, 429 *N.J. Super.* 34, 43-44, 56 *A.3d* 882 (App. Div. 2012); *N.J.S.A.* 2C:25-18.

enables them to consider the best interests of the child in determining the vital issue of child custody in divorce, using their "special expertise in the field of domestic relations." In so doing, the court must consider "the safety of the child and the safety of either parent from physical abuse by the other parent." *N.J.S.A.* 9:2-4.[68]

In one case, the Defendant appealed from an amended FRO that denied his request for joint legal custody of the party's son three years. The court acknowledged that under New Jersey law, where there has been a finding of domestic violence, a presumption arises, favoring an award in custody (both legal and physical) to "the non-abusive spouse," pursuant to *N.J.S.A.* 2C:25-29(b)(11). However, the court also noted that the presumption weakens as time passes without any conduct which can be said to jeopardize the "non-abusive spouse" or the child.[69]

There is a different standard in domestic violence matters as opposed to custody matters litigated in the Family Court as domestic violence is one of the factors for consideration per *N.J.S.A.* 9:2-4.

See Appendix B Needs of the Battered Woman.

---

[68] *R.K. v. F.K.*, 437 *N.J. Super.* 58, 65-67, 96 *A.3d* 291 (App. Div. 2014)(formatting altered from original and internal citations omitted).

[69] *Grover v. Terlaje* 379 *N.J. Super* 400, 879 *A.2d* 138 (App. Div 2005).

2.5 FILING THE COMPLAINT FOR A TEMPORARY RESTRAINING ORDER

A. WHERE

Municipal Court anytime, or Superior Court (8:30 a.m. to 3:30 p.m. Monday – Friday).

Superior Court – Domestic Violence Intake Unit (8:30 a.m. to 4:00 p.m. Monday – Friday)

A complaint can either be filed in a Municipal Court, or in the Family Part of the Superior Court Domestic Violence Unit. Municipal Court judges are more inclined to sign a complaint based on less substantial allegations than a Family Court judge. A denial by a municipal court judge does not preclude the victim from filing the very same complaint with the Superior Court. Regardless of which court is utilized, the procedure to file a complaint for a temporary restraining Order is the same (*note: intake forms used to collect information differ*).

B. JURISDICTION

A complaint can be brought in New Jersey, if the domestic violence occurred in N.J., or in another state, if the victim or defendant resides or is sheltered in New Jersey.[70] In the event a victim has fled the state to protect themselves and seek shelter, the court should have a hearing as to whether or not it has jurisdiction.[71]

C. BY WHOM

In person by the victim, unless victim has fled or is injured

D. FOR

The criminal acts provided for protection under the Domestic Violence Act and the basis for the restraining order is as follows:

Harassment
Assault
Terroristic threats
Kidnapping
Criminal restraint
False imprisonment

---

[70] *Sperling v. Teplitsky*, 294 *N.J. Super.* 312, 683 *A.2d* 244 (Ch. Div. 1996); *State v. Reyes*, 172 *N.J.* 154, 796 *A.2d* 879 (2002).

[71] *J.N. v. D.S.*, 300 *N.J. Super.* 647, 650, 693 *A.2d* 571 (Ch. Div. 1996).

Sexual Assault
Criminal sexual assault
Criminal sexual contact
Lewdness
Criminal mischief
Burglary
Criminal trespass
Stalking
Homicide

E. RELIEF SOUGHT

You should be aware of what relief you can ask for, besides the restraint of the defendant contacting the victim. You can ask for further restraints, prohibiting the defendant from contacting any friends or family, either personally or by phone, or coming to the victim's place of business. Below is a partial list of the relief that may be sought under the Act. A full list is covered in the relief chapter discussed later in the book.

Forbidding abuser from home, work, etc., and relatives
Forbidding abuser from possessing any firearm
Ordering search and seizure of weapons
Child support and/or alimony – temporary
Anger management counseling for abuser
Compensation for medical bills, damages, etc
Drug testing
Counseling for children and victim
Attorney's fees
Return of personal items.

F. INTAKE

The complaint will be taken by a Municipal/Superior Court Judge (in person or by phone), a domestic violence hearing officer, or a police officer. The Intake Officer will ask a series of personal questions about the victim. These include in which police district they reside, social security numbers, employment information, description of the individual, what is the victim's connection or relationship with the individual, etc. They also ask children's names, whether the victim wants the abuser to have visitation and in what manner, and whether they will be seeking child support or medical coverage. Be prepared to answer these questions.

The individual taking the victim's complaint in a domestic violence case – whether it is a police officer, a clerk at municipal court, a probation worker, or even a judge at the superior court, will be the first obstacle to overcome. They are oftentimes judgmental, sinister, unknowledgeable, uncaring. It is important that the victim presents himself/herself properly to this intake officer, i.e. people talk. Remember that even if it's not written down, the person will transmit their impression of the victim and the case, to the judge, before any decision is made.

The Intake officer will prepare a visitation Risk Assessment Sheet, and an Interview and Summary Sheet, if necessary (See Appendix G), or an Evaluation of Interview. (See Appendix H). They will also prepare a Confidential Litigant Information Sheet. (See Appendix I) You should have a Confidential Victim Information Sheet prepared to ask for support, See Appendix J.

If there is an injury, have the victim photograph it and bring the photo with them. If there are any photographs or tape recordings, substantiating the claim, bring these as well.

Inform intake if the victims had a child present during the domestic violence, and how, if at all, they were affected physically and psychologically. If the defendant is on drugs or alcohol, bring the empty liquor bottles, and take photos of the drugs and or paraphernalia. If the Defendant has a criminal background, or exhibits aberrant behavior, tell them, and describe same.

Where there are children, and visitation is an issue, describe defendant's parenting skills or lack thereof. Also have the victim voice any concerns where defendant's presence around the child should be monitored or obviated. See Visitation Risk Assessment check list Appendix G.

If the defendant has threatened to harm the victim's family, restricted their movements, insulted, criticized, or humiliated the victim, explain that to the interviewer. If they have forced the victim to have sex, or perform sexual acts that they are not comfortable doing, do not be ashamed to relay this. If the defendant is the jealous type, and has accused the victim of infidelity, followed them, or unfairly questions them as to their whereabouts or activities, mention that as well.

G. VICTIM'S APPEARANCE

Appearance is important and says a lot about you. When appearing, be sure the victim is well dressed and clean. As to demeanor, he/she should be pleasant, calm and logical; not appear angry, vindictive, or confused. It is an emotional time, but it is essential that the victim maintains control, and expresses their thoughts clearly.

The essential facts the victim must let the interviewer know is that they are afraid due to what the defendant has done to them, and fear that he will harm them in the future.

H. THE COMPLAINT

In filling out the complaint, it is necessary that the victim be as specific and complete as possible, regarding all the events that occurred, even where the victim feels they are being rushed by the police, who want to go home, or the court clerk who wants to abbreviate the session. Leave out nothing! Also, mention and be very specific regarding any past acts of domestic violence. Failing to do any of this may result in the case being compromised, since the ensuing restraining order is limited to the facts contained in the domestic violence complaint. In addition, it is a violation of Defendant's due process to issue a restraining order based on acts of domestic violence, not mentioned in the complaint.

If the restraining order is denied on a certain set of facts, it cannot be issued at a later date on the same set of facts, as that violates the principals of res judicata and collateral estoppel. [72] However, if new facts come to exist, the Complaint can be amended. [73]

Alternatively, domestic violence complaints can be amended by the party, or by the trial Court, if there is a lack of prejudice, a continuance, and an adjournment. The rationale guiding this is the clear public intent against domestic violence, and the fact that complaints are usually drafted by non-attorneys, thus warranting liberality to be given so as to maximize protection. The court has a duty to protect the victim. The power to provide protection is within the discretion of the trial court and should not readily be severed. [74]

I. ISSUING THE RESTRAINING ORDER

At the time of the issuance of a restraining order, the victim will be put under oath and asked questions about the incident. The judge usually will have a report before them, prepared by either the police officer or the domestic violence hearing officer.

J. FREQUENTLY ASKED QUESTIONS

Does the Victim have to disclose a current address on forms, where they fear contact by the Defendant?

If the victim has fled the residence, for their protection, they need not give their new address or divulge where they are presently residing. [75] However, the information is confidential to the court, and the victim does usually provides the court with a telephone number to contact

---

[72] *J.F. v. B.K.*, 308 *N.J. Super.* 387, 392, 706 *A.2d* 203 (App. Div. 1998).

[73] *Fisher v. Yates*, 270 *N.J. Super.* 458, 637 *A.2d* 546 (App. Div. 1994).

[74] *N.J.S.A.* 2C:25-18; *N.J.S.A.* 2C:25-28(p); *N.J.S.A.* 2C:25-26; *Coastal Group Inc. v. Dryvit Systems Inc.*, 274 *N.J. Super.* 171, 643 *A.2d* 649 (App. Div. 1994).

[75] *N.J.S.A.* 2C:25-28.

them at, as well as an address they are residing, should the court have to communicate important information, such as Defendant's release from jail. The victim is also given special numbers to contact, in case they have to change their telephone number, and also provides the court with any additional addresses they can be contacted

Are there exceptions where the victim is not required to make a personal application?

Yes. If for some reason the victim is not available themselves to make the application, i.e., out of the state, they fled the area, or injured, the victim can swear to the complaint on the phone. If the person is physically or mentally incapable of filing a complaint, another person, representing the individual may do so. It is unclear under the law, whether "represent" means that you need an attorney, or somebody who just represents their interest. Before either one of these non-appearances can result in the issuance of a temporary restraining order, the court must be satisfied that there are exigent circumstances for the non appearance and making a personal application.

If the victim calls the police, but decides not to file a complaint against the Defendant, where domestic violence takes place, what happens?

Even if the victim does not want to sign a criminal complaint, the police officer may do so themselves if they believe an act of domestic violence has been committed.

What are the resources available to victims?

When a complaint is filed, the plaintiff is given advice concerning certain services, such as counseling, anger management programs, substance abuse clinics and counseling, as well as being told they have a right to file both a domestic violence complaint and a criminal complaint simultaneously, and one does not preclude the filing of the other.

Do I file a criminal or civil complaint?

Determining whether to file a criminal or civil complaint is oftentimes within the discretion of the victim (unless filed by police officer-see above). A "Notice to Victim" is given by the police to the victim which explains the difference between the two proceedings and provides a notice that "the Act was enacted in order to offer direct, emergent access to immediate protection and support of services," but was intended to compliment, not replace, the more permanent long term remedies available in the criminal and the family courts.

May I file in more than one court if my complaint has been dismissed?

The Domestic Violence Act provides that a denial of a restraining order by a Municipal

Court judge or even an administrative dismissal of the complaint does not bar the victim from filing a complaint in the Family Part on the same incident and getting the same relief that they would have gotten before. Thus, you might have two bites of the same apple or two judges to whom you can appeal for relief.[76]

K. DOMESTIC VIOLENCE AGAINST THE ELDERLY OR DISABLED

When a disabled person is subjected to an act of domestic violence, the procedures are the same. Where there is abuse of the elderly or disabled, by a person with a duty to care for them, the victim, or the police on behalf of the victim, may file a criminal charge against the offender under *N.J.S.A.* 2C:24-8 "Abandonment, neglect of elderly person, disabled adult.," which is a third degree crime.

A person can be charged, under this Act if they have:

(1) a legal duty to care for or has assumed continued responsibility for the care of a person

who is:

a. 60 years of age or older, or

b. a disabled adult,

(2) The person abandons the elderly person or disabled adult; or unreasonably neglects to do or fails to permit to be done any act necessary for the physical or mental health of the elderly person or disabled adult, is guilty of a crime of the third degree. (For purposes of this section "abandon" means the willful desertion or forsaking of an elderly person or disabled adult.)

Subsection (b) of that statue, provides an exemption from liability, which states:

> A person shall not be considered to commit an offense under this section for the sole reason that he provides or permits to be provided nonmedical remedial treatment by spiritual means through prayer alone in lieu of medical care, in accordance with the tenets and practices of the elderly person's or disabled adult's established religious tradition, to an elderly person or disabled

---

[76] *N.J.S.A.* 2C:25-28.

adult to whom he has a legal duty to care for or has assumed responsibility for the care of.

L. MUNICIPAL COURT

The Municipal Court is open during normal court hours. Judges are also available via telephone, on notice, at any time when they are called by police, not only to take the domestic violence complaint, but on behalf of the defendant to set bail.

In order to insure emergent access to the Municipal Court, each assignment judge of the county designates at least two additional Municipal Court judges for each municipal court in their vicinage to provide backup coverage for domestic violence cases as well as other emergent matters. Each municipal police station is given a list of the alternate municipal judges with whom they may call to sign orders in the absence of their judge.

The police in a municipality are instructed during regular court hours to transport the victims, if necessary, to the Superior Court.

Thus in order of priority, the judges to be contacted are as follows:

1. Sitting Municipal Court judge

2. Alternate Municipal Court judge

3. Presiding Municipal Court judge (where applicable)

A list of Municipal Courts addresses and telephone numbers is in Appendix K.

M. SUPERIOR COURT

The Superior Court is open during regular court hours. A victim who files in the Superior Court will usually see a domestic violence coordinator, who screens the allegations, before being allowed to present their cause of action to a judge or a domestic violence hearing officer. When filing a complaint in the Superior court, the intake hearing officer fills out a form, called the Confidential Victim Information Sheet. It asks questions similar to those asked by other individuals taking the victims complaint in a domestic violence case (ie. Police, municipal court officers or judges). After that is compiled, somewhere in the process, the court fills out a "Confidential Litigation Information Sheet" which asks for even more detailed information such as driver's license number, auto license plate number, healthcare provider, etc. A copy of that form is in Appendix I.

In the event the police are called to a home during or following a domestic violence incident, the police are instructed to transport the victim to the Municipal Court, or to the Family Part of the Superior Court. However, they will most likely simply telephone Municipal Court judge with whom they are familiar, requesting an emergent temporary restraining order.[77]

In counties where transportation to the Superior Court from municipalities is burdensome, a procedure has been established so that the victim may request emergent relief by telephone communication, from the local police station, to the designated family judge, who will hear and decide on the matter.

The scenarios described above are all ex parte actions, in which the victim is asking the judge to enter certain restraints, and grant relief immediately without the defendant's participation.

When filing a complaint in the Superior court, the intake hearing officer fills out a form, called the Confidential Victim Information Sheet. It asks questions similar to those asked by other individuals taking the victims complaint in a domestic violence case (ie. Police, municipal court officers or judges).

After that is compiled, somewhere in the process, the court fills out a "Confidential Litigation Information Sheet" which asks for even more detailed information such as driver's license number, auto license plate number, healthcare provider, etc. A copy of that form is in Appendix I.

The Emergent Duty Superior Court Judge

The Family Division, domestic violence unit, has been instructed to accept domestic violence complaints until at least 3:30 p.m. during days when the Superior Court is in session. They are further informed not to turn victims away, even if they are about to close. In such "after hours" cases, it is mandatory that the court officer telephonically communicate with the emergent duty judges, to hear the victim's complaint and decide whether or not to issue a temporary restraining order. This obviates having the victim go to the local police or municipal court, when they are already in the Superior Court, albeit after hours.

The purpose in having the emergent duty judge is to insure the courts are readily available to domestic violence victims. The intake officers who help in processing a domestic violence complaint are warned: "Under no circumstance should an officer prevent or discourage a victim from seeking immediate temporary relief merely because domestic violence

---

[77] *N.J. Ct. R.* 5:7A(b).

occurs after regular business hours."[78]

Due to the sheer number of complaints, most counties have "intake officers" to take down the incidental information. These officers are non judges and usually consist of untrained county employees. The intake officer will either issue or deny an order, or have the Domestic Violence Judge rubber stamp their recommendations. Thus, it is the intake officer who takes the information from the victim, prepares a fact sheet for the Judge (usually makes recommendations), and submits before a Judge who shall appear before and swear to the acts of violence. If the complaint is substantial, a temporary restraining order will be issued. Most times, the weakest of complaints are signed. The undeclared mantra is "when in doubt, throw him out." Evaluation of interview form that the intake officer uses is in Appendix H.

If a TRO is granted, the court will automatically ask if there are any weapons in the home, and the weapons will be seized. A search warrant may be necessary in order to seize the weapons, and the court will issue a search warrant asking for specific weapons and defining the scope of the search. In addition a restraint will be ordered, prohibiting the defendant from possessing any firearms *(Note: there are some exceptions for police officers.)*

The restraining order can also: Transfer custody of the children to the victim and forbid visitation with the minor children until the return date for the safety of the victim and the children; Restrain the defendant from the parties home as there are no longer provisions for in-house restraining orders (allowing the abuser to stay in the house yet still being restrained from contact with the victim) in either a Temporary Restraining Order or a Final Restraining Order.[79] *(Note: restraints are not only valid in this state but also nationwide.)*

Make sure that you tell the police where the defendant can be served, so the defendant is made immediately aware of the restraints. The police may not ask the victim to serve the defendant.

Remember, filing a domestic violence complaint does not foreclose the victim from pursuing a criminal complaint. In all but the most grievous cases, criminal complaints are not filed against the abuser.

Even if the victim has left the residence for whatever reason(s), the Complaint cannot be delayed or dismissed.

The defendant can ask that the police accompany them to the scene of the domestic violence, if that is the home, in order to pick up their personal belongings.

---

[78] *State of New Jersey Domestic Violence Procedures Manual*, p.II-1 (2008).
[79] *N.J.S.A. 2C:25-28.1.*

The Act mandates that the final hearing take place within ten days and, upon proper application by defense counsel, the time can be shortened to two days. Unfortunately, this mandate is not always feasible given the court's backlog. Temporary Restraining Order further setting forth all the questions that will be asked and the relief that can be granted is in Appendix L.

Once granted the court submits an order. The defendant can apply to accelerate the date of the final hearing "if the interest of justice dictates," by filing an "application for appeal" and order. The request is usually granted, so long as the Court has time to hear it, and reasonable notice is given to the adverse party, indicating that this acceleration is being sought and the type of relief defendant will be asking for at the hearing. The form for the application is in Appendix N.[80]

---

[80] *Vendetti v. Meltz*, 359 *N.J. Super.* 63, 818 *A.2d* 357 (Ch. Div. 2002).

2.6   RELIEF UNDER THE TEMPORARY RESTRAINING ORDER

Once the *ex parte* complaint is brought and the restraining Order is issued, it remains in effect until the plenary hearing, or until a court enters a modification or dissolution.

Examples of the boiler plate relief the Temporary Restraining Order (TRO) may possibly grant are as follows:

1. Forbidding the defendant from returning to the scene of the domestic violence.
2. Forbidding the defendant from possessing any firearms or weapon.
3. Ordering the search and seizure of any weapon, at any location, where the judge has reasonable cause to believe the weapon is located (the judge must state with specificity their reasons for said belief and define the scope of the search and seizure).
4. Permitting the defendant to return to the scene to pick up personal belongings and effects. The police may accompany the defendant to the residence, where they will supervise the removal of the personal belongings. The time may be immediately after the service of the complaint, or at a subsequent time, specified in the order. Any times and items to be removed are limited by the specification set forth in the TRO.[81]
5. Restraining the defendant from committing further acts of domestic violence against the victim
6. Exclusive possession of the residence
7. Parenting time and risk assessment
8. Monetary Compensation – Compensatory and punitive damages
9. Professional domestic violence counseling
10. Restraints from specified locations
11. Restraints from contact
12. Rent or mortgage payments
13. Possession of personal property
14. Support for victim and minor children
15. Temporary custody of a minor child
16. Police to Accompany removal of personality
17. Miscellaneous relief, including monitoring of ordered relief
18. Psychiatric evaluation of defendant/ Anger Management
19. Prohibition against weapons
20. Prohibition against firearms
21. Prohibition against defendant stalking
22. "Indefinite" temporary restraining order
23. Drug Testing
24. Attorney Fees

---

[81] *Vendetti v. Meltz*, 359 *N.J. Super.* 63, 68, 818 *A.2d* 357 (Ch. Div. 2002).

25. Permits the defendant to return to the scene to pick up personal items
(*Note*: *See also Relief Under the Act Chapter Nine and Chapter Ten*)

The order should be neatly prepared and, if amended, it should not have substantial interlineations, added paragraphs, or cross-outs. This is to avoid any error or confusion.[82]

After the order is granted, a copy of the order, along with the complaint, is forwarded either to the Sheriff (during business hours,) or to the police in the municipality the defendant resides, in order to facilitate service upon the defendant. The service can be by personal service or substituted service. Plaintiff is NOT to serve the defendant personally. This Act also provides that "at no time shall the plaintiff be asked or required to serve any order on the defendant."

The order is effective throughout the State, as well as the country under the Full Faith and Credit Clause of the constitution.[83]

Make sure your restraining Order is as specific as possible regarding what your client needs to insure his or hers safety. Take for example a case where the parties TRO, did not contain a paragraph, specifying that the victim had exclusive use and possession of the house. The defendant in that case, visited the home while the wife was away, and was found to have not violated the order.

In a similar matter, the Appellate Division has held that a charge of contempt was defective because the restraining order was "unclear" and "the defendant's actions that prompted the contempt charge could not, as a matter of law, be found to constitute a knowing violation of an existing domestic violence restraining order.[84]

It is also important to be aware that the restraining order does not, unless specified, protect the victim from being in the "same place at the same time" as the Defendant, which would permit both to attend school events, baseball games, etc.[85]

---

[82] *Fillippone v. Lee*, 304 *N.J. Super.* 301, 700 *A.2d* 384 (App. Div. 1997).
[83] *N.J.S.A.* 2C:25-28 and 18 *U.S.C.A.* §2265.
[84] *State v. S.K.*, 423 *N.J. Super.* 540, 33 *A.3d* 1255 (App. Div. 2012).
[85] *Finamore v. Aronson*, 382 *N.J. Super.* 514, 889 *A.2d* 1114 (App. Div. 2006).

2.7 POLICE INTERVENTION:

A. CALL MUNICIPAL POLICE WHERE DOMESTIC VIOLENCE OCCURRED

If there is a domestic violence incident, the first step is to call the police. When the police respond to a domestic violence incident, they have an affirmative obligation to inform the victim of their rights, which advises them of available court action.[86]

The police must arrest the assailant if:

1. The victim exhibits signs of injury caused by domestic violence
2. A warrant is in effect - Pre-existing
3. There is probably cause to believe a weapon was used to commit an act of domestic violence. In this situation the officer must search and seize any weapons in the house as well.
   or
4. There is probable cause to believe a no contact court Order has been violated.[87]

A police officer who has determined there is probable cause to believe domestic violence has occurred, is required to then assist the victim in filing a complaint, and for providing transportation to court or directing the victim in doing so.

Even if the victim refuses to press charges, the police can independently do so, if they find probable cause to believe domestic violence has occurred. The officer is required to arrest the alleged perpetrator, especially where the victim shows signs of physical injury. The police officer is given discretion to make the decision as he sees fit,[88] even if the officer's acts or omissions might be to open to some criticism.[89] Generally speaking, the officer's course of action in dealing with a domestic violence case is protected under the Tort Claims Act, and they are immune to Civil Prosecution for same.[90]

B. FILING THE COMPLAINT-IN REVIEW

WHERE: Municipal Court or Superior Court, or via emergency call to either of the respective court judges, when after hours.

JURISDICTION: Where plaintiff lives, is sheltered in, or where incident occurred.

---

[86] *N.J.S.A.* 2C:25-23.
[87] *Ibid.*
[88] *N.J.S.A.* 59:3-2(a); *N.J.S.A.* 59:2-3(d).
[89] *S.P. v. Newark Police Department*, 428 *N.J. Super.* 210, 229, 52 *A.2d* 178 (App. Div. 2012).
[90] *N.J.S.A.* 59:1 to 59:12-3.

<u>CITE THE "PREDICATE EVENT" IN DETAIL</u>

<u>GIVE A COMPLETE HISTORY OF DOMESTIC VIOLENCE -(NOTE: ONLY ONE ACT IS NECESSARY)</u>

C. CONDITIONS WARRANTING ARREST DETAILED

1. The victim exhibits signs of injury caused by an act of domestic violence.

The word "exhibits" is to be liberally construed to mean any indication that a victim has suffered bodily injury, which shall include physical pain or any impairment of physical condition. Probable cause to arrest may also be established when the police officer observes any manifestation of an internal injury suffered by the victim.

If there are no visible signs of injury, but the victim states that an injury occurred, the officer should then consider other relevant factors in determining whether there is probable cause to believe an act of domestic violence has been committed, thus warranting an arrest. This determination is solely within their discretion. Relevant factors would include a history of domestic violence.[91]

2. A warrant for defendant exists.

There is not a definition or explanation of what kind of warrant qualifies. One can assume it is a pre-existing domestic violence warrant, but a criminal warrant may do, and maybe perhaps a traffic warrant may also qualify.

The most strenuous argument that must be made to police in the event that the abuser does have an outstanding warrant against them is that it is mandatory for them to make an arrest.

3. There is probable cause to believe that a weapon was used to commit domestic violence.[92]

4. There is probable cause to believe a no contact court order has been violated. If the victim does not have a copy of the Order, the officer may verify with the appropriate law enforcement agency.[93]

---

[91] *State of New Jersey Domestic Violence Procedures Manual,* p. III-6 to III-7 (2008).
[92] *N.J.S.A.* 2C:25-21(a)(1) to (4).
[93] *Ibid.*

In one case, where an estranged husband violated a final restraining Order, by showing up at the home of his estranged wife, the officer did not arrest the man as he was required to. The failure to make the mandatory arrest resulted in the perpetrator coming back and shooting his estranged wife. The court did not give the police officers or the police department immunity from suit. [94]

In some domestic violence cases, the parties file cross complaints against each other, with each party exhibiting signs of injury. Who do they police arrest in this situation? In this type of case, the Manual on Domestic Violence provides that determining which party in a domestic violence incident is the victim, where both parties' exhibit signs of injury, the officer should consider:

A. The comparative extent of the injuries suffered;
B. The history of domestic violence between the parties, if any;
C. The presence of wounds associated with defense or considered defensive wounds; or
D. Other relevant factors, including checking the Domestic Violence Registry (*N.J.S.A.* 2C:25-21(c)(2))

When you talk to the police, you will find that they are usually intransigent in their positions. Either they have been instructed by their department to arrest everybody, arrest only the man, or look the other way. You might want to convince them to arrest the abuser, for the protection of the victim, and you can point out the mandatory arrest requirements if applicable.

If the abuser exhibits signs of injury, and the police wish to arrest the victim as well, plea to the officer that the marks were merely made in self defense. The statute provides that the victim is to be granted relief, and not arrested or charged with an act, if they use reasonable force in self defense against a domestic violence abuser.

D. WITNESS NOTIFICATION FORM

At the time of the arrest, the officer is required to provide the victim with a witness notification form. This provides the victim with information about their rights under the Domestic Violence Act. These rights include, but are not limited to the following:

You have the right to go to court to get an order called a temporary restraining order, also known as a TRO, which may protect you from more abuse by your attacker. The officer who handed you this card can tell you how to obtain a TRO. The relief a judge can

---

[94] *Campbell v. Campbell*, 294 *N.J. Super.* 18, 682 *A.2d* 272 (Law Div. 1996).

order in a TRO may include:

(1)   That your attacker be temporarily forbidden from entering the home you live in;

(2)   That your attacker be temporarily forbidden from having contact with you or your relatives;

(3)   That your attacker be temporarily forbidden from bothering you at work;

(4)   That your attacker must pay temporary child support or support for you;

(5)   That you be given temporary custody of your children;

(6)   That your attacker must pay you back any money you have to spend for medical treatment, or repairs caused by the violence.

There are other things the court can order as well.

The police officer or a member of the court staff will explain the Procedure, and help the victim fill out the papers for a TRO. On weekends, holidays and other times, when the courts are closed, the victim can still get a TRO. The police officer responding to the domestic violence call will help the victim get in touch with a judge, who can give the victim a TRO. The victim is also instructed they also have the right to file a criminal complaint against their attacker. The police officer will tell the victim how to file a criminal complaint. (*Note as previously mentioned, that even if the victim does not want to file a criminal complaint, the police officer may do so themselves if they believe an act of domestic violence has been committed.*)

If there are any weapons in the home that the victim is aware of, even if the weapon was not used in committing the domestic violence, instruct the victims to tell the officer, so said weapons can be seized. If the whereabouts of said weapon have been concealed by the abuser, or even where there may be additional unknown weapons, the victim should insist that a search be made for those weapons. See Appendix O: Affidavit in Support of Search Warrant for a Weapon; See Appendix P: Search Warrant for Weapon.

2.8   BAIL; POST-INCIDENT

The defendant's prior record must be considered by the judge prior to setting bail. Bail is to be set as soon as possible, but no later than 24 hours after the arrest.[95]

The Court can also impose conditions on the allowance of bail such as:

(a) Prohibiting contact with the victim; [96]

(b) Prohibiting the possession of weapons;

(c) Restraining the Defendant from victim's residence or any other place where victim may be, ie. their work or school;

(d) Restraining the defendant from harassing/stalking the victim, victim's
relatives or friends in any way;

(e) Permitting the search and seizure of any weapons at any location which the judge has reasonable cause to believe that the weapons are located.

(f) Prohibiting the defendant from having any contact with the children of the relationship, or animals the parties own in common.[97]

In the event the defendant wishes to reduce the bail imposed, notice must be given to the victim. The police officer making the arrest is to contact the appropriate judge in person or by phone. The judge who imposed the original bail should hear the bail application unless the judge is unavailable. A substitute judge may reduce bail only where the amount of the original bail is available, and set forth in the record.[98]

---

[95] *N.J.S.A.* 2C:25-26(d).
[96] *State of New Jersey Domestic Violence Procedural Manual*, p. III-17.
[97] *N.J.S.A.* 2C:25-26(a).
[98] *N.J.S.A.* 2C:25-26(e).

2.9   APPLICATION FOR AN EARLY HEARING

After a Temporary Restraining Order is issued, the Court sets a "return date" for a hearing to determine whether a Permanent Restraining Order should issue. The time frame is usually between 7 to 10 days in order to provide a sufficient time, wherein, the defendant can be served, and the case listed with an appropriate Judge.

The defendant can apply to accelerate the date of the final hearing "if the interest of justice dictates." This is done by filing an "application for appeal" and order. The request is usually granted, so long as the Court has time to hear it, and reasonable notice is given to the adverse party, indicating that this acceleration is being sought and the type of relief defendant will be asking for at the hearing.[99]

If a final Restraining Order is issued, the defendant is fingerprinted and photographed. Failure to do so is a disorderly person's offense under *N.J.S.A.* 53:1-15. See Appendix N, Application for an Appeal and Order.[100]

---

[99] *Vendetti v. Meltz*, 359 *N.J. Super.* 63, 818 *A.2d* 357 (Ch. Div. 2002).
[100] *State of New Jersey Domestic Violence Procedure Manual*, p. IV-23, (2008); *see also N.J.S.A.* 53:1-15.

CHAPTER THREE

THE PROSECUTION AND DEFENSE OF DOMESTIC VIOLENCE CASES

3.1 POST INCIDENT

A. CLIENT PREPARATION CHECK LIST

For the Defense:

[ ] Provide a summary of events, including any previous history of domestic violence.

[ ] Appeal the temporary restraining order, and have it set for earlier date. Do this quickly as TROs have short return dates.

[ ] Provide an exact narrative of the alleged predicate event.

[ ] Review the complaint and certification.

[ ] Theorize the real motivation for alleging the incident, i.e. revenge, custody etc.

[ ] Substantiate your clients' theory of real motivation with evidence, i.e. tape recordings, prior writings, witnesses.

[ ] Conduct Discovery- Notice for Production of Documents *N.J. Ct. R.* 4:18-1.

[ ] Notice in lieu of subpoena *N.J. Ct. R.*1:9-1 and *N.J. Ct. R.* 1:9-2.

[ ] Make a list of witnesses to be used at the hearing, both lay and expert, specifying what they will testify to.

[ ] Produce any and all photographs, tape recordings, etc., pertaining to case.

[ ] Collect and inspect any physical evidence - torn clothing, broken dishes.

[ ] Visit the scene of domestic violence, taking pictures or diagram.

[ ] Collect experts' reports, hospital records, and medical records.

[ ]   Produce testimonial evidence - subpoena and interview fact witnesses.

[ ]   Subpoena police, police reports, and all tapes.

[ ]   Subpoena medical reports.

[ ]   Obtain transcripts of any hearing(s) to obtain temporary restraints, and any resulting order(s) (if Municipal Court - tape recording) See Appendix Q: Protective Order.

[ ]   Prepare financial information.

[ ]   If the client is using drugs or alcohol, have them stop in case tests are ordered.

[ ]   Have times set for prospective visitation, and names of any intermediary accessible to facilitate visitation.

[ ]   Have alternative living arrangements.

[ ]   Have time set up for the client to pick up their personal belongings. (provide the victim with a list of the belongings and financial information to be picked up).

[ ]   Consider a Civil Restraining Order to avoid trial, and settle the matter.

3.2   INTERVIEWING AND PREPARING YOUR CLIENT

The initial decision you are going to have to make is whether you want to wait until the return date of the *ex parte* restraining order, which is within 10 days of the issuance of the temporary restraining order, or whether you wish to accelerate the action, and move to ask for an immediate final hearing, to set aside the temporary restraining order.[101] There are, of course, advantages and disadvantages to each.

A falsely accused defendant, who has been thrown out of their home may have no place else to live, but a motel. They may have lost interim custody and are usually even denied visitation with their children. In these instances, you would want to move as quickly as possible to alleviate the hardship that they are enduring, even if this results in less time to available prepare their case.

If the client decides they wish to accelerate, an application should be made to immediately dissolve, modify, or appeal the temporary restraining order. A plenary hearing *de novo* can be held immediately before the judge who heard the original temporary restraining order, or any judge who has access to the file. The defendant can receive a hearing on the appeal immediately, upon notice to the plaintiff. See Appendix N.

On the other hand, if the defendant has satisfactory living arrangements available, and can bear not seeing his children for 10 days (if that's one of the reliefs that is requested), then it may be advantageous to wait until final hearing, utilizing that time to thoroughly prepare the case.[102]

If both parties appear for the plenary hearing on the appeal, and both agree to proceed on the record, the court may simultaneously move forward with the final hearing. The case will then either be dismissed, or a final order will be issued. If proper notice is given, and the Plaintiff's due process rights respected, failure to show on notice can also result in dismissal.[103]

Upon interviewing your client regarding the domestic violence incident, have them give you an exact narrative of the alleged predicate event, as well as whether there was any history of domestic violence in the past. Inquire as to whether there were any other false allegations made against them, and what became of them? Additional questions to ask include: Has the same matter been litigated previously? Is there a history of the alleged victim trying to get the defendant out of the house by other means, such as court motions? Is there any other motivating factor behind the alleged incident, i.e., revenge, custody, or strategic positioning in a

---

[101] *N.J.S.A.* 2C:25-29(a-d).
[102] *N.J.S.A.* 2C:25-29(a).
[103] *Vendetti v. Meltz*, 359 *N.J. Super.* 63, 818 *A.2d* 357 (Ch. Div. 2002).

matrimonial case?

Explore all avenues and determine whether there is any kind of proof available to support your client's position, such as a witness who has heard the alleged victim talk about these motivations, or documentary proof such as tape recordings, letters, or other admissions.

See Appendix G, H, and I: Visitation Risk Assessment, Evaluation of Interview, and Confidential Litigant Information Sheet, all used by the intake officer.

Prepare financial information. If you can, it is to your benefit to prepare a complete Case Information Statement; alternatively, you may simply prepare a weekly budget sheet, which is all that is required.

If your client is abusing drugs or alcohol, have them stop immediately, if for no other reason, that the court might order that immediate tests be done.

Have alternative housing available for your client. In some cases, even if your client is blameless, they may not want to return to the house, as this may risk additional domestic violence complaints or a finding against them. If the parties are already living in separate habitats, and/or your client does not wish to return to the house, certain consents and restraints can be incorporated into a matrimonial proceeding, if one is pending, or the domestic violence case can be delayed until one is instituted. There are also no longer "in house restraining orders," which permitted the restraints, but allowed the parties to live in the same house.[104]

Make arrangements to pick up your client's personal belongings and supplies, including clothes, financial documents, insurance policies, prescription drugs and insurance cards. The Act provides that the defendant may return to the house, with the assistance of the police, to retrieve their personal items. However, the times available to pick up these items, as well as amount of time the party are allowed to be in the home, are strictly limited.[105]

Develop a parenting time schedule, with visitation or parenting time dates, times of pickup/drop off, and alternative people to act as intermediaries. The victim may resent certain people being involved, so it is wise to have a few choices. Have alternative places for pick up/drop off, other than curb side, and as a last resort, do so at the local police station.

It is important to prepare for the possibility that you might lose the case no matter how innocent your client is. Domestic violence actions are determined in the context of "credibility".

---

[104] *N.J.S.A.2C:25-28.1.*
[105] *N.J.S.A. 2C:25-28(k).*

It is the victim's word against your client's. In addition, the burden of proof is only "the preponderance of evidence". Lastly, the judicial climate is such that most judges, no matter what the allegations, and no matter what the defense, would order a restraint because it is safer to enter one than to deny it. It is easier for a judge to rationalize the imposition of a restraining order, than to face the wrath of the victim, their superiors, and/or the press, in the event they are wrong and harm befalls the victim as a result of the wrong decision.

Look for a possible settlement if you believe that the facts are strongly against you. Be aware that domestic violence law provides that a consent order may only issue where there is an admission of guilt. A matrimonial restraint does not carry an admission of guilt or any criminal sanctions for violation of a restraint as they do in a domestic violence case. Perhaps even mutual restraints can be negotiated.

See Appendix L: Temporary Restraining Order. If the victim's case is proven, a Final Restraining Order is issued. See Appendix R. There is also a mandatory $50 fine which is imposed in addition to other relief that may be granted under the Act. See Chapter Nine.

A. DISCOVERY

As stated previously, domestic violence matters are considered summary actions, and thus discovery is minimally if at all permitted. *N.J. Ct. R.* 5:5-1 provides: Except for summary actions discovery in civil family actions shall be permitted. Furthermore, *N.J. Ct. R.* 5:5-1(d) states: "All other discovery in family actions shall be permitted only by leave of court for good cause shown ..." In light of this, it would appear that interrogatories and other forms of depositions can only be done where there has been "good cause shown." The exception to this is the production of documents (*N.J. Ct. R.* 4:18-1); requests for admissions (*N.J. Ct. R.* 4:22-1); and copies of documents, related to in pleadings (*N.J. Ct. R.* 4:18-2), which are permitted as of right.

One type of discovery tool that is not permitted in domestic violence cases is the taking of the plaintiff's deposition. The rationale for excluding the plaintiff's deposition is rooted in the belief that a victim of domestic violence, who may be suffering from "battered woman's syndrome," is not likely to proceed with the final restraining order after being subjected to depositions. In one case addressing the taking of a Plaintiff's deposition, the court noted that a deposition is an intimidating process especially for a victim of domestic violence. The court further explained that the intimidation is exasperated by the absence of a judge to protect the victim, who may or may not be represented by an attorney.[106]

It is however not fully accurate to say that the taking of a plaintiff's deposition is never

---

[106] *Depos v. Depos*, 307 *N.J. Super.* 396, 704 *A.2d* 1049 (Ch. Div. 1997).

permitted, where domestic violence has occurred. Depositions of the plaintiff are permitted in a matrimonial action, even where the parties have had a history of domestic violence. Safeguards are however available.

A party may exclude an alleged abuser from a deposition or hearing upon demonstrating exceptional circumstances. *N.J. Ct. R:* 4:10-3 allows a trial court, for good cause shown and when justice requires, to enter a protective order to protect a party who is being deposed from annoyance, embarrassment, oppression, or undue burden. In doing so, a court may order the following:

(1)   that discovery not be had;

(2)   that the discovery may be had only on specified terms and conditions, including a designation of the time or place;

(3)   that the discovery may be had only by a method of discovery other than that selected by the party seeking discovery; and

(4)   that certain matters may not be inquired into, or that the scope of the discovery be limited to certain matters...[107]

In one case, a plaintiff/wife moved to exclude her husband from her deposition, after a restraining order had been entered. The court held that the wife did not establish sufficient exceptional circumstances to warrant the exclusion of the husband from the deposition. The court held that the wife did not establish good cause, necessitating the prohibition of the defendant's presence at her deposition.[108]

The above court stated that when determining whether to enter a protective Order, the courts look to the following: ✓

1. Past history of domestic violence between the parties;
2. Any violations of a domestic violence restraining order;
3. Past disregard of the judicial process, by the party sought to be excluded from the deposition;
4. Anticipation of misconduct during deposition, which would harass, alarm or frighten the party being deposed;
5. The party's fear of the party sought to be excluded;
6. The mental and emotional health of both parties;
7. General security concerns for the safety of the party being deposed;
8. The good faith of the party being deposed in asking to exclude the other party from the deposition; and

---

[107] *Mugrage v. Mugrage*, 335 *N.J. Super.* 653, 763 *A.2d* 347 (Ch. Div. 2000).
[108] *Ibid.*

9. Any other factor deemed relevant by the court

In *Mugrage*, the defendant had never physically hit the plaintiff and was respectful of the judicial process. However, the plaintiff still was fearful of defendant. The court ultimately concluded that although the defendant was permitted to be present at the Plaintiff's depositions, certain conditions should be imposed including the following:

> The depositions should be held in a conference room in the courthouse, and that all persons who enter are required to go through weapons check. The alleged abuser shall not have any contact or communication with the victim, and shall not speak out loud in her presence. The parties shall sit on the same side of the room, but not at the same table. The alleged abuser shall arrive 15 minutes before the victim, and shall remain in the room to avoid contact with the victim.[109]

In order to produce both physical and testamentary evidence, supporting your client's position, take advantage of the notice for the production of documents, the notice in lieu of subpoena, etc. Find out if there are any kinds of photographs or tape recordings that are available. Ask your client what documents are available, and to provide a list of those you may need.

Inspect any physical evidence, i.e., torn clothing, broken dishes, etc. You may also either visit the scene of the domestic violence, have pictures taken, or both, so that you can understand what happened, in the context of the exact surroundings.

In terms of witnesses, be sure to get a list of witnesses from your client prior to hearing. There will be lay witnesses who know the background of the case, or were actual eye witnesses to the occurrence. There are also expert witnesses, such as doctors and police. It is important to interview all witnesses prior to the hearing. Be sure to find out what the witness will testify to, and determine whether the testimony will be in your client's favor. Also be sure to subpoena expert witnesses, as well as secure any expert witness records, including hospital and medical records, as well as police reports.

The Rules provide that when the alleged victim makes their application for a temporary restraining order, whether in person or by telephone, it has to be taken by means of a tape-recorded interview, a stenographic machine a, or as a last resort, "adequate longhand notes summarizing what is said," made by the judge.[110] Get copies of the transcript of the proceedings or copies of the notes to compare with the actual testimony at the time of trial, by

---

[109] *Ibid.*

[110] *N.J. Ct. R.* 5:7A; *see also State of New Jersey Domestic Violence Procedural Manual*, p. IV-2.

applying for a Protective Order. See Appendix Q.

If the police were witnesses or were able to see the condition of the premises, or the victim post incident, obtain their police reports. You might also wish to subpoena the officer(s), as well as any 911 tapes and/or emergency tapes of the responding police department. The tapes may help in assessing the Plaintiff's candor, by revealing their tone and temperament during the call to the police.

Interview the witnesses in person or by telephone. Only where it is a last resort, should you subpoena the witness to court, without having interviewed them first. Your opportunity to interview them may be at the time of trial, at which point you can make the decision to either have them testify or release them. The danger in such a case is that the adverse party will also be given the opportunity to interview the witness, which is problematic, where you decide not to use them as a witness, since the adverse party might.

Most unwilling witnesses, who have been avoiding talking to you before the subpoena, will call you immediately thereafter, in order to discuss the case and possibly avoid their appearance.

3.3   THE TRIAL OF DOMESTIC VIOLENCE CASE

Our firm has been trying domestic violence cases since the initial enactment of the domestic violence law. Unfortunately, we have seen the deterioration of the process, due to interference by the Administrative Office of the Courts, and the inadequacy of the judges, both in numbers and experience. Many of the judges are ignorant of the law, and arrogant in their approach to it. The Judge is given wide discretion, and their decisions are at times guided by the fear of criticism, or of losing their jobs.

The court proceeding itself has become a circus and a "court of comparative perjury". It is a "free for all" with the Judge being afraid to control the proceeding, or the attorneys, resulting in a "Cole Porter Courtroom," where "anything goes".

The Judges, who are first appointed to the bench, with the least amount of experience, are initially appointed to the Family Court to handle domestic violence matters. It is a "weigh station", where they eagerly await exit. Those who remain are usually those who can do or wish to do little else. The major problem is that they remain ignorant as to how to handle these very delicate domestic violence matters. They are trained in "judge's school" to be more sensitive to the needs and the plights of the victim, but not the practicalities of applying the law.

This ignorance has been acknowledged by state lawmakers as well. In October 2014, New Jersey Assembly Woman, Caroline Casagrande, stated:

"Right now, as it stands, we have victims going into the courtroom, where the people have minimal training."

In preparing a bill to establish a separate Domestic Violence Court, Cassagrande went on to say that the bill will enable the judges to be "knowledgeable in criminal law and procedure, particularly in relation to intimate partner violence. It's really an attempt to get these victims and perpetrators into a court that really understands the problem."

In the years that have passed, it is so disappointing to see many of these judges do not know basic Rules of Evidence, are afraid of criticism, and fear that they might make the wrong decision, not granting a Restraining Order, when it is clearly inappropriate.

There also seems to be a sort of gender bias, favoring granting restraining orders to women, while denying the same to a man. We had an incident where the male victim accused the wife of striking him, and she readily admitted to the offense. The man exhibited visible cuts and bruising. The judge still refused to give the victim a Restraining Order, because in his estimation, the man was so strong that the wife did not hurt him. Clearly, due to his injuries and pursuant to the law, this does not entitle a perpetrator to one free smack. The judge clearly made a mistake.

On the other hand, if the alleged victim is a woman, every menial act is viewed as an act of domestic violence, (i.e, "he hovered over me" or "he threw a pickle at me" or "I am afraid of him") and courts will grant a Temporary Restraining Order.

The judge is not the only problem in the domestic violence process. There are also the administrative officers. During standard procedures, the Intake Officers sometimes coach the victims (through leading questions) on what to say and how to say it, essentially putting words in their mouths, stressing how afraid they are of the supposed abuser. For the above reason, we order transcripts of the proceeding before the Intake Officer. This allows us to see if that story is consistent with the complaint, and how much the victim has been coached by the Intake Officer when making their statement. Too often words are spoon fed to the victims, such as asking the victim if they "are afraid of the defendant?" Contrast that with the more appropriate question of "how do you feel about the defendant?"

Obtaining the transcripts poses a problem of itself, since the courts put obstacles in the way of receiving the transcript. However, eventually the court will release the transcript with a Protective Order. Note that to not release the transcript would be in violation of the defendant's Constitutional Rights of Confrontation under the Constitution of the United States, and the Constitution of New Jersey.

If the complaint was made via telephone, which is permitted, that conversation can be secured. It is valuable in order to determine the tone of the alleged victim at the time the incident occurred.

These remarks are not meant to dissuade true victims of domestic abuse from using the system correctly in order to protect them, but to illustrate the reality of the situation. Lawyers themselves abuse the system, using domestic violence complaints to "gain a leg up in the matrimonial process," especially where custody is an issue. It is sad, but true.

A. DEPORTMENT

The first thing I stress to a client is the importance of their appearance and deportment. Their reaction to the alleged victim's allegations, and their responses to any inquires made, are as important as the evidence that is presented in the court. I warn the client that the intake officer of the Probation Department, the court clerk, law clerk, and the Sheriff's officers are all observing the parties, and will report any adverse behavior to the judge. Your client must be vigilant and alert from the minute they walk into the court house, until the end of trial as to what they say and how they behave.

You must instruct them that even if the most vile, salacious, and mendacious remarks are made by the victim, they should not react adversely and should sit at the counsel table stoically. They should not write copious notes in a hurried manner, tug at your jacket sleeve, and interrupt your train of thought as you are trying to listen to the testimony. They should not draw attention to themselves. There is no right to a jury trial in a domestic relations case.

B. STANDARD OF PROOF

As stated briefly earlier, the standard of proof in a domestic violence case, although *quasi* criminal in nature is not guilt beyond a reasonable doubt, it is not even the civil standard of clear and convincing evidence, but rather the "preponderance of the evidence standard."[111] Under this standard, the victim can establish their case by convincing the judge that the evidence establishes it is more probable than not, that the incident occurred. The act that brought the victim to court, called the "predicate act" must be established, in addition to providing evidence of immediate danger, and the victims continued fear of the defendant.

Since the domestic violence complaint is civil and not criminal, the penalties are civil and not criminal, and thus the preponderance "standard of proof" was deemed to better serve the purpose of the Act and protecting the victim of domestic violence.[112] The preponderance of proof standard is used in domestic violence cases, rather than the criminal standard of "beyond a reasonable doubt," was the recognition by the Legislature that allegations of domestic violence will frequently be difficult to prove due to the private nature of the acts between parties. There will be few, if any, eyewitnesses to marital discord or domestic violence, thus, making a judge's determination of credibility more difficult. A criminal standard of proof may be impossible for most victims to prove.

The term "preponderance of evidence" usually means that in weighing the evidence presented by both parties, the court finds that one side's evidence is more convincing than the other, and that party will prevail. This standard was found not to violate the due process clause of the Constitution.[113-114]

Applying the balancing test established in *Matthews v. Eldridge*,[115] the court concluded that the Act met constitutional muster, in line with the Appellate Division's holding in *Roe v. Roe*.[116] The court reasoned that the defendant's private interests carry far less weight than the

---

[111] *Cesare v. Cesare,* 302 *N.J. Super.* 57, 694 *A.2d* 603 (App. Div. 1997), *reversed,* 154 *N.J.* 394, 713 *A.2d* 390 (1998).

[112] *N.J.S.A.* 2C:25-29(a). This standard has been affirmed by the Appellate Division. *Roe v. Roe,* 253 *N.J. Super.* 418, 428, 601 *A.2d* 1201 (App. Div. 1992); *Crespo v. Crespo,* 408 *N.J. Super.* 25, 972 *A.2d* 1169 (App. Div. 2009), *aff'd,* 201 *N.J.* 207, 989 *A.2d* 827 (2010)

[113] *Crespo v. Crespo,* 408 *N.J. Super.* 25, 972 *A.2d* 1169 (App. Div. 2009).

[114] *N.J.S.A.* 2C:25-29(a).

[115] *Mathews v. Eldridge, 424 U.S. 319,* 96 *S. Ct.* 893, 47 *L. Ed.* 2d 18 *(1976).*

[116] *Roe v. Roe,* 253 *N.J. Super.* 418, 601 *A.2d* 1201 (App. Div. 1992).

governmental interest in eliminating domestic violence, and in affording immediate and effective protection to victims of domestic violence. In addition, given the private nature of domestic violence acts where most cases turn on the trial judge's assessment of the credibility of plaintiff and defendant, a standard more demanding than the preponderance standard would undermine the social purposes of the Act.

C. INTEREST OR BIAS

New Jersey Courts have long recognized the fact that if a witness has a particular interest, motive, bias, or prejudice, this may affect their credibility.[117] A witnesses' bias is relevant to their credibility because bias would affect the witness either consciously or subconsciously. One rule of court permits the introduction of extrinsic evidence, affecting a witness' credibility, regardless of whether that evidence is relevant to any other issue in the case.[118]

The relationship of a witness to one of the parties is also a fact, showing bias. Mothers, fathers, sisters, brothers, etc. all have a bias to their blood relatives. To deny the bias before the Judge, runs contrary to human understanding and would go to undermine their testimony.

The "general method of examining a witness's credibility is through cross-examination. Cross-examination is the most effective device known to our trial procedure for seeking the truth."[119]

In *Franklin v. Sloskey*, the court held it was error to issue a TRO where the defendant was not afforded the opportunity to cross-examine the plaintiff, and it was clear she was unaware of her ability to do so. Moreover, by not allowing the defendant to cross examine her accuser, the court also violated her due process rights.[120]

The Court Stated:

> We understand that in a pro se trial a judge often has to focus the testimony and take over the questioning of the parties and witnesses. That should be done in an orderly and predictable fashion however, and not at the expense of the parties' due process rights.[121]

---

[117] *State v. Taylor*, 38 *N.J. Super.* 6, 25, 118 *A.2d* 46 (App. Div. 1955).

[118] *N.J. R. Evid.* 607.

[119] *Peterson v. Peterson*, 374 *N.J. Super.* 116, 863 *A.2d* 1059 (App. Div. 2005).

[120] *Franklin v. Sloskey*, 385 *N.J. Super.* 534, 897 *A.2d* 1113 (App. Div. 2006).

[121] *Ibid.*

In the absence of the critical safeguards afforded by cross-examination, "the integrity of the fact-finding process" is compromised because the trial court is unable to fully and fairly assess credibility.[122]

D. STATE OF MIND

In order to hold a defendant liable, his culpability must be established, with respect to each material element of the offense.[123] The state of mind of the defendant, when committing an act, must be discerned, to determine whether he knowingly, purposefully, recklessly or negligently committed said acts.[124]

The Code of Criminal Justice provides:

"A person is not guilty of an offense unless he acted purposely, knowingly, recklessly, or negligently as the law may require, with respect to each material element of the offense."[125]

The statute in its various parts defines the various kinds of culpability, specifically, definitions of purposely, knowingly, recklessly and negligently.

Theoretically, the plaintiff must establish that each and every act of domestic violence occurred, no matter how many acts of domestic violence a plaintiff alleges, as each allegation goes to a Plaintiff's credibility. However, as long as a Plaintiff proves that one of the acts occurred, the defendant will be found guilty.

E. CONSISTENCY

The testimony of the alleged victim should comport with the allegations set forth in the domestic violence complaint. It has been found that it is a violation of due process to issue a restraining order based on acts of violence not mentioned in the complaint.[126] It is clearly improper to base a finding of domestic violence upon acts and conduct not mentioned in the Complaint.[127]

Unfortunately this precept is oftentimes ignored, and complaints are liberally amended, even being done so at trial, placing the defendant in an overwhelming position. Where this happens, it is prudent to ask for an adjournment to delay the procedure, and allow time to

---

[122] *Ibid(citing Davis v. Alaska*, 415 *U.S.* 308, 316, 94 *S. Ct.* 1105, 1110, 39 *L. Ed. 2d* 347 (1974)).
[123] *N.J.S.A.* 2C:2-2(a).
[124] *N.J.S.A.* 2C-2-2(b).
[125] *N.J.S.A.* 2C:-2(a).
[126] *J.F. v. B.K.*, 308 *N.J. Super.* 387, 706 *A.2d* 203 (App. Div. 1998).
[127] *L.D. v. W. D.*, 327 *N.J. Super.* 1, 742 *A.2d* 588 (App. Div. 1999).

formulate a proper response.

> "Due process requires that a party in a judicial hearing receive notice defining the issues and an opportunity to prepare. It forbids the trial court from converting a hearing on one act of domestic violence into a hearing on other acts that are not alleged in the complaint. In a case where the plaintiff was permitted to expand upon the alleged prior incidents not cited in the complaint, during the hearing, the court ruled that defendant's due process rights were violated and an adjournment should have been granted to defendant."[128]

F. STATUTORY DEFENSES

As in any criminal case, there are specific statutory defenses to any crime, and thus to any act of domestic violence. Although technically they all apply, in reality some are inapplicable in the domestic violence arena, such as mutual consent, joint participation, intoxication, duress, ignorance or mistake and even justification.

The only viable statutory defenses for domestic violence actions are self-defense and *de minimis* infractions.

G. SELF DEFENSE

Under the domestic violence statute, a person is justified in using force upon another person, when the actor reasonably believes that such force is immediately necessary for the purpose of protecting himself against the use of unlawful force by such other person on the present occasion.[129]

Otherwise stated, self defense is the right of a person to defend against any unlawful force. Self defense is also the right of a person to defend against seriously threatened unlawful force that is actually pending or reasonably anticipated.

When a person is in imminent danger of bodily harm, the person has the right to use force or even deadly force when that force is necessary to prevent the use against (him/her) of unlawful force. The force used by the defender must be proportionate to the unlawful force threatened or used against the defender.

However, in reality, you have two parties, one appearing weaker and the other stronger.

---

[128] *J.D. v. M.D.F.*, 207 *N.J.* 458, 25 *A.3d* 1045 (2011).
[129] *N.J.S.A.* 2C:3-4.

The court is not going to believe that the stronger party used self-defense in order to fend off the advances of the weaker party. For example, if a woman attacks a man, scratching his face, and he simply holds her off, causing her bruises in the process, nine times out of ten, the court is not going to believe that the bruises on the woman are as a result of a man defending himself, but rather an aggressive behavior on his part.

H. De MINIMIS

The rules also provide for *de minimis* infractions in which the actions are "too trivial to warrant the condemnation of conviction for these actions cannot reasonably be regarded as envisaged by the Legislature in forbidding the offense."[130]

See comments in other section such as harassment in which the courts have used this statute to dismiss warrantless actions.

I. CREDIBILITY OF THE VICTIM

Most domestic violence cases revolve around one party's version of an incident against another. He said, she said. There are rarely witnesses to the incidents, video tapes or tape recordings. Thus, the defense of a case hinges on testimonial evidence, both direct and circumstantial. <u>More importantly a good defense will focus on inconsistencies in the Plaintiff's statements</u>, casting doubt on their credibility.

Testimonial evidence, of course, is evidence obtained from individuals who take the witness stand and testify to events. Direct evidence is evidence in which an individual testifying establishes as directly proving a fact. Circumstantial evidence is evidence that proves the existence of a fact, based on an inference, which may be logically and reasonably drawn from another factor or group of facts. Both direct and circumstantial evidence are accepted as means of proof and have various degrees of persuasiveness.

In a domestic violence situation, direct evidence would be that the victim saw the defendant pull the phone out of the wall. Circumstantial evidence would be that when the victim left the house, the phone was intact, and when they returned, the defendant was there and the phone was on the ground. The direct evidence goes to prove that the defendant tore the telephone out of the wall; the circumstantial evidence establishes the facts from which the inference can be drawn that the defendant tore the phone out of the wall.

When looking to undermine the Plaintiff's credibility, some question to be asked include whether the plaintiff's testimony is different than:

---

[130] *N.J.S.A.* 2C:2-11.

1. Allegations in the certification to the complaint;
2. Testimony at the time of the request for a temporary restraining order;
3. What they reported happened in 911 tapes to the police, as reflected in a police report.
4. Statements made in a pending matrimonial action, which do not mention any acts of violence.

Other factors to consider would include whether the Plaintiff has filed any prior frivolous domestic violence complaints, which were dismissed, and whether the parties had un-coerced sexual relations with the other after the incident. While this latter element alone is not sufficient to void the complaint, it does contradict the claim of fear of immediate danger.

Another factor influencing credibility is time lapse; in other words, how much time has elapsed between the act of domestic violence and the report to the police, and/or the filing of the complaint? Although this is not conclusive of anything in itself, the longer the time period the parties continued to cohabit, the less likely the Plaintiff can satisfactorily convince a judge that they fear the defendant.

J. WITNESS COMPETENCY AND PRIVILEGE

The rules provide a presumption that a witness is competent to testify. A witness may however be deemed incompetent to testify, if the defense counsel can establish that there is an impediment as to their perception or memory.

The rules of Evidence provide, a witness may not testify to a matter unless evidence is introduced sufficient to support a finding that the witness has personal knowledge of the matter. A witness can acquire personal knowledge through any of their senses. The person is deemed to be competent if he can observe, remember, narrate and recognize the duty to tell the truth. Thus, a trial judge may reject the testimony of a witness if they lack personal knowledge, or if the witness's perception as to the facts of a particular matter are questionable.[131]

In order to preclude the evidence, the judge must reject the testimony of the witness, where he finds that no trier of fact would reasonably believe that the witness actually perceived the matter. (*Note: that a lack of mental capacity is no longer sufficient grounds to establish a witness's incompetency.*)

Obviously, if an eye witness was present at, and observed the event in question, they would be competent (unless their perception is flawed). On the other hand, if the witness did not see the event happen, but they were told about it by someone else, they do not have

---

[131] *N.J. R. Evid.* 602.

personal knowledge of the matter and would not be competent to testify. If the witness saw the event happen, but was not wearing necessary glasses or contacts at the time, their perception is put into question as well, and their testimony may be deemed incompetent.

If you are challenging a witness on the grounds of lack of personal knowledge, ask the judge for permission to *voir dire* the witness before they give their testimony. For example, if the testimony proffered is that the witness saw a particular event, you might be able to show that the witness was unable to see the event because of an obstructed view, distance problems, problems with eyesight, etc. At the very beginning of their testimony, throw doubt as to their conclusions. The court may only allow you to question witness competency upon cross examination. Often the court will rightly allow such testimony, other times judges view these attacks upon personal knowledge as going to the weight of the evidence, rather than the witnesses competency to testify and will thereby preclude it.

Individuals in a domestic violence case may want to provide children as witnesses, which presents a special problem. Remember that under the Rules of Evidence, there is a presumption that all witnesses are competent, even a child. The younger the child, the more the presumption of competency is refutable, and the child is deemed incompetent to testify. This is, of course, not the case if it can be shown that the child has the capacity to testify. If this can be shown, the child will be allowed as a witness.

In order for a child to testify, the proponent must demonstrate that the child:

1.   Has the ability to observe the event about which they are about to testify;

2.   Has the ability to remember the event about which they are to testify;

3.   Has the ability to narrate to the judge that which they observed;

4.   That they understand the oath that is taken, i.e. the child recognizes that they have a duty to tell the truth and they understand what the truth is.

Any attack upon these foundations may nullify a child witness, especially with the predilections of the court to not have them testify.

The proper time to *voir dire* the child as to their competency would be prior to them testifying. The court will most likely not want a child testifying against either one of their parents, and may be looking for a way to avoid this confrontation.

1. Privileges:

In a domestic violence situation, if the victim and the defendant are spouses, the witness spouse is not to be barred from testifying. On the other hand, if the domestic violence is between non-spouses, and the spouse (non-party to litigation) is a witness, they may be deemed incompetent to testify because of the spousal privilege under *New Jersey Rule of Evidence* 501. Per *New Jersey Rule of Evidence* 501(2), the spousal immunity does not attach under the "Offended Spouse" exception.[132-133]

An attorney for the defendant can also be prohibited from testifying under the lawyer/client privilege under *New Jersey Rule of Evidence* 504. This, of course, extends not only to what a lawyer may have seen, but also to disclosure of any communication between himself and his client.

Lastly, there is no parent/child privilege that would forbid a child from testifying against their parents.[134] There is no parent/child privilege, but the courts are loathed to get children involved in this situation. Unless a child is absolutely essential to the case, he or she should not be dragged into it, where there is another alternative.

K. IMPEACHMENT

The most effective tool of defense is to attack the credibility of the victim or witness by impeaching their testimony through cross examination.

This serves to contradict and thus <u>neutralize</u>, the harmful testimony given by the witness. As a result, the witnesses' statements are proven to be incorrect.[135]

The Methods of impeachment are as follows:

1. Showing the witnesses' statement is inconsistent with some prior testimony;

2. Proving that the witness is biased in some respect (family relationship, through hostility to the other party, financial interest in the outcome, etc.);

3. Attacking to the character of the witness and prior criminal convictions;

4. Contradicting the witness through other witnesses' testimony.

Testimony in a domestic violence trial can be used for purposes of cross-examination in

---

[132] *State v. Marriner*, 93 *N.J.L.* 273, 108 *A.* 306, 1919 *N.J. Sup. Ct. (1919), aff'd,* 95 *N.J.L.* 265, 111 *A.* 688 (E & A 1920).
[133] *N.J. R. Evid.* 501(2), 509, and *N.J.S.A.* 2A:84A-22.
[134] *Matter of Gail D.*, 217 *N.J. Super.* 226, 525 *A.2d* 337 (App. Div. 1987).
[135] *State v. Gallicchio*, 44 *N.J.* 540, 210 *A.2d* 409 (1965); *State v. Johnson*, 216 *N.J. Super.* 588,524 *A.2d* 826 (App. Div. 1987).

a related criminal trial, despite the language of *N.J.S.A.* 2C:25-29(a) that precludes the use of testimony of either party in a domestic violence hearing in a related criminal proceeding against the defendant. Courts have held the statute cannot be interpreted so broadly that it conflicts with a criminal defendant's constitutional rights under the Confrontation Clause. The trial testimony of a domestic violence complainant must be made available for use by a criminal defendant during cross-examination to impeach contradictory or inconsistent testimony that is material to the charges against the defendant or to show bias, prejudice or ulterior motives on the part of the witness. Likewise, if a criminal defendant chooses to testify in the criminal action, he or she would be subject to cross-examination to the same extent as the domestic violence complainant.[136]

L. INCONSISTENT PRIOR STATEMENTS

This tool utilizes the statements made by the witness at trial, and statements they have previously attested to, exhibiting any and all inconsistencies. The purpose here is not merely to contradict the testimony of the witness by way of the witnesses' prior testimony, but to impeach the witness, proving that they are not worthy of being believed. The previous statements of the witness could be written or oral. This is where the previously obtained police reports, medical reports, tape recordings, etc., become important yet again. The fact that the statements are inconsistent is relevant to credibility, sincerity, or memory.

New Jersey Rule of Evidence 613 provides that an attorney, when examining a witness concerning the prior statement, need not show or disclose to the witness at the time of cross examination, their prior statement. Thus, you do not have to show the witness the prior statement and ask them to explain the difference between that and their present testimony. If opposing counsel asks for it to be disclosed to them, they are entitled to receive a copy of it.

Prior inconsistent statements may also be used as substantive evidence and not solely for impeachment purposes.[137] However, if there is extrinsic evidence alluded to in inconsistent statements of the witness, a witness is to be afforded an opportunity to explain or deny the statement.

M. CRIMINAL RECORD WITNESS

A witness's criminal convictions are admissible, and "may be given in evidence to affect his (her) credit as a witness."[138] This is not the case where there has been an arrest of the witness, but no conviction. Inquiry concerning an arrest, or any reference to simply an arrest, is

---

[136] *State v. Duprey*, 427 *N.J. Super.* 314, 48 *A.3d* 419 (App. Div. 2012).
[137] *N.J. R. Evid.* 803(a)(1).
[138] *N.J.S.A.* 2A:81-12; *State v. Hawthorne*, 49 *N.J.* 130, 228 *A.2d* 682 (1967).

prohibited.[139]

The rationale for allowing this is based on the belief that criminals are not worthy of belief. Thus, if there is any crime that the witness has been convicted of, such as a prior domestic violence conviction, it can be used to impeach the credibility of the witness.

N. CHARACTER OF THE WITNESS

The credibility of a witness may be attacked or supported by evidence, which may come in the form of an opinion or their reputation. The evidence introduced must only relate to the witness' character for truthfulness or untruthfulness. Evidence of truthful character is admissible only after the character of the witness for truthfulness has been attacked by opinion or reputation evidence or otherwise. Except as otherwise provided by *New Jersey Rule of Evidence* 609 and by paragraph (b) of *New Jersey Rule of Evidence* 608, a trait of character cannot be proved by specific instances of conduct.[140]

O. OTHER WITNESSES' TESTIMONY

The most effective means of attacking one witnesses' testimony is through the testimony of another witness. Other witness testimony should be utilized in order to convince the Judge that your witnesses' statement is more credible than the other witnesses' statement.

P. BATTERED WOMEN'S SYNDROME

The classic concept of battered women's syndrome originally arose as a defense for women in criminal homicide trials. It was used to explain why a woman committed the murder of their intimate partner, where self-defense did not apply.

The defense of Battered Women Syndrome was introduced to explain behavioral and emotional patterns of women suffering from repeated physical abuse inflicted by their husbands/lovers, and to explain why these women continue to live with their abusers even though beatings continue over long periods of time. Expert testimony in this growing psychological field has been permitted across the nation and beginning in New Jersey in 1984 as a defense.[141]

The defense of Battered Women's Syndrome differs from typical self defense. Self defense cases, as mentioned previously, involve a person using force against someone who is about to attack, or is attacking them. Self defense also requires that the claimant be in

---

[139] *State v. Hutchins*, 241 *N.J. Super.* 353, 575 *A.2d* 35 (App. Div. 1990); *N.J. R. Evid.* 609.
[140] *N.J. R. Evid.* 404 and 608.
[141] *State v. Kelly*, 97 *N.J.* 178, 193, 478 *A.2d* 364 (1984).

imminent danger of bodily harm, and more importantly that the force used by the defender be proportionate to the unlawful force threatened or used against the defender.

On the other hand, cases dealing with Battered Women Syndrome usually involve the woman killing her abuser a good deal of time before an attack occurred, or sometime thereafter, when there is no immediate threat present. In these cases the woman has experienced a long history of battering. The Battered Woman Syndrome does not involve insanity, mental disabilities or diminished capacity. Rather, it bears on the self defense issue of honesty and reliability of defendant's belief that she was in immediate danger of serious injury.[142]

Lenore Walker, the preeminent researcher in the field of Battered Women's Syndrome, and the one most quoted by the courts, succinctly sets forth the doctrine, and the resultant theory has been known as the "Walker Cycle Theory."

Walker defines a battered woman as any woman "18 years of age or older, who is or has been in an intimate relationship with a man who repeatedly subjects or subjected her to forceful physical and/or psychological abuse, moderate coerce her to do something he wants her to do without any concern for her rights..In order to be classified as a battered women, the women must go through the battery cycle at least twice."[143] She states that the relationship between the woman and the abuser goes through three phases.

The three phases of the battering cycles are as follows:

- The "tension-building stage," during which the battering male engages in minor battering incidents and verbal abuse while the woman, beset by fear and tension, attempts to be as placating and passive as possible in order to stave off more serious violence.
- The "acute battering incident." At some point during phase one, the tension between the battered woman and the batterer becomes intolerable and more serious violence inevitable. The triggering event that initiates phase two is most often an internal or external event in the life of the battering male, but provocation for more severe violence is sometimes provided by the woman who can no longer tolerate or control her phase-one anger and anxiety.
- Extreme contrition and loving behavior on the part of the battering male. During this period the man will often mix his pleas for forgiveness and protestations of devotion with promises to seek professional help, to stop drinking, and to refrain from further violence. For some couples, this period of relative calm may last as long as several months, but in a battering relationship the affection and

---

[142] *State v. Myers*, 239 *N.J. Super.* 158, 570 *A.2d* 1260 (App. Div. 1990).
[143] *The Battered Women's Syndrome. L. Walker*, (1984).

contrition of the man will eventually fade and phase one of the cycle will start anew.[144]

According to this cycle theory, the battered woman is reduced to a state of fear and anxiety during the first two phases of the cycle, and her perception of danger extends beyond the time of the battering episodes themselves. The woman is consumed with a constant fear of harm which results in a "cumulative terror". This terror continues even through the peaceful interlude between episodes of abuse.

Walker stresses that the woman experiences a growing tension in phase one, develops a fear of death or serious bodily harm during phase two, and, if she is to strike out at the abuser, it has to be before the next attack occurs usually during the most peaceful of times, such as in phase three.

Walker observes:

> Sometimes, (the battered woman) strikes back during a calm period, knowing that the tension is building towards another acute battering incident, where this time she may die.

The common sense question asked by all who have not been involved in this kind of relationship is why doesn't the woman simply leave? Walker explains this by the second part of her theory called "Learned Helplessness."[145]

Walker adapted this theory from that of another researcher, Martin Seligman, who worked with laboratory dogs. These dogs, after being subjected to repeated shocks over which they had no control, "learned that they were helpless, and when placed in an escapable situation, the dogs failed to escape." Walker applies this theory to the problems of battered women and explains that:

> The women's experiences... of their attempts to control the violence would, over time, produce learned helplessness and depression as the 'repeated batterers, like electric shocks, diminish the woman's motivation to respond.[146]

The third phase of this cycle theory, "the loving contrition phase," also ties in with the "learned helplessness" theory to explain why battered women fail to leave violent relationships. According to Walker, the batterer's "extreme loving, kind and contrite behavior"

---

[144] *See State v. Kelly*, 97 *N.J.* 178, 478 *A.2d* 364 (1984).
[145] *The Battered Women's* Syndrome, *L. Walker,* p. 86
[146] *Id.* at 87

operates as a "process of reinforcement for remaining in the relationship." This new contrition following the acute battering incident softens the woman's recollection of the extremely negative preceding phase.

With all of these factors combined, the learned helplessness due to the uncontrollable beatings, the promises, and hope that things will be different, all contribute to the reason that she does not leave the home.

Victims are usually at their highest risk of injury when they try to leave their abusers, and those who do leave are justified in their continued fear because of the many cases where victims are assaulted or killed by former partners.

Walker rejects the beliefs that "battered women are masochistic, that they stay with their mates because they like beatings, that the violence fulfills a deep seated need within each partner, or that they are free to leave such relationships if that is what they really want to do."[147]

Studies have found that those who commit acts of domestic violence have an unhealthy need to control and dominate their partners and frankly do not stop their abusive behavior despite court orders.

In an earlier case, the Court determined that before a Court could consider a defense of "Battered Women's Syndrome", the action of the defendant must be viewed from an objective point of view to see if it meets the test, i.e. whether the provocation alleged was "sufficient to arouse the passions of an ordinary (person) beyond the power of his (or her) control."[148]

Now the test has shifted to a subjective point of view. The latest criminal case held that prior abuse was relevant in assessing the honesty and reasonableness of defendant's belief in the need to use deadly force.[149]

1. Battered Woman's Syndrome as a Cause of Action

Not only is Battered Woman's Syndrome a defense in domestic violence, but it has also been recognized as an affirmative cause of action under the laws of New Jersey (as a tort).[150]

---

[147] See L. Walker (1984) *The Battered Women's Syndrome*.

[148] *State v. McClain*, 248 *N.J. Super.* 409, 591 *A.2d* 652 (App. Div. 1991); Contrast this with the change from objective to subjective tests, to set forth in *State v. Hoffman*, 149 *N.J.* 564, 695 *A.2d* 236 (1997) described under the harassment part of this book.

[149] *State v. Gartland*, 149 *N.J.* 456, 694 *A.2d* 564 (1997).

[150] *Cusseaux v. Pickett*, 279 *N.J. Super.* 335, 652 *A.2d* 789 (Law Div. 1994).

Miss Cusseaux lived with Wilson Pickett, Jr., the rock-n-roll legend for about 10 years. During this period, he continuously battered her, and on a number of occasions, she had to seek medical attention. The complaint against Pickett alleged that he mistreated Cusseaux, "jeopardized her health and well-being, and caused her physical injuries, on numerous occasions," as "part of a continuous course of conduct and constituted a pattern of violent behavior, frequently associated with being intoxicated." The judge used a Louisiana case[151] to support his decision to recognize the cause of action, but modified the case's decision. (The Louisiana court rejected the argument that the battered-woman's syndrome constituted a continuing tort, and instead found that each incident of battery and assault was a separate cause of action. Thus, the plaintiff was precluded from recovering damages for incidents that occurred beyond the effective statute of limitations period.) In its decision, the court stated:

> It would be contrary to the public policy of this state, not to mention cruel, to limit only those individual incidents of assault and battery, for which the applicable (two year) statute of limitation has not run. The mate who was responsible for creating the condition suffered by the battered woman must be made to account for his actions, all his actions.[152]

Although stating that the "Battered-Woman's Syndrome" was not previously an affirmative cause of action in this state, and only cognizable under the laws of defense in criminal actions, the court nonetheless recognized it as a new cause of action, stating that the New Jersey Supreme Court has expressly held that trial courts must accord any plaintiff's complaint a "meticulous" and "indulgent" examination.[153]

The court pointed to the Prevention of Domestic Violence Act, wherein the Legislature found that domestic violence was a serious crime against society, and that there are thousands of persons in this state who are regularly beaten, tortured, and in some cases even killed by their spouses and cohabitants. Moreover, the court stated that it is the responsibility of the courts to protect victims of violence that occurs in a family or family-like settings:

> The efforts of the Legislature to this end should be applauded. However, there are but steps in the right direction. As in a case with the domestic statute where existing criminal statutes were inadequate, so too are the civil laws of assault and battery insufficient to address the harm suffered as a result of Domestic violence. Domestic violence is a plague on our social structure

---

[151] *Laughlin v. Breux*, 515 *So.2d* 480 (La. App. 1 Cir. 1987).

[152] *Cusseaux v. Pickett*, 279 N.J. Super. 335, 652 A.2d 789 (Law Div. 1994).

[153] *Printing Mart Morristown v. Sharp Electronics Corp.*, 116 N.J. 739, 772, 653 A.2d 31 (1989)

and frontal assault on the institutions of the family. The Battered Woman's Syndrome is but one of the pernicious symptoms of that plague. Although the court could be hard pressed to prescribe the panacea for all domestic violence, they are entrusted with the power to fashion a palliative when necessary. The underpinning of our common law and public policy demand that where the Legislature has not gone far enough, the courts must fill the interstices.

The court then set down the four standards the plaintiff must prove to establish a cause of action for Battered Woman's Syndrome:

1. Involvement in a marital or a marital-like intimate relationship; and

2. Physical or psychological abuse perpetrated by the dominant partner to the relationship over an extended period of time; and

3. The afore stated abuse has caused recurring physical or psychological injury over the course of the relationship; and

4. A past or present inability to take any action or improve or alter the situation unilaterally."[154]

2. Last Note on the Role of Expert Witnesses

The existence and impact of the Battered Woman's Syndrome is an appropriate subject for expert testimony. This expert testimony may be used to support a witness' credibility.[155]

A person can be an expert witness in support of the defense of Battered Woman's Syndrome even if they have never testified in court before if they have the necessary expertise to testify both in terms of practice and study, and have a sufficient basis upon which to offer an opinion from both their personal interview with the victim and their knowledge of the case.[156]

If a person asserts Battered Woman's Syndrome, and intends to introduce expert testifying with regard to it, she must submit to an examination of the state's expert(s) who may be called to rebut the defense.[157]

---

[154] *Cusseaux v. Pickett,* 279 *N.J. Super.* 335, 344, 652 *A.2d* 789 (Law. Div. 1994).
[155] *State v. Kelly,* 97 *N.J.* 178, 478 *A.2d* 364 (1984).
[156] *State v. Frost,* 242 *N.J. Super.* 601, 577 *A.2d* 1282 (App. Div. 1990).
[157] *State v. Myers,* 239 *N.J. Super.* 158, 169, 570 *A.2d* 1260 (App. Div. 1990).

If relief is granted, the Court will Order a Permanent Restraining Order.

3.4 MAGIC WORDS TO A JUDGE FROM PLAINTIFF

The following are terms, sentences, and phrases that can assist an attorney when before the court and should be utilized strategically in the appropriate situation. Same has been categorized as follows.

A. GENERAL

At its core, the 1991 Domestic Violence Act effectuates the notion that the victim of domestic violence has the right to be left alone. Not only do victims of domestic violence have the right to be left alone, but each and every person has the fundamental right to be left alone and to feel safe, especially within their own home. These assurances are protected under the umbrella of the right to privacy afforded by both the U.S. and N.J. Constitutions.

Domestic violence disputes "are not private wars. Acts of domestic violence are often crimes. The public has an interest, wholly apart from that of the litigants, in the fair and effective resolution of these cases." [158]

The Act is intended to assist those who are truly the victims of domestic violence. It should not be trivialized by its misuse in situations which do not involve violence, or threats of violence. Previously expressed, the Act is at times misused in order to gain advantage in a companion matrimonial action, or where custody or visitation is at issue.

The courts are conscious of the burgeoning domestic violence case load in the Superior Court, and that jurisdictional scrutiny is necessary to insure that the Act is not trivialized and the Superior Court is not overrun with disorderly person cases probably allocable to the municipal courts. [159]

There is an "atmosphere of hostility in this household culminating in the threat." [160]

"Subjective fear" is the fear produced by and within the mind of the victim as the victim understands and communicates it." "Rather, the test is one of objective fear, i.e. that fear which a reasonable victim similarly situated would have under the circumstances" [161]

The public has an interest, wholly apart from that of the litigants, in the fair and effective resolution of these cases. Victims come from a variety of circumstances, but the optimism that often underlies their forgiveness of the abusers should not deny them protection

---

[158] *A.B. v. L.M.*, 89 *N.J. Super.* 125, 672 *A.2d* 1296 (App. Div. 1996).

[159] *Smith v. Moore*, 298 *N.J. Super.* 121, 689 *A.2d* 145 (App. Div. 1997).

[160] *Roe v. Roe*, 253 *N.J. Super.* 418, 601 *A.2d* 1201 (App. Div. 1992).

[161] *Stevenson v. Stevenson*, 314 *N.J. Super.* 350, 714 *A.2d* 986 (Ch. Div. 1998).

of law when confronted with the party's request.[162]

B. HARASSMENT

When deciding whether the harassment statutes have been violated, the courts must consider the totality of the circumstances.[163]

The scales of justice remind us that the public as well as the victim have a right to feel safe when alone in their own home. Each and every one of us has the fundamental right to be left alone.[164]

The defendant's conduct taken in the aggregate constitutes domestic violence and defendant had intended to harass plaintiff.[165]

Purposeful is "the highest form of *mens rea* contained in our penal code and the most difficult to establish."[166]

A single communication can be sufficient to constitute domestic violence, even with no history of abuse between the parties, a court can also determine that an ambiguous incident qualify as prohibited conduct based on finding of violence on the parties part.[167]

"Placing oneself in a location and remaining there for some time may constitute a 'course of conduct'."[168] The court may rely upon prior conduct and common sense to infer that the defendant had intended, and had the necessary purpose to harass his victim.[169]

"Any abuser who spontaneously appears or makes surprising communications without any legitimate purpose enhances the victim's apprehension. The fears of a domestic violence victim and the turmoil she or he has experienced should not be trivialized."[170]

The method and manner of communication established a harassing intent to annoy or alarm.

---

[162] *A.B. v. L.M.*, 289 N.J. *Super.* 125, 131, 672 *A.2d* 1296 (App. Div. 1996).

[163] *Cesare v. Cesare*, 154 *N.J.* 394, 713 *A.2d* 390 (1998).

[164] *State v. Mosch*, 214 N.J. *Super.* 457, 519 A.2d 937 (App. Div. 1986), *certif. den.*, 107 *N.J.* 131, 526 *A.2d* 147 (1987).

[165] *J.N.S. v. D.B.S.*, 302 N.J. *Super.* 525, 527, 695 *A.2d* 730 (App. Div. 1997).

[166] *State v. Duncan*, 376 N.J. *Super.* 253, 262, 870 *A.2d* 30 (App. Div. 2005).

[167] *Cesare v. Cesare*, 154 *N.J.* 394, 713 *A.2d* 390 (1998).

[168] *State v. J.T.*, 294 N.J. *Super.* 540, 545, 683 *A.2d* 1166 (App. Div. 1996).

[169] *E.K. v. G.K.*, 241 N.J. *Super.* 567, 573 *A.2d* 883 (App. Div. 1990).

[170] *State v. Hoffman*, 149 *N.J.* 564, 586, 695 *A.2d* 236, 247 (1997).

A mere expression of an option utilizing offensive language is not sufficient to prove harassment ("senile old bitch").[171]

It is not whether she is in mortal fear of her life, but whether the statements meet the statutory requirement. "Pre-divorce statements respecting absence of affections and physical desire alone are not intended to be sufficient to fulfill the elements of purposeful alarm or serious annoyance necessary to constitute harassment under the statute."[172]

Evidence of a past incident of domestic violence, between defendant and a previous spouse, who is not a party in the action, is admissible to prove that an ambiguous comment is made with a purpose to annoy or alarm plaintiff so as to constitute harassment.[173]

---

[171] *E.M.B. v. R.F.B.*, 419 *N.J. Super.* 177, 183, 16 *A.3d* 463 (App. Div. 2011).
[172] *Murray v. Murray*, 267 *N.J. Super.* 406, 411, 631 *A.2d* 984 (App. Div. 1993).
[173] *Rosiak v. Melvin*, 351 *N.J. Super.* 322, 798 *A.2d* 156 (Ch. Div. 2002).

3.5   MAGIC WORDS TO JUDGE FOR THE DEFENSE

A. GENERAL

The integrity of the trial courts fact finding was compromised by the failure of the defendant to...

Defendant was merely responding honestly to his wife's inquiries. Despite the fact that these statements were made to belittle and demean the plaintiff, they were not made for that purpose, although they might have had that effect.[174]

"This finding is insufficient as a matter of law to meet the statutory standard."[175]

Actions were "accidental and unanticipated."[176]

The criminalization of inconsequential acts that the Legislature never intended to prohibit will not solve this problem.[177]

The courts are conscious of the burgeoning domestic violence case load in the Superior Court, and jurisdictional scrutiny is necessary to insure that the Act is not trivialized and the Superior Court is not overrun with disorderly person cases probably allocable to the municipal courts.[178]

Defendant did not have any reasonable basis for her belief that she was terrified by defendant's actions.[179]

That conduct cannot be found by a preponderance of the evidence that constitutes domestic violence.[180]

Defendant's conduct may have been inappropriate or improper. However, there is some justification for his or her conduct.

This matter fits into a category of domestic contretemps more than a "matter of

---

[174] *Murray v. Murray*, 267 *N.J. Super.* 406, 408, 631 *A.2d* 984 (App. Div. 1993).

[175] *Peranio v. Peranio*, 280 *N.J. Super.* 47, 55, 654 *A.2d.* 495 (App. Div. 1995).

[176] *E.K. v. G.K.*, 241 *N.J. Super.* 569, 573 *A.2d* 883 (App. Div. 1990).

[177] *N.J.S.A.* 2C:25-29(a) (1) and (2).

[178] *Smith v. Moore*, 298 *N.J. Super.* 121, 689 *A.2d* 145 (App. Div. 1997).

[179] *J.N.S v. D.B.S..*, 302 *N.J. Super.* 525, 530, 695 *A.2d* 730 (App. Div. 1997).

[180] *Cesare v. Cesare*, 302 *N.J. Super.* 57, 694 *A.2d* 603, (App. Div. 1997), *reversed*, 154 *N.J.* 394, 713 *A.2d* 348 (1997).

consequence."[181]

The difficult task facing each judge who must rule on domestic violence complaints is that they never know with certainty which persons, among the many each day who swear out complaints seeking protection from alleged domestic violence, are actually at risk.

The court with necessity must distinguish between bickering between the parties from prohibitive acts of domestic violence.

Plaintiff's repeated and petty complaints to the local police department evidence a lack of perspective and a sense of proportion that led to the filing of this complaint are consistent with the conclusion that the Court should not believe the plaintiff.

By dismissing the complaint, we are not asking the court to condone the offense of inappropriate behavior of the defendant, but merely to reassert the importance of the Prevention of Domestic Violence Act by denying its application to trivial and petty communications between separated spouses who appear to be misusing the Act.

Ongoing disputes between the parties should have been referred to the Family Part judge to whom the pending divorce action was assigned. This judge would have the authority to take effective action to protect the children from harmful and offensive conduct that is done by either one of the parties in their presence. The parties' disputes over custody, visitation, support, and assets are already before the court in their matrimonial litigation.[182] His efforts were those of a loving suitor trying to repair the relationship and did not constitute house member.[183-184]

There is insufficient credible evidence to support the plaintiff's accusation of domestic violence.

The invocation of the domestic violence law in this instance trivializes the plight of true victims of domestic violence and would violate the true spirit of the Legislature's purpose.

The Legislature did not intend to commission any of these acts automatically would warrant the issuance of a domestic violence order. The law mandates that acts claimed by the plaintiff to be domestic violence must be evaluated in light of the previous history of domestic violence between the plaintiff and defendant including previous threats, harassment, and physical abuse, and in light of whether immediate danger to the person or the property is

---

[181] *N.B. v. T.B.* 297 *N.J. Super.* 35, 41, 687 *A.2d* 766 (App. Div. 1997)(*quoting Corrente v. Corrente*, 281 *N.J. Super.* 243, 250, 657 *A.2d* 440 (App. Div. 1995)).

[182] *J.N.S. v. D.B.S.*, 302 *N.J. Super.* 525, 532, 695 *A.2d* 730 (App. Div. 1997).

[183] *Bresocnik v. Gallegos*, 367 *N.J. Super.* 178, 842 *A.2d* 276 (App. Div. 2004).

[184] *Sweeney v. Honachefsky*, 313 *N.J. Super.* 443, 712 *A.2d* 1274 (App. Div. 1998).

present. This requirement reflects the reality that domestic violence is ordinarily more than an isolated aberrant act and incorporates the Legislative intent to provide a vehicle to protect victims whose safety is threatened. This is the backdrop on which the defendant's acts must be evaluated.[185-186]

We are mindful that the dissolution of a marriage is often acrimonious but such acrimony should not be used as a weapon to gain strategic advantage in the matrimonial court, thus trivializing and distorting the beneficial purpose of the Act to protect against regular abusive behavior. Matters such as the present case, do not rise to the level of domestic violence and can be addressed by the Chancery Division, Family Part, under its equitable powers.[187]

These are not acts which can be characterized as alarming or seriously annoying.[188]

These findings indicate that the focus of the Legislature was regular serious abuse between spouses. That this is so is underscored by the reference to torture, battery, beatings and killing in the findings.[189]

Separate and apart from these evidential insufficiencies which preclude a finding of the predicate act of harassment, defendant's conduct were plainly never contemplated by the Legislature when it addressed the serious social problem of domestic violence. Plaintiff's complaint asserted that there was no history of domestic violence, and there was no finding by the judge of a history of abuse or an immediate threat to safety. What occurred between these parties, whose relationship had ended and who were living apart, was a conflict over finances and possession of the marital premises. During an argument, tempers flared and defendant threatened drastic measures. He carried out his threat with the childish act of turning off the phone. While this was not conduct to be proud of, plaintiff was neither harmed (except in the most inconsequential way) nor was she subjected to potential injury. As such, the invocation of the domestic violence law trivialized the plight of true victims of domestic violence and misused the legislative vehicle which was developed to protect them. It also had a secondary negative effect: the potential for unfair advantage to a matrimonial litigant.

Some people, in seeking a restraining order, come to court with the intent of gaining an advantage in a pending divorce action in order to obtain custody of the children or possession of the home, or both.

---

[185] *Corrente v. Corrente*, 281 *N.J. Super.* 243, 248, 657 *A.2d* 440 (App. Div. 1995).

[186] *N.J.S.A.* 2C:25-29(a) (1) and (2).

[187] *Cesare v. Cesare*, 302 *N.J. Super.* 57, 68, 694 *A.2d* 603, 609 (App. Div. 1997), *reversed*, 154 *N.J.* 394, 713 *A.2d* 390 (1998).

[188] *J.N.S. v. D.B.S.*, 302 *N.J. Super.* 525, 531, 695 *A.2d* 730 (App. Div. 1997).

[189] *N.J.S.A.* 2C:25-29(a)(1) and (2).

There are "serious" policy implications of permitting allegations of this nature to be branded as domestic violence and used by either spouse to secure a ruling on critical issues such as support, exclusion from marital residence, and property disposition, particularly when or where a matrimonial action is pending or about to begin.[190]

We recognize that in the area of domestic violence, as in some other areas of our law, some people may attempt to use the process as a sword rather than as a shield. The Judicial System must once again rely on the trial courts as the gatekeeper. The Legislature has established a self-regulating provision in the Act so they can be used to protect against frivolous prosecutions under the Act. The gap filler of the nature is the *de minimis* infraction provision, *N.J.S.A.* 2C:2-11.[191]

As was said by the Appellate Division in *Murray*:

We are concerned, too, with the serious policy implications of permitting allegations of this nature to be branded as domestic violence and used by either spouse to secure rulings on critical issues such as support, exclusion from marital residence and property disposition, particularly when aware that a matrimonial action is pending or about to begin.[192]

Neither the harassment statute nor the Prevention of Domestic Violence Act were intended to place trial judges in the role of superior monitors over modern-day parenting. In our view, plaintiffs repeated and petty complaints to the local police department evidence a lack of perspective and sense of proportion that led to the filing of this complaint and are consistent with the judge's own conclusion that he believed "neither the plaintiff nor the defendant."[193]

Domestic violence is ordinarily something more than an isolated abhorrent event.[194]

"It must be understood that [the] decision today does not in any way condone the offensive and inappropriate behavior of either party." The point is to "reassert the importance of the Prevention of Domestic Violence Act by denying its application to trivial and petty communications between separated spouses who appear to be misusing that Act."[195]

---

[190] *Murray v Murray,* 267 N.J. Super. 406, 410, 631 *A.2d* 984 (App. Div. 1993).

[191] *State v. Hoffman,* 149 N.J. 564, 586, 695 *A.2d* 236, 247 (1997).

[192] *J.N.S. v. D.B.S.,* 302 N.J. Super. 525, 531, 695 *A.2d* 730 (App. Div. 1997).

[193] *J.N.S v. D.B.S.,* 302 N.J. Super. 525, 532, 695 *A.2d* 730 (App. Div. 1997).

[194] *Peranio v. Peranio,* 280 N.J. Super. 47, 54, 654 *A.2d* 495 (App. Div. 1995).

[195] *J.N.S. v. D.B.S.,* 302 N.J. Super. 525, 532, 695 *A.2d* 734 (App. Div. 1997).

B. HARASSMENT

The evidence does not support a finding of harassment.

This may be an "over-the-top, in-your-face gesture, but it was not likely to neither alarm nor seriously annoy a reasonable person. On the contrary, it is merely a minor irritant attached to a legitimate legal communication.[196]

"Human nature being what it is, this is unfortunately the kind of infantile tweaking we have come to expect of litigants whose hopes and dreams for their marriage and family life have been dashed."[197]

The Legislature did not intend to criminalize "irksome or vexing communications."[198]

Certainly, defendant, as the natural father of the child, had a right to express disapproval at the way the child was being punished. Although he may have chosen other words, his conduct did not rise to the level of harassment.[199]

Plaintiffs disputed allegations, even if true, are trivial because there is insufficient evidence that defendant acted with the required "intent to harass" the plaintiff.

Despite the vulgarities that both parties obviously exchanged on numerous occasions and the inappropriate behavior to which they exposed their children, defendant's behavior cannot fairly be said to have violated the criminal code or to have been evidence or risk of escalating or future violence.

Neither the harassment statute nor the Prevention of Domestic Violence Act was intended to place trial judges in the role of super monitors over modern day parenting.

There can be no finding of intent to harass with respect to the actions of the defendant against the plaintiff, only that the defendant was alarmed by them, which fall short of the mandate of the statute.[200]

Verbal harassment is not merely "offensive language." It's got to be more than a mere

---

[196] *State v. B.H.*, 290 *N.J. Super.* 588, 599, 676 *A.2d.* 565 (App. Div. 1996), *reversed in part and affirmed in part*, 149 N.J. 564, 695 *A.2d* 236 (1997).

[197] *Ibid.*

[198] *State v. Hoffman*, 149 *N.J.* 564, 578, 695 *A.2d* 236, 243 (1997).

[199] *State v. D.C.*, 269 *N.J. Super.* 458, 462, 635 *A.2d* 1002 (App. Div. 1994).

[200] *State v. B.H.*, 290 *N.J. Super.* 588, 608, 676 *A.2d.* 565 (App. Div. 1996).

expression of opinion using offensive language.[201]

One cannot proscribe mere speech, use of language, or other forms of expression. The First Amendment permits regulation of conduct, not mere expression.[202]

There was no purpose to harass, and defendant's speech was merely "offensive language" as opposed to verbal harassment.[203]

"It is a trivial, non-actionable event."[204]

"Objective fear" is that fear which a reasonable victim similarly situated would have had under the circumstances.[205]

"The Domestic Violence Act affords critically needed protections in appropriate situations. It was not intended to attempt to regulate and adjudicate every loss of temper, angry word, or quarrel between persons connected by familial relationship."[206]

A violation of *N.J.S.A.* 2C:33-4(c) requires proof of a course of conduct, which may consist of conduct that is alarming, or it may be a series of repeated acts if done with the purpose "to alarm or seriously annoy" the intended victim.[207]

---

[201] *State v. Finance American Corp.* 182 *N.J. Super.* 33, 36, 440 *A.2d* 28 (App. Div. 1981).

[202] *State v. L.C.* 283 *N.J. Super.* 441, 450, 662 *A.2d* 577 (App. Div. 1995).

[203] *State v. L.C.* 283 *N.J. Super.* 441, 451, 662 *A.2d* 577 (App. Div. 1995).

[204] *State v. Wilmouth*, 302 *N.J. Super.* 20, 23, 694 *A.2d* 584 (App. Div. 1997).

[205] *Carfagno v. Carfagno*, 288 *N.J. Super.* 424, 437, 672 *A.2d* 751 (Ch. Div. 1995).

[206] *State v. Wilmouth*, 302 *N.J. Super.* 20, 694 *A.2d* 584 (App. Div. 1997); *see State v. L.C.*, 283 *N.J. Super.* 441, 662 *A.2d* 577 (App. Div. 1995), *certif. denied*, 143 *N.J.* 325, 670 *A.2d* 1066 (1996); *Corrente v. Corrente*, 281 *N.J. Super.* 243, 657 *A.2d* 440 (App. Div. 1995); *Peranio v. Peranio*, 280 *N.J. Super.* 47, 654 *A.2d* 495 (App. Div. 1995); *Murray v. Murray*, 267 *N.J. Super.* 406, 631 *A.2d* 984 (App. Div. 1993); *see also State v. Brown*, 394 *N.J. Super.* 492, 927 *A.2d* 569 (App. Div. 2007); *Signorile v. City of Perth Amboy*, 523 *F.Supp.2d* 428 (2007).

[207] *J.D. v. M.D.F.*, 207 *N.J.* 458, 25 *A.3d* 1045 (App. Div. 2011).

CHAPTER FOUR

THE ACT

4.1   HISTORY OF THE ACT

Prior to the enactment of the domestic violence law, courts would skeptically look at a criminal action filed by a spouse (usually the wife), against her husband, while still married. They believed that the problem did not really exist, and was merely exaggerated by the dependent spouse in order to get some kind of advantage in the matrimonial situation. Even worse, it was also believed by not only the court, but by individuals in general, that acts of domestic violence were part of marriage and should be endured by the victim.

This attitude has been engendered over centuries and is best described by Judge Angelo DiCamillo in his report entitled: "Domestic Violence Law of New Jersey":

> There are numerous examples of the way in which domestic violence has been 'embraced' by the legal system as a means of maintaining order and the hierarchical status quo. One of the most famous descriptions of a husband's 'right' to physically 'discipline' his wife is found in *Blackstone's Commentaries*, Chapter IV, 442-445 (1765).

> The husband also, by the old law, might give his wife moderate correction. For, as he is to answer for her misbehavior, the law thought it reasonable to entrust him with this power of restraining her, by domestic chastisement, in the same moderation that a man is allowed to correct his apprentices or children; for whom the master or parent is also liable in some cases to answer. But this power of correction was confined within reasonable bounds, and the husband was prohibited from using any violence to his wife, *aliter quam ad virum, ex causa regiminis et castigationis uxoris suae, licite et rationabiliter pertinet* ("except it belongs to the man to licitly and reasonably discipline and castigate his wife".) The civil law gave the husband the same, or a larger, authority over his wife: allowing him, for some misdemeanors, *flagellis et fustibus acriter verberare uxorem* ("to strongly flagellate and discipline his wife"); for others, only *modicam castigationem adhibere* ("moderate castigation was permitted"). But with us, in the politer reign of Charles the second, this power of correction began to be doubted; and a wife may now have security of the peach against her husband; or, in

return, a husband against his wife. Yet the lower rank of people, who were always fond of the old common law, still claim and exert their ancient privilege: and the courts of law will still permit a husband to restrain a wife of her liberty, in case of any gross misbehavior.

Under the common law rule of coverture, upon marriage, women lost their legal identity as independent persons and immediately became 'covered' under the protection and authority of their husbands. It was said that upon marriage, 'the man and the woman became one and the man was 'The One'." Since a husband could be held legally responsible for his wife's misconduct, the common law permitted and even encouraged husbands to 'control' their wives through violence.

The domestic violence laws in New Jersey and across the country grew out of the Battered Woman's Movement in the early 1970's. This movement had three tenets: empowerment, social change, and safety. The goal of the movement was to bring the secrets of wife abuse, which like incest, was rarely mentioned or acknowledged as existing, out of the closet. The victims sought recognition of their plight, the cooperation of police to protect them, and for judges to enforce the laws.

It was not until there was vast social change with the struggle for women's equality that this epidemic upon society was finally recognized. Women's shelters were established to house the women and the children who were victims of domestic violence; physicians were recognizing the unmistakable signs of domestic abuse; but the police and the courts were still slow in responding. They viewed domestic disputes as less serious than "stranger" violence criminal complaints. These domestic relations crimes were further complicated by the very nature of parties' relationship.

Over the years, various commissions have studied the full extent of the domestic violence problem. As a result of becoming more familiar with domestic violence, the commissions realized that its impact is not only upon women and children, but extends to parents being abused by adult children; two partners in-traditional relationships as well as to persons sharing the same household. This culminated in the realization that the definition of "victim" of domestic violence had to be expanded.

In New Jersey, prior to 1981, recommendations were made to the State Legislature entitled "Battered Women in New Jersey", prepared by the New Jersey Advisory Committee to the United States Commission on Civil Rights, resulting from a series of meetings between mutual sponsors of the bill. These individuals included Senator Wynona M. Lipman and Senator Merlino, as well as Assemblywoman Barbara W. McConnell, representatives of the Commission on Sex Discrimination, the New Jersey Departments of Community Affairs and Human Services, the New Jersey Coalition for Battered Women led by Sandy Clark, Legal Services of New Jersey, the Administrative Office of the Courts and County Prosecutors. Their goal in their initial proposal of legislation was the strengthening of civil and criminal remedies, and the creation of additional remedies in a civil law context, which they believed would offer a broader more flexible relief to battered women.

In the explanation to the original Senate Bill No. 3127 dated December 14, 1981, the sponsors noted:

> The increasing prevalence of domestic violence--particularly battered women--is a critical national problem. The United States Department of Justice report entitled 'Crimes in the United States - 1979' revealed that 30% of the homicides committed in this country are victims of domestic violence. In the vast majority of these family homicide cases, police had previously been called to the house because of physical violence. Although there are no conclusive statistics on the incidents of domestic violence in New Jersey, a recent New Jersey Advisory Committee report to the United States Commission on Civil Rights, 'Battered Women in New Jersey,' did document the problems facing battered women in selected localities. The intent of this Bill in many instances closely parallels the recommendations of the Advisory Committee report.

> The New Jersey Coalition for Battered Women and Legal Services of New Jersey realized the need for exclusive changes in the legal system and represented a proposal to the sponsors of this Legislature and the Commission on Sex Discrimination.

> ... Domestic violence has a detrimental effect on families; there are alarming correlations between spouse and child abuse and between violent families and delinquency. This Act presents a comprehensive response to the recurrent problem of domestic violence by insuring victims the maximum protection of the law. It prevents repeated occurrences of violence by facilitating a prompt and thorough response to the complaints.

When Senator Lipman introduced the bill in the Legislature in January of 1981, she stated:

"Domestic violence is a critical problem that until recently has been ignored. The attitude contained in the Old English proverb 'A woman, a spaniel, a walnut tree, the more you beat them the better they be' must be eradicated through affirmative legislation".

The bill was introduced to the Assembly in March of 1981, by Assemblyman Barbara McConnell, who stated:

> Once every minute in this country, an act of domestic violence occurs. Many people still think of the crime as a private matter between family members, and a nuisance to police. What they don't realize is that one third of all murder victims in this country are victims of domestic violence. And by the time that final, violent attack occurs, often the victim has been abused time and again, with the knowledge of the police. In half the reported incidents of domestic violence, police have been called to the home five times or more.
>
> It is obvious that lawmakers in this state are not giving the police and the courts the tools to break this deadly cycle of violence in our homes. The legislation I have introduced is designed to put those tools to work.
>
> We are not proposing any radical changes in the laws, or in the structure of our families. Some of the initial resistance this bill has received, I believe, is due to confusion over its purpose and its ultimate effect.
>
> Very simply, we want to guarantee victims the maximum protection they deserve under the law, and we want to treat the abuser, as well as the abused, by providing the counseling and help that will heal our wounded families.

In 1981, the New Jersey State Legislature first enacted into law the original "Prevention of Domestic Violence Act", which was subsequently amended in 1982, 1987, 1988, and 1989. A complete revision of the Law was enacted on November 12, 1991 with the "Prevention of Domestic Violence Act of 1990.

The Act was made more extensive by amendments signed in 1994. In that year, by Joint Resolution No. 2, the Legislature expressed that they wanted to comprehensively address the serious crime of domestic violence, which required an immediate response by law enforcement personnel, judges, and court personnel, while also educating the public, and assuring the victims of domestic violence that the law would protect them. At the signing of amendments to the Prevention of Domestic Violence Law on August 12, 1994, Governor Christine Whitman said:

> I'm here to encourage the victims to seek the protection of the law; to say to them that from now on, you are going to receive that protection...We are now sending a very clear signal that we expect action and that there are certain activities that are not going to be tolerated, whether they take place behind closed doors, between people who know one another or among strangers on the street.[208]

One of the changes made to the Act was the addition a new class of victims, i.e., people involved in a dating relationship. Two new offenses, murder and stalking, were also recognized under the act. Another change to the Act was the authorization of municipal court judges to issue *ex parte* orders, and providing that the orders for emergency relief were immediately appealable before any judge of the family part, where the plaintiff lived or was sheltered. The amendments also stated that in the event a court denied the temporary restraining order, or where a complaint was dismissed, the victim would not be barred from re-filing, based upon the same incident.

The Act also supplemented available emergent relief, allowing for orders for search and seizure of weapons at locations where the judge had reasonable cause to believe the weapons are located (*Note: the judge when doing this is required to specifically state reasons for and the scope of the search.*) The amendments additionally provided procedures for implementation, in that an order granting emergency relief must be immediately afforded to the sheriff for immediate service upon the defendant, that the complaint be immediately forwarded for service on the defendant and the municipal police where plaintiff lived or was sheltered, and authorizing the court to order appropriate substituted service if necessary upon the defendant.

The Act has been upheld as constitutional, even the *ex parte* temporary restraining process. It has been held that the ex parte temporary restraining order does not deprive a defendant of due process under the rationale that the statute gives careful attention to the balancing of the rights of both the defendant and the victim. The temporary restraining order is only entered into if it appears the plaintiff is in danger of domestic violence. Any such restraining order is subject to dissolution/modification on 24 hours' notice or immediately appealable for a plenary hearing de novo before a judge of the family party (as well as subject to a mandatory hearing within 10 days).[209]

---

[208] *Ivette Mendez, Shielding the Victim-Whitman Enacts Broader Tougher Domestic Abuse Laws, The Star Ledger,* August 12, 1994, at 113.

[209] *Grant v. Wright,* 222 *N.J. Super.* 191, 536 *A.2d* 319 (App. Div.), *certif. denied,* 111 *N.J.* 562, 546 *A.2d* 493 (1988).

The Act itself is not aimed at punishing a person who committed an act of domestic violence, but rather to protect the victims.[210] The Act's purpose, reiterated case after case, is to protect victims who are in a domestic relationship from their abusers, while being cognizant that these particular situations are unique from the usual criminal assault and crime situations. The additional complications present in domestic relationships, which are not present in "stranger violence" cases include: the victim's love for the abuser, the victim's economic dependency on the abuser, the victim's fear of increased or escalated "separate violence", the victim's belief that she can help the abuser or that the abuser needs her help, the victim's belief that she caused the abuse by "misbehaving", the victim and the abuser having children in common, the victim's isolation from friends and resources, the victim's lack of support from her family for "allowing" the relationship to deteriorate, etc.

Various courts have restated the principles set forth in the Legislature's findings and declarations, utilizing them as foundations for their decisions when determining whether to grant a final restraining order or not. *i.e.* Courts have stated that "thousands of persons in the state are regularly beaten, tortured and in some cases even killed," but that there are also individuals who claim to be victims of domestic violence in order to get a leg up in other proceedings. Thus, the courts stress that the act should only be uses where there is serious abuse, and not distorted or trivialized by misuse.[211] The purpose of the focus of the Legislature was "regular serious abuse."[212] (*Note: Contrast this with the Supreme Court declaration that "there is no such thing as an act of domestic violence that was not serious."[213]*)

Courts will often cite that it is the intent of the Legislature "to assure the victims of domestic violence the maximum protection from abuse the law can provide."[214] In that vein, courts have in difficult and questionable situations, justified their action based on the rationale that the Legislature has mandated that the courts liberally construe the remedies available to protect victims of violence. They stress a flexible approach and state that the Legislature has recognized the court's equitable powers are particularly appropriate in the context of domestic relations cases.[215]

The courts have also found that there is a positive correlation between spousal abuse and child abuse, thereby necessitating the possible need for a best interest investigation (for visitation or parenting time.) On the other hand, judges are also aware that this is a double edged sword since a claim of abuse may be a baseless tool utilized by a person seeking custody. These individuals know that if they can prove some form of domestic violence against their

---

[210] *Carfagno v. Carfagno*, 288 N.J. Super. 421, 434, 672 A.2d 751 (Ch. Div. 1995).

[211] *N.B. v. T.B.*, 297 N.J. Super. 35, 42, 687 A.2d 766 (App. Div. 1997).

[212] *D.C. v. F.R.*, 286 N.J. Super. 589, 608, 670 A.2d 51 (App. Div. 1996).

[213] *Brennan v. Orban*, 145 N.J. 282, 678 A.2d 667 (1996).

[214] *Cesare v. Cesar*, 154 N.J. 394, 399, 713 A.2d. 390, 392 (1998)(*citing N.J.S.A. 2C:25-18*)).

[215] *Carr v. Carr*, 120 N.J. 336, 576 A.2d 872 (1990).

spouse, they have an advantage in receiving final custody in their case.

The Legislative findings pertaining to domestic violence not only recognized the victims of the domestic violence, but also some of the societal and sociological implications of violence within the family setting. They found that police and the courts have not in the past responded adequately to the problem; nor have the victims been treated fairly by the courts and police. Rather they have had "substantial difficulty in getting access protection from the judicial system, particularly due to that system's inability to generate a prompt response to the emergency situation."[216]

It is important to remember that domestic violence does not only influence those directly involved in it, but the public at large. The legislature stated that the public has an interest in acts of domestic violence, which are not private wars or disputes, but crimes against society:

> The public has an interest, wholly apart from that of the litigants, in the fair and effective resolution of these cases. Victims come from a variety of circumstances, but the optimism that often underlies their forgiveness of the abusers should not deny them protection of law when confronted with the party's request. It also bears repeating that these disputes are not private wars. Acts of domestic violence are often crimes. The public has an interest wholly apart from the litigants, and a fair and effective resolution of these cases. Victims come from a variety of circumstances, but the optimism that often underlies their forgiveness of their abusers should not deny them the protection of the law.[217]

---

[216] *Ibid.*
[217] *A.B. v. L.M.*, 289 *N.J. Super.* 125, 131, 672 *A.2d* 1296 (App. Div. 1996).

4.2   COMMON LAW RESTRAINING ORDERS

Prior to the Domestic Violence Act being passed, the only recourse available to a party who experienced harm or the threat of harm, from their spouse, in the household, was to oust the other spouse from the home they both owned as "tenants by the entirety." This relief was granted in the form of injunctive relief pursuant to the general equity power of the court on a positive showing of certain and immediate necessity to protect the safety of person or property. In essence, this constituted a common law restraining order.[218]

There are still opportunities to receive this type restraining order by filing a motion before the court. These restraining orders can be substituted for the domestic violence final restraining order when there is an existing matrimonial case in progress, or either a matrimonial (divorce complaint) or a support or custody case can be filed simultaneously as a means to have some proceeding available to enter a consent order that is issued in the matrimonial case.

The adoption of a restraining order in the civil action obviates the necessity of the defendant pleading guilty or trial in the domestic violence matter, but does not have the strength of provisions of the Act or the possibility of the violator of the criminal order going to jail. The civil restraint should be used selectively. If you have a case you might lose, or you want to bring down the "heat" of the litigation, it is an alternate method of achieving some of your goals. The Civil Restraining Order can be effectuated and can include the following relief.

There is no provision in the Act for an issuance of the restraining order without finding a guilty plea.

A restraining order can be entered by consent, or upon regular motion, and the following are non-exclusive list of factors used in issuing a general restraining order:

(1) The character of the interest to be protected;

(2) The relative adequacy of the injunction to the plaintiff as compared with other remedies;

(3) The unreasonable delay in bringing suit;

(4) Any related misconduct by the plaintiff;

(5) The comparison of hardship to the plaintiff if relief is denied and hardship to defendant if relief is granted;

---

[218] *Roberts v. Roberts*, 106 *N.J. Super.* 108, 254 *A.2d* 323 (Ch. Div. 1969).

(6) The interest of others, including the public; and

(7) The practicality of framing the order or judgment.[219]

Typically an application would be made before the trial judge by an Order to Show Cause and a hearing would be scheduled by the judge giving both parties an opportunity to be heard and for the court to decide whether the application was genuine, and even if it was, the courts were loathed to throw one spouse out of the matrimonial home.

A hearing would only be held if the plaintiff had made a *prima facie* case under the law that the marital conflict was such that the spouse might be precluded from the home, and that application was opposed, creating conflicting certifications which would then make it necessary to have testimony in order to determine the factual disputes.[220]

According to *Roberts,* the plaintiff had to make a positive showing of certain and immediate necessity to oust the other spouse in order to protect the safety of personal property or person, and there needs to be the threat of future injury or damage if the spouse was not excluded from the home.

Subsequently, a court applied the Roberts holding to prevent the entry of mother into the home she owned with the father, when it determined that the mother's medical and alcoholic disabilities, her unannounced absences, and unannounced returns of irregular duration from the marital home were detrimental to the best interests of the children. The court recognized it had a duty to protect the child during matrimonial litigation under the *parens patriae* doctrine.[221]

Other cases followed which extended the principle. Husband who voluntarily left the house was prevented from coming back into the home after leaving for a period of 17 months, where no proof presented of actual physical or emotional injury to the plaintiff or children[222]

---

[219] *Restatement (2nd of Torts)* 936 (1977) *as cited* in *Sheppard v. Township of Frankford*, 261 *N.J. Super.* 5, 617 *A.2d* 666 (App. Div. 1992).

[220] Historically there have been other applications before *Roberts* for the expulsion of the husband from the matrimonial home; *see also Berger v. Berger*, 6 *N.J. Super.* 52, 69 *A.2d* 741 (App. Div. 1949); *R.S.*2:50-37 (now *N.J.S.A.* 2A:34-23).

[221] *S. v. A.*, 118 *N.J. Super.* 69, 285 *A.2d* 588 (Ch. Div. 1972).

[222] *Babushik v. Babushik*, 157 *N.J. Super.* 128, 384 *A.2d* 574 (Ch. Div. 1978); *Degenaars v. Degenaars*, 186 *N.J. Super.* 233, 452 *A.2d* 222 (Ch. Div. 1982).

4.3 THE ACT

The entire Act is presented here for easy reference.

This act shall be known and may be cited as the "Prevention of Domestic Violence Act of 1991."[223]

N.J.S.A. 2C:25-18.   FINDINGS, DECLARATIONS

The Legislature finds and declares that domestic violence is a serious crime against society; that there are thousands of persons in this State who are regularly beaten, tortured and in some cases even killed by their spouses or cohabitants; that a significant number of women who are assaulted are pregnant; that victims of domestic violence come from all social and economic backgrounds and ethnic groups; that there is a positive correlation between spousal abuse and child abuse; and that children, even when they are not themselves physically assaulted, suffer deep and lasting emotional effects from exposure to domestic violence. It is therefore, the intent of the Legislature to assure the victims of domestic violence the maximum protection from abuse the law can provide.

The Legislature further finds and declares that the health and welfare of some of its most vulnerable citizens, the elderly and disabled, are at risk because of incidents of reported and unreported domestic violence, abuse and neglect which are known to include acts which victimize the elderly and disabled emotionally, psychologically, physically and financially; because of age, disabilities or infirmities, this group of citizens frequently must rely on the aid and support of others; while the institutionalized elderly are protected under *P.L.*1977, *c.* 239 (*C.* 52:27G-1 et seq.). Elderly and disabled adults in non-institutionalized or community settings may find themselves victimized by family members or others upon whom they feel compelled to depend.

The Legislature further finds and declares that violence against the elderly and disabled, including criminal neglect of the elderly and disabled under section 1 of *P.L.*1989, *c.* 23 (*C.* 2C:24-8), must be recognized and addressed on an equal basis as violence against spouses and children in order to fulfill our responsibility as a society to protect those who are less able to protect themselves.

The Legislature further finds and declares that even though many of the existing criminal statutes are applicable to acts of domestic violence, previous societal attitudes concerning domestic violence have affected the response of our law enforcement and judicial systems, resulting in these acts receiving different treatment from similar crimes when they occur in a domestic context. The Legislature finds that battered adults presently experience

---

[223] *N.J.S.A.* 2C:25-17.

substantial difficulty in gaining access to protection from the judicial system, particularly due to that system's inability to generate a prompt response in an emergency situation.

It is the intent of the Legislature to stress that the primary duty of a law enforcement officer when responding to a domestic violence call is to enforce the laws allegedly violated and to protect the victim. Further, it is the responsibility of the courts to protect victims of violence that occurs in a family or family-like setting by providing access to both emergent and long-term civil and criminal remedies and sanctions, and by ordering those remedies and sanctions that are available to assure the safety of the victims and the public. To that end, the Legislature encourages the training of all police and judicial personnel in the procedures and enforcement of this act, and about the social and psychological context in which domestic violence occurs; and it further encourages the broad application of the remedies available under this act in the civil and criminal courts of this State. It is further intended that the official response to domestic violence shall communicate the attitude that violent behavior will not be excused or tolerated, and shall make clear the fact that the existing criminal laws and civil remedies created under this act will be enforced without regard to the fact that the violence grows out of a domestic situation.

N.J.S.A. 2C:25-19.   DEFINITIONS

As used in this act:

a. "Domestic violence" means the occurrence of one or more of the following acts inflicted upon a person protected under this act by an adult or an emancipated minor:

(1) Homicide *N.J.S.* 2C:11-1 et seq.
(2) Assault *N.J.S.* 2C:12-1
(3) Terroristic threats *N.J.S.* 2C:12-3
(4) Kidnapping *N.J.S.* 2C:13-1
(5) Criminal restraint *N.J.S.* 2C:13-2
(6) False imprisonment *N.J.S.* 2C:13-3
(7) Sexual assault *N.J.S.* 2C:14-2
(8) Criminal sexual contact *N.J.S.* 2C:14-3
(9) Lewdness *N.J.S.* 2C:14-4
(10) Criminal mischief *N.J.S.* 2C:17-3
(11) Burglary *N.J.S.* 2C:18-2
(12) Criminal trespass *N.J.S.* 2C:18-3
(13) Harassment *N.J.S.* 2C:33-4
(14) Stalking *P.L.*1992, *c.* 209 (*C.*2C:12-10)

When one or more of these acts is inflicted by an unemancipated minor upon a person protected under this act, the occurrence shall not constitute "domestic violence," but may be the basis for the filing of a petition or complaint pursuant to the provisions of section 11 of *P.L.*1982, *c.*77 (*C.*2A:4A-30).

b.　　"Law enforcement agency" means a department, division, bureau, commission, board or other authority of the State or of any political subdivision thereof which employs law enforcement officers.

c.　　"Law enforcement officer" means a person whose public duties include the power to act as an officer for the detection, apprehension, arrest and conviction of offenders against the laws of this State.

Victim of domestic violence" means a person protected under this act and shall include any person who is 18 years of age or older or who is an emancipated minor and who has been subjected to domestic violence by a spouse, former spouse, or any other person who is a present or former household member. "Victim of domestic violence" also includes any person, regardless of age, who has been subjected to domestic violence by a person with whom the victim has a child in common, or with whom the victim anticipates having a child in common, if one of the parties is pregnant. "Victim of domestic violence" also includes any person who has been subjected to domestic violence by a person with whom the victim has had a dating relationship.

"Emancipated minor" means a person who is under 18 years of age but who has been married, has entered military service, has a child or is pregnant or has been previously declared by a court or an administrative agency to be emancipated.

N.J.S.A. 2C:25-20.　　DEVELOPMENT OF TRAINING COURSE; CURRICULUM

a. (1) The Division of Criminal Justice shall develop and approve a training course and curriculum on the handling, investigation and response procedures concerning reports of domestic violence and abuse and neglect of the elderly and disabled. This training course and curriculum shall be reviewed at least every two years and modified by the Division of Criminal Justice form time to time as need may require. The Division of Criminal Justice shall distribute the curriculum to all local police agencies.

(2) The Attorney General shall be responsible for ensuring that all law enforcement officers attend initial training within 90 days of appointment or transfer and annual in service training of at least four hours as described in this section.

b. (1) The Administrative Office of the Courts shall develop and approve a training course and a curriculum on the handling, investigation and response procedures concerning allegations of domestic violence. This training course shall be reviewed at least every two years and modified by the Administrative Office of the Courts from time to time as need may require.

(2) The Administrative Director of the Courts shall be responsible for ensuring that all judges and judicial personnel attend initial training within 90 days of appointment or transfer and annual in-service training as described in this section.

(3) The Division of Criminal Justice and the Administrative Office of the Courts shall provide that all training on the handling of domestic violence matters shall include information concerning the impact of domestic violence on society, the dynamics of domestic violence, the statutory and case law concerning domestic violence, the necessary elements of a protection order, policies and procedures as promulgated or ordered by the Attorney General or the Supreme Court, and the use of available community resources, support services, available sanctions and treatment options. Law enforcement agencies shall: (1) establish domestic crisis teams or participate in established domestic crisis teams, and (2) train individual officers in methods of dealing with domestic violence and neglect and abuse of the elderly and disabled. The teams may include social workers, clergy or other persons trained in counseling, crisis intervention or in the treatment of domestic violence and neglect and abuse of the elderly and disabled victims.

N.J.S.A. 2C:25-21. ARREST OF ALLEGED ATTACKER; SEIZURE OF WEAPONS, ETC.

a. When a person claims to be a victim of domestic violence, and where a law enforcement officer responding to the incident finds probable cause to believe that domestic violence has occurred, the law enforcement officer shall arrest the person who is alleged to be the person who subjected the victim to domestic violence and shall sign a criminal complaint if:

(1)   The victim exhibits signs of injury caused by an act of domestic violence;

(2)   A warrant is in effect;

(3)   There is probable cause to believe that the person has violated *N.J.S.* 2C:29-9, and there is probable cause to believe that the person has been served with the order alleged to have been violated. If the victim does not have a copy of a purported order, the officer may verify the existence of an order with the appropriate law enforcement agency; or

(4)   There is probable cause to believe that a weapon as defined in *N.J.S.* 2C:39-1 has been involved in the commission of an act of domestic violence.

b. A law enforcement officer may arrest a person, or may sign a criminal complaint against that person, or may do both, where there is probable cause to believe that an act of domestic violence has been committed, but where none of the conditions in subsection a. of this section applies.

c.   (1) As used in this section, the word "exhibits" is to be liberally construed to mean any indication that a victim has suffered bodily injury, which shall include physical pain or any impairment of physical condition. Where the victim exhibits no visible sign of injury, but states that an injury has occurred, the officer should consider other relevant factors in determining whether there is probable cause to make an arrest.

(2) In determining which party in a domestic violence incident is the victim where both parties' exhibit signs of injury, the officer should consider the comparative extent of the injuries, the history of domestic violence between the parties, if any, and any other relevant factors.

(3) No victim shall be denied relief or arrested or charged under this act with an offense because the victim used reasonable force in self defense against domestic violence by an attacker.

d.   (1) In addition to a law enforcement officer's authority to seize any weapon that is contraband, evidence or an instrumentality of crime, a law enforcement officer who has probable cause to believe that an act of domestic violence has been committed shall:

> (a) Question persons present to determine whether there are weapons on the premises; and

> (b) Upon observing or learning that a weapon is present on the premises, seize any weapon that the officer reasonably believes would expose the victim to a risk of serious bodily injury. If a law enforcement officer seizes any firearm pursuant to this paragraph, the officer shall also seize any firearm purchaser identification card or permit to purchase a hand gun issued to the person accused of the act of domestic violence.

(2) A law enforcement officer shall deliver all weapons, firearm purchaser identification cards and/or permits to purchase a hand gun seized pursuant to this section to the county prosecutor and shall append an inventory of all seized weapons to the domestic violence report.

(3) Weapons seized in accordance with the above "Prevention of Domestic Violence Act of 1991" *P.L.* 1991, *c.* 261 (*C.* 2C:25-17 et seq.) shall be returned to the owner except upon order of the Superior Court. The prosecutor who has possession of the seized weapons may, upon notice to the owner, petition a judge of the Family Part of the Superior Court, Chancery Division, within 45 days

of seizure, to obtain title to the seized weapons, or to revoke any and all permits, licenses and other authorizations for the use, possession, or ownership of such weapons pursuant to the law governing such use, possession, or ownership, or may object to the return of the weapons on such grounds as are provided for the initial rejection or later revocation of the authorizations, or on the grounds that the owner is unfit or that the owner poses a threat to the public in general or a person or persons in particular.

A hearing shall be held and a record made thereof within 45 days of the notice provided above. No formal pleading and no filing fee shall be required as a preliminary to such hearing. The hearing shall be summary in nature. Appeals from the results of the hearing shall be to the Superior Court, Appellate Division, in accordance with the law.

If the prosecutor does not institute an action within 45 days of seizure, the seized weapons shall be returned to the owner.

After the hearing, the court shall order the return of the firearms, weapons and any authorization papers relating to the seized weapons to the owner if the court determines the owner is not subject to any of the disabilities set forth in *N.J.S.* 2C:58-3 c. and find that the complaint has been dismissed at the request of the complainant and the prosecutor determines that there is insufficient probable cause to indict; or if the defendant is found not guilty of the charges; or if the court determines that the domestic violence situation no longer exists. Nothing in this act shall impair the right of the State to retain evidence pending a criminal prosecution. Nor shall any provision of this act be construed to limit the authority of the State or a law enforcement officer to seize, retain or forfeit property pursuant to chapter 64 of Title 2C of the New Jersey Statutes.

If, after the hearing, the court determines that the weapons are not to be returned to the owner, the court may:

(a)   With respect to weapons other than firearms, order the prosecutor to dispose of the weapons if the owner does not arrange for the transfer or sale of the weapons to an appropriate person within 60 days; or

(b)   Order the revocation of the owner's firearms purchaser identification card or any permit, license or authorization, in which case the court shall order the owner to surrender any firearm seized and all other firearms possessed to the prosecutor and shall order the prosecutor to dispose of the firearms if the owner does not arrange for the sale of the firearms to a registered dealer of the firearms within 60 days; or

(c)   Order such other relief as it may deem appropriate. When the court orders the weapons be forfeited to the State, or the prosecutor is required to dispose of the weapons, the prosecutor shall dispose of the property as provided in *N.J.S.* 2C:64-6.

(4) A civil suit may be brought to enjoin a wrongful failure to return a seized firearm where the prosecutor refuses to return the weapon after receiving a written request to do so and notice of the owner's intent to bring a civil action pursuant to this section. Failure of the prosecutor to comply with the provisions of this act shall entitle the prevailing party in the civil suit to reasonable costs, including attorney's fees, provided that the court finds that the prosecutor failed to act in good faith in retaining the seized weapon.

(5) No law enforcement officer or agency shall be held liable in any civil action brought by any person for failing to learn of, locate or seize a weapon pursuant to this act, or for returning a seized weapon to its owner.

N.J.S.A. 2C:25-21.1. RULES, REGULATIONS CONCERNING WEAPONS PROHIBITIONS AND DOMESTIC VIOLENCE

.   The Attorney General may adopt, pursuant to the "Administrative Procedure Act," *P.L.*1968, *c.*410 (*C.*52:14B-1 et seq.), rules and regulations necessary and appropriate to implement this act.

N.J.S.A. 2C:25-22.   IMMUNITY FROM CIVIL LIABILITY

A law enforcement officer or a member of a domestic crises team or any person who, in good faith, reports a possible incident of domestic violence to the police shall not be held liable in any civil action brought by any party for an arrest based on probable cause, enforcement in good faith of a court order, or any other act or omission in good faith under this act.

N.J.S.A. 2C:25-23.   DISSEMINATION OF NOTICE TO VICTIM OF DOMESTIC VIOLENCE

A law enforcement officer shall disseminate and explain to the victim the following notice, which shall be written in both English and Spanish:

"You have the right to go to court to get an order called a temporary restraining order, also called a TRO, which may protect you from abuse by your attacker. The officer who handed you this card can tell you how to get a TRO."

The kinds of things a judge can order in a TRO may include:

(1)   That your attacker is temporarily forbidden from entering the home you live in;

(2)   That your attacker is temporarily forbidden from having contact with you or your relatives;

(3)   That your attacker is temporarily forbidden from bothering you at work;

(4)   That your attacker has to pay temporary child support or support for you;

(5)   That you be given temporary custody of your children;

(6)   That your attacker pays you back any money you have to spend for medical treatment or repairs because of the violence. There are other things the court can order, and the court clerk will explain the procedure to you and will help you fill out the papers for a TRO.

You also have the right to file a criminal complaint against your attacker. The police officer who gave you this paper will tell you how to file a criminal complaint.

On weekends, holidays, or other times when the courts are closed, you still have a right to get a TRO. The police officer who gave you this paper can help you get in touch with a judge who can give you a TRO.

N.J.S.A. 2C:25-24.   DOMESTIC VIOLENCE OFFENSE REPORT

a. It shall be the duty of a law enforcement officer who responds to a domestic violence call to complete a domestic violence offense report. All information contained in the domestic violence offense report shall be forwarded to the appropriate county bureau of identification and to the State bureau of records and identification in the Division of State Police in the Department of Law and Public Safety. A copy of the domestic violence offense report shall be forwarded to the municipal court where the offense was committed unless the case has been transferred to the Superior Court.

b. The domestic violence offense report shall be on a form prescribed by the supervisor of the State Bureau of Records and Identification which shall include, but not be limited to, the following information:

(1) The relationship of the parties;
(2) The sex of the parties;
(3) The time and date of the incident;
(4) The number of domestic violence calls investigated;
(5) Whether children were involved, or whether the alleged act of domestic violence had been committed in the presence of children;

(6) The type and extent of abuse;

(7) The number and type of weapons involved;

(8) The action taken by the law enforcement officer;

(9) The existence of any prior court orders issued pursuant to this act concerning the parties;

(10) The number of domestic violence calls alleging a violation of a domestic violence restraining order;

(11) The number of arrests for a violation of a domestic violence order; and

(12) Any other data that may be necessary for a complete analysis of all circumstances leading to the alleged incident of domestic violence.

c. It shall be the duty of the Superintendent of the State Police with the assistance of the Division of Systems and Communications in the Department of Law and Public Safety to compile and report annually to the Governor, the Legislature and the Advisory Council on Domestic Violence on the tabulated data from the domestic violence offense reports, classified by county.

N.J.S.A. 2C:25-25.   CRIMINAL COMPLAINT; PROCEEDINGS

The court in a criminal complaint arising from a domestic violence incident:

a. Shall not dismiss any charge or delay disposition of a case because of concurrent dissolution of a marriage, other civil proceedings, or because the victim has left the residence to avoid further incidents of domestic violence;

b. Shall not require proof that either party is seeking dissolution of a marriage prior to institution of criminal proceedings;

c. Shall waive any requirement that the victim's location be disclosed to any person.

N.J.S.A. 2C:25-26.   RELEASE FROM CUSTODY BEFORE TRIAL; CONDITIONS

a. When a defendant charged with a crime or offense involving domestic violence is released from custody before trial on bail or personal recognizance, the court authorizing the release may, as a condition of release, issue an order prohibiting the defendant from having any contact with the victim including, but not limited to, restraining the defendant from entering the victim's residence, place of employment or business, or school, and from harassing or stalking the victim or victim's friends, co-workers, or relatives in any way. The court may also enter an order prohibiting the defendant from having any contact with any animal owned, possessed, leased, kept, or held by either party or a minor child residing in the household. In addition, the court may enter an order directing the possession of the animal and providing that the animal shall not be disposed of prior to the disposition of the crime or offense. The court may enter an order prohibiting the defendant from possessing any firearm or other weapon enumerated in subsection r. of *N.J.S.* 2C:39-1 and ordering the search for and seizure of any such weapon at any location where the judge has reasonable cause to believe the weapon is located. The judge shall state with specificity the reasons for and scope of the search and seizure authorized by the order.

b. The written court order releasing the defendant shall contain the court's directives specifically restricting the defendant's ability to have contact with the victim or the victim's friends, co-workers or relatives or any animal owned, possessed, leased, kept or held by either party, or a minor child residing in the household. The clerk of the court or other person designated by the court shall provide a copy of this order to the victim forthwith.

c. The victim's location shall remain confidential and shall not appear on any documents or records to which the defendant has access.

d. Before bail is set, the defendant's prior record shall be considered by the court. The court shall also conduct a search of the domestic violence central registry. Bail shall be set as soon as is feasible, but in all cases within 24 hours of arrest.

e. Once bail is set, it shall not be reduced without prior notice to the county prosecutor and the victim. Bail shall not be reduced by a judge other than the judge who originally ordered bail, unless the reasons for the amount of the original bail are available to the judge who reduces the bail and are set forth in the record.

f. A victim shall not be prohibited from applying for, and a court shall not be prohibited from issuing, temporary restraints pursuant to this act because the victim has charged any person with commission of a criminal act.

N.J.S.A. 2C:25-26.1. NOTIFICATION OF VICTIM OF RELEASE OF DEFENDANT

Notwithstanding any other provision of law to the contrary, whenever a defendant charged with a crime or an offense involving domestic violence is released from custody, the prosecuting agency shall notify the victim.

N.J.S.A. 2C:25-27. CONDITIONS OF SENTENCING IF DEFENDANT FOUND GUILTY OF DOMESTIC VIOLENCE

a. When a defendant is found guilty of a crime or offense involving domestic violence, and a condition of sentence restricts the defendant's ability to have contact with the victim, the victim's friends, co-workers, or relatives, or an animal owned, possessed, leased, kept, or held by either party, or a minor child residing in the household, that condition shall be recorded in an order of the court and a written copy of this order shall be provided to the victim by the clerk of the court or other person designated by the court. In addition to restricting a defendant's ability to have contact with the victim, the victim's friends, co-workers, or relatives, or an animal owned, possessed, leased, kept, or held by either party, or a minor child residing in the household, the court may require the defendant to receive professional counseling from either a private source or a source appointed by the court, and if the court so orders, the court shall require the defendant to provide documentation of attendance at the professional counseling. In any case where the court order contains a requirement that the defendant receive professional counseling, no application by the defendant to dissolve the restraining order shall be granted unless, in addition to any other provisions required by law or conditions ordered by the court, the defendant has completed all required attendance at such counseling.

b. In addition, the court may enter an order directing the possession of an animal owned, possessed, leased, kept, or held by either party, or a minor child residing in the household. Where a person has abused or threatened to abuse such animal, there shall be a presumption that possession of the animal shall be awarded to the non-abusive party.

N.J.S.A. 2C:25-28. FILING COMPLAINT ALLEGING DOMESTIC VIOLENCE IN FAMILY PART; PROCEEDING

a. A victim may file a complaint alleging the commission of an act of domestic violence with the Family Part of the Chancery Division of the Superior Court in conformity with the rules of court. The court shall not dismiss any complaint or delay disposition of a case because the victim has left the residence to avoid further incidents of domestic violence. Filing a complaint pursuant to this section shall not prevent the filing of a criminal complaint for the same act.

On weekends, holidays and other times when the court is closed, a victim may file a complaint before a judge of the Family Part of the Chancery Division of the Superior Court or a municipal court judge who shall be assigned to accept complaints and issue emergency *ex parte* relief in the form of temporary restraining orders pursuant to this act.

A plaintiff may apply for relief under this section in a court having jurisdiction over the place where the alleged act of domestic violence occurred, where the defendant resides, or where the plaintiff resides or is sheltered, and the court shall follow the same procedures applicable to other emergency applications. Criminal complaints filed pursuant to this act shall be investigated and prosecuted in the jurisdiction where the offense is alleged to have occurred. Contempt complaints filed pursuant to *N.J.S.* 2C:29-9 shall be prosecuted in the county where the contempt is alleged to have been committed and a copy of the contempt complaint shall be forwarded to the court that issued the order alleged to have been violated.

b. The court shall waive any requirement that the petitioner's place of residence appear on the complaint.

c. The clerk of the court, or other person designated by the court, shall assist the parties in completing any forms necessary for the filing of a summons, complaint, answer or other pleading.

d. Summons and complaint forms shall be readily available at the clerk's office, at the municipal courts and at municipal and State police stations.

e. As soon as the domestic violence complaint is filed, both the victim and the abuser shall be advised of any programs or services available for advice and counseling.

f. A plaintiff may seek emergency, *ex parte* relief in the nature of a temporary restraining order. A municipal court judge or a judge of the Family Part of the Chancery Division of the Superior Court may enter an *ex parte* order when necessary to protect the life, health or well-being of a victim on whose behalf the relief is sought.

g. If it appears that the plaintiff is in danger of domestic violence, the judge shall, upon consideration of the plaintiff's domestic violence complaint, order emergency *ex parte* relief, in the nature of a temporary restraining order. A decision shall be made by the judge regarding the emergency relief forthwith.

h. A judge may issue a temporary restraining order upon sworn testimony or complaint of an applicant who is not physically present, pursuant to court rules, or by a person who represents a person who is physically or mentally incapable of filing personally. A temporary restraining order may be issued if the judge is satisfied that exigent circumstances exist sufficient to excuse the failure of the applicant to appear personally and that sufficient grounds for granting the application have been shown.

i. An order for emergency *ex parte* relief shall be granted upon good cause shown and shall remain in effect until a judge of the Family Part issues a further order. Any temporary order hereunder is immediately appealable for a plenary hearing *de novo* not on the record before any judge of the Family Part of the county in which the plaintiff resides or is sheltered if that judge issued the temporary order and sets forth in the record the reasons for the modification or dissolution. The denial of a temporary restraining order by a municipal court judge and subsequent administrative dismissal of the complaint shall not bar the victim from re-filing a complaint in the Family Part based on the same incident and receiving an emergency, *ex parte* hearing *de novo* not on the record before a Family Part judge, and every denial of relief by a municipal court judge shall so state.

j. Emergency relief may include forbidding the defendant from returning to the scene of the domestic violence, forbidding the defendant to possessing any firearm or other weapon enumerated in subsection *r.* of *N.J.S.* 2C:39-1, ordering the search for and seizure of any such weapon at any location where the judge has reasonable cause to believe the weapon is located, and any other appropriate relief. Other appropriate relief may include, but is not limited to n order directing the possession of any animal owned, possessed, leased, kept, or held by either party, or a minor child residing in the household, and providing that the animal shall not be disposed of prior to the entry of a final order pursuant to section 13 of *P.L.* 1991 *c.* 261 (*C.2C:25-29*).

The judge shall state with specificity the reasons for, and scope of the search, and seizure authorized by the order. The provisions of this subsection prohibiting a defendant from possessing a firearm or other weapon shall not apply to any law enforcement officer while actually on duty, or to any member of the Armed Forces of the United States or member of the National Guard while actually on duty or traveling to or from an authorized place of duty.

k. The judge may permit the defendant to return to the scene of the domestic violence to pick up personal belongings and effects but shall, in the order granting relief, restrict the time and duration of such permission and provide for police supervision of such visit.

l. An order granting emergency relief, together with the complaint or complaints, shall immediately be forwarded to the appropriate law enforcement agency for service on the defendant, and to the police of the municipality in which the plaintiff resides or is sheltered, and shall immediately be served upon the defendant by the police, except that an order issued during regular court hours may be forwarded to the sheriff for immediate service upon the defendant in accordance with the rules of court. If personal service cannot be affected upon the defendant, the court may order other appropriate substituted service. At no time shall the plaintiff be asked or required to serve any order on the defendant.

m. (Deleted by amendment, *P.L.* 1994, *c.* 94.)

n. Notice of temporary restraining orders issued pursuant to this section shall be sent by the clerk of the court or other person designated by the court to the appropriate chiefs of police, members of the State Police and any other appropriate law enforcement agency or court.

o. (Deleted by amendment, *P.L.* 1994, *c.* 94.)

p. Any temporary or final restraining order issued pursuant to this act shall be in effect throughout the State, and shall be enforced by all law enforcement officers.

q. Prior to the issuance of any temporary or final restraining order issued pursuant to this section, the court shall order that a search be made of the domestic violence central registry with regard to the defendant's record.

N.J.S.A. 2C:25-28.1.   IN-HOUSE RESTRAINING ORDERS PROHIBITED

Notwithstanding any provision of *P.L.*1991, *c.* 261 (*C.* 2C:25-17 et seq.) to the contrary, no order issued by the Family Part of the Chancery Division of the Superior Court pursuant to section 12 or section 13 of *P.L.*1991, *c.* 261 (C.2C:25-28 or 2C:25-29) regarding emergency, temporary or final relief shall include an in-house restraining order which permits the victim and the defendant to occupy the same premises, but limits the defendant's use of that premises.

N.J.S.A. 2C:25-29.   HEARING PROCEDURES; RELIEF

a. A hearing shall be held in the Family Part of the Chancery Division of the Superior Court within 10 days of the filing of a complaint pursuant to section 12 of *P.L.*1991, *c.*261 (C.2C:25-28) in the county where the *ex parte* restraints were ordered, unless good cause is shown for the hearing to be held elsewhere. A copy of the complaint shall be served on the defendant in conformity with the Rules of Court. If a criminal complaint arising out of the same incident which is the subject matter of a complaint brought under *P.L.*1981, *c.* 426 (C.2C:25-1 et seq.) or *P.L.*1991, *c.* 261 (C.2C:25-17 et seq.) has been filed, testimony given by the plaintiff or defendant in the domestic violence matter shall not be used in the simultaneous or subsequent criminal proceeding against the defendant, other than domestic violence contempt matters and where it would otherwise be admissible hearsay under the rules of evidence that govern where a party is unavailable. At the hearing, the standard for proving the allegations in the complaint shall be by a preponderance of the evidence. The court shall consider, but not be limited to the following factors:

(1) The previous history of domestic violence between the plaintiff and defendant, including threats, harassment and physical abuse;

(2) The existence of immediate danger to person or property;

(3) The financial circumstances of the plaintiff and defendant;

(4) The best interests of the victim and any child;

(5) In determining custody and parenting time, the protection of the victim's safety; and

(6) The existence of a verifiable order of protection from another jurisdiction.

An order issued under this act shall only restrain or provide damages payable from a person against whom a complaint has been filed under this act and only after a finding or an admission is made that an act of domestic violence was committed by that person. The issue of whether or not a violation of this act occurred, including an act of contempt under this act, shall not be subject to mediation or negotiation in any form. In addition, where a temporary or final order has been issued pursuant to this act, no party shall be ordered to participate in mediation on the issue of custody or parenting time.

b. In proceedings in which complaints for restraining orders have been filed, the court shall grant any relief necessary to prevent further abuse. In addition to any other provisions, any restraining order issued by the court shall bar the defendant from purchasing, owning, possessing or controlling a firearm and from receiving or retaining a firearms purchaser identification card or permit to purchase a handgun pursuant to *N.J.S.* 2C:58-3 during the period in which the restraining order is in effect, or two years, whichever is greater, except that this provision shall not apply to any law enforcement officer while actually on duty, or to any member of the Armed Forces of the United States or member of the National Guard while actually on duty or traveling to or from an authorized place of duty. At the hearing, the judge of the Family Part of the Chancery Division of the Superior Court may issue an order granting any or all of the following relief:

(1) An order restraining the defendant from subjecting the victim to domestic violence, as defined in this act.

(2) An order granting exclusive possession to the plaintiff of the residence or household regardless of whether the residence or household is jointly or solely owned by the parties, or jointly or solely leased by the parties. This order shall not in any manner affect title or interest to any real property held by either party or both jointly. If it is not possible for the victim to remain in the residence, the court may order the defendant to pay the victim's rent at a residence other than the one previously shared by the parties if the defendant is found to have a duty to support the victim and the victim requires alternative housing.

(3) An order providing for parenting time. The order shall protect the safety and well-being of the plaintiff and minor children and shall specify the place and frequency of the parenting time. Parenting time arrangements shall not compromise any other remedy provided by the court by requiring or encouraging contact between the plaintiff and defendant. Orders for parenting time may include a designation of a place of parenting time away from the plaintiff, the participation of a third party, or supervised parenting time.

(a) The court shall consider a request by a custodial parent who has been subjected to domestic violence by a person with parenting time rights to a child in the parent's custody for an investigation or evaluation by the appropriate agency to assess the risk of harm to the child prior to the entry of a parenting time order. Any denial of such a request must be on the record and shall only be made if the judge finds the request to be arbitrary or capricious.

(b) The court shall consider suspension of the parenting time order and hold an emergency hearing upon an application made by the plaintiff certifying under oath that the defendant's access to the child pursuant to the parenting time order has threatened the safety and well-being of the child.

(4) An order requiring the defendant to pay to the victim monetary compensation for losses suffered as a direct result of the act of domestic violence. The order may require the defendant to pay the victim directly, to reimburse the Victims of Crimes Compensation Office for any and all compensation paid by the Victims of Crime Compensation Office directly to or on behalf of the victim, and may require that the defendant reimburse any parties that may have compensated the victim, as the court may determine. Compensatory losses shall include, but not be limited to, loss of earnings or other support, including child or spousal support, out-of-pocket losses for injuries sustained, cost of repair or replacement of real or personal property damaged or destroyed or taken by the defendant, cost of counseling for the victim, moving or other travel expenses, reasonable attorney's fees, court costs, and compensation for pain and suffering. Where appropriate, punitive damages may be awarded in addition to compensatory damages.

(5) An order requiring the defendant to receive professional domestic violence counseling from either a private source or a source appointed by the court and, in that event, requiring the defendant to provide the court, at specified intervals, with documentation of attendance at the professional counseling. The court may order the defendant to pay for the professional counseling. No application by the defendant to dissolve a final order which contains a requirement for attendance at professional counseling pursuant to this paragraph shall be granted by the court unless, in addition to any other provisions required by law or conditions ordered by the court, the defendant has completed all required attendance at such counseling.

(6) An order restraining the defendant from entering the residence, property, school, or place of employment of the victim or of other family or household members of the victim, and requiring the defendant to stay away from any specified place that is named in the order and is frequented regularly by the victim or other family or household members.

(7) An order restraining the defendant from making contact with the plaintiff or others, including an order forbidding the defendant from personally, or through an agent, initiating any communication likely to cause annoyance or alarm including, but not limited to, personal, written, or telephone contact with the victim or other family members, or their employers, employees, or fellow workers, or others with whom communication would be likely to cause annoyance or alarm to the victim.

(8) An order requiring that the defendant make, or continue to make, rent or mortgage payments on the residence occupied by the victim if the defendant is found to have a duty to support the victim or other dependent household members, provided that this issue has not been resolved or is not being litigated between the parties in another action.

(9) An order granting either party temporary possession of specified personal property, such as an automobile, checkbook, documentation of health insurance, an identification

documents, a key, and other personal effects.

(10) An order awarding emergency monetary relief, including emergency support for minor children, to the victim and other dependents, if any. An ongoing obligation of support shall be determined at a later date pursuant to applicable law.

(11) An order awarding temporary custody of a minor child. The court shall presume that the best interests of the child are served by an award of custody to the non-abusive parent.

(12) An order requiring that a law enforcement officer accompany either party to the residence or any shared business premises to supervise the removal of personal belongings in order to ensure the personal safety of the plaintiff when a restraining order has issued. This order shall be restricted in duration.

(13) (deleted by Amendment *P.L.* 1995, *C.* 242)

(14) An order granting any other appropriate relief for the plaintiff and dependent children, provided that the plaintiff consents to such relief, including relief requested by the plaintiff at the final hearing, whether or not the plaintiff requested such relief at the time of the granting of the initial emergency order.

(15) An order that requires that the defendant report to the intake unit of the Family Part of the Chancery Division of the Superior Court for monitoring of any other provision of the order.

(16) In addition to the order required by this subsection prohibiting the defendant from possessing any firearm, the court may also issue an order prohibiting the defendant from possessing any other weapon enumerated in subsection *r.* of *N.J.S.* 2C:39-1 and ordering the search for and seizure of any firearm or other weapon at any location where the judge has reasonable cause to believe the weapon is located. The judge shall state with specificity the reasons for and scope of the search and seizure authorized by the order.

(17) An order prohibiting the defendant from stalking or following, or threatening to harm, to stalk or to follow, the complainant or any other person named in the order in a manner that, taken in the context of past actions of the defendant, would put the complainant in reasonable fear that the defendant would cause the death or injury of the complainant or any other person. Behavior prohibited under this act includes, but is not limited to, behavior prohibited under the provisions of *P.L.*1992, *c.* 209 (*C.* 2C:12-10).

(18) An order requiring the defendant to undergo a psychiatric evaluation.

(19) An order directing the possession of any animal owned, possessed, leased, kept, or held by either party or a minor child residing in the household. Where a person has abused or threatened to abuse such animal, there shall be a presumption that possession of the animal shall be awarded to the non-abusive party.

(c) Notice of orders issued pursuant to this section shall be sent by the clerk of the Family Part of the Chancery Division of the Superior Court or other person designated by the court to the appropriate chiefs of police, members of the State Police and any other appropriate law enforcement agency.

(d) Upon good cause shown, any final order may be dissolved or modified upon application to the Family Part of the Chancery Division of the Superior Court, but only if the judge who dissolves or modifies the order is the same judge who entered the order, or has available a complete record of the hearing or hearings on which the order was based.

(e) Prior to the issuance of any order pursuant to this section, the court shall order that a search be made of the domestic violence central registry.

N.J.S.A. 2C:25-29.1.   CIVIL PENALTY FOR CERTAIN DOMESTIC VIOLENCE OFFENDERS

In addition to any other disposition, any person found by the court in a final hearing pursuant to section 13 of *P.L.* 1991, *c.*261 (*C.* 2C:25-29) to have committed an act of domestic violence shall be ordered by the court to pay a civil penalty of at least $50, but not to exceed $500. In imposing this civil penalty, the court shall take into consideration the nature and degree of injury suffered by the victim. The court may waive the penalty in cases of extreme financial hardship.

N.J.S.A. 2C:25-29.2.   COLLECTION, DISTRIBUTION OF CIVIL PENALTIES COLLECTED

All civil penalties imposed pursuant to section 1 of *P.L.* 2001, *c.* 195 (*C.*2C:25-29.1) shall be collected as provided by the Rules of Court. All moneys collected shall be forwarded to the Domestic Violence Victims' Fund established pursuant to section 3 of *P.L.* 2001, *c.* 195 (*C.*30:14-15).

N.J.S.A. 2C:25-29.3.   RULES OF COURT

The Supreme Court may promulgate Rules of Court to effectuate the purposes of this act [2C:25-29.1 et al.].

\

N.J.S.A.2C:25-29.4.   SURCHARGE FOR DOMESTIC VIOLENCE OFFENDER TO FUND GRANTS

In addition to any other penalty, fine or charge imposed pursuant to law, a person convicted of an act of domestic violence, as that term is defined by subsection a. of section 3 of *P.L.* 1991, *c.*261 (*C.*2C25-19), shall be subject to a surcharge in the amount of $100 payable to the Treasurer of the State of New Jersey for use by the Department of Human Services to fund grants for domestic violence prevention, training and assessment.

N.J.S.A. 2C:25-30.   VIOLATIONS, PENALTIES

Except as provided below, a violation by the defendant of an order issued pursuant to this act shall constitute an offense under subsection b. of *N.J.S.* 2C:29-9 and each order shall so state.   All contempt proceedings conducted pursuant to N.J.S. 2C:29-9 involving domestic violence orders, other than those constituting indictable offenses, shall be heard by the Family Part of the Chancery Division of the Superior Court.   All contempt proceedings brought pursuant to *P.L.*1991, *c.* 261 (*C.* 2C:25-17 et seq.) shall be subject to any rules or guidelines established by the Supreme Court to guarantee the prompt disposition of criminal matters. Additionally, and notwithstanding the term of imprisonment provided in *N.J.S.* 2C:43-8, any person convicted of a second or subsequent non-indictable domestic violence contempt offense shall serve a minimum term of not less than 30 days.   Orders entered pursuant to paragraphs (3), (4), (5), (8), and (9) of subsection *b.* of section 13 of this act shall be excluded from enforcement under subsection b. of *N.J.S.* 2C:29-9; however, violations of these orders may be enforced in a civil or criminal action initiated by the plaintiff or by the court, on its own motion, pursuant to applicable court rules.

N.J.S.A. 2C:25-31.   CONTEMPT, LAW ENFORCEMENT PROCEDURES

Where a law enforcement officer finds that there is probable cause that a defendant has committed contempt of an order entered pursuant to the provisions of *P.L.*1981, *c.* 426 (*C.* 2C:25-1 et seq.) or *P.L.* 1991, *c.* 261 (*C.* 2C:25-17 et seq.), the defendant shall be arrested and taken into custody by a law enforcement officer.   The law enforcement officer shall follow these procedures:

The law enforcement officer shall transport the defendant to the police station or such other place as the law enforcement officer shall determine is proper.   The law enforcement officer shall:

(a) Conduct a search of the domestic violence central registry and sign a complaint concerning the incident which gave rise to the contempt charge;

(b) Telephone or communicate in person or by facsimile with the appropriate judge assigned pursuant to this act and request bail be set on the contempt charge;

(c) If the defendant is unable to meet the bail set, take the necessary steps to insure that the defendant shall be incarcerated at police headquarters or at the county jail; and

(d) During regular court hours, the defendant shall have bail set by a Superior Court judge that day. On weekends, holidays and other times when the court is closed, the officer shall arrange to have the clerk of the Family Part notified on the next working day of the new complaint, the amount of bail, the defendant's whereabouts and all other necessary details. In addition, if a municipal court judge set the bail, the arresting officer shall notify the clerk of that municipal court of this information.

N.J.S.A. 2C:25-32.   ALLEGED CONTEMPT, COMPLAINT'S PROCEDURE

Where a person alleges that a defendant has committed contempt of an order entered pursuant to the provisions of *P.L.*1981, *c.* 426 (*C.2C:25-1 et seq.*) or *P.L.* 1991, *c.* 261, but where a law enforcement officer has found that there is not probable cause sufficient to arrest the defendant, the law enforcement officer shall advise the complainant of the procedure for completing and signing a criminal complaint alleging a violation of *N.J.S.* 2C:29-9. During regular court hours, the assistance of the clerk of the Family Part of the Chancery Division of the Superior Court shall be made available to such complainants. Nothing in this section shall be construed to prevent the court from granting any other emergency relief it deems necessary.

N.J.S.A. 2C:25-33.   RECORD OF APPLICATIONS FOR RELIEF; CONFIDENTIALITY; FORMS

(a) The Administrative Office of the Courts shall, with the assistance of the Attorney General and the county prosecutors, maintain a uniform record of all applications for relief pursuant to sections 9, 10, 12, and 13 of *P.L.* 1991, *c.* 261 (*C.* 2C:25-25, *C.*2C:25-26, *C.*2C:25-27, *C.*2C:25-28, and *C.*2C:25-29). The record shall include the following information:

(1) The number of criminal and civil complaints filed in all municipal courts and the Superior Court;

(2) The sex of the parties;

(3) The relationship of the parties;

(4) The relief sought or the offense charged, or both;

(5) The nature of the relief granted or penalty imposed, or both, including, but not limited to the following:

A. custody;

B. child support;

C. the specific restraints ordered;

D. any requirements or conditions imposed pursuant to the paragraphs (1) through (18) of subsection b. of section 13 of *P.L.* 1991, *c.*261 (*C.*2C:25-29), including, but not limited to, professional counseling or psychiatric evaluations;

(6) The effective date of each order issued; and

(7) In the case of a civil action in which no permanent restraints are entered, or in the case of a criminal matter that does not proceed to trial, the reason or reasons for the disposition.

It shall be the duty of the Director of the Administrative Office of the Courts to compile and report annually to the Governor, the Legislature and the Advisory Council on Domestic Violence on the data tabulated from the records of these orders.

All records maintained pursuant to this act shall be confidential and shall not be made available to any individual or institution except as otherwise provided by law.

In addition to the provisions of subsection a. of this section, the Administrative Office of the Courts shall, with the assistance of the Attorney General and the county prosecutors, create and maintain uniform forms to record sentencing, bail conditions and dismissals. The forms shall be used by the Superior Court and by every Municipal Court to record any order in a case brought pursuant to this act. Such recording shall include, but not be limited to, the specific restraints ordered, any requirements or conditions imposed on the defendant, and any conditions of bail.

N.J.S.A. 2C:25-34   DOMESTIC VIOLENCE RESTRAINING ORDERS, CENTRAL REGISTRY.

The Administrative Office of the Courts shall establish and maintain a central registry of all persons who have had domestic violence restraining orders entered against them, all persons who have been charged with a crime or offense involving domestic violence, and all persons who have been charged with a violation of a court order involving domestic violence. All records made pursuant to this section shall be kept confidential and shall be released only to:

(a) A public agency authorized to investigate a report of domestic violence;

(b) A police or other law enforcement agency investigating a report of domestic violence, or conducting a background investigation involving a person's application for a firearm permit or employment as a police or law enforcement officer or for any other purpose authorized by law or the Supreme Court of the State of New Jersey;

(c) A court, upon its finding that access to such records may be necessary for determination of an issue before the court;

(d) A surrogate, in that person's official capacity as deputy clerk of the Superior Court, in order to prepare documents that may be necessary for a court to determine an issue in an adoption proceeding; or

(e) The Division of [Youth and Family Services]Child Protection and Permanency in the Department of Children and Families when the division is conducting a background investigation involving:

(1) an allegation of child abuse or neglect, to include any adult member of the same household as the individual who is the subject of the abuse or neglect allegation; or

(2) an out-of-home placement for a child being placed by the Division of [Youth and Family Services] Child Protection and Permanency, to include any adult member of the prospective placement household.

Any individual, agency, surrogate or court which receives from the Administrative Office of the Courts the records referred to in this section shall keep such records and reports, or parts thereof, confidential and shall not disseminate or disclose such records and reports, or parts thereof; provided that nothing in this section shall prohibit a receiving individual, agency, surrogate or court from disclosing records and reports, or parts thereof, in a manner consistent with and in furtherance of the purpose for which the records and reports or parts thereof were received.

Any individual who disseminates or discloses a record or report, or parts thereof, of the central registry, for a purpose other than investigating a report of domestic violence, conducting a background investigation involving a person's application for a firearm permit or employment as a police or law enforcement officer, making a determination of an issue before the court, conducting a background investigation as specified in subsection e. of this section, or for any other purpose other than that which is authorized by law or the Supreme Court of the State of New Jersey, shall be guilty of a crime of the fourth degree.

N.J.S.A. 2C:25-35 RULES OF COURT CONCERNING CENTRAL REGISTRY FOR DOMESTIC VIOLENCE

The Supreme Court of New Jersey may adopt Rules of Court appropriate or necessary to effectuate the purposes of this act.

CHAPTER FIVE

THE CRIMES

In accordance with the Legislature intent, courts are to liberally approach and construe the remedies available to protect any victims of domestic violence.

Since the domestic violence complaint is civil and not criminal, the penalties are civil and not criminal, and thus the preponderance "standard of proof" better serves the purpose of the Act and protecting the victim of domestic violence. The reason that the preponderance of the proof standard is used in domestic violence cases, rather than the criminal standard of "beyond a reasonable doubt," is based upon the Legislative recognition that allegations of domestic violence will frequently be difficult to prove, due to the private nature of the acts between parties. There will be few, if any, eyewitnesses to marital discord or domestic violence, thus, making judge's determination of credibility more difficult. A criminal standard of proof may all but be impossible for most victims to prove and would undermine the social purpose of the Act. [224]

The Act does not create new crimes, redefine prohibited conduct, and does not substitute or supersede the protection offered by the Criminal Code, but instead offers additional protection to those victims of domestic violence. [225] Accordingly, instead of redefining prohibited conduct, the law simply incorporates [certain criminal statutes], and provides civil remedies to the victims. [226]

The original Act listed only 10 crimes. It was with the amendment in 1994 that the additional crimes of homicide, terroristic threats, criminal trespass, and stalking were added. Only enumerated acts qualify under the statute.

Before listing the various acts which have been incorporated into the Domestic Violence Act, it is important to note that under the statute, only one act is necessary in order to constitute domestic violence. One exception is under Section 13, harassment, as can be seen *infra*, where one incident in and of itself may not qualify to establish enough of a basis for domestic violence under the Harassment Statute.

"Domestic violence," under the Act means the occurrence of one or more of the following acts inflicted upon a person protected under this act by an adult or an emancipated minor:

---

[224] *N.J.S.A.* 2C:25-29(a); *Roe v. Roe,* 253 *N.J. Super.* 418, 428, 601 *A.2d* 1201 (App. Div. 1992).

[225] If no domestic relations exist, the victim must look to the Criminal Code; *see Sperling v. Teplitsky,* 294 *N.J. Super.* 312, 683 *A.2d* 244 (Ch. Div. 1996).

[226] *N.B. v. T.B.,* 297 *N.J. Super.* 35, 40, 687 *A.2d* 766 (App. Div. 1997).

(1) Homicide
(2) Assault
(3) Terroristic threats
(4) Kidnapping
(5) Criminal restraint
(6) False imprisonment
(7) Sexual assault
(8) Criminal sexual contact
(9) Lewdness
(10) Criminal mischief
(11) Burglary
(12) Criminal trespass
(13) Harassment
(14) Stalking

The practitioner should note that if an act is perpetrated by an un-emancipated minor to a victim protected by the Act, i.e., a child against a parent in the home, it does not fall within the Domestic Violence Act, but in fact falls under the provisions of *N.J.S.A.* 2A:4A-30.

5.1   HARASSMENT[227]

This matter is listed first because it is the most used in all domestic violence matters.

Except as provided in subsection *e.*, a person commits a petty disorderly person's offense if, with purpose to harass another, he:

a. Makes, or causes to be made, a communication or communications anonymously or at extremely inconvenient hours, or in offensively coarse language, or any other manner likely to cause annoyance or alarm;

b. Subjects another to striking, kicking, shoving, or other offensive touching, or threatens to do so; or

c. Engages in any other course of alarming conduct, or of repeatedly committed acts with purpose to alarm or seriously annoy such other person.

A communication under subsection a. may be deemed to have been made either at the place where it originated or at the place where it was received.

d. (Deleted by amendment, *P.L.*2001, *c.*443).

e. A person commits a crime of the fourth degree if, in committing an offense under this section, he was serving a term of imprisonment or was on parole or probation as the result of a conviction of any indictable offense under the laws of this State, any other state or the United States.[228]

The Legislative purpose in enacting the harassment statute is to make criminal, private annoyances that are not entitled to constitutional protection.[229]

Harassment is the most controversial of the domestic violence offenses, and as such has been the subject of much scrutiny. Between the years 1988 and 2015 there have been 26 reported Appellate decisions and two Supreme Court cases dealing with domestic violence harassment. Nine of the cases found that there was insufficient evidence of harassment, and seven cases found that there was sufficient evidence. As the years progressed, the Appellate courts began to reverse the trial court's determinations of domestic violence, based on harassment.

---

[227] *N.J.S.A.* 2C:33-4.

[228] *L.*1978, *c.*95; *amended* 1983, *c.*334; 1990, *c.*87, *s.*2; 1995, *c.*211, *s.*2; 1998, c.17, s.4; 2001, *c.*443, *s.*3.

[229] The *final report of the New Jersey Criminal Law Revision Commission, Commentary* to *N.J.S.A.* 2C:33-4 at 296 (1971) ("*Final Report*").

Upon the enactment of the Domestic Violence Statute, our firm's senior partner had a case in which a woman threw a gherkin pickle at her husband, while he was sitting on the couch watching television with a friend, and alluded to the fact that it represented his manhood. The court found this amounted to harassment under the Domestic Violence Act. As a result, they ordered her to leave the marital home, and left a full time working man with the custody of three children.

One of the seminal cases dealing with harassment and terroristic threats is *Cesare.* In *Cesare*, the court addressed the standard role that past history of abuse should play under the Act in evaluating a domestic violence complaint that alleges terroristic threats and harassment, and the standard of review that an Appellate Court should apply in reviewing a trial court's decision.[230] The court held that when deciding whether the harassment statute has been violated, the courts must consider the totality of the circumstances. The Court determined that even one sufficiently egregious action may constitute domestic violence under the Act, even with no history of abuse between the parties, but a court may also determine that an ambiguous incident qualifies as prohibited conduct, based upon a finding of previous violence in the parties past. Although a court is not obligated to find a past history of abuse before determining that an act of domestic violence has been committed in a particular situation, a Court must at least consider that factor in the course of its analysis. In this case, the court found the defendant's phrase "I do have a choice" and his repeated attempts to convince plaintiff to come upstairs, where he had guns, (which plaintiff testified was unusual) after an argument, could be viewed as communications likely to cause annoyance or alarm made with the purpose to harass. The trial court reviewed defendant's history of threats and violence, including threatening to tie his wife to the railroad tracks, blowing her up in a shed, as well as the fact that there were guns in the house, and found that "there was some other motive in this case." That motive, presumably an attempt to harass, could be found to "disturb, irritate or bother" a women in plaintiff's situation.[231]

In another case, the court held that the single act of sending provocative photographs to a victim's family member constitutes harassment sufficient for the entry of a final restraining order. "The act of mailing graphic pornographic pictures to a third-party (plaintiff's sister), and implying that they may be sent to the victim's workplace and to her son is egregious." The

---

[230] *Cesare v. Cesare*, 154 *N.J.* 394, 713 *A.2d* 390 (1998).

[231] *See J.F. v. B.K.*, 308 *N.J. Super.* 387, 706 *A.2d* 203 (App. Div. 1998)(observing that absent a showing of surrounding circumstances which could support a finding that such ordinarily innocuous conduct constituted an act of harassment within the intent of *N.J.S.A.* 2C:33-4, such conduct could not establish the predicate crime for a finding of domestic violence.); *See also J.D. v. M.D.F.*, 207 *N.J.* 458, 25 *A.3d* 1045, (App. Div. 2011) (stating that whether conduct "rises to the level of harassment or not is fact-sensitive. The smallest additional fact or the slightest alteration in context, particularly if based on a history between the parties, may move what otherwise would appear to be non-harassing conduct into the category of actions that qualify for issuance of a restraining order)).

Appellate Division confirmed the trial court's entry of the final restraining order when it considered the act in question against the landscape of the parties' history, despite any prior history of domestic violence.[232]

Defendant's actions of using "offensively coarse" language ("pig," "whore," "slut," "fucking bitch") directed toward the plaintiff in a public setting, in front of their children, and parents of their children's friends, qualified as harassment per New Jersey law. The Court ruled that this conduct falls squarely within the statutory limits of harassment because (1) the defendant communicated with the plaintiff; (2) the defendant's purpose in communicating was to harass the plaintiff; and (3) the communication was made in a manner that was likely to cause annoyance or alarm to its intended recipient. While the defendant argued that his actions lacked the second element of intent, because he was angered by a mistaken municipal court order, the court looked to the "totality of the circumstances" and found that the nature, manner of delivery, and the attendant circumstances of the verbal attack "strongly suggest a purpose to harass."[233]

In *Tribuzo,* the Defendant and plaintiff (former lovers) had not been together in 3 years. Defendant had in his possession, a set of car keys and a book that belonged to Plaintiff, which he kept in his car, hoping to encounter her and return said items. During the predicate incident, the Defendant approached plaintiff at a supermarket to give back these items, and became angered when she refused to talk to him. When the Plaintiff went to her automobile to leave, the defendant blocked her in with his automobile. Based upon the incident and additional factors, the court found that plaintiff was protected, despite the intervening hiatus of three years. The court further found that during the 3 year hiatus, the Defendant engaged in a course of frequent, unwanted contacts, which demonstrated defendant's continuing emotional attachment to the Plaintiff and an effort to control plaintiff's behavior. In that time, Defendant drove up and down Plaintiff's street, set up a web page using her business name (without her authorization, sent flowers, gifts, and letters, and constantly contacted her. The Court held that Defendant's conduct constituted harassment, whereby he was angry and frustrated at plaintiff for rebuffing him, used coarse and offensive language, and blocked in plaintiffs car, which was to be considered in light of his multiple prior unwanted and upsetting contacts with plaintiff...[234]

The custodian of a child, and the child's biological father, shared "a child in common," warranting the custodians protection under New Jersey's Prevention of Domestic Violence Act, where the father violated the harassment portion of the statute. In this case, the Plaintiff established by a preponderance of the evidence that defendant engaged in harassing conduct in violation of *N.J.S.A.* 2C:33-4(a), by making calls in offensively coarse language at inconvenient

---

[232]*McGowan v. O'Rourke*, 391 *N.J. Super.* 502, 918 *A.2d* 716 (App. Div. 2007).

[233]*C.M.F. v. R.G.F.*, 418 *N.J. Super.* 396, 13 *A.3d* 905 (App. Div. 2011).

[234] *Tribuzio v. Roder*, 356 *N.J. Super.* 590, 813 *A.2d* 1210 (App. Div. 2003).

hours which caused plaintiff alarm. It was also proven: (1) defendant threatened to kill plaintiff with the purpose to put her in imminent fear of death; (2) plaintiff reasonably believed the immediacy of these threats; and (3) there was a likelihood the threats would be carried out. *N.J.S.A.* 2C:12-3(b). Plaintiff testified she was, and still is, in fear for her safety.[235]

Objective Standard of Being Terrified

Defendant's threat to kill the Plaintiff or to have someone else kill her, during a heated argument, was held to be harassment, even though the plaintiff waited eight days before filing the complaint and continued to live in the marital home The court stated as a matter of in dicta (statements made to elaborate): "it is not whether she is in mortal fear of her life, it is whether the Plaintiff made a statement which meets the criteria in *N.J.S.A.* 2C 33-4." The Appellate Division found there was sufficient evidence to support a harassment finding because the specific communication of a threat to kill the Plaintiff, by the Defendant or another, was done so in "a manner likely to cause annoyance or alarm under the statute."[236]

Words are not always necessary - action can amount to enough to constitute harassment

A violation of *N.J.S.A. 2C:33-4(c)* requires proof of a course of conduct, which may consist of conduct that is alarming, or it may be a series of repeated acts if done with the purpose "to alarm or seriously annoy" the intended victim.[237]

Where a Defendant waited outside on the grounds of an adjacent property, staring at the plaintiff as she exited her home, standing up at that time, without saying anything to her, his actions were found to be harassment because of defendant positioning himself in a location where his wife could see him. Defendant was in plain sight, announcing his presence to his wife. In the courts opinion, this action constituted a "passive form of a threat" and was done with the purpose to cause annoyance or alarm to the Plaintiff.[238]

The Supreme Court addressed a similar issue in *State v. Hoffman*, where is was questioned with whether the act of mailing a torn up support order on two separate occasions, by one former spouse to another, constituted harassment under the statute. *(Note: The court also addressed a second issue, whether the mailings constituted violations of an earlier restraining order, which is discussed under the contempt section of the book.)*[239]

---

[235] *D.V. v. A.H.*, 394 *N.J. Super.* 388, 926 *A.2d* 887 (Ch. Div. 2007).

[236] *Roe v. Roe*, 253 *N.J. Super.* 418, 601 *A.2d* 1201 (App. Div. 1992).

[237] *J.D. v. M.D.F.*, 207 *N.J.* 458, 25 *A.3d* 1045 (App. Div. 2011).

[238] *State v. J.T.*, 294 *N.J. Super.* 540, 683 *A.2d* 1166 (App. Div. 1996).

[239] *State v. Hoffman*, 149 *N.J.* 564, 576, 695 *A.2d* 236, 238 (1997).

In its decision, the court reiterated that the harassment statute had three separate parts, and that the three subsections are each "freestanding because each defines an offense in its own right.[240] The plain language of subdivision (a) provides that a person commits a petty disorderly persons offence if he or she:

Makes, or causes to be made, a communication anonymously or at extremely inconvenient hours, or in offensive course language, or any other manner likely to cause annoyance or alarm.

A violation of this subsection requires the following elements:

1.   Defendant made or caused to be made a communication;
2.   Defendant's purpose in making or causing the communication to be made was to harass another person; and
3.   The communication was one of the specified manners or any other manner similarly likely to cause annoyance or alarm to intended recipient.

The court determined that the substantive criminal offense prescribed by this subsection "is directed at the purpose behind and motivation for" making or causing the communication to be made.[241] It was the duty of the State to prove beyond a reasonable doubt, that defendant's purpose in mailing the communications was to harass. "Purposely" is defined by the New Jersey Code of Criminal Justice as follows: "A person acts purposely with respect to the nature of his conduct or a result thereof if it is his conscious object to engage in contact of that nature or to cause such a result."[242] Finding that there was no legitimate purpose for the defendant's actions, the Supreme Court decided the trial court could reasonably infer that the defendant acted with the purpose to harass the plaintiff.[243]

Having determined that the second element was met and it being conceded that the first element was present (Defendant made the communication), the court then looked to the third crucial requirement of subsection (a) of the harassment statute, that the two mailings were made in a "manner likely to cause annoyance or alarm."

Noting that subsection (a), unlike subsection (c), did not contain any adjective to quantify the degree of annoyance required (that is the word "seriously"), the court went on to find that the difference between "annoyance" and "serious annoyance" is a matter of degree,

---

[240] See State v. Mortimer, 135 N.J. 517, 525, 641 A.2d 257 (1994).

[241] State v. Hoffman, 149 N.J. 564, 576, 695 A.2d 236, 238 (1997).

[242] N.J.S.A. 2C:2-2(b)(1).

[243] State v. McDougald, 120 N.J. 523, 566-67, 577 A.2d 419 (1990); State v. Avena, 281 N.J. Super. 327, 340, 657 A.2d 883 (App. Div. 1995). Common sense and experience may inform that determination. State v. Richards, 155 N.J. Super. 106, 118, 382 A.2d 407 (App. Div. 1978), certif. den., 77 N.J. 478, 391 A.2d 493 (1978).

and concluded that the Legislature made a conscious choice that the level of annoyance caused by communications directed to a person with the purpose to harass need not be as serious in paragraph (a) as it is in paragraph (c) in order to constitute harassment.

The court was then faced with defining and quantifying what "to annoy or alarm" was. It found that the Legislature intended that the term "annoyance" should derive its meaning from the conduct that was being scrutinized. Based upon a thorough examination of legislative intent, the court decided that the Legislature intended that the scheduled provision encompass only those types of communication that are "also invasive of the recipients privacy, and should only be interpreted and applied to those modes of communicative harassment that intrude into the individual's "legitimate expectations of privacy." "Speech that does not invade one's privacy by its anonymity, offensive coarseness, or extreme inconvenience, does not lose constitutional protection even when it is annoying."[244]

Although finding that defendant could not be criminally convicted for harassment, the Court declared:

> The fears of a domestic violence victim and the turmoil she or he has experienced should not be trivialized. In different contexts, a recipient of a torn-up court order may not be alarmed or seriously annoyed, but some victims of domestic violence may rightly view a course of communicative conduct as seriously annoying, alarming, or threatening, or all of those things.

According to the Court, conduct that does not constitute an invasion of privacy to the ordinary victim under subsection (a) might constitute harassment to the victim of past domestic abuse. Therefore, the Court maintained, "in determining whether a defendant's conduct is likely to cause the required annoyance or alarm to the victim that defendant's past conduct toward the victim and the relationship's history must be taken into account. As to the second issue, the court also found that the two mailings were in violation of the restraining order.[245]

<u>Evidence of a past incident of domestic violence, between defendant and a previous spouse, who is not a party in the action, is admissible to prove that an ambiguous comment is made with a purpose to annoy or alarm plaintiff so as to constitute harassment.</u>

In one case, the Plaintiff accused the Defendant of harassment and sought a Restraining Order. The evidence revealed that earlier in their relationship the defendant told the plaintiff that he had previously spent time in jail for assaulting his second wife. The court held that the admission, when combined with numerous telephone calls, and an ambiguous statement by defendant that plaintiff "will get it," constituted harassment within the meaning of the

---

[244] *State v. Hoffman*, 149 *N.J.* 564, 583-584, 695 *A.2d* 238, 246 (1997).
[245] *Ibid.*

Prevention of Domestic Violence Act. The court found that the vague statement, when viewed in light of defendant's incarceration for a previous domestic violence act, could reasonably frighten, disturb, or trouble plaintiff. (*Note: The statement was admissible under New Jersey Rule of Evidence 401, since a statement about "spending time in jail" could be admitted to prove intent to harass. Furthermore, it was a statement by a party and an admission.*)[246]

Cases Where Court Did Not Find Harassment

A normal marital argument, where a former husband admitted he stood in former wife's doorway and yelled at her regarding the child's behavior, did not constitute harassment. In this case, the court found Defendant did not act or speak with purpose to harass, annoy, or alarm. The argument was simply an "expression of a lack of affection of a crumbling marriage and cannot be considered an act of harassment for purposes of the Prevention of Domestic Violence Act."[247]

In *Grant v. Wright,* the Plaintiff alleged harassment against the defendant for conduct consisting of putting her belongings in storage while she was gone for the weekend, knowing that this action would anger and upset her. The Plaintiff also claimed that the Defendant had anger rants, wherein he slapped and slammed door, had violent outbursts, and threw objects about. The court found this was not harassment because actions did not rise to the level of a "course of alarming conduct or repeated acts to alarm within the meaning of the statute. The court also found that although the defendant's purpose was to harass or annoy plaintiff by moving her stuff, such a purpose to harass, is not sufficient to satisfy the definition upon which the court relied. Moreover, the trial court (who initially found harassment) did not consider certain relevant factors. The Prevention of Domestic Violence Act requires that:

a.   A hearing shall be held in juvenile and domestic relations court within 10 days of the filing of a complaint.... At the hearing the standard for proving the allegations in the complaint shall be by a preponderance of the evidence. The court shall consider but not be limited to the following factors:

(1)   The previous history of domestic violence between the cohabitants including threats, harassment and physical abuse
(2)   The existence of immediate danger to person or property.... [*N.J.S.A.* 2C:25-13(a).][248]

Note: Danger to person or property is prerequisite

---

[246] *Rosiak v. Melvin*, 351 *N.J. Super.* 322, 798 *A.2d* 156 (Ch. Div. 2002).
[247] *Chernesky v. Fedorczyk*, 346 *N.J. Super.* 34, 786 *A.2d* 881 (App. Div. 2001).
[248] *Grant v. Wright*, 222 *N.J. Super.* 191, 536 *A.2d* 319 (App. Div.), *certif. denied*, 111 *N.J.* 562, 546 *A.2d* 493 (1988).

In a case where a mother (M.A.) filed a domestic violence complaint against defendant/stepfather, alleging he sexually abused her 15-year-old daughter, M.P., the Superior Court of New Jersey, Chancery Division, Family Part, dismissed the action since the daughter was not a "victim" as defined in the New Jersey Prevention of Domestic Violence Act. In addition, the mother was not permitted to bring an action on behalf of her daughter. Moreover, the court dismissed mother's contemporaneous charge alleging harassment committed against her, by the sexual abuse to her daughter. In regard to the harassment charge, the court found that neither subsection (a) nor (b) applied. Additionally, subsection (c) did not apply, because even though defendant's alleged sexual assaults on M.P. were surely "alarming," there is nothing in the record to suggest that defendant assaulted M.P. for the purpose of "alarming" M.P.'s mother rather than for his own sexual gratification.[249]

Purpose to Harass is Necessary

Where a defendant made seemingly alarming comments to his wife's uncle, the court found there was no harassment, as the purpose of defendant's conversation with his wife's uncle was not to harass his wife, or to cause the uncle to make a communication in a "manner likely to cause annoyance or alarm" to his wife under *N.J.S.A.* 2C:33-4(a).[250]

A mere expression of an opinion utilizing offensive language is not sufficient to prove harassment. It was not harassment under the Prevention of Domestic Violence Act, *N.J.S.A.* 2C:25-19 (a), for defendant to call his mother a "senile old bitch." Under *N.J.S.A.* 2C:25-19, the court should not assess the effect of the speech on the victim, who was clearly upset, but rather the intent of the actor in making the communication.[251] In its decision, the court cited *State v. L.C.*:

> Because the First Amendment to the United States Constitution "permits regulation of conduct, not mere expression," the speech punished by the harassment statute "must be uttered with the specific intention of harassing the listener." A restraining order based on harassment cannot be entered "if based on a mere expression of opinion utilizing offensive language."[252]

The theft of personal property alone does not qualify as harassment. In order to qualify as harassment, the act must be committed with the "purpose to harass," or in other words,

---

[249] *M.A. v. E.A.*, 388 *N.J. Super.* 612, 909 *A.2d* 1168 (App. Div. 2006).

[250] *State v. Castagno*, 387 *N.J. Super.* 598, 905 *A.2d* 415 (App. Div. 2006).

[251] *E.M.B. v. R.F.B.*, 419 *N.J. Super.* 177, 16 *A.3d* 463 (App. Div. 2011).

[252] *State v. L.C.*, 283 *N.J. Super.* 441, 450, 662 *A.2d* 577 (App. Div. 1995), *certif. denied*, 143 *N.J.* 325, 670 *A.2d* 1066 (1996).

with the intent to alarm or seriously annoy such other person. Moreover, the court stated theft by itself, does not qualify as a predicate act enumerated in *N.J.S.A.* 2C:25-19.[253]

When evaluating whether an individual acted with the requisite purpose, our courts must be especially vigilant in domestic violence cases involving the interactions of couples in the midst of a breakup.[254]

The purpose to harass required "may be inferred from the evidence presented. Common sense and experience may inform that determination."[255]

Court Did Not Find Purpose to Harass or Seriously Annoy

"Not all offensive or bothersome behavior, however constitutes harassment." In the criminal context, the Appellate Division has cautioned against "overextending a criminal statute to rude behavior which is not directed to anyone specifically, but only towards an institution in general."[256] In *State v. Duncan*, the court found that venting feelings of frustration or irritation, in addition to the use of obscenities during a 911 call did not demonstrate a purpose to harass, thus making a restraining order inappropriate. Moreover, the court noted that purposeful is "the highest form of *mens rea* contained in our penal code and the most difficult to establish."[257]

In another case, the Defendant disciplined the party's children in a manner her husband disapproved of, despite this, the defendant continued to discipline the children in the same manner. The Appellate Division reversed the trial court's finding of harassment because it held that the defendant was not shown to have disciplined the children with "a purpose" to harass plaintiff. The court further found that even if defendant had purposely harmed the child, the Plaintiff would still have to prove that the Defendant acted with the requisite element of a purpose to harass Plaintiff.[258]

The court deemed it was not harassment where the defendant/ex-husband sent ex-wife 18 text messages during a three hour period. Although the Defendant's conduct may have been dysfunctional, the trial court did not find, nor did the evidence show, that Defendant sent the

---

[253] *E.M.B. v. R.F.B.*, 419 *N.J. Super.* 177, 16 *A.3d* 463 (App. Div. 2011).

[254] *See Franklin v. Sloskey*, 385 *N.J. Super.* 534, 544, 897 *A.2d* 1113 (App. Div. 2006) (concluding that evidence established only a "dispute between a couple in the midst of a breakup, disagreeing over the future of their unborn child" rather than intent to harass"); *Bresocnik v. Gellegos*, 367 *N.J. Super.* 178, 842 *A.2d* 276 (App. Div. 2004) (concluding that letter expressing regret and continued affection did not reveal intent to harass.)

[255] *State v. Hoffman,* 149 *N.J.* 564, 695 *A.2d* 236 (1997).

[256] *J.D. v. M.D.F.*, 207 *N.J.* 458, 25 *A.3d* 1045 (2011).

[257] *State v. Duncan*, 376 *N.J. Super.* 253, 262, 870 *A.2d* 307 (App. Div. 2005).

[258] *E.K. v. G.K.*, 241 *N.J. Super.* 567, 575 *A.2d* 883 (App. Div. 1990).

text messages for the purpose of harassing his ex-wife. Defendant sent the messages for the purpose of obtaining information about their daughter, and had Plaintiff provided him with the information, the Defendant's messaging would have stopped.[259] The purpose of defendant's messages was not to harass plaintiff. Although defendant's behavior may have been dysfunctional, if plaintiff provided the information to defendant, the messages would have stopped.

It is not harassment when what occurred between the parties is merely a matrimonial argument concerning money, property, the anticipation of divorce or similar marital disputes (*Note: the courts in those cases observed that there was no history of threats, abuse, or domestic violence between the parties.*)[260]

Where Defendant repeatedly told the Plaintiff that she is not sexually attractive, and he doesn't love her, the trial court found these "types of statements that have been meant to belittle her and to demean her and inflict emotional abuse upon her," constituted harassment. Defendant did not dispute telling his wife that he didn't love her or have sexual feelings for her. Rather, Defendant maintained he was merely responding honestly to his wife's inquiries. The Appellate Division reversed the decision as there was no evidence of record to sustain a finding that the *purpose* of defendant's remarks was to repeatedly alarm or annoy the plaintiff, although it may have had that effect. The domestic violence complaint along with Plaintiff's own testimony, support Defendant's contention that he was planning to leave and divorce the Plaintiff, and had made this known. The court held that pre-divorce statements respecting absence of affection or physical desire alone were not intended to be sufficient to fulfill the elements of purposeful alarm or serious annoyance necessary to constitute harassment under either statute.[261]

In *D.C. v. V. T.H., a* Defendant went to his child's daycare and threatened to stick his foot up Plaintiff's boyfriend's ass if the boyfriend physically disciplined his child again. The Plaintiff also alleged (though denied by Defendant), that Defendant threatened to kick her ass as well. The Appellate Division found the defendant was not guilty of harassment under *N.J.S.A.* 2C:33-4(a), since he did not make the statement concerning plaintiff's boyfriend's with the purpose of harassing plaintiff. (*Note: It as necessary that the Defendant directed the threatening remarks to the victim, not a 3rd party.*) Rather, defendant's evident purpose in making the statement was to dissuade plaintiff's boyfriend from inflicting further discipline to his child.[262]

The court did not find harassment where a Defendant secretively monitored the Plaintiff by installing a concealed camera and microphone in her bedroom. The Appellate Division found

---

[259] *L.M.F. v. J.A.F.*, 421 *N.J. Super.* 523, 24 *A.3d* 849 (App. Div. 2011).

[260] *Cesare v. Cesare*, 154 *N.J.* 394, 713 *A.2d* 390 (1998)(*citing Corrente v. Corrente*, 281 *N.J. Super.* 243, 250, 657 *A.2d* 440 (App. Div. 1995)).

[261] *Murray v. Murray*, 267 *N.J. Super.* 406, 408-411, 631 *A.2d* 984 (App. Div. 1993).

[262] *D.C. v. T.H.*, 269 *N.J. Super.* 458, 461, 635 *A.2d* 1002 (App. Div. 1994).

that since the camera was concealed in a manner so as to avoid detection, Defendant did not intend to annoy or alarm the Plaintiff, but meant only to observe her.[263]

The court did uphold the stalking conviction and went on to differentiate findings necessary for stalking as opposed to harassment. A person is guilty of stalking if he purposefully or knowingly engages in a course of conduct directed at a specific person that *would cause a reasonable person to fear bodily injury* to himself or a member of his immediate family or to fear the death of himself or a member of his immediate family." *N.J.S.A.* 2C:12-10(b). Stalking requires:

1.   Defendant engaged in speech or conduct directed at or toward a person;
2.   That speech or conduct occurred on at least 2 occasions;
3.   Defendant purposely engaged in speech or course of conduct that is capable of causing a reasonable person to fear for herself or her immediate family bodily injury or death.

Victim need not be aware of stalking or conduct when it happens.[264]

Note: Motivation

A Defendant's statements that the parties were "beyond words" and that he would "bury" the Plaintiff, following a dispute, did not rise to the level of harassment. The court found that it was not the Defendant's purpose to harass the Plaintiff. Furthermore, the Defendant did not engage in a course of conduct or repeated acts, intended to alarm or seriously annoy the Plaintiff, even if his comments were alarming to her. The court noted in its dicta that the statute prohibits "regular serious abuse" where there is a previous history of violence between the parties.[265]

Note: Serious Annoyance

In *Corrente v. Corrente,* the court held that Defendant's acts of calling the Plaintiff at work, asking for money, and threatening to take "drastic measures" if plaintiff did not produce the money, as well as disconnecting plaintiff's phone service, was not harassment. The court found defendant did not make the calls with the purpose to harass the Plaintiff, even though she felt alarmed by said calls. While the judge did find intent to harass in the turning off of the phone, that act was neither repeated nor a course of conduct. In addition, neither the phone calls (which plaintiff testified requested her to move out of the house and pay her share of the

---

[263] *H.E.S. v. J.C.S.*, 349 *N.J. Super.* 332, 793 *A.2d* 780 (Ch. Div. 2002), *aff'd. in part and rev. in part*, 175 *N.J.* 309, 815 *A.2d* 405 (2003).

[264] *Ibid.*

[265] *Peranio v. Peranio*, 280 *N.J. Super.* 47, 51, 654 *A.2d* 495 (App. Div. 1995).

household costs), nor the turning off of the phone, were acts which can be characterized as alarming or seriously annoying.[266]

While picking up/dropping off parties children, the Defendant made obscene gestures at the plaintiff, called her vulgar names, made ethnic and sexual remarks about plaintiff's new boyfriend, and kicked over a garbage can. The court found this was not harassment, despite the fact that plaintiff testified she was terrified of the defendant. The Appellate Division found that the evidence did not support any reasonable basis on her behalf that she was in fact terrified by this action and found there was insufficient credible evidence that defendant intended to "alarm" plaintiff but only that the parties were mutually annoyed at each other. "Neither the harassment statute nor the Prevention of Domestic Violence Act were intended to place trial judges in the role of super monitors over modern-day parenting."[267]

Note: Course of Alarming Conduct

Defendant's reference to her husband's female friend as a "whore" and a "slut" in front of their children did not reveal a "purpose to harass" and defendant's speech was merely an expression of opinion utilizing "offensive language" as opposed to "verbal harassment."[268]

A Defendant's attempt to walk into his wife's bedroom and pick up his child, which resulted in a pushing and shoving match (although inappropriate), was not harassment. The defendant did not engage in a "course of alarming conduct, nor did he repeatedly commit acts with the purpose to alarm or seriously annoy." The judge here also did not find that the husband acted with a purpose to harass his wife.[269]

Where a Defendant communicated to his wife, through a co-worker, that he had moved her desk, the court found nothing in the record to support a determination that the defendant's purpose was to harass. In addition, the communication was not made in the manner likely to cause annoyance or alarm.[270] Rather, the parties' activity was one of mutual annoyance not domestic violence.

Note: An individual act previously rejected as insufficient to constitute domestic violence may take on greater significance if the act is later repeated in a manner that may amount to a course of conduct, prohibited by N.J.S.A. 2C:33-4(c) (harassment) and/or N.J.S.A. 2C:12-10(b) (stalking). In such situations, the prior act may be considered along with the new conduct to determine

---

[266] *Corrente v. Corrente*, 281 *N.J. Super.* 243, 249, 657 *A.2d* 440 (App. Div. 1995).

[267] *J.N.S. v. D.B.S.*, 302 *N.J. Super.* 525, 532, 695 *A.2d* 730 (App. Div. 1997)(The Wife filed two complaints against the defendant for the two mailings; each complaint alleged two distinct defenses: harassing communications and domestic violence contempt)).

[268] *State v. L.C.*, 283 *N.J. Super.* 441, 448, 662 *A.2d* 577 (App. Div. 1995).

[269] *N.B. v. T.B.*, 297 *N.J. Super.* 35, 38-41, 687 *A.2d* 766 (App. Div. 1997).

[270] *L.D. v. W.D.*, 327 *N.J. Super.* 1, 742 *A.2d* 588 (App. Div. 1999).

whether a plaintiff has established domestic violence based on a subsequent complaint. If not, it may be barred under principles of res judicata.[271]

A not guilty finding of harassment in the Municipal Court cannot be used as a "res judicata" in the domestic violence case because the burden of proof in the municipal case is beyond a reasonable doubt and the burden of proof in a domestic violence proceeding is the lesser standard, preponderance of evidence.

---

[271] *T.M. v. J.C.*, 348 *N.J. Super.* 101, 791 *A.2d* 300 (App. Div. 2002).

5.2   HOMICIDE

N.J.S.A. 2C:25-19(a)(1) lists "homicide" which includes all offenses relating to the causing of death or serious bodily injury resulting in death, and cites "*N.J.S.A.* 2C:11-1 *et. seq.*" That sections states:

a.   "Bodily injury" means physical pain, illness or any impairment of physical condition;

b.   "Serious bodily injury" means bodily injury which creates a substantial risk of death or which causes serious, permanent disfigurement, or protracted loss or impairment of the function of any bodily member or organ;

c.   "Deadly weapon" means any firearm or other weapon, device, instrument, material or substance, whether animate or inanimate, which in the manner it is used or is intended to be used, is known to be capable of producing death or serious bodily injury or which in the manner it is fashioned would lead the victim reasonably to believe it to be capable of producing death or serious bodily injury;

d.   "Significant bodily injury" means bodily injury which creates a temporary loss of the function of any bodily member or organ, or temporary loss of any one of the five senses.[272]

In *State v. Lee,* the court was confronted with the question, whether the imposition of the Domestic Violence surcharge for convictions based on acts of domestic violence can be applied if the defendant is charged with attempted murder.[273] The court found that neither attempts, generally, nor attempted murder, specifically, are included in *N.J.S.A.* 2C:25-19(a), which lists the offenses which can constitute domestic violence. Therefore, such crimes are not subject to the domestic violence surcharge under *N.J.S.A.* 2C:25-29.4.

N.J.S.A. 2C:11-2 CRIMINAL HOMICIDE

a.   A person is guilty of criminal homicide if he purposely, knowingly, recklessly or, under the circumstances set forth in section 2C:11-5, causes the death of another human being.
b.   Criminal homicide is murder, manslaughter or death by auto.

N.J.S.A. 2C:11-3 MURDER[274]

a.   Except as provided in *N.J.S.* 2C:11-4, criminal homicide constitutes murder when:

---

[272] *N.J.S.A.* 2C:11-1 et seq.
[273] *State v. Lee*, 411 *N.J. Super.* 349, 986 *A.2d* 42 (App. Div. 2010).
[274] *N.J.S.A.* 2C:11-3 (2014)

(1) The actor purposely causes death or serious bodily injury resulting in death; or

(2) The actor knowingly causes death or serious bodily injury resulting in death; or

(3) It is committed when the actor, acting either alone or with one or more other persons, is engaged in the commission of, or an attempt to commit, or flight after committing or attempting to commit robbery, sexual assault, arson, burglary, kidnapping, carjacking, criminal escape or terrorism pursuant to section 2 of *P.L.*2002, *c.*26 (*C.*2C:38-2), and in the course of such crime or of immediate flight there from, any person causes the death of a person other than one of the participants; except that in any prosecution under this subsection, in which the defendant was not the only participant in the underlying crime, it is an affirmative defense that the defendant:

> (a) Did not commit the homicidal act or in any way solicit, request, command, importune, cause or aid the commission thereof; and
> (b) Was not armed with a deadly weapon, or any instrument, article or substance readily capable of causing death or serious physical injury and of a sort not ordinarily carried in public places by law-abiding persons; and
> (c) Had no reasonable ground to believe that any other participant was armed with such a weapon, instrument, article or substance; and
> (d) Had no reasonable ground to believe that any other participant intended to engage in conduct likely to result in death or serious physical injury.

b. (1) Murder is a crime of the first degree but a person convicted of murder shall be sentenced, except as provided in paragraphs (2), (3) and (4) of this subsection, by the court to a term of 30 years, during which the person shall not be eligible for parole, or be sentenced to a specific term of years which shall be between 30 years and life imprisonment of which the person shall serve 30 years before being eligible for parole.

(2) If the victim was a law enforcement officer and was murdered while performing his official duties or was murdered because of his status as a law enforcement officer, the person convicted of that murder shall be sentenced by the court to a term of life imprisonment, during which the person shall not be eligible for parole.

(3) A person convicted of murder shall be sentenced to a term of life imprisonment without eligibility for parole if the murder was committed under all of the following circumstances:

(a) The victim is less than 14 years old; and

(b) The act is committed in the course of the commission, whether alone or with one or more persons, of a violation of *N.J.S.A. 2C:14-2* or *N.J.S.A. 2C:14-3.*

(4) Any person convicted under subsection a.(1) or (2) who committed the homicidal act by his own conduct; or who as an accomplice procured the commission of the offense by payment or promise of payment of anything of pecuniary value; or who, as a leader of a narcotics trafficking network as defined in *N.J.S.A. 2C:35-3* and in furtherance of a conspiracy enumerated in *N.J.S.A. 2C:35-3*, commanded or by threat or promise solicited the commission of the offense, or, if the murder occurred during the commission of the crime of terrorism, any person who committed the crime of terrorism, shall be sentenced by the court to life imprisonment without eligibility for parole, which sentence shall be served in a maximum security prison, if a jury finds beyond a reasonable doubt that any of the following aggravating factors exist:

(a) The defendant has been convicted, at any time, of another murder. For purposes of this section, a conviction shall be deemed final when sentence is imposed and may be used as an aggravating factor regardless of whether it is on appeal;

(b) In the commission of the murder, the defendant purposely or knowingly created a grave risk of death to another person in addition to the victim.

(c) The murder was outrageously or wantonly vile, horrible or inhuman in that it involved torture, depravity of mind, or an aggravated assault to the victim;

(d) The defendant committed the murder as consideration for the receipt, or in expectation of the receipt of anything of pecuniary value.

(e) The defendant procured the commission of the murder by payment or promise of payment of anything of pecuniary value;

(f) The murder was committed for the purpose of escaping detection, apprehension, trial, punishment or confinement for another offense committed by the defendant or another;

(g) The murder was committed while the defendant was engaged in the commission of, or an attempt to commit, or flight after committing or attempting to commit murder, robbery, sexual assault, arson, burglary, kidnapping, carjacking or the crime of contempt in violation of subsection (b) of *N.J.S.A. 2C:29-9;*

(h) The defendant murdered a public servant, as defined in *N.J.S.A. 2C:27-1,* while the victim was engaged in the performance of his official duties, or because of the victim's status as a public servant;

(i) The defendant: (i) as a leader of a narcotics trafficking network as defined in *N.J.S.A. 2C:35-3* and in furtherance of a conspiracy enumerated in *N.J.S.A. 2C:35-3,* committed, commanded or by threat or promise solicited the commission of the murder or (ii) committed the murder at the direction of a leader of a narcotics trafficking network as defined in *N.J.S.A. 2C:35-3* in furtherance of a conspiracy enumerated in *N.J.S.A. 2C:35-3*;

(j) The homicidal act that the defendant committed or procured was in violation of paragraph (1) of subsection a. of *N.J.S.A. 2C:17-2*;

(k) The victim was less than 14 years old; or

(l) The murder was committed during the commission of, or an attempt to commit, or flight after committing or attempting to commit, terrorism pursuant to section 2 of *P.L.*2002, c.26 (*C.*2C:38-2).

(5) A juvenile who has been tried as an adult and convicted of murder shall be sentenced pursuant to paragraph (1), (2) or (3) of this subsection.

c. (Deleted by amendment, *P.L.2007, c.204*).

d. (Deleted by amendment, *P.L.2007, c.204*).

e. (Deleted by amendment, *P.L.2007, c.204*).

f. (Deleted by amendment, *P.L.2007, c.204*).

g. (Deleted by amendment, *P.L.2007, c.204*).

h. (Deleted by amendment, *P.L.2007, c.204*).

i. For purposes of this section the term "homicidal act" shall mean conduct that causes death or serious bodily injury resulting in death.

j. In a sentencing proceeding conducted pursuant to this section, the display of a photograph of the victim taken before the homicide shall be permitted.

5.3 ASSAULT [275]

a. Simple assault. A person is guilty of assault if he:

(1) Attempts to cause or purposely, knowingly or recklessly causes bodily injury to another; or

(2) Negligently causes bodily injury to another with a deadly weapon; or

(3) Attempts by physical menace to put another in fear of imminent serious bodily injury.

Simple assault is a disorderly persons offense unless committed in a fight or scuffle entered into by mutual consent, in which case it is a petty disorderly person's offense.

b. Aggravated assault. A person is guilty of aggravated assault if he:

(1) Attempts to cause serious bodily injury to another, or causes such injury purposely or knowingly or under circumstances manifesting extreme indifference to the value of human life recklessly causes such injury; or

(2) Attempts to cause or purposely or knowingly causes bodily injury to another with a deadly weapon; or

(3) Recklessly causes bodily injury to another with a deadly weapon; or

(4) Knowingly under circumstances manifesting extreme indifference to the value of human life points a firearm, as defined in section 2C:39-1(f)., at or in the direction of another, whether or not the actor believes it to be loaded; or

(5) Commits a simple assault as defined in subsection a. (1), (2) or (3) of this section upon:

(a) Any law enforcement officer acting in the performance of his duties while in uniform or exhibiting evidence of his authority or because of his status as a law enforcement officer; or
(b) Any paid or volunteer fireman acting in the performance of his duties while in uniform or otherwise clearly identifiable as being engaged in the performance of the duties of a fireman; or

---

[275] *N.J.S.A. 2C:12-1.*

(c) Any person engaged in emergency first-aid or medical services acting in the performance of his duties while in uniform or otherwise clearly identifiable as being engaged in the performance of emergency first-aid or medical services; or

(d) Any school board member, school administrator, teacher, school bus driver or other employee of a public or nonpublic school or school board while clearly identifiable as being engaged in the performance of his duties or because of his status as a member or employee of a public or nonpublic school or school board or any school bus driver employed by an operator under contract to a public or nonpublic school or school board while clearly identifiable as being engaged in the performance of his duties or because of his status as a school bus driver; or

(e) Any employee of the Division of Child Protection and Permanency while clearly identifiable as being engaged in the performance of his duties or because of his status as an employee of the division; or

(f) Any justice of the Supreme Court, judge of the Superior Court, judge of the Tax Court or municipal judge while clearly identifiable as being engaged in the performance of judicial duties or because of his status as a member of the judiciary; or

(g) Any operator of a motorbus or the operator's supervisor or any employee of a rail passenger service while clearly identifiable as being engaged in the performance of his duties or because of his status as an operator of a motorbus or as the operator's supervisor or as an employee of a rail passenger service; or

(h) Any Department of Corrections employee, county corrections officer, juvenile corrections officer, State juvenile facility employee, juvenile detention staff member, juvenile detention officer, probation officer or any sheriff, undersheriff, or sheriff's officer acting in the performance of his duties while in uniform or exhibiting evidence of his authority; or

(i) Any employee, including any person employed under contract, of a utility company as defined in section 2 of *P.L.*1971, *c.*224 (*C.2A*:42-86) or a cable television company subject to the provisions of the "Cable Television Act," *P.L.*1972, *c.*186 (*C.*48:5A-1 *et seq.*) while clearly identifiable as being engaged in the performance of his duties in regard to connecting, disconnecting or repairing or attempting to connect, disconnect or repair any gas, electric or water utility, or cable television or telecommunication service; or

(j) Any health care worker employed by a licensed health care facility to provide direct patient care, any health care professional licensed or otherwise authorized pursuant to Title 26 or Title 45 of the Revised Statutes to practice a health care profession, except a direct care worker at a State or county psychiatric hospital or State developmental center or veterans' memorial home, while clearly identifiable as being engaged in the duties of providing direct patient care or practicing the health care profession; or

(k) Any direct care worker at a State or county psychiatric hospital or State developmental center or veterans' memorial home, while clearly identifiable as being engaged in the duties of providing direct patient care or practicing the health care profession, provided that the actor is not a patient or resident at the facility who is classified by the facility as having a mental illness or developmental disability; or

(6) Causes bodily injury to another person while fleeing or attempting to elude a law enforcement officer in violation of subsection b. of *N.J.S.A. 2C:29-2* or while operating a motor vehicle in violation of subsection c. of *N.J.S.A. 2C:20-10*. Notwithstanding any other provision of law to the contrary, a person shall be strictly liable for a violation of this subsection upon proof of a violation of subsection b. of *N.J.S.A. 2C:29-2* or while operating a motor vehicle in violation of subsection c. of *N.J.S.A. 2C:20-10* which resulted in bodily injury to another person; or

(7) Attempts to cause significant bodily injury to another or causes significant bodily injury purposely or knowingly or, under circumstances manifesting extreme indifference to the value of human life recklessly causes such significant bodily injury; or

(8) Causes bodily injury by knowingly or purposely starting a fire or causing an explosion in violation of *N.J.S.A. 2C:17-1* which results in bodily injury to any emergency services personnel involved in fire suppression activities, rendering emergency medical services resulting from the fire or explosion or rescue operations, or rendering any necessary assistance at the scene of the fire or explosion, including any bodily injury sustained while responding to the scene of a reported fire or explosion. For purposes of this subsection, "emergency services personnel" shall include, but not be limited to, any paid or volunteer fireman, any person engaged in emergency first-aid or medical services and any law enforcement officer. Notwithstanding any other provision of law to the contrary, a person shall be strictly liable for a violation of this paragraph upon proof of a violation of *N.J.S.A. 2C:17-1* which resulted in bodily injury to any emergency services personnel; or

(9) Knowingly, under circumstances manifesting extreme indifference to the value of human life, points or displays a firearm, as defined in subsection f. of *N.J.S.A. 2C:39-1*, at or in the direction of a law enforcement officer; or

(10) Knowingly points, displays or uses an imitation firearm, as defined in subsection f. of *N.J.S.A. 2C:39-1,* at or in the direction of a law enforcement officer with the purpose to intimidate, threaten or attempt to put the officer in fear of bodily injury or for any unlawful purpose; or

(11) Uses or activates a laser sighting system or device, or a system or device which, in the manner used, would cause a reasonable person to believe that it is a laser sighting system or device, against a law enforcement officer acting in the performance of his duties while in uniform or exhibiting evidence of his authority. As used in this paragraph, "laser sighting system or device" means any system or device that is integrated with or affixed to a firearm and emits a laser light beam that is used to assist in the sight alignment or aiming of the firearm.

Aggravated assault under subsections b.(1) and b.(6) is a crime of the second degree; under subsections b.(2), b.(7), b.(9) and b.(10) is a crime of the third degree; under subsections b.(3) and b.(4) is a crime of the fourth degree; and under subsection b.(5) is a crime of the third degree if the victim suffers bodily injury, otherwise it is a crime of the fourth degree. Aggravated assault under subsection b.(8) is a crime of the third degree if the victim suffers bodily injury; if the victim suffers significant bodily injury or serious bodily injury it is a crime of the second degree. Aggravated assault under subsection b.(11) is a crime of the third degree.

c. (1) A person is guilty of assault by auto or vessel when the person drives a vehicle or vessel recklessly and causes either serious bodily injury or bodily injury to another. Assault by auto or vessel is a crime of the fourth degree if serious bodily injury results and is a disorderly persons offense if bodily injury results. Proof that the defendant was operating a hand-held wireless telephone while driving a motor vehicle in violation of section 1 of *P.L.*2003, *c.*310 (*C.*39:4-97.3) may give rise to an inference that the defendant was driving recklessly.

(2) Assault by auto or vessel is a crime of the third degree if the person drives the vehicle while in violation of *R.S.*39:4-50 or section 2 of *P.L.*1981, c.512 (*C.*39:4-50.4a) and serious bodily injury results and is a crime of the fourth degree if the person drives the vehicle while in violation of *R.S.*39:4-50 or section 2 of *P.L.*1981, *c.*512 (*C.*39:4-50.4a) and bodily injury results.

(3) Assault by auto or vessel is a crime of the second degree if serious bodily injury results from the defendant operating the auto or vessel while in violation of *R.S.*39:4-50 or section 2 of *P.L.*1981, *c.*512 (*C.*39:4-50.4a) while:

(a) on any school property used for school purposes which is owned by or leased to any elementary or secondary school or school board, or within 1,000 feet of such school property;
(b) driving through a school crossing as defined in *R.S.*39:1-1 if the

municipality, by ordinance or resolution, has designated the school crossing as such; or

(c) driving through a school crossing as defined in *R.S.*39:1-1 knowing that juveniles are present if the municipality has not designated the school crossing as such by ordinance or resolution.

Assault by auto or vessel is a crime of the third degree if bodily injury results from the defendant operating the auto or vessel in violation of this paragraph.

A map or true copy of a map depicting the location and boundaries of the area on or within 1,000 feet of any property used for school purposes which is owned by or leased to any elementary or secondary school or school board produced pursuant to section 1 of *P.L.*1987, *c.*101 (*C.*2C:35-7) may be used in a prosecution under subparagraph (a) of paragraph (3) of this subsection.

It shall be no defense to a prosecution for a violation of subparagraph (a) or (b) of paragraph (3) of this subsection that the defendant was unaware that the prohibited conduct took place while on or within 1,000 feet of any school property or while driving through a school crossing. Nor shall it be a defense to a prosecution under subparagraph (a) or (b) of paragraph (3) of this subsection that no juveniles were present on the school property or crossing zone at the time of the offense or that the school was not in session.

(4) Assault by auto or vessel is a crime of the third degree if the person purposely drives a vehicle in an aggressive manner directed at another vehicle and serious bodily injury results and is a crime of the fourth degree if the person purposely drives a vehicle in an aggressive manner directed at another vehicle and bodily injury results. For purposes of this paragraph, "driving a vehicle in an aggressive manner" shall include, but is not limited to, unexpectedly altering the speed of the vehicle, making improper or erratic traffic lane changes, disregarding traffic control devices, failing to yield the right of way, or following another vehicle too closely.

As used in this section, "vessel" means a means of conveyance for travel on water and propelled otherwise than by muscular power.

d.   A person who is employed by a facility as defined in section 2 of *P.L.*1977, *c.*239 (*C.*52:27G-2) who commits a simple assault as defined in paragraph (1) or (2) of subsection a. of this section upon an institutionalized elderly person as defined in section 2 of *P.L.*1977, *c.*239

(C.52:27G-2) is guilty of a crime of the fourth degree.

e.   (Deleted by amendment, *P.L.*2001, *c.*443).

f.   A person who commits a simple assault as defined in paragraph (1), (2) or (3) of subsection a. of this section in the presence of a child under 16 years of age at a school or community sponsored youth sports event is guilty of a crime of the fourth degree. The defendant shall be strictly liable upon proof that the offense occurred, in fact, in the presence of a child under 16 years of age. It shall not be a defense that the defendant did not know that the child was present or reasonably believed that the child was 16 years of age or older. The provisions of this subsection shall not be construed to create any liability on the part of a participant in a youth sports event or to abrogate any immunity or defense available to a participant in a youth sports event. As used in this act, "school or community sponsored youth sports event" means a competition, practice or instructional event involving one or more interscholastic sports teams or youth sports teams organized pursuant to a nonprofit or similar charter or which are member teams in a youth league organized by or affiliated with a county or municipal recreation department and shall not include collegiate, semi-professional or professional sporting events.

A court may issue a temporary restraining order to a party, based on a single act of assault by the perpetrator.[276]

Where a defendant knocked plaintiff to the floor, pulled her hair, hit her, and threatened her with additional violence, requiring Plaintiff to seek emergency room treatment, a permanent restraining order was issued.[277]

In *South v. North*, a defendant (household member) purposefully struck the plaintiff with a cane, pushed her out of her home, and locked the doors, continuing a course of abusive action, which he had exacted on plaintiff for several years.[278] The court here ultimately found that defendant committed acts of assault, criminal restraint and harassment. The court in making its determination, stated that the entry of a Final Restraining Order, under the Act requires:

> (I) a determination that plaintiff is a "victim of domestic violence" defined in *N.J.S.A.* 2C:25-19(d),
>
> (II) a determination that defendant committed an act of

---

[276] *Comas v. Comas*, 257 *N.J. Super.* 585, 608 *A.2d* 1005 (Ch. Div. 1992)(no analysis made other than that statement).

[277] *Bryant v. Burnett*, 264 *N.J. Super,* 222, 223, 624 *A.2d* 584 (App. Div. 1993).

[278] *South v. North*, 304 *N.J. Super.* 104, 108, 698 *A.2d* 553 (App. Div. 1997).

"domestic violence" defined in *N.J.S.A.* 2C:25-19(a); and

(III) a consideration of the nonexclusive factors found in *N.J.S.A.* 2C:25-29(a).

(These factors include but are not limited to previous history of domestic violence between the plaintiff and defendant, including threats, harassment and physical abuse; The existence of immediate danger to person or property; and the existence of a verifiable order of protection from another jurisdiction)

The Court in *Silver v. Silver* enunciated a more stringent standard when determining whether or not to issue a domestic violence restraining order for an assault complaint.[279] That court stated that the commission of one of the enumerated predicate acts of domestic violence does not automatically mandate the entry of a domestic violence restraining order. The court stated with authority:

> It is clear that the Legislature did not intend that the commission of any one of these acts [contained in *N.J.S.A.* 2C:25-19(a)] automatically mandates the issuance of a domestic violence order. Domestic violence is ordinarily more than an isolated aberrant non-violent act. Indeed, the Act mandates that the court, in determining whether an act of domestic violence has occurred, consider the previous history of domestic violence between the parties including threats, harassment and physical abuse, *N.J.S.A.* 2C:25-29(a)(1), and the existence of immediate danger to person or property, *N.J.S.A.* 2C:25-29(a)(2). While a single sufficiently egregious action may constitute domestic violence even if there is no history of abuse between the parties, a court may also determine that an ambiguous incident qualifies as domestic violence based on finding previous acts of violence.

In *Silver*, the court held that a trial court must engage in a two-step analysis in domestic violence cases: first, it must decide whether a plaintiff has proven one or more predicate acts after considering previous history of domestic violence, and second, it must decide whether an FRO is needed "to protect the victim from an immediate danger or to prevent further abuse," after again considering previous domestic violence history. The court elaborated on the analysis, stating:

---

[279] *Silver v. Silver*, 387 *N.J. Super.* 112, 903 *A.2d* 446 (App. Div. 2006)(some internal citations omitted and altered from original).

First, the judge must determine whether the plaintiff has proven, by a preponderance of the credible evidence, that one or more of the predicate acts set forth in *N.J.S.A.* 2C:25-19(a) has occurred. *See N.J.S.A.* 2C:25-29(a) (stating that "the standard for proving the allegations in the complaint shall be by a preponderance of the evidence"). In performing that function, "the Act does require that 'acts claimed by a plaintiff to be domestic violence . . . be evaluated in light of the previous history of violence between the parties.'" Stated differently, when determining *whether* a restraining order should be issued based on an act of assault or, for that matter, any of the predicate acts, the court must consider the evidence in light of whether there is a previous history of domestic violence, and whether there exists immediate danger to person or property. *See N.J.S.A.* 2C:25-29(a)(1) and (2).

The second inquiry of whether a domestic violence restraining order should be issued is most often perfunctory and self-evident, the guiding standard is whether a restraining order is necessary, upon an evaluation of the factors set forth in *N.J.S.A.* 2C:25-29(a)(1) to -29(a)(6), to protect the victim from an immediate danger or to prevent further abuse. *See N.J.S.A.* 2C:25-29(b)

Simple assault is not a "misdemeanor crime of domestic violence," as defined in the Lautenberg Amendment, because it does not have as an element the use or attempted use of physical force, or the threatened use of a deadly weapon. N.J.S.A. 2C:12-1(a)(3) provides that a person is guilty of simple assault if he attempts by physical menace to put another in fear of imminent serious bodily injury. This type of assault may be committed simply by physical menace without actual or attempted use of physical force. "For example, an assailant could violate the assault statute, by raising a clenched fist in a menacing manner, without hitting or attempting to hit the victim." In effect, those persons found guilty of violating the simple assault statute are not prohibited from carrying a firearm under the Lautenberg Amendment, which prohibits any person who has been convicted of a "misdemeanor crime of domestic violence" from possessing any firearm that has been shipped or transported in interstate commerce.[280]

---

[280] *Frazier v. Northern State Prison, Dept. of Corrections,* 392 *N.J. Super.* 514, 921 *A.2d* 479 (App. Div. 2007).

5.4   TERRORISTIC THREATS[281]

a.   A person is guilty of a crime of the third degree if he threatens to commit any crime of violence with the purpose to terrorize another or to cause evacuation of a building, place of assembly, or facility of public transportation, or otherwise to cause serious public inconvenience, or in reckless disregard of the risk of causing such terror or inconvenience. A violation of this subsection is a crime of the second degree if it occurs during a declared period of national, State or county emergency. The actor shall be strictly liable upon proof that the crime occurred, in fact, during a declared period of national, State or county emergency. It shall not be a defense that the actor did not know that there was a declared period of emergency at the time the crime occurred.

b.   A person is guilty of a crime of the third degree if he threatens to kill another with the purpose to put him in imminent fear of death under circumstances reasonably causing the victim to believe the immediacy of the threat and the likelihood that it will be carried out.

Proof of terroristic threats must be measured by an objective standard.   The requirements are:

(1) Defendant in fact threatened the plaintiff;
(2) Defendant intended to so threaten the plaintiff;
(3) A reasonable person would have believed of the threat.[282]

The elements of the crime of terroristic threats implicitly require the identification of the intended victim. "Without knowing the identity of the victim, the statutory phrase "*with the purpose to terrorize another*" is rendered devoid of substance."[283]

Despite recognizing that under the objective standard, the Court should not consider the victim's actual fear, the court held that it must consider a plaintiff's individual circumstances and background in determining whether a reasonable person in that situation would have believed the defendant's threat.[284]

The threat does not have to be communicated directly to the victim to be actionable, "the legal sufficiency of the evidence" is controlled not by the identity of the hearer as such, but by considering the hearer's identity as part of the surrounding circumstances."[285] It is sufficient

---

[281] *N.J.S.A.* 2C:12-3.

[282] *Cesare v, Cesare*, 154 *N.J.* 394, 713 *A.2d* 390 (1998).

[283] *State v. Tindell*, 417 *N.J. Super* 530, 553, 10 *A.3d* 1203 (App. Div. 2011).

[284] *State v. Smith*, 262 *N.J. Super.* 487, 515, 621 *A.2d* 493 (App. Div.), *certif. denied*, 134 *N.J.* 476, 634 *A.2d* 523 (1993); *State v. Nolan*, 205 *N.J. Super.* 1, 500 *A.2d* 1 (App. Div. 1985).

[285] *State v. Milano*, 167 *N.J. Super.* 318, 323, 400 *A.2d* 854 (Law Div. 1979), *aff'd*, 172 *N.J. Super.* 361, 412 *A.2d* 129 (App. Div. 1979), *certif. denied*, 84 *N.J.* 421, 420 *A.2d* 333 (1980).

that "the threat be made under circumstances under which it carries the serious promise of death."[286]

In *Cesare*, the Appellate Division found sufficient evidence existed for the trial court to have found that defendant committed terroristic threats, when during an argument regarding custody and equitable distribution of marital home that would occur if the parties divorced, Defendant made the statement "As I've told you before, I do have a choice, and you will not get either of those things." At defendant trial his prior acts of domestic violence were admissible for the limited purpose of demonstrating that the victim had reason to believe he would carry out threats to kill her.[287] The court further found that based upon plaintiff's testimony that defendant had previously used the word "choice" in the context of a threat to kill, a court could properly find that defendant intended his words on July 9 to be another such threat. In addition, Defendant's later insistence that plaintiff come up to the bedroom, where the guns were kept, and Plaintiff's testimony about defendant's previous threats, intimidation, and abuse of their children were such that a reasonable victim in plaintiff's situation would have felt fear.

The defendant's words do not have to contain an explicit threat to kill. [288] The gravamen of the offense involves the communication of a threat to kill in such terms as would in the attendant circumstances convey to an ordinary individual that the language seriously threatened death.[289]

In the case of *State v. Butterfoss*,[290] the court outlined the requisites for sufficiently sustaining an indictment for terroristic threats. Therein, the court reasoned that the question of whether defendant made terroristic threats depended on:

> Whether the surrounding circumstances were such that an ordinary person in the mother's position would have felt threatened and whether the defendant intended to frighten her; whether he intended to carry out the threat or whether the fear of the victim was actually induced or immaterial considerations.

---

[286] *State v. Dispoto*, 189 *N.J.* 108, 913 *A.2d* 791 (2007)(*citing State v. Nolan*, 205 *N.J. Super.* 1,4, 500 *A.2d* 1 (App. Div. 1985)).

[287] *Cesare v. Cesare*, 154 *N.J.* 394, 713 *A.2d* 390 (1998).

[288] *Ibid.*

[289] *State v. Kaufman,* 118 *N.J. Super.* 472, 288 *A.2d* 581 (App. Div.), *certif. den.,* 60 *N.J.* 467, 291 *A.2d* 17 (1972); *State v. Johns* 111 *N.J. Super.* 574, 270 *A.2d* 59 (App. Div. 1970), *certif. den.* 60 *N.J.* 467, 291 *A.2d* 17(1972); *State v. Smith*, 262 *N.J. Super.* 487, 621 *A.2d* 493 (App. Div.), *certif. den.,* 134 *N.J.* 476, 634 *A.2d* 523 (1993); *Brunswick Corp v. Director, Division of Taxation*, 134 *N.J.* 476, 634 *A.2d.* 523 (1993).

[290] *State v. Butterfoss*, 234 *N.J. Super.* 606, 611-612, 561 *A.2d* 312 (Law Div. 1988).

In *Butterfoss*, the Plaintiff went to pick up her child who was attending a nursery school. Defendant, who had not seen either of them for several months, drove in, picked up the child and put her in the back seat of his car, instructing Plaintiff to get into the front seat. He told Plaintiff he was going to take his daughter to California. Upon noticing a paper bag on the floor containing small pieces of rope and cloth, Defendant told Plaintiff he planned to break into her house, tie her up, gag her if she was uncooperative, and then take the child. Subsequently, Defendant did take the child to California, and called the mother, asking her to join them, in an effort to get the family back together. Plaintiff obliged, after having trouble finding the child.

The court found that these circumstances presented the Grand Jury with some evidence of a present threat to commit a crime of violence with purpose to terrorize the mother. She was threatened by the expected loss of her daughter. She was confronted with ropes and gags. She was told of a prior intention to assault her, tie her and gag her. This is enough to satisfy statutory requirements.

On the contrary *see DC v. TH,* where after testimony, the court specifically found that defendant did not commit acts of terroristic threats and did not threaten to do bodily harm to plaintiff. In this case Defendant did threaten Plaintiff's boyfriend with bodily harm if he disciplined his child again (with the purpose to dissuade him from doing so), and there were conflicting statements by both Plaintiff and Defendant as to whether the Plaintiff was threatened by physical harm as well. The Defendant's position that he did not threaten the Plaintiff was also supported by his sister who served as witness.[291]

Defendant's communications to the plaintiff, wherein he threatened physical harm to both the Plaintiff and her boyfriend, in addition to threats of her immanent deportment, constituted terroristic threats or harassment.[292]

---

[291] *D.C. v. T.H.* 269 *N.J. Super.* 458, 262, 635 *A.2d.* 1002 (App. Div. 1994).
[292] *J.S. v. J.F,* 410 *N.J. Super* 611, 983 *A.2d* 1151 (App. Div. 2009).

142

5.5   KIDNAPPING [293]

a.   Holding for ransom, reward, or as a hostage. A person is guilty of kidnapping if he unlawfully removes another from the place where he is found or if he unlawfully confines another with the purpose of holding that person for ransom or reward or as a shield or hostage.

b.   Holding for other purposes. A person is guilty of kidnapping if he unlawfully removes another from his place of residence or business, or a substantial distance from the vicinity where he is found, or if he unlawfully confines another for a substantial period, with any of the following purposes:

(1) To facilitate commission of any crime or flight thereafter;

(2) To inflict bodily injury on or to terrorize the victim or another;

(3) To interfere with the performance of any governmental or political function; or

(4) To permanently deprive a parent, guardian or other lawful custodian of custody of the victim.

c.   Grading of kidnapping. (1) Except as provided in paragraph (2) of this subsection, kidnapping is a crime of the first degree and upon conviction thereof, a person may, notwithstanding the provisions of paragraph (1) of subsection a. of *N.J.S.A. 2C:43-6,* be sentenced to an ordinary term of imprisonment between 15 and 30 years. If the actor releases the victim unharmed and in a safe place prior to apprehension, it is a crime of the second degree. (2) Kidnapping is a crime of the first degree and upon conviction thereof, an actor shall be sentenced to a term of imprisonment by the court, if the victim of the kidnapping is less than 16 years of age and if during the kidnapping:

(a) A crime under *N.J.S.A. 2C:14-2* or subsection a. of *N.J.S.A. 2C:14-3* is committed against the victim;

(b) A crime under subsection b. of *N.J.S.A. 2C:24-4* is committed against the victim; or

(c) The actor sells or delivers the victim to another person for pecuniary gain other than in circumstances which lead to the return of the victim to a parent, guardian or other person responsible for the general supervision of the victim.

Notwithstanding the provisions of paragraph (1) of subsection a. of *N.J.S.A.*

---

[293] *N.J.S.A. 2C:13-1.*

2C:43-6, the term of imprisonment imposed under this paragraph shall be either a term of 25 years during which the actor shall not be eligible for parole, or a specific term between 25 years and life imprisonment, of which the actor shall serve 25 years before being eligible for parole; provided, however, that the crime of kidnapping under this paragraph and underlying aggravating crimes listed in subparagraph (a), (b) or (c) of this paragraph shall merge for purposes of sentencing. If the actor is convicted of the criminal homicide of a victim of a kidnapping under the provisions of chapter 11, any sentence imposed under provisions of this paragraph shall be served consecutively to any sentence imposed pursuant to the provisions of chapter 11.

d. "Unlawful" removal or confinement. A removal or confinement is unlawful within the meaning of this section and of sections *2C:13-2* and *2C:13-3,* if it is accomplished by force, threat or deception, or, in the case of a person who is under the age of 14 or is incompetent, if it is accomplished without the consent of a parent, guardian or other person responsible for general supervision of his welfare.

e. It is an affirmative defense to a prosecution under paragraph (4) of subsection b. of this section, which must be proved by clear and convincing evidence, that:

(1) The actor reasonably believed that the action was necessary to preserve the victim from imminent danger to his welfare. However, no defense shall be available pursuant to this subsection if the actor does not, as soon as reasonably practicable but in no event more than 24 hours after taking a victim under his protection, give notice of the victim's location to the police department of the municipality where the victim resided, the office of the county prosecutor in the county where the victim resided, or the Division of Child Protection and Permanency in the Department of Children and Families;

(2) The actor reasonably believed that the taking or detaining of the victim was consented to by a parent, or by an authorized State agency; or

(3) The victim, being at the time of the taking or concealment not less than 14 years old, was taken away at his own volition by his parent and without purpose to commit a criminal offense with or against the victim.

It is an affirmative defense to a prosecution under paragraph (4) of subsection b. of this section that a parent having the right of custody reasonably believed he was fleeing from imminent physical danger from the other parent, provided that the parent having custody, as soon as reasonably practicable:

(1) Gives notice of the victim's location to the police department of the

municipality where the victim resided, the office of the county prosecutor in the county where the victim resided, or the Division of Child Protection and Permanency in the Department of Children and Families; or

(2) Commences an action affecting custody in an appropriate court.

g. As used in subsections e. and f. of this section, "parent" means a parent, guardian or other lawful custodian of a victim.

Kidnapping is a specially-graded offense; for first-degree kidnapping the maximum authorized sentence is thirty years with fifteen years of parole ineligibility.[294]

Where a Defendant was convicted of kidnapping, sexual assault, aggravated assault, terroristic threats, and possession of a shotgun for an unlawful purpose, following the kidnapping of his ex-girl friend, the Appellate Division reversed the conviction because the trial court failed to give the jury limiting instructions on the difference between substantive use and limited use of expert testimony concerning the Battered Woman's Syndrome, which could be used to explain a victim's reactions or late reporting of the events and not as evidence that the crime occurred. The court found this omission was plain error.[295]

---

[294] *State v. Louis,* 117 *N.J.* 250, 566 *A.2d.* 511 (1989).
[295] *State v. Ellis,* 280 *N.J. Super.* 533, 656 *A.2d* 25 (App. Div. 1995).

5.6   CRIMINAL RESTRAINT [296]

A person commits a crime of the third degree if he knowingly:

a.   Restrains another unlawfully in circumstances exposing the other to risk of serious bodily injury; or

b.   Holds another in a condition of involuntary servitude.

The creation by the actor of circumstances resulting in a belief by another that he must remain in a particular location shall, for purposes of this section, be deemed to be a holding in a condition of involuntary servitude.

In any prosecution under subsection b., it is an affirmative defense that the person held was a child less than 18 years old and the actor was a relative or legal guardian of such child and his sole purpose was to assume control of such child.

In the case of *South v. North*, the court found that the Defendant committed acts of "domestic violence," where he purposely struck plaintiff with a cane, which constituted assault, and pushed her out of her home, locking the door, which constituted criminal restraint and/or harassment under *N.J.S.A.* 2C:13-2 and *N.J.S.A.* 2C:33-4.[297]

5.7   FALSE IMPRISONMENT [298]

A person commits a disorderly person's offense if he knowingly restrains another unlawfully so as to interfere substantially with his liberty. In any prosecution under this section, it is an affirmative defense that the person restrained was a child less than 18 years old and that the actor was a relative or legal guardian of such child and that his sole purpose was to assume control of such child.

There are no cases dealing with criminal restraint and domestic violence.

---

[296] *N.J.S.A.* 2C:13-2.
[297] *South v. North*, 304 *N.J. Super.* 104, 698 *A.2d.* 553 (Ch. Div. 1997).
[298] *N.J.S.A.* 2C:13-3.

5.8   SEXUAL ASSAULT [299]

a.   An actor is guilty of aggravated sexual assault if he commits an act of sexual penetration with another person under any one of the following circumstances:

(1) The victim is less than 13 years old;

(2) The victim is at least 13 but less than 16 years old; and

> (a) The actor is related to the victim by blood or affinity to the third degree, or

> (b) The actor has supervisory or disciplinary power over the victim by virtue of the actor's legal, professional, or occupational status, or

> (c) The actor is a resource family parent, a guardian, or stands in loco parentis within the household;

(3) The act is committed during the commission, or attempted commission, whether alone or with one or more other persons, of robbery, kidnapping, homicide, aggravated assault on another, burglary, arson or criminal escape;

(4) The actor is armed with a weapon or any object fashioned in such a manner as to lead the victim to reasonably believe it to be a weapon and threatens by word or gesture to use the weapon or object;

(5) The actor is aided or abetted by one or more other persons and the actor uses physical force or coercion;

(6) The actor uses physical force or coercion and severe personal injury is sustained by the victim;

(7) The victim is one whom the actor knew or should have known was physically helpless or incapacitated, intellectually or mentally incapacitated, or had a mental disease or defect which rendered the victim temporarily or permanently incapable of understanding the nature of his conduct, including, but not limited to, being incapable of providing consent.

Aggravated sexual assault is a crime of the first degree.

---

[299] *N.J.S.A.* 2C:14-2.

Except as otherwise provided in subsection d. of this section, a person convicted under paragraph (1) of this subsection shall be sentenced to a specific term of years which shall be fixed by the court and shall be between 25 years and life imprisonment of which the person shall serve 25 years before being eligible for parole, unless a longer term of parole ineligibility is otherwise provided pursuant to this Title.

b. An actor is guilty of sexual assault if he commits an act of sexual contact with a victim who is less than 13 years old and the actor is at least four years older than the victim.

c. An actor is guilty of sexual assault if he commits an act of sexual penetration with another person under any one of the following circumstances:

(1) The actor uses physical force or coercion, but the victim does not sustain severe personal injury;
(2) The victim is on probation or parole, or is detained in a hospital, prison or other institution and the actor has supervisory or disciplinary power over the victim by virtue of the actor's legal, professional or occupational status;
(3) The victim is at least 16 but less than 18 years old and

(a) The actor is related to the victim by blood or affinity to the third degree; or
(b) The actor has supervisory or disciplinary power of any nature or in any capacity over the victim; or
(c) The actor is a resource family parent, a guardian, or stands in loco parentis within the household.

(4) The victim is at least 13 but less than 16 years old and the actor is at least four years older than the victim.

Sexual assault is a crime of the second degree.

d. Notwithstanding the provisions of subsection a. of this section, where a defendant is charged with a violation under paragraph (1) of subsection a. of this section, the prosecutor, in consideration of the interests of the victim, may offer a negotiated plea agreement in which the defendant would be sentenced to a specific term of imprisonment of not less than 15 years, during which the defendant shall not be eligible for parole. In such event, the court may accept the negotiated plea agreement and upon such conviction shall impose the term of imprisonment and period of parole ineligibility as provided for in the plea agreement, and may not impose a lesser term of imprisonment or parole or a lesser period of parole ineligibility than that expressly provided in the plea agreement. The Attorney General shall develop guidelines to ensure the uniform exercise of discretion in making determinations regarding a negotiated reduction in the term of imprisonment and period of parole ineligibility set forth in subsection a. of this section.

A Defendant was properly convicted of raping his own wife in violation of *N.J.S.A* *2A:138-1* (now *N.J.S.A* *2C:14-2*) where a restraining order issued against the defendant, and his agreement not to molest her precluded any common law exemption for the act. [300]

Another court found that the State was entitled to prosecute a defendant under *N.J.S.A.* *2A:138-1* (now *N.J.S.A.* *2C:14-2*), for raping his estranged wife and that defendant could not invoke an outdated and doubtful rule exempting men from prosecution for spousal rape. [301]

Where a husband on several occasions physically abused his wife, and had nonconsensual sex with her, the trial court found that the nonconsensual sex did not constitute sexual assault or criminal sexual contact because the husband did not have the requisite criminal intent, as he believed his conduct was permitted by his religion. The Appellate Division reversed, holding that neither crime specified a mental state. Thus the husband's knowing conduct was sufficient to establish the elements of both offenses. Furthermore, the court found that the Free Exercise Clause of the First Amendment, did not require the trial court to exempt the husband, a practicing Muslim, from a finding that he committed the predicate acts of sexual assault and criminal sexual contact and thus violated the PDVA.[302]

In a case where a mother filed a domestic violence complaint against defendant/stepfather, alleging he sexually abused her 15-year-old daughter, the Superior Court of New Jersey, Chancery Division, Family Part, dismissed the action since the daughter was not a "victim" as defined in the New Jersey Prevention of Domestic Violence Act. In addition the mother was not permitted to bring an action on behalf of her daughter. [303]

---

[300] *State v. Morrison*, 85 N.J. 212, 426 A.2d 47 (1981).
[301] *State v. Smith*, 85 N.J. 193, 426 A.2d 38 (1981).
[302] *S.D. V. M.J.R.*, 415 N.J. Super. 417, 2 A.3d 412 (App. Div. 2010).
[303] *M.A. v. E.A.*, 388 N.J. Super. 612, 909 A.2d 1168 (App. Div. 2006).

5.9   CRIMINAL SEXUAL CONTACT [304]

a.   An actor is guilty of aggravated criminal sexual contact if he commits an act of sexual contact with the victim under any of the circumstances set forth in *2C:14-2* a(2) through (7).

Aggravated criminal sexual contact is a crime of the third degree.

b.   An actor is guilty of criminal sexual contact if he commits an act of sexual contact with the victim under any of the circumstances set forth in section *2C:14-2* c(1) through (4).

Criminal sexual contact is a crime of the fourth degree.

(*Note: N.J.S.A. 2C:14-2 referenced herein, is the Sexual Assault Statue discussed in the previous section*)

See *S.D. v. M.J.*, discussed in the previous section as it pertains to both Sexual Assault and Criminal Sexual Contact.[305]

5.10   LEWDNESS [306]

a.   A person commits a disorderly persons offense if he does any flagrantly lewd and offensive act which he knows or reasonably expects is likely to be observed by other non consenting persons who would be affronted or alarmed.

b.   A person commits a crime of the fourth degree if:

(1) He exposes his intimate parts for the purpose of arousing or gratifying the sexual desire of the actor or of any other person under circumstances where the actor knows or reasonably expects he is likely to be observed by a child who is less than 13 years of age where the actor is at least four years older than the child.

(2) He exposes his intimate parts for the purpose of arousing or gratifying the sexual desire of the actor or of any other person under circumstances where the actor knows or reasonably expects he is likely to be observed by a person who because of mental disease or defect is unable to understand the sexual nature of the actor's conduct.

---

[304] *N.J.S.A.* 2C:14-3.

[305] *S.D. v. M.J.R.*, 415 *N.J. Super.* 417, 2 *A.3d* 412 (App. Div. 2010).

[306] *N.J.S.A.* 2C:14-4.

c. As used in this section:

"lewd acts" shall include the exposing of the genitals for the purpose of arousing or gratifying the sexual desire of the actor or of any other person.

5.11 CRIMINAL MISCHIEF [307]

a.   Offense defined. A person is guilty of criminal mischief if he:

(1) Purposely or knowingly damages tangible property of another or damages tangible property of another recklessly or negligently in the employment of fire, explosives or other dangerous means listed in subsection a. of *N.J.S.A.* 2C:17-2; or

(2) Purposely, knowingly or recklessly tampers with tangible property of another so as to endanger person or property, including the damaging or destroying of a rental premises by a tenant in retaliation for institution of eviction proceedings.

b.   Grading.

(1) Criminal mischief is a crime of the third degree if the actor purposely or knowingly causes pecuniary loss of $ 2,000.00 or more.

(2) Criminal mischief is a crime of the fourth degree if the actor causes pecuniary loss in excess of $ 500.00 but less than $ 2000.00. It is a disorderly persons offense if the actor causes pecuniary loss of $ 500.00 or less.

(3) Criminal mischief is a crime of the third degree if the actor damages, defaces, eradicates, alters, receives, releases or causes the loss of any research property used by the research facility, or otherwise causes physical disruption to the functioning of the research facility. The term "physical disruption" does not include any lawful activity that results from public, governmental, or research facility employee reaction to the disclosure of information about the research facility.

(4) Criminal mischief is a crime of the fourth degree if the actor damages, removes or impairs the operation of any device, including, but not limited to, a sign, signal, light or other equipment, which serves to regulate or ensure the safety of air traffic at any airport, landing field, landing strip, heliport, helistop or any other aviation facility; however, if the damage, removal or impediment of the device recklessly causes bodily injury or damage to property, the actor is guilty of a crime of the third degree, or if it recklessly causes a death, the actor is guilty of a crime of the second degree.

---

[307] *N.J.S.A.* 2C:17-3.

(5) Criminal mischief is a crime of the fourth degree if the actor interferes or tampers with any airport, landing field, landing strip, heliport, helistop or any other aviation facility; however if the interference or tampering with the airport, landing field, landing strip, heliport, helistop or other aviation facility recklessly causes bodily injury or damage to property, the actor is guilty of a crime of the third degree, or if it recklessly causes a death, the actor is guilty of a crime of the second degree.

(6) Criminal mischief is a crime of the third degree if the actor tampers with a grave, crypt, mausoleum or other site where human remains are stored or interred, with the purpose to desecrate, destroy or steal such human remains or any part thereof.

(7) Criminal mischief is a crime of the third degree if the actor purposely or knowingly causes a substantial interruption or impairment of public communication, transportation, supply of water, oil, gas or power, or other public service. Criminal mischief is a crime of the second degree if the substantial interruption or impairment recklessly causes death.

(8) Criminal mischief is a crime of the fourth degree if the actor purposely or knowingly breaks, digs up, obstructs or otherwise tampers with any pipes or mains for conducting gas, oil or water, or any works erected for supplying buildings with gas, oil or water, or any appurtenances or appendages therewith connected, or injures, cuts, breaks down, destroys or otherwise tampers with any electric light wires, poles or appurtenances, or any telephone, telecommunications, cable television or telegraph wires, lines, cable or appurtenances.

c. A person convicted of an offense of criminal mischief that involves an act of graffiti may, in addition to any other penalty imposed by the court, be required to pay to the owner of the damaged property monetary restitution in the amount of the pecuniary damage caused by the act of graffiti and to perform community service, which shall include removing the graffiti from the property, if appropriate. If community service is ordered, it shall be for either not less than 20 days or not less than the number of days necessary to remove the graffiti from the property.

d. As used in this section:

"Act of graffiti" means the drawing, painting or making of any mark or inscription on public or private real or personal property without the permission of the owner.

e. A person convicted of an offense of criminal mischief that involves the damaging or destroying of a rental premises by a tenant in retaliation for institution of eviction proceedings, may, in addition to any other penalty imposed by the court, be required to pay to the owner of the property monetary restitution in the amount of the pecuniary damage caused by the damage or destruction.

5.12   BURGLARY [308]

a.   Burglary defined. A person is guilty of burglary if, with purpose to commit an offense therein or thereon he:

(1) Enters a research facility, structure, or a separately secured or occupied portion thereof unless the structure was at the time open to the public or the actor is licensed or privileged to enter;
(2) Surreptitiously remains in a research facility, structure, or a separately secured or occupied portion thereof knowing that he is not licensed or privileged to do so; or
(3) Trespasses in or upon utility company property where public notice prohibiting trespass is given by conspicuous posting, or fencing or other enclosure manifestly designed to exclude intruders.

b.   Grading. Burglary is a crime of the second degree if in the course of committing the offense, the actor:

(1) Purposely, knowingly or recklessly inflicts, attempts to inflict or threatens to inflict bodily injury on anyone; or
(2) Is armed with or displays what appear to be explosives or a deadly weapon.

Otherwise burglary is a crime of the third degree.

An act shall be deemed "in the course of committing" an offense if it occurs in an attempt to commit an offense or in immediate flight after the attempt or commission.

In an Appellate Division decision, the court found that a defendant's entry into an apartment, in violation of a domestic violence restraining order, cannot serve as a basis to convict him of burglary. The defendant could only be convicted of burglary if his purpose upon entry was to commit a separate offense subsequent to his entry.[309]

In another case, the court found the Defendant guilty of (1) entering with intent to rob pursuant to former *N.J.S.A.* 2A:94-1 (now *N.J.S.A.* 2C:18-2), (2) robbery under *N.J.S.A.* 2A:141-1, and (3) robbery pursuant to former *N.J.S.A.* 2A:151-5, where the record showed that he entered the victim's kitchen armed with a barbecue fork, choked her, knocked her to the floor, gagged her, forced her to lie on the floor, and escaped in her automobile after demanding money and taking her wedding rings.[310]

---

[308] *N.J.S.A.* 2C:18-2.
[309] *State v. Marquez,* 277 *N.J. Super.* 162, 649 *A.2d* 114, (App. Div. 1994).
[310] *State v. Mann,* 171 *N.J. Super.* 173, 408 *A.2d* 440 (App. Div. 1979).

5.13 CRIMINAL TRESPASS [311]

a. Unlicensed entry of structures. A person commits an offense if, knowing that he is not licensed or privileged to do so, he enters or surreptitiously remains in any research facility, structure, or separately secured or occupied portion thereof, or in or upon utility company property, or in the sterile area or operational area of an airport. An offense under this subsection is a crime of the fourth degree if it is committed in a school or on school property. The offense is a crime of the fourth degree if it is committed in a dwelling. An offense under this section is a crime of the fourth degree if it is committed in a research facility, power generation facility, waste treatment facility, public sewage facility, water treatment facility, public water facility, nuclear electric generating plant or any facility which stores, generates or handles any hazardous chemical or chemical compounds. An offense under this subsection is a crime of the fourth degree if it is committed in or upon utility company property. An offense under this subsection is a crime of the fourth degree if it is committed in the sterile area or operational area of an airport. Otherwise it is a disorderly person's offense.

b. Defiant trespasser. A person commits a petty disorderly persons offense if, knowing that he is not licensed or privileged to do so, he enters or remains in any place as to which notice against trespass is given by:

> (1) Actual communication to the actor; or
> (2) Posting in a manner prescribed by law or reasonably likely to come to the attention of intruders; or
> (3) Fencing or other enclosure manifestly designed to exclude intruders.

c. Peering into windows or other openings of dwelling places. A person commits a crime of the fourth degree if, knowing that he is not licensed or privileged to do so, he peers into a window or other opening of a dwelling or other structure adapted for overnight accommodation for the purpose of invading the privacy of another person and under circumstances in which a reasonable person in the dwelling or other structure would not expect to be observed.

d. Defenses. It is an affirmative defense to prosecution under this section that:

> (1) A structure involved in an offense under subsection a. was abandoned;
> (2) The structure was at the time open to members of the public and the actor complied with all lawful conditions imposed on access to or remaining in the structure; or
> (3) The actor reasonably believed that the owner of the structure, or other person empowered to license access thereto, would have licensed him to enter

---

[311] *N.J.S.A.* 2C:18-3.

or remain, or, in the case of subsection c. of this section, to peer.

In order for the defendant to be convicted of Criminal Trespass, the State must prove the following elements beyond a reasonable doubt:

- The defendant attempted to enter, or surreptitiously remained in the structure. (structure can include a dwelling or other property.)

- The defendant did so knowing he had no right to enter or to be there at the time.

The Criminal Trespass Statute also has a provision against "peeping." In Order to establish a person has violated the peeping provision, the State must prove beyond a reasonable doubt that defendant: (1) "peered into" a window or other opening of a dwelling or other structure adapted for overnight accommodations, (2) had the purpose to invade the privacy of another individual, (3) the circumstances were such that a reasonable person in the dwelling or structure would not expect to be observed; and (4) that defendant knew he was not licensed or privileged to peer into the window or other opening of the dwelling. [312] Furthermore, the prohibited "peering into" must be from a location outside, and into, the window or other opening of a dwelling or other structure adapted for overnight accommodations.

In *Kaman v. Egan,* the plaintiff had filed a complaint against the defendant, his daughter, under the PDVA seeking a restraining order based on a single act of trespass unaccompanied by a violent act or threat thereof. The daughter had supervised visitation with her children in the home of plaintiff, who was the legal custodian of his grandchildren. Defendant appeared at plaintiff's house for visitation with her children on an unscheduled date, and at a time when the plaintiff was not at home. When asked to leave three times by her stepmother defendant refused, stating she wanted to see her children. When her stepmother threatened to call the police, defendant left. The plaintiff then filed a complaint against his daughter, founded on the predicate act of criminal trespass.

The Appellate Division found that "the judge correctly concluded that defendant had committed an act of criminal trespass by entering plaintiff's home knowing that she was not licensed or privileged to do so on that occasion." However, the court noted that the finding of the predicate act did not end the inquiry, stating:

> It is clear that the Legislature did not intend that the commission of any one of these acts [contained in *N.J.S.A.* 2C:25-19(a)] automatically mandates the issuance of a domestic violence order...is ordinarily more than an isolated aberrant non-violent

---

[312] *State v. Burke,* 362 *N.J. Super.* 55, 59, 826 *A.2d* 808 (App. Div. 2003).

act. Indeed domestic violence, the Act mandates that the court, in determining whether an act of domestic violence has occurred, consider the previous history of domestic violence between the parties including threats, harassment and physical abuse, *N.J.S.A.* 2C:25-29(a)(1), and the existence of immediate danger to person or property, *N.J.S.A.* 2C:25-29(a)(2). While a single sufficiently egregious action may constitute domestic violence even if there is no history of abuse between the parties, a court may also determine that an ambiguous incident qualifies as domestic violence based on finding previous acts of violence.[313]

Accepting the factual findings of the trial judge, The Appellate court concluded "that the judge erred in his legal conclusion that this single act of trespass unaccompanied by violence or a threat of violence was sufficient to justify issuance of a restraining order under the Act." Although acknowledging that the defendant's acts technically constituted a trespass, they "did not involve violence or a threat of violence" Under the circumstances the court conclude that the acts complained of were nothing more than an ordinary domestic contretemps which the Act was never intended to address.

---

[313] *Kamen v. Egan*, 322 *N.J. Super.* 222, 227-228, 730 *A.2d* 873 (App. Div. 1999)(citations omitted and formatting altered from original).

5.14 STALKING [314]

The stalking statute itself has been in effect since 1981. The purpose of the stalking law was to protect a victim of repeated harassing or threatening behavior, before the victim has actually been physically attacked. [315]

In 1992, the Legislature included stalking as a domestic violence crime. The act was modeled after a 1990 California Statute. The stalking statute was amended in 1992 to make it clear that relief may be given in a Final Restraining Order.

In 1996, a revision to the Act made a judgment of conviction for stalking operate as an application for a permanent restraining order, limiting the contact of the defendant and the victim who was stalked. It provided a hearing for a permanent restraining order at the time of the service or guilty plea, unless the victim requests otherwise. This hearing shall be before the Superior Court in which the following relief can be granted:

1. An order restraining the defendant from entering the residence, property, school or place of employment of the victim and requiring the defendant to stay away from any specified place that is named in the order and is frequented by the victim.

2. An order restraining the defendant from making contact with the victim, including an order forbidding the defendant from personally or through an agent initiating any communication likely to cause annoyance or alarm including, but not limited to, personal, written, or telephone contact with the victim, the victim's employers, employees, or fellow workers, or others who through communication would be likely to cause annoyance or alarm to the victim.

The permanent restraining order was permitted to be dissolved upon application of the victim, to the court which granted the Order.

The current stalking statute provides:

a.   As used in this act:

(1) "Course of conduct" means repeatedly maintaining a visual or physical proximity to a person; directly, indirectly, or through third parties, by any action, method, device, or means, following, monitoring, observing, surveilling, threatening, or communicating to or about, a person, or interfering with a

---

[314] *P.L.* 1992, *c.* 209; *N.J.S.A.* 2C:12-10.

[315] *State v. Saunders*, 302 *N.J. Super.* 509, 695 *A.2d* 722 (App. Div.), *cert. den.*, 151 *N.J.* 470,   700 *A.2d* 881 (1997); *State v. Zeidell*, 151 *N.J.* 470, 700 *A.2d* 881 (1997).

person's property; repeatedly committing harassment against a person; or repeatedly conveying, or causing to be conveyed, verbal or written threats or threats conveyed by any other means of communication or threats implied by conduct or a combination thereof directed at or toward a person.

(2) "Repeatedly" means on two or more occasions.

(3) "Emotional distress" means significant mental suffering or distress.

(4) "Cause a reasonable person to fear" means to cause fear which a reasonable victim, similarly situated, would have under the circumstances.

b.   A person is guilty of stalking, a crime of the fourth degree, if He purposefully or knowingly engages in a course of conduct directed at a specific person that would cause a reasonable person to fear for his safety or the safety of a third person or suffer other emotional distress.

c.   A person is guilty of a crime of the third degree if he commits the crime of stalking in violation of an existing court order prohibiting the behavior.

d.   A person who commits a second or subsequent offense of stalking against the same victim is guilty of a crime of the third degree.

e.   A person is guilty of a crime of the third degree if he commits the crime of stalking while serving a term of imprisonment or while on parole or probation as the result of a conviction for any indictable offense under the laws of this State, any other state or the United States.

f.   This act shall not apply to conduct which occurs during organized group picketing.

A conviction for stalking requires proof beyond a reasonable doubt of the following elements:

- A showing that defendant purposefully or knowingly engaged in a course of conduct (conduct was repeated i.e. on 2 or more occasions) directed at a specific person;
- Defendant's conduct was such that it would cause a reasonable person to fear bodily injury or death to herself or to a member of her immediate family.[316]

---

[316] *State v. Gandhi*, 201 *N.J.* 161, 989 *A.2d* 256 (2010).

As discussed in an earlier section, a Husband was properly found to have stalked his wife, where he had set up video and audio surveillance in her bedroom, which allowed him to know her whereabouts, her phone conversations, and where she placed things in that room. In that case, the husband also threatened that their marriage would only end through death, which caused her to have a reasonable fear of bodily injury or death.[317] Although the court stated that this behavior did not constitute harassment (as there was no intent to harass), defendant's actions made plaintiff feel she was always being watched and constitute stalking. Notably, the court clarified that a stalking conviction can occur even if the victim is not aware of the stalking or conduct when it happens.[318]

The anti-stalking statute reaches and punishes a person who engages in a course of stalking conduct, even if that person is operating under the motivation of an obsessed and disturbed love that purportedly obscures appreciation of the terror that his or her conduct would reasonably cause to the victimized person.[319] The court stated:

> The anti-stalking statute that criminalized defendant's actions provided that a person is guilty of stalking "if he purposefully or knowingly engages in a course of conduct directed at a specific person that would cause a reasonable person to fear bodily injury to himself or a member of his immediate family or to fear the death of himself or a member of his immediate family." *N.J.S.A.* 2C:12-10(b). Based on that language and the history of this statutory offense, we do not discern a legislative intent to limit the reach of the anti-stalking statute to a stalker-defendant who purposefully intended or knew that his behavior would cause a reasonable person to fear bodily injury or death. Rather, we read the offense to proscribe a defendant from engaging in a course of repeated stalking conduct that would cause such fear in an objectively reasonable person. We view the statute's course-of-conduct focus to be on the accuser's conduct and what that conduct would cause a reasonable victim to feel, not on what the accused intended. Indeed, a person accused of stalking conduct very well may have intended to be amorous, but if he or she purposefully or knowingly engages in course of conduct and the effect of that conduct is terrorizing to a reasonable victim, then the anti-stalking statute criminalizes the conduct.
>
> We hold that the statutory offense reaches and punishes a person

---

[317] *H.E.S. v. J.C.S.*, 175 *N.J.* 309, 815 *A.2d* 405 (2003).

[318] *H.E.S. v. J.C.S.,* 175 *N.J.* 309, 315, 815 *A.2d* 405, 411 (2003).

[319] *State v. Gandhi,* 201 *N.J.* 161, 989 *A.2d* 256 (2010).

who engages in a course of stalking conduct even if the person is operating under the motivation of an obsessed and disturbed love that purportedly obscures appreciation of the terror that his or her conduct would reasonably cause to the victimized person. [320]

A Defendant's conduct constituted stalking and harassment when Defendant picketed at plaintiff's residence, as well as threatening plaintiff by means of offensive hand gestures, shouting curses at her, and blocking her exiting from her property.[321]

N.J.S.A. 2C:12-10.1 STALKING, CONVICTION TO OPERATE AS APPLICATION FOR PERMANENT RESTRAINING ORDER; HEARING; DISSOLUTION OF ORDER; NOTICE; VIOLATIONS.

a.   A judgment of conviction for stalking shall operate as an application for a permanent restraining order limiting the contact of the defendant and the victim who was stalked.

b.   A hearing shall be held on the application for a permanent restraining order at the time of the verdict or plea of guilty unless the victim requests otherwise. This hearing shall be in Superior Court. A permanent restraining order may grant the following specific relief:

(1) An order restraining the defendant from entering the residence, property, school, or place of employment of the victim and requiring the defendant to stay away from any specified place that is named in the order and is frequented regularly by the victim.

(2) An order restraining the defendant from making contact with the victim, including an order forbidding the defendant from personally or through an agent initiating any communication likely to cause annoyance or alarm including, but not limited to, personal, written, or telephone contact, or contact via electronic device, with the victim, the victim's employers, employees, or fellow workers, or others with whom communication would be likely to cause annoyance or alarm to the victim. As used in this paragraph, "communication" shall have the same meaning as defined in subsection q. of N.J.S. 2C:1-14.

c.   The permanent restraining order entered by the court subsequent to a conviction for stalking as provided in this act may be dissolved upon the application of the stalking victim to the court which granted the order.

---

[320] *State v. Gandhi*, 201 *N.J.* 161, 169-170, 989 *A.2d* 256 (2010).

[321] *N.G. v. J.P.*, 426 *N.J. Super* 398, 402, 45 *A.3d* 371 (App. Div 2012).

d. Notice of permanent restraining orders issued pursuant to this act shall be sent by the clerk of the court or other person designated by the court to the appropriate chiefs of police, members of the State Police and any other appropriate law enforcement agency or court.

e. Any permanent restraining order issued pursuant to this act shall be in effect throughout the State, and shall be enforced by all law enforcement officers.

f. A violation by the defendant of an order issued pursuant to this act shall constitute an offense under subsection a. of *N.J.S.* 2C:29-9 and each order shall so state. Violations of these orders may be enforced in a civil or criminal action initiated by the stalking victim or by the court, on its own motion, pursuant to applicable court rules. Nothing in this act shall preclude the filing of a criminal complaint for stalking based on the same act which is the basis for the violation of the permanent restraining order.

A court found that the former stalking statute was not unconstitutionally vague where it did not define certain words and phrases, since it was clear what type of conduct is proscribed.[322]

Another case dealing with stalking, also addressed the interplay of stalking and harassment, with the principle of res judicata. The court stated that an individual act previously rejected as insufficient to constitute domestic violence may take on greater significance if the act is later repeated in a manner that may amount to a course of conduct prohibited by *N.J.S.A.* 2C:33-4 (c) and/or *N.J.S.A.* 2C:12-10(b). In such an instance, the prior act may be considered along with the new conduct in determining whether a plaintiff has established domestic violence based on a subsequent complaint. If not, it may be barred under principles of *res judicata.*[323]

In *State v. Lozada,* the defendant was charged and convicted of stalking (elevated to a third-degree offense because the alleged criminal conduct occurred while defendant was subject to a domestic violence restraining order), and fourth-degree contempt of a restraining order. On appeal, the Appellate Court held that the trial court erred in denying the defendant's motion to sever, because "the jury's knowledge that there has been a restraining order is likely to prejudice defendant's right to a fair trial of the issue of whether he is guilty of conduct constituting stalking." In light of the required severance, both convictions had to be reversed.[324]

---

[322] *State v. Saunders*, 302 N.J. Super. 509, 695 A.2d 722 (App. Div. 1997).

[323] *T.M. v. J.C.*, 348 N.J. Super. 101, 104, 791 A.2d 300 (App. Div. 2002).

[324] *State v. Lozada,* 357 N.J. Super. 468, 472, 815 A.2d 1002 (App. Div. 2003).

CHAPTER SIX

ARREST AND SEIZURE OF WEAPONS [325]

6.1   ARREST

When the police are called to respond to an incident of domestic violence and find probable cause to believe that domestic violence has occurred, they are mandated to arrest the perpetrator and sign a criminal complaint themselves, even if the victim will not.

The police are required to make a mandatory arrest and file a criminal complaint specifically where the following circumstances exist:

- The victim exhibits signs of injury caused by the acts of domestic violence.
- A warrant for defendant is in effect.
- That there is probable cause that the perpetrator has violated a No Contact Order, and there is probable cause to believe that the person has been served with the order alleged to have been violated.
- There is probable cause to believe that a <u>weapon has been involved</u> in the commission of an act of domestic violence.

(1) The victim exhibits signs of injury caused by the acts of domestic violence.

The Domestic Violence Procedure's Manual provides guidelines on domestic violence response procedures for the police. The police are instructed that the word "exhibits" is to be liberally construed to mean any indication that a victim has suffered bodily injury, which includes physical pain or impairment of physical condition.

The police may arrest a perpetrator upon seeing outward signs of a victims injuries, such as scars or bruises, but may also do so where there are no visible signs of injury, when a victim states that an injury has occurred. In the later scenario, the officer should consider surrounding relevant factors in determining whether there is probable cause to make an arrest, which includes the officer's observations of the victim's manifestations of an internal injury. Since other "relevant factors" state in the manual, are not defined, great liberality is given to the observations of the police officer, and an arrest can be made even though there is no outward sign of physical injury, where that officer sees fit.

In domestic violence incidents, where both parties exhibit signs of injury, the officer must then decide which party (or parties) to arrest. The manual leaves it to his discretion based upon the following considerations:

---

[325] *N.J.S.A.* 2C:25-21.

The comparative extent of injury suffered to each party;
The history of domestic violence between the parties, if any;
The presence of wounds associated with defense, or considered defensive wounds; or
Other relevant factors, including checking the DV Central Registry.
N.J.S.A. 2C:25-21(c)(2).

The manual does provide for an exception, where both parties show signs of injury for a victim acting in self defense. It provides that the investigating officer must insure that "no victim shall be denied relief or arrested or charged under this act with an offense because the victim used reasonable force in self-defense against domestic violence by an attacker." *N.J.S.A.* 2C:25-21(c)(3).

Theoretically, since one cannot predict how each officer will judge a situation, if one party is more injured than the other, it would indicate that the less injured party should not be arrested. If both parties are injured, but one of the parties has a history of inflicting domestic violence, then it is probably the assumption that the injuries inflicted upon the perpetrator were the result of the victim defending themselves, and the person with the history of domestic violence should be arrested.

(2) A warrant for defendant is in effect.

There is no definition of the word warrant, but it can be presumed that a previous warrant for Domestic Violence Act is what is meant. Certainly an argument can be made that any warrant would permit making a mandatory arrest, including a warrant for non-support or failure to pay a traffic ticket.

(3) That there is probable cause that the perpetrator has violated a No Contact Order, and there is probable cause to believe that the person has been served with the order alleged to have been violated.

This means that if there was a previous restraining order in effect at the time of the arrest the police must arrest. The police are instructed that in case the victim does not have a copy of the previous court order, the officer may verify the existence of an order by calling their own police headquarters, another police headquarters, or the court from which it was issued, to determine whether an order exists. A question arises of whether or not the defendant should be arrested for violating an order, where one has been issued, but the defendant has not been served. As the manual provides and as oftentimes occurs, the police will make the arrest anyway, if they have probable cause to believe the person has been served.

(4)   There is probable cause to believe that a <u>weapon has been involved</u> in the

commission of an act of domestic violence.

What is and what is not a weapon is left to the definitions in *N.J.S.A.* 2C:39-1, "Firearms, other dangerous weapons and instruments of crime."

The following cases address when arrest is or is not warranted, how probable cause is interpreted, and seizure of weapons under *N.J.S.A.* 2C:25-21(d)(3).

A charge of contempt of a Final Restraining Order does not require an arrest warrant unless there is a reasonable basis in the complaint to conclude that the defendant's contempt was dangerous to others, himself or property. In cases where a warrant is unwarranted, a summons should issue, which does not require that an arrest be made.[326]

The police were justified in making an arrest when a concerned citizen reported that they heard the defendant using loud and abusive language, and threatened to throw knives at his wife, despite the fact that the victim and husband denied that an act of domestic violence had occurred. The issue in this case was whether probable cause existed to arrest defendant or, alternatively, whether it was objectively reasonable for the officers to believe that probable cause existed at the time of plaintiff's arrest. The court stated that probable cause exists if at the time of the arrest "the facts and circumstances within the officers' knowledge and of which they had reasonably trustworthy information were sufficient to warrant a prudent man in believing that the suspect had committed or was committing an offense. In addition, the court noted that probable cause to arrest can be based on the statement of a witness or informant. Generally, however, some verification of an anonymous informant's disclosures of criminal activity, as well as a demonstration of his trustworthiness, are necessary in order to establish his credibility, so that such information may fairly and reasonably be assimilated as a proper basis for appropriate police action. The court concluded that the officer's analysis, based on the totality of the circumstances, indicated that he acted reasonably in the defendant's arrest. [327]

---

[326] *State v. Krivoshik*, 289 *N.J. Super.* 132, 672 *A.2d* 1315 (Ch. Div. 1995); *N.J. Ct. R.* 3:3-1; *N.J. Ct. R.* 3:3-3.
[327] *Wildoner v. Borough of Ramsey*, 162 *N.J.* 375, 745 *A.2d* 1146 (2000)

6.2 BAIL

Where an officer finds that there is probable cause to believe a defendant has committed contempt of an order, the defendant will be arrested and taken into custody by said officer. The officer is then required to follow the procedures below:

The law enforcement officer shall transport the defendant to the police station or such other place as the law enforcement officer shall determine is proper. The law enforcement officer shall:

a. Conduct a search of the domestic violence central registry and sign a complaint concerning the incident which gave rise to the contempt charge;

b. Telephone or communicate in person or by facsimile with the appropriate judge assigned pursuant to this act and request bail be set on the contempt charge;

c. If the defendant is unable to meet the bail set, take the necessary steps to insure that the defendant shall be incarcerated at police headquarters or at the county jail; and

d. During regular court hours, the defendant shall have bail set by a Superior Court judge that day. On weekends, holidays and other times when the court is closed, the officer shall arrange to have the clerk of the Family Part notified on the next working day of the new complaint, the amount of bail, the defendant's whereabouts and all other necessary details. In addition, if a municipal court judge set the bail, the arresting officer shall notify the clerk of that municipal court of this information.[328]

Bail is either set by:

A Superior Court Judge during normal Court hours (8:30 a.m. to 4:00 p.m.); or an

Emergent Superior Court Judge when courts are closed; or an

Municipal Court Judge, if designated by the Assignment Judge of the Court to set bail for a contempt charge, where the violation is petty disorderly offense, or if the defendant had disobeyed a no contact restraining order.[329]

A Court administrator cannot set bail.

Before bail is set, the defendant's prior record must be considered by the court,

---

[328] *N.J.S.A. 2C:25-31 (a) to (d).*
[329] *Chapter 64 of Title 2C of New Jersey Statutes.*

including a search of the domestic violence central registry. Bail should be set as soon as is feasible, but in all cases within 24 hours of arrest.[330]

The Court can impose conditions on the allowance of Defendant's bail including but not limited to:

> Prohibiting the defendant from having any contact with the victim;
> Prohibiting the defendant from possessing weapons;
> Restraining defendant from victim's residence or any other place where victim may be any other condition to protect the victim;
> Restraint defendant from harassing the victim or victim's relatives in any way;
> Permitting the search and seizure of any weapon at any location which the judge has reasonable cause to believe that the weapon is located.[331]

In the event the defendant wishes to reduce the bail imposed on them, notice must be given to the prosecutor and victim. The original judge who imposed the original bail should hear the bail application unless the judge is unavailable, in which case the substitute judge should have the entire record of the proceeding before them.[332]

---

[330] N.J.S.A. 2C:25-26(d).
[331] N.J.S.A. 2C:25-26(a).
[332] N.J.S.A. 2C:25-26(e).

6.3   SEIZURE OF WEAPONS

A. GENERALLY

The Domestic Violence Act provides for the seizure of weapons. These seizures are however subject to the restraints imposed by the Fourth Amendment and New Jersey's constitutional guarantee against unreasonable search and seizures.

Generally speaking:

> A person convicted of a misdemeanor crime of domestic violence is "unfit," under New Jersey law, from using, possessing, or owning any firearms that have been shipped or transported in interstate or foreign commerce. Therefore, the weapons forfeiture and return provisions contained in *N.J.S.A.* 2C:25-21d(3) and 18 *U.S.C.A.* § 922(g)(9) are in harmony and the doctrine of federal preemption is inapplicable to these circumstances.[333]

B. SEARCH AND SEIZURE PURSUANT TO POLICE RESPONSE TO DOMESTIC VIOLENCE CALL

When a police officer has been called to a domestic violence incident and has probable cause to believe that an act of domestic violence has been committed, said officer has a duty to question all persons present to determine whether there are weapons on the premises. In addition, if the officer sees or learns that a weapon is on the premises of a domestic violence incident and reasonably believes that the weapon would expose the victim to a risk of serious bodily injury, the officer is obligated to attempt to gain possession of the weapon. If a law enforcement officer seizes any firearm, the officer shall also seize any firearm purchaser identification card or permit to purchase a handgun issued to the person accused of the act of domestic violence.[334]

Where the weapon is in plain view, the officer should seize the weapon. If the weapon is not in plain view, but is located on the premises owned by the victim or jointly owned by both the perpetrator and the victim, the officer should obtain consent, preferably in writing, and then search for and seize the weapon.

If the weapon is not on the premises, the officer should attempt to obtain possession of the weapon by a voluntary surrender of the weapon. Where the perpetrator or the possessor of the weapon refuses to surrender the weapon, or to allow the officer to search for the

---

[333] *State v. Wahl*, 365 *N.J. Super.* 356, 360, 839 *A.2d* 120 (App. Div. 2004).
[334] *N.J.S.A. 2C:25-26 and N.J.S.A. 2C:25-28(j).*

specified weapon, the officer should obtain a Domestic Violence Warrant for the Search and Seizure of Weapons.

In *Hoffman v. Union Country*, plaintiff brought a replevin action for the return of his rifles, shotguns and a Japanese saber that were turned over to the Rahway Police Department by his wife. The weapons had been removed following a domestic dispute. The court found that plaintiff no longer qualified for a firearms purchaser identification card and dismissed his replevin complaint. In its decision, the court found that the police officer came into lawful possession of plaintiff's weapons. The court also found that the police officers' concern for plaintiff's wife's safety, based on the plaintiff's pattern of violent behavior and alcohol abuse, was reasonable and prudent; thus, the police conduct was not overreaching or offensive. [335]

C. SEARCH AND SEIZURE PURSUANT TO COURT ORDERS[336]

In addition to the authority granted to officers to a conduct search and seizure of weapons when responding to a domestic violence incident, the officers may also do so where there is a Court Order. This may take place after the issuance of a Temporary or a Final Restraining Order by the Court.

The court order is limited in scope by the fourth amendment and the New Jersey Constitution. As such, the Order may allow for "the search for and seizure of any such weapon at any location where the judge has reasonable cause to believe the weapon is located. The judge shall state with specificity the reasons for and scope of the search and seizure authorized by the order."[337]

If a domestic violence victim obtains a TRO or FRO directing that the domestic violence assailant surrender a named weapon, the officer enforcing the Order, should demand that the person surrender the named weapon.

If the perpetrator or the possessor of the weapon refuses to surrender it, the officer should:

1. Inform the person that the court order authorizes a search and seizure
of the premises for the named weapon, and
2. Arrest the person, if the person refuses to surrender the named
weapon, for failing to comply with the court order, [338]
and

---

[335] *Hoffman v. Union County Prosecutor*, 240 *N.J. Super.* 206, 572 *A.2d* 1200 (Law. Div. 1990).
[336] *N.J.S.A. 2C:25-26 and N.J.S.A. 2C:25-28(j).*
[337] *N.J.S.A. 2C:25-26(a).*
[338] *N.J.S.A. 2C:29-9.*

3. Conduct a search of the named premises for the named weapon.

The police, in executing a search warrant for weapons, authorized by a TRO, were told by the victim, that a gun was in a cubby hole above the Defendant's bed. In order to get to the cubby hole, the police had to move a pillow and observed a small quantity of cocaine lying in the bed. The trial court denied the defendant's motion to suppress and said that the municipal judge's motive to prevent possible acts of domestic violence permitted the expansion of the search to the entire apartment.[339] The court stated that this was acceptable, even though there was no probable cause to believe the gun was illegally possessed, or that it was evidence of a crime. In addition, plaintiff never indicated that the firearm was used against her in any act of domestic violence. The police were simply taking steps to remove a firearm from the possession of a person in a potentially dangerous domestic violence situation. Their purpose was not to seek evidence of a crime.[340]

In so holding, the court set forth the rationale justifying its decision:

> Protection of the victim is the clear and unequivocal message. Law enforcement personnel and the courts are encouraged to insure, indeed charged with insuring, the safety of all victims exposed to actual or potential acts of domestic violence or abuse.[341]

Rejecting the argument that the Domestic Violence Act's "reasonable cause" standard is unconstitutional, the court, in *Burdin* held:

> Even without the traditional probable cause requirement having been met, the search under the facts and circumstances of this case passes constitutional scrutiny. A limited police entry is allowed to remove an item of potential danger in the volatile setting of domestic violence, especially when that item is a handgun.[342]

Compare to *Frazier*, where a senior corrections officer was allowed to carry a firearm even after his conviction for simple assault under the Domestic Violence Act.[343]

---

[339] *State v. Burdin,* 313 N.J. Super. 468, 712 A.2d 1286 (Law Div. 1998)

[340] *State v. Solomon,* 262 N.J. Super. 618, 621-622, 621 A.2d 559(Ch. Div. 1993).

[341] *State v. Saavedra,* 276 N.J. Super. 289, 292, 647 A.2d 1348 (App. Div. 1994).

[342] *State v. Burdin,* 313 N.J. Super. 468, 712 A.2d 1286 (Law Div. 1998).

[343] *Frazier v. Northern State Prison, Dept. of Corrections,* 392 N.J. Super. 514, 921 A.2d 479 (App. Div. 2007).

D. WHERE POLICE OBTAIN CONSENT TO SEARCH AND SEIZE A WEAPON, THEY ARE LIMITED IN SCOPE BY ADDITIONAL CONSIDERATIONS

In *Younger*, the defendant's grandmother consented to the search of her eleven-year old granddaughter's bedroom for a gun. The defendant had arrived at the grandmother's house, with his belongings, and had been sleeping in said bedroom. The grandmother gave the police consent to search the room, for a gun. During the search, an officer moved one of the bags containing the defendant's clothing and found a small vinyl change purse. The officer opened the change purse and found drugs.[344] The court suppressed this evidence because the search of the purse exceeded the scope of the authority inherent in the consent, as a gun could not possibly have been concealed in the change purse. In addition the court found "no capacity to consent to a search of possessions in which another person has or should be reasonably believed to have an exclusive right of control or right of privacy."[345]

E. SEARCH AND SEIZURES WHERE THERE ARE NO WARRANTS AND/OR NO APPARENT DOMESTIC VIOLENCE

A warrantless search of a home is presumptively invalid, thus the state bears the burden of establishing that such a search falls within one of the few "well-delineated exceptions to the warrant requirement."[346]

A warrantless search is not to be justified or validated by an officer having probable cause that a domestic violence action occurred. The permissible scope in each case will be dependent on the circumstances, including the extent and nature of the officer's probable cause to believe there is a dangerous weapon on the premises and the degree of exigency of the situation.

In one case, the police were dispatched to render police assistance to Plaintiff for Defendant's violation of a domestic violence restraining order and because Plaintiff "felt that her life was being threatened" by Defendant's presence. (The restraining order had in fact been vacated days prior because neither party appeared at the final hearing. Thus, no warrant was in place). When the officers approached the house they heard the male and female arguing. After knocking on the door, the police were invited in by the victim, who stated she wanted defendant out of the house. The defendant advised the police that he would leave the house, but asked that he be permitted to get dressed and get some personal items. The police then followed him into the bedroom, in accordance with regular police procedures, where they said they say saw marijuana in plain view and seized same. The Defendant was charged with possession and subsequently moved to suppress the evidence. The trial court granted

---

[344] *State v. Younger*, 305 *N.J. Super.* 250, 702 *A.2d* 477 (App. Div. 1997).
[345] *Ibid.*
[346] State v. Frankel, 179 N.J. 586, 847 A.2d 561 (2004).

defendant's motion to suppress said evidence as being the fruit of an unlawful search, since there was no warrant in place, and the police had no probable cause to believe an act of domestic violence had taken place when responding to the alleged domestic violence incident, thus an arrest was unwarranted.

The Appellate Division affirmed the trial court, but the Supreme Court reversed and said that the search was valid because the search was held within the context of the statute, [347] which authorizes an arrest if an officer has probable cause to believe a person has violated the terms of a domestic violence order, or where there is probable cause that domestic violence has been committed. The court held that the officer had probable cause, and need not have checked upon the truth of the statements that were given by the dispatcher to them, indicating that a temporary restraining order was in effect. Furthermore, there was no evidence in the negative to suggest that the officer had cause to believe that the temporary restraining order was not in effect and not served.

The court also determined that given all the circumstances, the officers had reason to believe that the defendant had previously engaged in a course of alarm and conduct and now presented an immediate danger to the victim of domestic violence, and that they had a right to serve defendant in the matter in which they did within the home.

> Whether he was investigating a domestic violence complaint or waiting to enforce an order, Mathis was following reasonable procedures directed toward protecting police officers as well as domestic violence victims, when he accompanied defendant into the bedroom.[348]

F. EFFECTS OF A WARRANT WHEN PROCEDURE IS NOT FOLLOWED

Before a domestic violence temporary restraining order and accompanying search warrant can be issued, the court must find probable cause to believe that an offense of domestic violence has occurred. If the record of an ex parte proceeding does not disclose "a proper basis for a finding of exigency for the telephonic application, probable cause to believe that the offense of domestic violence has occurred, and a reason to permit a search for weapons in a location removed from the place where the domestic violence allegedly occurred," the search warrant is invalid.[349]

---

[347] *N.J.S.A.* 2C:25-21(g).

[348] *State v. Scott*, 231 *N.J. Super.* 258, 555 A.2d 667 (App. Div. 1989), *rev.*, 118 *N.J.* 406, 571 *A.2d* 1304 (1990).

[349] *State v. Dispoto*, 189 *N.J.* 108, 913 *A.2d* 791 (2007)(*citing State v. Cassidy*, 179 *N.J.* 150, 163-64, 843 *A.2d* 1132 (2004)).

Where a police officer telephoned the municipal court judge seeking a temporary restraining order, the judge took testimony telephonically, but did not administer an oath to the victim or officer, and did not record the proceedings. The TRO was subsequently issued authorizing a search for weapons, resulting in the discovery of weapons. The defendant appealed. The Supreme Court held that the TRO was invalid, and that no exception to the warrant requirement applied, since there was no exigency, as no one claimed that defendant had threatened to use his guns, and the assault occurred a month before the search. In regard to the emergency aid exception, the home police searched was not the scene of the assault and the situation was not then volatile.[350]

> The Act recognizes that, in certain circumstances, removal of weapons will be necessary to protect a victim. When an officer has "probable cause" to believe an act of domestic violence has been committed, the officer may "question persons *present* to determine whether there are weapons *on the premises*" and seize any weapon that the officer reasonably believes would expose the victim to harm.[351]

In regard to improper procedure the court noted:

> The record of the *ex parte* proceeding must disclose a proper basis for a finding of exigency for the telephonic application, probable cause to believe that the offense of domestic violence has occurred, and a reason to permit a search for weapons in a location removed from the place where the domestic violence allegedly occurred.[352]

G. UTILIZATION OF SEIZED PRODUCTS IN CRIMINAL PROCEEDINGS

In a case decided in 2003, the court held that weapons obtained pursuant to a domestic violence search warrant generally may not be admitted in a subsequent criminal proceeding. The court specified that evidence found pursuant to searches authorized under *N.J.S.A.* 2C:25-21(d)(1) and *N.J.S.A.* 2C:25-28(j) are constitutional, so long as the seized items were not used in criminal prosecution, unless the factual circumstances justify a search under a recognized exception to the warrant requirement.[353]

---

[350] *State v. Cassidy*, 179 *N.J.* 150,163-164, 843 *A.2d.* 1132 (2004); *N.J.S.A.* 2C:25-21(d).
[351] *Ibid.*
[352] *Ibid.*
[353] *State v. Perkins*, 358 *N.J. Super.* 151, 817 *A.2d* 364 (App. Div. 2003).

Subsequently, in *State v. Harris*, the court was called upon to consider the relationship between a search conducted pursuant to a domestic violence warrant (which permits issuance of a warrant upon reasonable cause), Article I, paragraph 7 of the New Jersey Constitution, and the Fourth Amendment of the United States Constitution; both of which state that no warrant may issue "except upon probable cause." Specifically, the court was faced with the question of whether weapons recovered from a defendant's premises during a search conducted pursuant to a Domestic Violence warrant may be admitted in a subsequent criminal prosecution of defendant for possession of those weapons. The court concluded that items seized during a search conducted pursuant to a warrant issued under the Prevention of Domestic Violence Act can serve as the basis for a subsequent criminal prosecution if their illegal nature is immediately apparent.[354]

H. SEIZURE OF WEAPON IDENTIFICATION CARDS

In addition to the statute providing for the seizure of weapons, it also authorizes the officer to seize any firearm purchaser identification card or permit(s) to purchase a handgun, issued to the person accused of the act of domestic violence weapon, incidental to an appropriate search for weapons.[355]

This protection was recognized by courts, even before it was codified in the current statute.

> This enhancement of victims protection, through temporary seizure of authorization papers is specifically sanctioned by the Act; and that even if that were not the case, the benefit to the alleged victim is nonetheless exactly what the Legislature contemplated and sought to achieve through passage of the Act. In either instance, seizure of the card incidental to an appropriate search for weapons is lawful.[356]

The firearms purchaser's identification card should be denied if there is a domestic violence restraining order against the applicant.[357] (*Note: there are limited circumstances where a card will be allowed to issue.*)

Even when a Final Restraining Order is vacated by agreement, the firearms purchaser's identification card is not to be released because *N.J.S.A.* 2C:58-3(c)(8) prohibits the issuance of a card when a firearm is seized pursuant to the Domestic Violence Act and the prohibition

---

[354] *State v. Harris,* 211 *N.J.* 566, 50 *A.3d* 15 (2012).

[355] *N.J.S.A* 2C:25-28(j).

[356] *Matter of Seized Firearms Identification Card of Hand,* 304 *N.J. Super.* 360, 700 *A.2d* 904 (Ch. Div. 1997).

[357] *Adler v. Levack,* 308 *N.J. Super.* 219, 705 *A.2d* 1218 (App. Div. 1998); *N.J.S.A.* 2C:58-3(c)(1) to (6).

stands even if the restraining order is later vacated.[358]

---

[358] *M.S. v. Millburn Police Dept.*, 395 *N.J. Super.* 638, 930 *A.2d* 481 (App. Div. 2007), *rev. and rem.*, 197 *N.J.* 236, 962 *A.2d* 515 (2008).

6.4   SEIZURE OF MARIJUANA

The purpose of a search warrant is to protect the victim of domestic violence from further violence; it is not a tool for finding evidence of criminality.

An earlier court decision dealing with this issue is *Johnson*. In *Johnson*, the Defendant moved to suppress the marijuana found as a result of a search. The court stated that the "family part judge had reasonable cause to believe that an act of domestic violence had been perpetrated by defendant against plaintiff, and that defendant was in possession of, or had access to the weapon that created a heightened risk of injury" to plaintiff. However, the court stated that there was an insufficient basis in the record to provide reasonable cause to believe that defendant's access to a weapon posed additional risk of harm to his spouse.[359]

The *Johnson* court stated that accordingly, the analysis of whether a domestic violence search warrant passes constitutional muster should not be guided by probable cause, which requires a well-grounded suspicion that a crime has been or is being committed. Instead, this court used the less stringent standard of "reasonable cause." The court stated that in order to support the issuance of a search warrant, the judge must find there exists reasonable cause to believe that, (1) the defendant has committed an act of domestic violence, (2) the defendant possesses or has access to a firearm or other weapon specified in *N.J.S.A.* 2C:39-1(r), and (3) the defendant's possession or access to the weapon poses a heightened risk of injury to the victim. Additionally, a description of the weapon and its believed location must be reasonably specified in the warrant. These requirements are consistent with the constitutional guarantees against unreasonable searches and seizures afforded to a defendant by the United States and New Jersey Constitutions.[360]

Significantly, the court in *Dispoto*, specifically disapproved of the first prong of the *Johnson* standard, holding that "before a domestic violence temporary restraining order and *accompanying search warrant* can be issued, the court must find probable cause to believe that an offense of domestic violence has occurred."[361]

In *Dispoto*, an informant told police that defendant planned to kill his wife; the claim was uncorroborated. A police officer told the wife of the threat and urged her to obtain a temporary restraining order against defendant, which she did. Pursuant to *N.J.S.A.* 2C:25-28(j) of the New Jersey Prevention of Domestic Violence Act, *N.J.S.A.* 2C:25-17 to -33, the police obtained a domestic violence warrant to search defendant's home and office for weapons. The police found a gun during the search, and questioned Defendant as to the contents of his safe;

---

[359] *State v. Johnson*, 352 *N.J. Super.* 15, 799 *A.2d* 608 (App. Div. 2002); *See also State v. Frankel*, 179 *N.J.* 586, 847 *A.2d* 561 (App. Div. 2004).

[360] *Ibid*.

[361] *State v. Dispoto*, 189 *N.J.* 108, 913 *A.2d* 791 (2007).

he said it contained marijuana. They then obtained a warrant to search for drugs. The intermediate appellate court held that as defendant was not in custody when he was mirandized, the failure to re-administer the warning after his arrest required suppression of his statement. The Supreme Court affirmed on other grounds. It held that as the informant's statement did not supply probable cause to believe that a terroristic threat was made, the domestic violence search warrant was invalid. Therefore, evidence that was produced through defendant's compliance with that warrant was the fruit of the poisonous tree and had to be suppressed.[362] The Court reasoned:

> The temporary restraining order's purpose is to provide the domestic violence victim with a buffer zone of safety and shield the victim from the risk of contact with an abuser. Similarly, he purpose of a domestic violence search warrant "is to protect a victim of domestic violence from further violence, not to discover evidence of criminality." Accordingly, before a domestic violence temporary restraining order and accompanying search warrant can be issued, the court must find probable cause to believe that an offense of domestic violence has occurred. If the record of an ex parte proceeding does not disclose "a proper basis for a finding of exigency for the telephonic application, probable cause to believe that the offense of domestic violence has occurred, and a reason to permit a search for weapons in a location removed from the place where the domestic violence allegedly occurred," the search warrant is invalid. In the absence of an exception to the warrant requirement, "evidence seized pursuant to a defectively authorized search warrant" is inadmissible in a subsequent criminal prosecution.[363]

> The remedial protections afforded under the New Jersey Prevention of Domestic Violence Act (NJPDVA), *N.J.S.A.* 2C:25-17 to -33, are intended for the benefit of victims of domestic violence and are not meant to serve as a pretext for obtaining information to advance a criminal investigation against an alleged abuser.[364]

The court in *Harris* went further requiring probable cause for each of the three elements specified in *Johnson*. The court stated that so long as the court makes a determination that there is (1) probable cause to believe that an act of domestic violence has been committed by

---

[362] *State v. Dispoto*, 189 *N.J.* 108, 120, 913 *A.2d* 791 (2007)(formatting and citations altered from original).

[363] *Ibid*(internal citations omitted and altered from original).

[364] *Ibid.*

the defendant, (2) probable cause to believe a search for and seizure of weapons is "necessary to protect the life, health or well-being of a victim on whose behalf the relief is sought," [365]; and (3) probable cause to believe that the weapons are located in the place to be searched, a warrant issued under this statute is constitutionally sound. These refinements would keep *N.J.S.A.* 2C:25-28(j) from running afoul of the Fourth Amendment.

---

[365] *N.J.S.A.* 2C:25-28(f).

6.5   RETURN OF WEAPONS

Weapons seized in accordance with the "Prevention of Domestic Violence Act of 1991", shall be returned to the owner, except upon order of the Superior Court. The prosecutor, in possession of the seized weapons may, upon notice to the owner, petition a judge of the Family Part of the Superior Court, Chancery Division, within 45 days of seizure, to obtain title to the seized weapons, or to revoke any and all permits, licenses and other authorizations for the use, possession, or ownership of such weapons pursuant to the law governing such use, possession, or ownership, or may object to the return of the weapons on such grounds as are provided for the initial rejection or later revocation of the authorizations, or on the grounds that the owner is unfit or that the owner poses a threat to the public in general or a person or persons in particular.[366]

A hearing is to be held and a record made thereof within 45 days of the notice provided above. No formal pleading and no filing fee shall be required prior to the hearing. The hearing shall be summary in nature. Appeals from the results of the hearing shall be to the Superior Court, Appellate Division, in accordance with the law.[367]

If the prosecutor does not institute an action within 45 days of seizure, the seized weapons shall be returned to the owner.[368]

After a forfeiture hearing, the court shall order the return of the firearms, weapons and any authorization papers relating to the seized weapons to the owner if the court determines the owner is not subject to any of the disabilities set forth in *N.J.S.A. 2C:58-3(c)* and finds that the complaint has been:

1.   Dismissed at the request of the complainant and the prosecutor determines that there is insufficient probable cause to indict; or
2.   If the defendant is found not guilty of the charges; or
3.   If the court determines that the domestic violence situation no longer exists.[369]

Note: Nothing in the act impairs the right of the State to retain evidence pending a criminal prosecution. In addition, no provision of the act limits the authority of the State or a law enforcement officer to seize, retain or forfeit property pursuant to chapter 64 of Title 2C of the New Jersey Statutes.

---

[366] *N.J.S.A.* 2C:25-21(d)(3).
[367] *N.J.S.A.* 2C:25-21(d)(3).
[368] *N.J.S.A.* 2C:25-21(d)(3).
[369] *N.J.S.A.* 2C:25-21 (d)(3).

If, after the hearing, the court determines that the weapons are not to be returned to the owner, the court may:

(1) With respect to weapons other than firearms, order the prosecutor to dispose of the weapons if the owner does not arrange for the transfer or sale of the weapons to an appropriate person within 60 days; or

(2) Order the revocation of the owner's firearms purchaser identification card or any permit, license or authorization, in which case the court shall order the owner to surrender any firearm seized and all other firearms possessed to the prosecutor and shall order the prosecutor to dispose of the firearms if the owner does not arrange for the sale of the firearms to a registered dealer of the firearms within 60 days; or

(3) Order such other relief as it may deem appropriate. When the court orders the weapons forfeited to the State or the prosecutor is required to dispose of the weapons, the prosecutor shall dispose of the property as provided in *N.J.S.A. 2C:64-6.*[370]

A civil suit may be brought to enjoin a wrongful failure to return a seized firearm where the prosecutor refuses to return the weapon after receiving a written request to do so and notice of the owner's intent to bring a civil action pursuant to this section. Failure of the prosecutor to comply with the provisions of this act shall entitle the prevailing party in the civil suit to reasonable costs, including attorney's fees, provided that the court finds that the prosecutor failed to act in good faith in retaining the seized weapon.[371]

No law enforcement officer or agency shall be held liable in any civil action brought by any person for failing to learn of, locate or seize a weapon pursuant to this act, or for returning a seized weapon to its owner.[372]

When interpreting the law, courts have for the most part held that even the late filing of a forfeiture petition is permitted to ensure "maximum protection" for a potential victim of domestic violence through the "broad application" of the prosecutorial power. In one case, the court permitted a late filing where the state moved to file "as expeditiously as possible." The court allowed for the late filing as there was no evidence that the State slept on its rights or that "the delay resulted in prejudice to an innocent party." The court further reasoned that the Legislature is certainly cognizant of the fact that the calendars of our courts are busy ones. Accordingly, the State will not be penalized for its inability to obtain an earlier hearing date on its petition for forfeiture.[373]

---

[370] *N.J.S.A. 2C:25-21 (d)(3)(a-c).*
[371] *N.J.S.A. 2C:25-21 (d)(4).*
[372] *N.J.S.A. 2C:25-21 (d)(5).*
[373] *State v. Volpini,* 291 *N.J. Super.* 401, 677 *A.2d* 780 (App. Div. 1996).

The trial court properly denied defendant's motion to dismiss a weapons forfeiture petition, based upon the prosecutor's failure to file the forfeiture petition within forty-five days of the seizures as required by *N.J.S.A.* 2C:25-21(d)(3).[374] The Appellate Division affirmed the trial court's determination that the filing was timely under the circumstances presented. The 45 day period within which the application for forfeiture must be filed by the county prosecutor does not begin to run on the date of "seizure" by law enforcement agencies but, instead, the date on which the county prosecutor came into possession of the weapon or had knowledge of its seizure.[375]

The court in *State v. S.A.*, held that the state's failure to seek forfeiture within 45 days under state statute did not give defendant the automatic right to the return of the seized weapons, so long as the domestic violence restraining order was outstanding.[376]

Similarly, the Appellate Division found that, while there exists no specific statutory authorization for the seizure of "permits, licenses", or "any authorization papers", such as a firearms identification card, their seizure, incidental to an unsuccessful yet lawful search for weapons, is consistent with the provisions of the Act *(this is pre-amendment, as statute now expressly allows for such seizure.)* Even were the statute silent on the issue of "return", the seizure of authorization papers alone, incidental to search for weapons never found, would undeniably inhibit the ability of the owner or licensee to purchase lawfully other firearms.[377]

In *Hoffman v. Union County*, the Plaintiff's weapons were seized for "safe keeping" after a domestic violence incident involving his wife and son. The weapons were not seized as evidence of a crime or forfeited for unlawful use under *N.J.S.A.* 2C:65-1. The State had secured the possession of the firearms without a search warrant, court order, or any legal process, following a domestic violence complaint and based upon the victims fear that they would be used to harm her. The Plaintiff had a long history of alcohol abuse and disorderly conduct offenses. Accordingly, he was denied possession of the weapons while the court determined his fitness to possess them. The temporary seizing of plaintiff's weapons is in accord with a long-standing policy of the state of New Jersey to keep guns out of the hands of all dangerously unfit persons, criminal and non-criminal.[378]

---

[374] *State v. McGovern*, 385 *N.J. Super.* 428, 897 *A.2d* 434 (App. Div. 2006).

[375] *State v. McGovern*, 385 *N.J. Super.* 428, 897 *A.2d* 434 (App. Div. 2006); *State v. Saaveedra*, 276 *N.J. Super.* 289, 647 *A.2d* 1348 (App. Div. 1994); *Matter of Seized Firearms Identification Card of Hand*, 304 *N.J. Super.* 360, 700 *A.2d* 904 (Ch. Div. 1997).

[376] *State v. S.A.*, 290 *N.J. Super.* 240, 675 *A.2d* 678 (App. Div. 1996).

[377] *Matter of Seized Firearms Identification Card of Hand*, 304 *N.J. Super.* 360, 700 *A.2d* 904 (Ch. Div. 1997).

[378] *Hoffman v. Union County Prosecutor*, 240 *N.J. Super.* 206, 572 *A.2d* 1200 (Law. Div. 1990).

The *Hoffman* court referred to the earlier case of *State v. Cunningham*, wherein the defendant was charged with shooting his wife with a handgun. In refusing his request for the return of his handgun, the Appellate Division recognized that there are circumstances when, without a gun being unused unlawfully, the police would be authorized to seize the weapon to protect the public from danger.

> Clearly, the statutory design is to prevent firearms from coming into the hands of persons likely to pose a danger to the public. It seeks to achieve this result by providing for the revocation of a firearms purchaser identification card when its possessor has become disqualified under *N.J.S.A.* 2C:58-3(c) subsequent to the issuance of the card. We note that forfeiture is another remedy that can be invoked, in an appropriate case. Forfeiture applies when a gun is possessed or used for a criminal purpose, whether or not its owner has been convicted. *But we can imagine many circumstances when, without the owner using a gun unlawfully, the police would be authorized to seize a gun in order to protect the public from danger.* This might be done as a parallel to the exercise of the common law right to abate a nuisance summarily when the safety of the public is threatened. This could occur, for example, if an owner carelessly allowed his children to play with a loaded gun, or if an owner became insane and was carelessly handling a gun, resulting in a threat to the public safety. Such conduct would not be criminal, but would justify the denial of a permit to acquire a gun. To further the legislative policy, we conclude that the police need not return a gun to its owner in such a case, although the owner had not used the gun unlawfully and no one had yet been injured. But the owner would have the right to a hearing to determine if he is disqualified on the standards of *N.J.S.A.* 2C:58-3(c) from receiving the gun."[379]

The *Hoffman* court further noted that domestic violence is a serious crime, which is on the rise. The police officers, when responding to domestic violence calls are required to make on the scene evaluations and take appropriate actions, based upon common sense and experience. When the officers were asked by the victim to take her husband's weapons from the premises following a dispute between the victim and her son, common sense would dictate that any weapons be removed from a house where domestic violence is ongoing. The court stated that the officers concerns for the victims safety, as well as her personal concerns, were reasonable and prudent, and the seizure of the weapons by the police was not overreaching or

---

[379] *State v. Cunningham*, 186 *N.J. Super.* 502, 511-513, 453 *A.2d* 239 (App. Div. 1982)(emphasis supplied).

offensive. The court noted that the Legislature has gone so far as to permit a violent cohabitant to be ejected from his own home on an *ex-parte* application, which is more intrusive than the temporary possession of his guns, while the court determines his fitness to own them.

> Seeking judicial approval prior to the seizure of Mr. Hoffman's weapons would jealously guard Mr. Hoffman's right to his property while leaving Mrs. Hoffman in jeopardy. Temporarily detaining the weapons and then giving plaintiff an opportunity to be heard in court was the practical solution used by the police. The court recognizes that Mr. Hoffman's right to enjoy his property has been infringed. In this case the rights of Mr. & Mrs. Hoffman and the State all must be balanced.

After balancing these rights, the court finally determined that because of the plaintiffs disturbing pattern of domestic violence, and his alcohol abuse, he no longer qualified for a firearms purchaser identification card, which was then revoked.

Regardless of the exact wording of the Act, case law has determined that under the acts provisions, there are instances when a State need not return the weapons, aside from retaining the weapons for evidence, or pursuant to an order of forfeiture.

The State has a right to retain the evidence pending a criminal prosecution, and they still have the right to seize them according to other statutes, particularly Chapter 64 of Title 2C of the New Jersey Statutes.

In one case, where a domestic violence complaint was filed by the victim and a criminal complaint was filed by the police department, the firearms were not returned to the husband. While the criminal complaint was subsequently withdrawn, the domestic violence complaint moved forward, resulting in restraints being entered against the Defendant. The court noted there are three situations where a gun may be returned, ie where the complaint (*note: court specified this referred to the domestic violence complaint.*) was dismissed at the request of the complainant and the prosecutor determines that there is insufficient probable cause to indict; or if the defendant is found not guilty of the charges; or if the court determines that the domestic violence situation no longer exists. Applying this to the facts, the court concluded that the Defendant posed a threat to his wife, and the domestic violence complaint was not dismissed. Since the Defendant did not qualify for the return of the weapons, the retention of said weapons was permissible.[380]

Where weapons were confiscated in connection with a domestic violence charge, the state had a right to retain the weapons, even though no criminal or domestic violence charges

---

[380] *State v. Solomon*, 262 *N.J. Super.* 618, 621 *A.2d* 559 (Ch. Div. 1993).

remained, and the domestic violence situation had abated. The court noted a "gap" in the provisions of the Firearms Purchase Law and the Domestic Violence Act and determined that they should be read in light of each other in order to further the legislative intent.

> It is the "fundamental tenet of statutory construction that every effort should be made to harmonize the law relating to the same subject matter."

Reading *N.J.S.A.* 2C:58-3(c) and *N.J.S.A.* 2C:25-21(d)(3) together, the Supreme Court found that the Legislature intended that courts not return guns to a defendant in a domestic violence action, even after the dismissal of the complaint, if the court finds that the defendant poses a threat to public health, safety, or welfare. The Supreme Court remanded the matter to the Family Part for further factual findings on the issue of whether the defendant posed a threat to public health, safety or welfare.[381]

The withdrawal of the domestic violence complaint by the complainant does not automatically require the dismissal of the forfeiture application under the Act. The court in *Volpini* held that prior to the return of any seized weapons, to ensure "maximum protection" for a potential victim of domestic violence through the "broad application" of the prosecutorial power, the motion judge should consider the merits of the State's forfeiture petition.[382]

The Appellate Division has also determined that the state is permitted to retain weapons even where it has failed to move for forfeiture pursuant to *N.J.S.A.* 2C:25-21(d)(1), within 45 days. The Court relied upon an amendment to "the gun control act", 18 *U.S.C.S.* 922(g)(8), which forbids firearms possession by anyone subject to a domestic-violence order. Since the Defendant was still subject to domestic restraints, he was not entitled to the return of his weapons. Furthermore, as the Federal Statute and State statues are not in actual conflict, the issue of federal preemption does not arise.[383]

In one case, the Appellate Division indicated that a court should refrain from returning weapons not only to one who poses a threat to the public safety and welfare, but also to a person who would be disqualified from retaining a firearms permit.[384] Moreover, the knowing violation of the gun laws in and of itself is a sufficient statutory basis for the court to order a forfeiture of seized weapons, without the necessity of the court also finding that the defendant

---

[381] *Matter of the Return of Weapons of J.W.D.*, 149 N.J. 108, 693 A.2d 92 (1997); *State v. Warrick*, 283 *N.J. Super.* 169, 661 *A.2d* 335 (App. Div. 1995).

[382] *State v. Volpini*, 291 N.J. Super. 401, 677 A.2d 780 (App. Div. 1996).

[383] *State v. S.A.*, 290 *N.J. Super.* 240, 675 *A.2d* 68 (App. Div. 1996).

[384] *State v. Freysinger*, 311 *N.J. Super.* 509, 514-17, 710 *A.2d* 596 (App. Div. 1998)(defendant's defense was that he was not drinking "presently" and thus was not a habitual drunkard as to deny him the return of his weapons); *N.J.S.A.* 2C:54-3.

is unfit or a danger to the public in general or persons in particular.[385]

In State (*E.L.*) *v. G.P.N*, a domestic violence complaint filed by defendant's former wife, resulted in the issuance of a temporary restraining order (TRO) and the confiscation of defendant's guns from his office and home. After the dismissal of the complaint and the restraining order, the State moved for forfeiture of the weapons and revocation of defendant's permit, because defendant did not reveal his New York drug conviction on his gun permit application. [386] The trial court granted the motion and defendant appealed. On appeal, the court affirmed and held that the nature of both the omission and the New York offense disqualified defendant from holding a permit. The court reasoned that the permit statute, *N.J.S.A.* 2C:58-3(c)(1), precluded anyone who had been convicted of a crime from acquiring a firearm or a firearms purchaser identification card. The court declared that defendant's New York conviction constituted a "crime" under the permit statute. In addition, the court held that the prosecution's forfeiture application was not time barred. The court reasoned that the permit statute explicitly provided that a permit is void at such time the holder becomes subject to any of the disabilities enumerated in *N.J.S.A.* 2C:58-3(c).

The court stated:

> The permit statute explicitly provides that a permit is void at such time the holder becomes subject to any of the disabilities enumerated in *N.J.S.A.* 2C:58-3(c) and *N.J.S.A.* 2C:58-3(f).
> Pursuant to this section, a permit may be revoked, after hearing upon notice, *at any time* upon a finding that the holder no longer qualifies for the permit. [387]

In a forfeiture proceeding pursuant to *N.J.S.A.* 2C:58-3(c)(5), following the dismissal of a domestic violence complaint, the Appellate Division held that the lower Court erred when it relied upon the petitioner's estranged wife as an expert on mental illness to support forfeiture. The Appellate Court held that the wife's qualifications as a certified nurse in the field of mental illness were not adequately established, and that *N.J.S.A.* 45:11-23 prohibits nurses from making medical diagnosis. This, along with her incomplete knowledge of the drug defendant was using, imprecise knowledge as to the diagnoses, and the obvious bias, resulted in a reversal. The court concluded the Wife's testimony constituted a net opinion, or a conclusion that was unsupported by factual evidence, and was thus inadmissible. Because the evidence did not support a finding that husband posed a threat, husband was entitled to reversal of the forfeiture order.[388]

---

[385] *State v. 6 Shot Colt .357*, 365 N.J. Super. 411, 417, 839 A.2d 155 (Ch. Div. 2003).

[386] *State (E.L.) v. G.P.N.*, 321 N.J. Super. 172, 728 A.2d 316 (App. Div. 1999).

[387] *State (E.L.) v. G.P.N.*, 321 N.J. Super. 172, 728 A.2d 316 (App. Div. 1999).

[388] *State v. One Marlin Rifle*, 319 N.J. Super. 359, 725 A.2d 144 (App. Div. 1999).

"The burden of proof is upon the State to show by a preponderance of the evidence, that forfeiture is legally warranted."[389] In *Cordoma*, the Defendant's weapon was seized pursuant to a domestic violence temporary restraining order (TRO) obtained by his former wife, which she voluntarily withdrew before entry of an FRO. Subsequently, the State instituted forfeiture proceedings, concerning defendant's fitness to possess a firearm, which resulted in a judgment ordering the forfeiture of his service handgun, etc. The defendant appealed. On appeal, the Appellate Court found there was insufficient evidence to support the trial court's finding that defendant was unfit to possess a firearm, but that evidence presented provided a rational basis to question defendant's suitability to possess a firearm. Thus the court vacated the judgment and the case was remanded.[390]

On the Federal front, the Attorney General in a memorandum dated April 4, 1997 on Federal Firearms Restrictions noted the various convictions for different offenses involving violence against family members, and stated that it is a violation of federal law for a person who has been convicted of 'misdemeanor crimes for domestic violence' to possess a firearm or ammunition.

This law applies to all persons including those employed in law enforcement or in the military.[391] It should be noted it applies to convictions under the criminal laws, but because the Domestic Violence Act is not a criminal statute, and a state law, the Federal Statute does not apply to domestic violence, civil complaints, or temporary or final restraining orders.

---

[389] *State v Cordoma*, 372 N.J. Super. 524, 533, 859 A.2d 756 (App. Div. 2004).
[390] *State v Cordoma*, 372 N.J. Super. 524, 533-34, 859 A.2d 756 (App. Div. 2004).
[391] 18 *U.S.C.S.* 922(d)(9).

6.6   WEAPONS – DEFINITION [392]

The following definitions apply to this chapter and to chapter 58:

a. "Antique firearm" means any rifle or shotgun and "antique cannon" means a destructive device defined in paragraph (3) of subsection c. of this section, if the rifle, shotgun or destructive device, as the case may be, is incapable of being fired or discharged, or which does not fire fixed ammunition, regardless of date of manufacture, or was manufactured before 1898 for which cartridge ammunition is not commercially available, and is possessed as a curiosity or ornament or for its historical significance or value.

b. "Deface" means to remove, deface, cover, alter or destroy the name of the maker, model designation, manufacturer's serial number or any other distinguishing identification mark or number on any firearm.

c. "Destructive device" means any device, instrument or object designed to explode or produce uncontrolled combustion, including (1) any explosive or incendiary bomb, mine or grenade; (2) any rocket having a propellant charge of more than four ounces or any missile having an explosive or incendiary charge of more than one-quarter of an ounce; (3) any weapon capable of firing a projectile of a caliber greater than 60 caliber, except a shotgun or shotgun ammunition generally recognized as suitable for sporting purposes; (4) any Molotov cocktail or other device consisting of a breakable container containing flammable liquid and having a wick or similar device capable of being ignited. The term does not include any device manufactured for the purpose of illumination, distress signaling, line-throwing, safety or similar purposes.

d. "Dispose of" means to give, give away, lease, loan, keep for sale, offer, offer for sale, sell, transfer, or otherwise transfer possession.

e. "Explosive" means any chemical compound or mixture that is commonly used or is possessed for the purpose of producing an explosion and which contains any oxidizing and combustible materials or other ingredients in such proportions, quantities or packing that an ignition by fire, by friction, by concussion or by detonation of any part of the compound or mixture may cause such a sudden generation of highly heated gases that the resultant gaseous pressures are capable of producing destructive effects on contiguous objects. The term shall not include small arms ammunition, or explosives in the form prescribed by the official United States Pharmacopoeia.

f. "Firearm" means any handgun, rifle, shotgun, machine gun, automatic or semi-automatic rifle, or any gun, device or instrument in the nature of a weapon from which may be fired or ejected any solid projectable ball, slug, pellet, missile or bullet, or any gas, vapor or other

---

[392] *N.J.S.A.* 2C:39-1.

noxious thing, by means of a cartridge or shell or by the action of an explosive or the igniting of flammable or explosive substances. It shall also include, without limitation, any firearm which is in the nature of an air gun, spring gun or pistol or other weapon of a similar nature in which the propelling force is a spring, elastic band, carbon dioxide, compressed or other gas or vapor, air or compressed air, or is ignited by compressed air, and ejecting a bullet or missile smaller than three-eighths of an inch in diameter, with sufficient force to injure a person.

g. "Firearm silencer" means any instrument, attachment, weapon or appliance for causing the firing of any gun, revolver, pistol or other firearm to be silent, or intended to lessen or muffle the noise of the firing of any gun, revolver, pistol or other firearm.

h. "Gravity knife" means any knife which has a blade which is released from the handle or sheath thereof by the force of gravity or the application of centrifugal force.

i. "Machine gun" means any firearm, mechanism or instrument not requiring that the trigger be pressed for each shot and having a reservoir, belt or other means of storing and carrying ammunition which can be loaded into the firearm, mechanism or instrument and fired there from.

j. "Manufacturer" means any person who receives or obtains raw materials or parts and processes them into firearms or finished parts of firearms, except a person who exclusively processes grips, stocks and other nonmetal parts of firearms. The term does not include a person who repairs existing firearms or receives new and used raw materials or parts solely for the repair of existing firearms.

k. "Handgun" means any pistol, revolver or other firearm originally designed or manufactured to be fired by the use of a single hand.

l. "Retail dealer" means any person including a gunsmith, except a manufacturer or a wholesale dealer, who sells, transfers or assigns for a fee or profit any firearm or parts of firearms or ammunition which he has purchased or obtained with the intention, or for the purpose, of reselling or reassigning to persons who are reasonably understood to be the ultimate consumers, and includes any person who is engaged in the business of repairing firearms or who sells any firearm to satisfy a debt secured by the pledge of a firearm.

m. "Rifle" means any firearm designed to be fired from the shoulder and using the energy of the explosive in a fixed metallic cartridge to fire a single projectile through a rifled bore for each single pull of the trigger.

n. "Shotgun" means any firearm designed to be fired from the shoulder and using the energy of the explosive in a fixed shotgun shell to fire through a smooth bore either a number of ball shots or a single projectile for each pull of the trigger, or any firearm designed to be fired from the shoulder which does not fire fixed ammunition.

o. "Sawed-off shotgun" means any shotgun having a barrel or barrels of less than 18 inches in length measured from the breech to the muzzle, or a rifle having a barrel or barrels of less than 16 inches in length measured from the breech to the muzzle, or any firearm made from a rifle or a shotgun, whether by alteration, or otherwise, if such firearm as modified has an overall length of less than 26 inches.

p. "Switchblade knife" means any knife or similar device which has a blade which opens automatically by hand pressure applied to a button, spring or other device in the handle of the knife.

q. "Superintendent" means the Superintendent of the State Police.

r. "Weapon" means anything readily capable of lethal use or of inflicting serious bodily injury. The term includes, but is not limited to, all (1) firearms, even though not loaded or lacking a clip or other component to render them immediately operable; (2) components which can be readily assembled into a weapon; (3) gravity knives, switchblade knives, daggers, dirks, stilettos, or other dangerous knives, billies, blackjacks, bludgeons, metal knuckles, sandclubs, slingshots, cesti or similar leather bands studded with metal filings or razor blades imbedded in wood; and (4) stun guns; and any weapon or other device which projects, releases, or emits tear gas or any other substance intended to produce temporary physical discomfort or permanent injury through being vaporized or otherwise dispensed in the air.

s. "Wholesale dealer" means any person, except a manufacturer, who sells, transfers, or assigns firearms, or parts of firearms, to persons who are reasonably understood not to be the ultimate consumers, and includes persons who receive finished parts of firearms and assemble them into completed or partially completed firearms, in furtherance of such purpose, except that it shall not include those persons dealing exclusively in grips, stocks and other nonmetal parts of firearms.

t. "Stun gun" means any weapon or other device which emits an electrical charge or current intended to temporarily or permanently disable a person.

u. "Ballistic knife" means any weapon or other device capable of lethal use and which can propel a knife blade.

v. "Imitation firearm" means an object or device reasonably capable of being mistaken for a firearm.

w. "Assault firearm" means:

(1) The following firearms:

Algimec AGM1 type

Any shotgun with a revolving cylinder such as the "Street Sweeper" or "Striker 12"

Armalite AR-180 type

Australian Automatic Arms SAR

Avtomat Kalashnikov type semi-automatic firearms

Beretta AR-70 and BM59 semi-automatic firearms

Bushmaster Assault Rifle

Calico M-900 Assault carbine and M-900

CETME G3

Chartered Industries of Singapore SR-88 type

Colt AR-15 and CAR-15 series

Daewoo K-1, K-2, Max 1 and Max 2, AR 100 types

Demro TAC-1 carbine type

Encom MP-9 and MP-45 carbine types

FAMAS MAS223 types

FN-FAL, FN-LAR, or FN-FNC type semi-automatic firearms

Franchi SPAS 12 and LAW 12 shotguns

G3SA type

Galil type Heckler and Koch HK91, HK93, HK94, MP5, PSG-1

Intratec TEC 9 and 22 semi-automatic firearms

M1 carbine type

M14S type

MAC 10, MAC 11, MAC 11-9mm carbine type firearms

PJK M-68 carbine type

Plainfield Machine Company Carbine

Ruger K-Mini-1 4/5F and Mini-1 4/5RF

SIG AMT, SIG 550SP, SIG 551SP, SIG PE-57 types

SKS with detachable magazine type

Spectre Auto carbine type

Springfield Armory BM59 and SAR-48 type

Sterling MK-6, MK-7 and SAR types

Steyr A.U.G. semi-automatic firearms

USAS 12 semi-automatic type shotgun

Uzi type semi-automatic firearms

Valmet M62, M71S, M76, or M78 type semi-automatic firearms

Weaver Arm Nighthawk.

(2) Any firearm manufactured under any designation which is substantially identical to any of the firearms listed above.

(3) A semi-automatic shotgun with either a magazine capacity exceeding six rounds, a pistol grip, or a folding stock.

(4) A semi-automatic rifle with a fixed magazine capacity exceeding 15 rounds.

(5) A part or combination of parts designed or intended to convert a firearm into an assault firearm, or any combination of parts from which an assault firearm may be readily assembled if

those parts are in the possession or under the control of the same person.

x. "Semi-automatic" means a firearm which fires a single projectile for each single pull of the trigger and is self-reloading or automatically chambers a round, cartridge, or bullet.

y. "Large capacity ammunition magazine" means a box, drum, tube or other container which is capable of holding more than 15 rounds of ammunition to be fed continuously and directly therefrom into a semi-automatic firearm.

z. "Pistol grip" means a well-defined handle, similar to that found on a handgun, that protrudes conspicuously beneath the action of the weapon, and which permits the shotgun to be held and fired with one hand.

aa. "Antique handgun" means a handgun manufactured before 1898, or a replica thereof, which is recognized as being historical in nature or of historical significance and either (1) utilizes a match, friction, flint, or percussion ignition, or which utilizes a pin-fire cartridge in which the pin is part of the cartridge or (2) does not fire fixed ammunition or for which cartridge ammunition is not commercially available.

bb. "Trigger lock" means a commercially available device approved by the Superintendent of State Police which is operated with a key or combination lock that prevents a firearm from being discharged while the device is attached to the firearm. It may include, but need not be limited to, devices that obstruct the barrel or cylinder of the firearm, as well as devices that immobilize the trigger.

cc. "Trigger locking device" means a device that, if installed on a firearm and secured by means of a key or mechanically, electronically or electromechanically operated combination lock, prevents the firearm from being discharged without first deactivating or removing the device by means of a key or mechanically, electronically or electromechanically operated combination lock.

dd. "Personalized handgun" means a handgun which incorporates within its design, and as part of its original manufacture, technology which automatically limits its operational use and which cannot be readily deactivated, so that it may only be fired by an authorized or recognized user. The technology limiting the handgun's operational use may include, but not be limited to: radio frequency tagging, touch memory, remote control, fingerprint, magnetic encoding and other automatic user identification systems utilizing biometric, mechanical or electronic systems. No make or model of a handgun shall be deemed to be a "personalized handgun" unless the Attorney General has determined, through testing or other reasonable means, that the handgun meets any reliability standards that the manufacturer may require for its commercially available handguns that are not personalized or, if the manufacturer has no such reliability standards, the handgun meets the reliability standards generally used in the industry for commercially available handguns.

CHAPTER SEVEN

IMMUNITY FROM CIVIL LIABILITY [393]

Under the New Jersey Tort Claims Act ("TCA"), *N.J.S.A.* 59:1-1 to 59:12-3, police officers are immune from injuries arising out of the failure to provide police protection, and failure to make an arrest. As long as they acted in good faith in the execution and enforcement of the law, and their response to a call was a discretionary act rather than an administerial act, they could not be held liable for their actions or lack of action.

The Domestic Violence Immunity Statute also protects law enforcement officers and others so situated, or any person who, in good faith, reports a possible incident of domestic violence from civil liability. Thus, if a neighbor mistakenly informs the police that a neighbor has committed domestic violence against their spouse, and is mistaken in their belief, causing the arrest of the supposed perpetrator, they are immune from civil liability as long as they acted in good faith in their notification.

In one instance the police arrested an alleged perpetrator when called by the apartment manager, who reported that she heard him using loud and abusive language, and that he was threatening to throw knives at the victim. The victim and the alleged perpetrator denied that an act of domestic violence had occurred. The court ruled that the officer acted properly in the totality of the circumstances and granted summary judgment as to immunity. [394]

There has also been a decision which denied the police from immunity for their failure to act, and found the individual policeman and police department responsible. In this case, a victim called the police to respond to her request to have her estranged husband removed from her home. There was already a Final Restraining Order issued against him, which prohibited contact with the victim. The police had notice of previous incidents of domestic violence at the victim's residence, and instead of arresting the defendant for his violation of the restraining order, they remained on the premises until he left, at which time they also left. A short time later, the defendant returned to the residence and shot the plaintiff. [395]

The police department and the individual officers were found liable and not immune from litigation on four bases:

(1) That they were not immune under *N.J.S.A.* 59:5-4 which protects against suits against public employees from failure to provide police protection or sufficient police protection. [396]

---

[393] *N.J.S.A.* 2C:25-22.
[394] *Wildoner v Borough of Ramsey*, 162 N.J. 375, 382, 744 A.2d 1146 (2000)
[395] *Campbell v. Campbell*, 294 N.J. Super. 18, 682 A.2d 272 (Law. Div. 1996).
[396] *Campbell v. Campbell*, 294 N.J. Super. 18, 682 A.2d 272 (Law. Div. 1996)(*citing Suarez v. Dosky*, 171 N.J.

The court held that this was inapplicable because the statute was intended to insulate State and Local Governments from liability for their policy decisions regarding whether or not to provide certain police services, not to immunize them from the consequences of their negligent actions.[397]

(2) Ministerial Act-The police argued that they were immune under *N.J.S.A.* 59:3-2(a), which protects a public employee from exercising judgment or discretion because they were performing a discretionary act when they responded to the call, and public employees are not liable for injuries resulting from the exercise or judgment of discretion in the performance of their duties.[398]

The court rejected this argument because there was a Final Restraining Order. The Act at *N.J.S.A.* 2C:25-1 et seq. allows no discretion. They must arrest when there is a violation of a previous restraining order. The court found that these discretionary acts are limited to discretionary acts at the highest levels of government in matters of policy or planning, and not to the discretionary acts of an individual police officer. The duty that is imposed on a police officer is ministerial and, therefore, not subject to immunity of *N.J.S.A.* 59:3-2(a) .[399]

(3) The police officers also asserted as a source of immunity *N.J.S.A.* 59:5-5 which relates to the failure of police officers to arrest the defendant. The court rejected this assertion on two grounds.

First, the court held that this immunity does not apply as the Legislature has made it clear that the police officer must enforce a domestic violence order and all other laws which protect domestic violence victims, and this mandate makes the immunity inapplicable as it is in conflict with *N.J.S.A.* 2C:25-31.

A second reason why immunity does not apply, was that the restraining order established a "special relationship" between the police and the plaintiff, and it creates an exception to the immunity statute,[400] which has been overruled and New Jersey does not recognize a "special relationship" as "[d]uty is not a consideration is whether an immunity applies and, if not, whether liability should attach. Therefore, there is no "special relationship" exception to the statute.[401]

Super. 1, 407 *A.2d* 1237 (1979)).

[397] *Ibid.*

[398] *See also S.P. v. Newark Police*, 428 *N.J. Super.* 210, 52 *A.3d* 178 (App. Div. 2012) (holding the police immune from liability).

[399] *Campbell v. Campbell*, 294 *N.J. Super.* 18, 23, 682 *A.2d* 272 (Law. Div. 1996)(*citing Tice v. Cramer*, 133 *N.J.* 347, 627 *A.2d* 1090 (1993)); *Costa v. Josey*, 83 *N.J.* 49, 415 *A.2d* 337 (1980).

[400] *Campbell v. Campbell*, 294 *N.J. Super.* 18, 23, 682 *A.2d* 272 (Law. Div. 1996)(*citing Lee v. Doe.*, 232 *N.J. Super.* 569, 557 *A.2d* 1045 (App. Div. 1989)).

[401] *Maculuso v. Knowles*, 341 *N.J. Super.* 112, 116, 775 *A.2d* 108 (App. Div. 2001); *see Blunt v. Klapproth*,

(4) The court further rejected the Defendant's argument that the statute immunized them because they acted in good faith. The police department and the police officers are also not immune under *N.J.S.A.* 59:3-3 which provides that a public employee is not liable if he acts in good faith in the execution of any law, and *N.J.S.A.* 59:3-5 which protects a public employee from any injury caused by the adoption or failure to enforce any law. The court determined that there was an exception to the statute, most specifically, the "special circumstances exception", which is defined as those involving emergent high risk perils to the public of which the governmental entity has actual or constructive notice. Because the police had constructive notice, perhaps actual notice of the existence of the restraining order, they were aware of the incidents of domestic violence involving the victim and defendant which had occurred at the residence on prior occasions.

The court stated that a domestic violence restraining order is the end product of a finding of the court that domestic violence has taken place. The restraining order itself, with the actual or constructive knowledge of the order, the history of prior incidents of domestic violence, and plaintiff's objections to the presence of the defendant at the premises, demonstrated the high risk situation was presented, and which required the police officers to enforce the arrest provision of the Domestic Violence Act.

A police officer does not have a constitutional obligation to protect a victim from an abuser.[402]

The failure of a police officer to arrest an alleged assailant after a victim reported to police that the assailant had groped and propositioned her prior did not subject the police to liability even though the victim was subsequently sexually assaulted the next day because the court found that the Prevention of Domestic Violence Act did not expressly create an exception to the immunity provisions of the Tort Claims Act such that the failure of police to arrest the alleged attacker subjected a public entity to liability for subsequent damages to the victim, where the officers determined she was not a victim of domestic violence and exhibited no visible injuries. [403]

---

309 *N.J. Super.* 493, 504, 707 *A.2d.* 1021 (App. Div.), *certif. den.*, 156 *N.J.* 387, 718 *A.2d* 1216 (1998).
[402] *Burella v. City of Philadelphia*, 501 *F.3d* 134 (3rd Cir. 2007).
[403] *S.P. v. Newark Police Department*, 428 *N.J. Super.* 210, 52 *A.3d* 178 (App. Div. 2012).

CHAPTER EIGHT

CONFIDENTIALITY OF VICTIM'S LOCATION; BAIL [404]

Integral to the Domestic Violence Act is a mandate that the victim's location remain confidential and not appear in any documents or records to which the defendant has access.[405] In a reported case involving the confidentiality of the location of a domestic violence victim, the court granted plaintiff (victim's) voter's request to register to vote without having her residential address made a matter of public record. The court ruled that because plaintiff was a victim of domestic violence, "the confidentiality of her address, to protect her from future abuse, as well as her right to vote, was to be protected."[406]

There is another confidentiality provision within the act, which states that all records maintained pursuant to the Act shall remain confidential and shall not be made available to any individual or institution except as provided by law.[407]

It is important to note that the confidentiality provision of this part of the act is not absolute. In a case where the parties in a domestic violence proceeding did not object to a newspaper's access to court records relating to the case, the court found *N.J.S.A.* 2C:25-33 did not preclude release of the confidential records. The court also found that pursuant to this section, under certain circumstances the court may permit access to that which has been designated confidential by statute. In accordance with that section, the court may make a case-by-case determination of the need for disclosure in order to narrowly tailor the confidentiality restrictions to the governmental interest served, and therefore the statute is constitutional and does not deny access implicitly guaranteed under the First Amendment. Once an application is made for access to the Clerk's file, the court must decide whether the release of the information will have a detrimental effect on the parties, particularly the victim and if so, whether it outweighs the public's interest of the right-to-know.[408]

The court in *Pepe* allowed for the access considering the following factors:

1. The facts surrounding the alleged act of domestic violence were already a matter of public record;
2. The pending complaint was public;
3. The names of the parties were known;
4. The release of the information will not have a detrimental effect on any of the

---

[404] *N.J.S.A.* 2C:25-26.
[405] *N.J.S.A.* 2C:25-26(a).
[406] *D.C. v. Superintendent of Elections*, 261 *N.J. Super.* 366, 618 *A.2d* 931 (Law Div. 1992).
[407] *N.J.S.A.* 2C:25-33(a).
[408] *Pepe v. Pepe*, 258 *N.J. Super.* 157, 609 *A.2d* 127 (Ch. Div. 1992).

parties, particularly the victim;

5. The parties did not object to the release; and
6. Under the circumstances of this case, the release of the court files will not discourage the victim from coming forward.

ADDRESS CONFIDENTIALITY PROGRAM ACT *N.J.S.A.* 47:4-1

Another statute created to address confidentiality for the victim of domestic violence is the "Address Confidentiality Program Act." Pursuant to the Act, program victims have their mail delivered to an address designated by the Secretary of State, deemed to be there address. The statute establishes criteria for participating in, and removal from the program.[409]

Where a husband filed a divorce complaint, he was unable to verify the wife's address for service of process due to an active domestic violence restraining order entered against him. The court did not give the defendant the address and provided that service must be effectuated by forwarding a copy of the summons and complaint, along with the order therein, via certified mail, by a representative of the court's domestic violence unit to the wife at her last address of record.[410] The court further stated:

> If service via certified mail is effectuated... the case may continue accordingly. Alternatively, if the domestic violence unit is unable to serve or otherwise contact wife, ...the unit will notify the court to determine any future additional action to effectuate alternate substitute service of the divorce complaint.[411]

---

[409] *N.J.S.A.* 47:4-1 to -6.
[410] *J.C. v. M.C.*, 438 *N.J. Super.* 325, 335, 103 *A.3d* 318 (App. Div. 2013).
[411] *Ibid.*

CHAPTER NINE

RELIEF THAT CAN BE GRANTED UNDER THE ACT

9.1   RELIEF UNDER THE ACT, GENERALLY

Following a hearing, and a finding of domestic violence, the court may issue an order granting any or all of the following relief, including any relief "necessary to prevent further abuse," under *N.J.S.A.* 2C:25-29(b).

(1) Barring the defendant from purchasing, owning, possessing or controlling a firearm and from receiving or retaining a firearms purchaser identification card or permit to purchase a handgun pursuant to during the period in which the restraining order is in effect, or two years whichever is greater...*N.J.S.A.* 2C:25-29(b).

(2) Restraining defendant from subjecting the victim to further domestic violence. *N.J.S.A.* 2C:25-29(b)(1)

(3) Exclusive possession of household, regardless of whether the residence or household is jointly or solely owned by the parties or jointly or solely leased by the parties. *N.J.S.A.* 2C:25-29(b)(2)

> (a) If it is not possible for the victim to remain in the residence, the court may order the defendant to pay the victim's rent at a residence other than the one previously shared by the parties if the defendant is found to have a duty to support the victim and the victim requires alternative housing [*Note: In-house restraining orders are specifically prohibited. N.J.S.A. 2C:25-28.1*]

(4) Parenting Time and Risk Assessments. Orders for parenting time must include the place and frequency of parenting time. The Orders may include a designation of a place of parenting time away from the plaintiff, the participation of a third party, or supervised parenting time. *N.J.S.A.* 2C:25-29(b)(3). The court shall consider a request by a custodial parent who has been the victim of domestic violence, for an investigation or evaluation (of the defendant/dv perpetrator), by the appropriate agency to assess the risk of harm to the child prior to the entry of a parenting time order. The custodial parent can also request an assessment of risk of harm to the child or children posed by unsupervised parenting time with the defendant prior to the entry of an order for parenting time.

(5) Compensatory payment for losses suffered as a direct result of the act of domestic violence, which shall include, but are not limited to:

Loss of Earnings or other support
Child and spousal support
Out-of-pocket losses for injuries sustained or any other Medical Expenses
Cost of repair or replacement of damaged or destroyed real or personal property
Cost of counseling for the victim
Moving or travel expenses
Reasonable attorney's fees
Court costs
Compensation for pain and suffering
Punitive Damages may be awarded in addition for compensatory damages.

[*N.J.S.A.* 2C:25-29(b)(4)]

(6) Professional counseling for defendant. A court may order the defendant to receive professional domestic violence counseling from either a private or court-appointed source, and pay for same. *N.J.S.A.* 2C:25-29(b)(5).

(7) Restraining the defendant from certain locations, including the residence, property, school, or place of employment of the victim or other family or household members of the victim and requiring the defendant to stay away from any specified place that is named in the order and is frequented regularly by the victim or other family or household members. *N.J.S.A.* 2C:25-29(b)(6)

(8) Restraining the defendant from making contact with the plaintiff or others, such as their family, household members, employers, employees or fellow workers.
This restraint forbids the defendant from directly or through an agent, initiating any communication likely to cause annoyance or alarm including, but not limited to, personal, written, or telephone contact with the victim or other family members, or their employers, employees, or fellow workers, or others with whom communication would be likely to cause annoyance or alarm to the victim. *N.J.S.A.* 2C:25-29(b)(7).

(9) Requiring the defendant to pay or continue to pay rent or mortgage payments on the residence occupied by the victim if the defendant is found to have a duty to support the victim or other dependent household members... *N.J.S.A.* 2C:25-29(b)(8).

(10) Granting either party temporary possession of specified property, such as an automobile, checkbook, documentation of health insurance, an identification document, a key, and other personal effects.

(11) Awarding emergency monetary relief, such as support for minor children, to the victim, and other dependents, if any. Any ongoing obligation of support is to be determined at a later time. N.J.S.A.2C:25-29(b)(10).

(12) Awarding temporary custody of a minor child, based on the best interest standard, favoring the non-abusive parent. *N.J.S.A.* 2C:25-29(b)(11).

(13) Requiring a law enforcement officer to accompany either party to the residence, or a shared business premises and supervise the removal of personal belongings, so as to ensure personal safety of the victim, where a restraining order has been issued. *N.J.S.A.* 2C:25-29(b)(12).

(14) Granting other appropriate relief for the plaintiff and dependent children, so long as plaintiff consents to such relief, including relief requested by the plaintiff at the final hearing, regardless of whether or not the plaintiff requested such relief at the time of the plenary hearing. *N.J.S.A.* 2C:25-29(b)(14).

(15) Requiring the defendant to report to the intake unit of the Family Division of the Chancery Division of the Superior Court, for monitoring adherence to any provision of the order. *N.J.S.A.* 2C:25-29(b)(15).

(16) Requiring the defendant to undergo a psychiatric evaluation. *N.J.S.A.* 2C:25-29(b)(18).

(17) Prohibiting the defendant from possessing any other weapon enumerated in N.J.S.A.2C:39-1(r), and ordering the search for and seizure of any firearm or other weapon at any location where the judge has reasonable cause to believe the weapon is located. *N.J.S.A.* 2C:25-29(b)(16).

(18) Prohibiting the defendant from stalking or following, or threatening to harm, to stalk or to follow, the complainant or any other person named in the order in a manner that, taken in the context of past actions of the defendant, would put the complainant in reasonable fear that the defendant would cause the death or injury of the complainant or any other person. *N.J.S.A.* 2C:25-29(b)(17).

(Note: See also Relief Under the Act Chapter 2.6 and 10.7)

CHAPTER TEN

PLENARY HEARING AND HEARING FACTORS [412]

10.1 HISTORY

In 1991, the Legislature declared domestic violence a serious crime against society. It found that thousands of people within the State were regularly beaten, tortured and in some cases killed by their spouses or cohabitants. The Legislature also found that many of the existing criminal statues were applicable to acts of domestic violence; however societal attitudes concerning domestic violence affected how law enforcement and judicial systems responded to same. As a result, acts received different treatment from similar crimes when they occurred in a domestic violence setting. In response, the Legislature necessitated the training requirements for police and judicial personnel in the procedure and enforcement of this act.

The New Jersey Domestic Violence Act provides for two forms of relief to a victim of domestic violence, consisting of civil and criminal relief.

In 1994, substantial amendments were made to the act. One of the changes provided for the hearing on domestic violence to be held in the county where the *ex parte* restraints were ordered, unless good cause was shown for the hearing to be held elsewhere. Another amendment required that the court consider requests made by the custodial parent, who was subjected to domestic violence by a person with visitation rights, for an assessment of "risk of harm" to a child prior to entering a visitation order. Previously this risk assessment could only be made by a plaintiff.

Further changes provided for the inclusion of additional relief in the form of compensatory losses, child or spousal support, and costs for the repair or replacement of property taken or destroyed by the defendant. The revision also included emergency support for minor children in orders awarding emergency monetary relief, as well as authorizing a law enforcement officer to accompany either party to supervise removal of personal belongings to them, including personal belongings at shared business premises.

The amendments additionaly authorized the court to issue an order restraining the defendant from making contact with the plaintiff, including any personal communication or communication to any agent if it was likely to alarm or annoy.

---

[412] *N.J.S.A.* 2C:25-27.

The revisions further authorized the search and seizure of weapons under specific conditions set forth, as well as allowing the court to order defendant to undergo a psychiatric evaluation.

10.2   TEMPORARY RESTRAINING ORDERS/INITIAL PROCEEDINGS

In each county there are designated domestic violence professionals who are instructed to interview each individual in a domestic violence matter, get a brief synopsis of the underlying events, and the relief sought.

In most counties, both parties will be instructed to fill out rudimentary financial sheets, so that the judge has some idea of the financial circumstances of the parties and what interim support they would be able to give, in the event restraints are granted.

Upon application for a Temporary Restraining Order (TRO), and after hearing testimony from the victim, the judge will issue or deny the TRO, setting forth the reasons therein. Where granted, the Order must be completed and signed by the judge. Copies shall be served upon, (1) the victim; (2) The law enforcement agency of the municipality in which the victim resides or is sheltered; and (3) the law enforcement agency which will serve the defendant with the Complaint/TRO.

In the event the judge grants the TRO, a return date for the Final Hearing is to be set within ten (10) days. The final hearing must be scheduled within ten days of the filing of the Complaint/TRO in the county where the Complaint/TRO was ordered, unless good cause is shown for the hearing to be held elsewhere. *N.J.S.A.* 2C:25-29 and *N.J. Ct. Rule* 5:7A.

A Domestic Violence matter may be transferred between vicinages by order of the presiding judge or his or her designee in the following situations:

1. Plaintiff or defendant works in family court in the original county of venue, consistent with the judiciary "Policy and Procedures for Reporting Involvement in Criminal/Quasi- Criminal Matters";

2. There is an FM or FD matter pending in the other county(In this situation, one party could then move for consolidation to have the matter heard in the county in which the matrimonial action is pending);

3. The filing of the TRO and FRO are where the act(s) occurred but plaintiff or both parties reside in another county, upon application by either party;

4. Such other matters for good cause shown.

At times, when a party has not been successful in the matrimonial county, they will go forum shopping in another county, seeking to gain an advantage. In other instances, one party may believe that the judge knows too much about the case or the individual, and may be looking for a fresh/unbiased judge in another county. In either situation, a motion can be made by simply writing a letter to the judge in the county you wish to have the domestic violence case transferred to, setting forth the reasons for the transfer, with a copy to the judge in the county that the domestic violence case is currently before. In accordance with human nature, in most instances, if a judge is given an excuse to transfer a case and lighten their caseload, they will likely grant the motion.

10.3   APPEALS OF AN EX-PARTE RESTRAINING ORDER

Any TRO is immediately appealable by plaintiff or defendant for a plenary hearing de novo, before any Superior Court, Family Division Judge in the county where the TRO was entered if that judge issued the temporary order or has access to the reasons for the issuance of the TRO and sets forth on the record the reason for the modification or dissolution. *N.J.S.A.* 2C:25-28(i). See Appendix N.

When presented with a request for an emergent appeal, the court staff is to obtain the reasons for the request of appeal and assist the appealing party in completing the "Appeal of Ex Parte Order," and present the request along with the file to the judge for consideration.

If the application is granted, an emergent hearing will be scheduled where there has been adequate notice provide to both parties, regarding the purpose of the hearing and the issues to be addressed.

At this appeal of the TRO, the judge may continue, modify or dissolve the TRO, and must place the reasons for doing so on the record. Where the application is denied, the reasons shall be set forth by the judge on the "Appeal of Ex Parte Order" form and the FRO hearing will proceed as initially scheduled.

If both parties appear for the plenary hearing, are prepared, and agree to proceed, the court may simultaneously proceed with the appeal and the final hearing in one proceeding.

The court may grant an adjournment or issue a continuance if either party requests an adjournment in order to obtain or consult with an attorney, secure witnesses, or other good cause, unless the delay would create an extreme hardship on the other party, or there has been an inordinate delay in seeking counsel.[413]

---

[413] *State of New Jersey Domestic Violence Procedural Manual*, p. IV-12.

10.4   NON APPEARANCE BY EITHER PARTY

If no one appears for the final hearing, the court shall attempt to contact the parties and find out the reasons for the non-appearance, presenting this information to the court for consideration prior to the dismissal of any Order. Where there is no appearance by either party, the matter shall be rescheduled unless the court is fully satisfied that a dismissal meets the standards set forth on the Order of Dismissal

If a Plaintiff does not appear, all efforts should be made to contact the plaintiff to determine the reason for the non-appearance. If only the defendant appears, the Manual instructs that the defendant shall be brought into the court room and questioned on the record, under oath, concerning the reasons for the plaintiff's failure to appear, and whether or not the defendant caused or is responsible for the non appearance.

If the plaintiff can be contacted, and after hearing both parties' explanations, the judge is satisfied that the plaintiff's failure to appear was not the result of coercion and/or duress, and that the plaintiff is not in danger of subsequent acts of violence committed by the defendant, an order of dismissal can be given. If not, or if the plaintiff cannot be contacted, the matter shall be rescheduled.

Where a plaintiff is unable to appear at the final hearing for good cause shown, arrangements shall be made for a telephonic appearance on the record.

The courts are also instructed not to issue a warrant to compel the presence of a plaintiff in court under any circumstances when the Plaintiff has failed to appear in court, or has allowed the defendant back in the home.

If only the plaintiff appears, the plaintiff's request for relief should be identified in accordance with the domestic violence procedures.

Where the defendant does not appear at the final hearing, and proof of service is provided, the court should conduct the final hearing and may enter a final default order. In appropriate cases, the court may also issue a bench warrant for defendant's non-appearance. [414]

If alternatively, the court file does not contain proof of service, the court should conduct a hearing, questioning the plaintiff as to:

---

[414] *State of New Jersey Domestic Violence Procedural Manual*, p. IV-11.

- Whether the plaintiff has seen the defendant in the court house or knows of the defendant's whereabouts;

- Whether the plaintiff is aware of whether the defendant was served and the basis for such knowledge;

- Whether the defendant has had any contact with the plaintiff since execution of the temporary restraining order; and

- Whether the same or different conditions exist in comparison to those at the time of the initial hearing;

- That the continuance of the restraint is necessary and that there is still a good cause to believe the life, health and well-being of the plaintiff is endangered by the defendant;

- The basis for each and every form of relief sought by the plaintiff.

If the court determines that the defendant had actual knowledge of the restraining order and hearing date, and states these finding on the record, the court may conduct the final hearing and may enter a final order by default.

If the court determines that the defendant has not been served, but finds there is reasonable likelihood of service on the defendant within a reasonable amount of time (e.g. the defendant's address is known, but they are on a business trip), a short postponement should be granted and a final hearing date scheduled, which is to be memorialized in a Continuance Order, or Amended TRO. The Continuance Order shall be served on the defendant with the Complaint/TRO. The court will continue the Temporary Restraining Order until specifically superseded by a further order of the court, and upon service on defendant being effectuated.

Where the plaintiff/appellant filed a domestic violence complaint against the defendant, and subsequently received his cross complaint alleging domestic violence against her on the day of the hearing, the court proceeded to hear the action. The Plaintiff was found guilty of domestic violence and the Defendant was acquitted. The court determined that each side had a full opportunity at the hearing to present a version of the critical events. Further, the court found that appellant was prepared for the hearing, and did not request a postponement.[415]

---

[415] *Mann v. Mann*, 270 *N.J. Super.* 269, 637 *A.2d* 170 (App. Div. 1993).

In another case where Plaintiff filed for domestic violence, the trial judge found that the plaintiff had also committed acts of violence against the defendant, and that defendant was a "victim" within the meaning of *N.J.S.A.* 2C:25-3(e), despite the fact that Defendant never filed a counterclaim.[416]

Where a Plaintiff filed a domestic violence complaint, alleging that her boyfriend slapped her, spit on her, made harassing phone calls, and threatened to kill her, a hearing was conducted and her complaint was dismissed. Several months later, plaintiff filed a second complaint under the Act, when defendant left a note on her car, indicating he would like to talk to Plaintiff. A different trial court granted plaintiff's request for a restraining order against defendant, after plaintiff told the court about events surrounding her first complaint. The decision was reversed since the defendant's action of leaving the note on plaintiff's car was not a violation of the Act, and more importantly because the trial court had made its decision based on a course of conduct that was not mentioned in the second complaint, which is a fundamental violation of due process. The Defendant could not be prepared to defend himself against charges that were not alleged until the day of the hearing. [417]

Note: When the allegations in the plaintiff's complaint are incomplete and/or at the final hearing the plaintiff seeks a restraining order based upon acts outside the complaint, the court, either on its own motion or on a party's motion, can amend the complaint to include those acts. Due process mandates that the judge inquire as to whether the defendant needs additional time to prepare in light of the amended complaint. If this is affirmative the judge may grant a brief adjournment where he determines that the defendant did not have adequate notice and needs time to prepare. If an adjournment is granted, a continuance order or an amended TRO shall be entered.

---

[416] *Maksuta v. Higson*, 242 *N.J. Super.* 452, 577 *A.2d* 185 (App. Div. 1990).
[417] *J.F. v. B.K.*, 308 *N.J. Super.* 387, 391, 706 *A.2d* 203 (App. Div. 1998).

10.5   STANDARD OF PROOF

At the hearing the standard for proving the allegations in the complaint is the lowest standard of evidence, the preponderance of the evidence. This standard of proof is applicable in normal civil cases.   Under this standard, the plaintiff, must establish that the desired inference is more probable than not. If the evidence is in equipoise, the burden has not been met. It is often said that the term "preponderance of evidence" means the greater weight of credible evidence in the case. This does not necessarily mean the evidence consists of a greater number of witnesses, etc., but means that evidence which carries the greater convincing power to our minds.[418]

A judge cannot abdicate his decision making role to an expert or other third party. In one case the court stated, "It is apparent from this record that the trial judge was prepared to abdicate his decision making responsibility and adjudicate the matter solely based on the results of a test administered by a court selected polygraph expert. Trial judges have been admonished many times and in various contexts not to abdicate decision making responsibilities to experts." Furthermore, credibility determinations are reserved to the trier of fact, judge or jury, not an expert.[419]

---

[418] *Cvelich v. Erie Railroad Co.*, 120 *N.J.L.* 414, *199 A. 771* (Sup. Ct.), *aff'd.*, 122 *N.J.L.* 26, 4 *A.2d* 271 (E&A 1938), *cert. den.*, 307 *U.S.* 633, 59 *S. Ct.* 1033, 83 *L. Ed.* 1516 (1939); *Rothman v. City of Hackensack*, 1 *N.J. Tax* 438, 441-443 (Tax Ct. 1980), *aff'd.*, 4 *N.J. Tax* 529 (App. Div. 1981); *State v. Lewis*, 67 *N.J.* 47, 49, 335 *A.2d* 12 (1975).

[419] *Capell v. Capell*, 358 *N.J. Super.* 107, 817 *A.2d* 337 (App. Div. 2003).

10.6   HEARING FACTORS

The court in making its determination shall use the following non-exclusive six factors:

> (1)   The previous history of domestic violence between the plaintiff and defendant, including threats, harassment and physical abuse;
> (2) The existence of immediate danger to person or property;
> (3) The financial circumstances of the plaintiff and defendant;
> (4) The best interests of the victim and any child;
> (5) In determining custody and parenting time, the protection of the victim's safety; and
> (6) The existence of a verifiable order of protection from another jurisdiction.

Allegations in a former domestic violence complaint, which was dismissed before reaching a final hearing, are relevant as to whether or not the defendant poses a threat to the public in general or a person or persons in particular, and is admissible in a subsequent domestic violence matter. Any previous history of domestic violence between the plaintiff and the defendant is always relevant.[420]

Prior acts of domestic violence are admissible, even if not subject to an adjudication of domestic violence.[421] But prior acts of domestic violence, which have been litigated and determined in a prior action, are barred by res judicata and collateral estoppel.[422]

Testimony is not limited to acts of domestic violence that fall within the Statute of Limitations.[423]

Two New Jersey courts have held that proof of Battered Women's Syndrome ("BWS") can affect the statue of limitations in civil cases. One Case held that the statute of limitations should be tolled where the plaintiff establishes by medical, psychiatric, or psychological evidence that she suffers from BWS.[424] Another court held that BWS must be treated the same as a continuing tort because it "is the result of a continuing pattern of abuse and violent

---

[420] *State v. Warrick, 283 N.J. Super. 169, 661 A.2d* 335 (App. Div. 1995).

[421] *Roe v. Roe, 253 N.J. Super. 418, 423, 601 A.2d* 1201 (App. Div. 1992).

[422] *State v. Gonzalez,* 75 N.J. 181, 186-87, 380 A.2d 1128 (1977); *Allesandra v. Gross,* 187 N.J. Super. 96, 103, 453 A.2d 904 (App. Div. 1982).

[423] *Cusseux v. Pickett,* 279 N.J. Super. 335, 652 A.2d 789 (Law Div. 1994).

[424] *Giovine v. Giovine,* 284 N.J. Super. 3, 18, 663 A.2d 109 (App. Div. 1995).

behavior that causes continuing damage."[425] In addition, criminal defendants are permitted to admit evidence of BWS in criminal cases to explain their allegedly criminal conduct.

It is important to note that the act prohibits mediation of any kind, on any issue, such as custody or parenting time, in domestic violence cases. *See N.J.S.A.* 2C:25-29(a)(6) and *New Jersey Court Rule* 1:40-5(a).This provision serves to prevent the victim from being exposed to the abuser under the pretext of settling the case or dealing with the children.

After a final hearing is conducted, the court can either enter an FRO, granting the appropriate relief, where there is a finding of domestic violence, or an admission of an act of domestic violence by the defendant. The court may also dismiss the Complaint/TRO and dissolve all restraints if domestic violence has not been established, or where appropriate, adjourn the final hearing and continue the restraints on an interim basis until a final determination can be made.

A Restraining Order will issue where the court finds that the defendant has committed domestic violence (findings must be set forth on the record), or upon admission by the Defendant that he committed the domestic violence. Where there is an admission of domestic violence by the defendant, the following additional requirements must be met:

- The parties must be sworn before any action is taken on the complaint;
- The defendant must provide a factual basis for the admission that an act of domestic violence has occurred; and
- Where it becomes clear that defendant does not agree that the conduct constituted an act of domestic violence, the hearing must proceed.

If there is a pending matrimonial case, under an FM Docket Number, as set forth in Chapter Two, it is possible to dismiss a domestic violence complaint, under the FV Docket Number, and agree to civil restraints in the Family Part Case under the FM Docket Number (Civil Restrains may also be placed in the FD Docket after dismissal of the FV.) It is good practice to enter into a consent order and sign same prior to dismissing the FV matter. Both an FV and FM matter may also proceed simultaneously with restraints and a FRO entered under the FV docket, but all other issues such as support or custody would be handled under the FM Docket.

Occasionally it is necessary to modify an FRO under the FV as things change in an FM. However, if there is a Final Restraining Order entered, FRO, and there is a pending Non-Dissolution Matter, under the FD Docket, with no Orders entered, the FD matter will be

---

[425] *Cusseaux v. Pickett*, 279 *N.J. Super.* 335, 344-45, 652 *A.2d* 789 (Law. Div. 1994).

dismissed and all applications/motions for relief sought shall be made under the FV Docket as long as long as the FV matter is still in effect.[426]

---

[426] *State of New Jersey Domestic Violence Procedural Manual*, p. IV-19 to -20.

10.7   RELIEF UNDER THE ACT

After a hearing has been held, and where there is a finding of domestic violence, the court may issue an order granting any or all of the following relief, including any relief "necessary to prevent further abuse," under *N.J.S.A.* 2C:25-29(b).

(1) RESTRAINING THE DEFENDANT FROM COMMITTING FURTHER ACTS OF DOMESTIC VIOLENCE AGAINST THE VICTIM.

Even though the Domestic Violence Act expressly bars the issuance of a restraining order in the absence of a finding of domestic violence, the court has the authority to issue an order restraining contact between the parties in furtherance of the state's domestic violence laws under its more general, equitable powers.[427]

(2) EXCLUSIVE USE AND POSSESSION OF THE RESIDENCE

The victim may be granted exclusive possession and use of the house where they and the defendant live, regardless of whether the household is jointly or solely owned by the parties or jointly or solely leased by the parties. The order does not however affect title or interest to any real property held by either party or both jointly. This provision aids victims who have felt powerless living in a home titled to the Defendant, who oftentimes believe they have no place to go, since the home was not technically "theirs.

If it is impossible or undesirable for the victim to remain in the residence (ie. the abuser will come back contrary to the restraining order), the court may order the defendant to pay for the costs of alternative housing, if the defendant is found to have a duty to support the victim and the victim requires alternative housing.
N.J.S.A. 2C:25-29(b)(2).

When requesting relief, ensure that the Order is as specific as possible and states everything necessary to ensure the victims safety. For instance, absent a paragraph in the order, specifying that the victim has exclusive use and possession of the house, the court could find that a defendant who visits the home while the wife is away, is not in violation of the Order.

"In-house restraining orders," which allow the victim to cohabit in the same household with the defendant, without having contact with each other, are prohibited under the Act.

---

[427] *P.J.G. v. P.S.S.*, 297 N.J. *Super.* 468, 688 A.2d 630 (App. Div. 1997).

Plaintiff obtained a TRO against the Defendant. In light of the fact that the Plaintiff worked and the Defendant was the primary caretaker for the parties 2 children, the family court awarded temporary custody of the children and exclusive use of the marital home to defendant. On appeal, the Appellate Court found that the trial court erred in granting defendant exclusive possession of the marital home and in granting defendant temporary custody of the couple's two children. The court found that the facts of the case did not justify the transgression from the presumption embodied in *N.J.S.A.* 2C:25-29(b)(11), stating that the best interests of the children were served by an award of custody to the non-abusive parent. In addition, the court held that the facts cannot support an order granting exclusive possession of the marital home to the party guilty of committing domestic abuse.[428]

(3) PARENTING TIME AND RISK ASSESSMENT

In the event restraints are granted, An Order providing for parenting time (visitation) can be established for the defendant to have access to the minor children, unless he or she is a danger to them.

An Order for parenting time shall protect the safety and well-being of the plaintiff and children and shall specify the place and frequency of parenting time. Orders may also include a designation of a place for parenting time, the participation of a third party, or whether supervised is necessary. Parenting time arrangements must not compromise any other remedies provided by the court Order, such as requiring contact between the plaintiff and defendant. [*N.J.S.A.* 2C:25-29(b)(3).]

Usually curbside pickup occurs, so that the parties have no direct contact with each other, assuming the children are old enough to bring themselves from the house to the car. A third party can also act as a go between, possibly by providing an alternative place to pick up or drop off the child(ren). In the worst case situations, pick up/drop off can be done at the local police stations. Such a setting may give the victim a feeling a security, given the police presence. However, this is usually a last resort, since a person would not want to subject their child(ren) to the elements present in a police station. In addition, the police do not like to act as intermediaries and are less then cooperative.

Defendant's request to have visitation with the parties' child at his apartment in Manhattan was not prohibited by the act or *N.J.S.A.* 9:2-2, which prohibits removal of a child from the state. The court found that the prohibition does not apply to temporary departures,

---

[428] *J.D. v. M.A.D.*, 429 *N.J. Super.* 34, 56 *A.3d* 882 (App. Div. 2012).

and that the visitation was in the child's best interest.[429]

RISK ASSESSMENT-*N.J.S.A.* 2C:25-29(b)(3)(a).

A custodial parent, who has been the victim of domestic violence from the person requesting parenting time may request an investigation or evaluation, by the appropriate agency (usually the county probation department), to assess the risk of harm to the child prior to the entry of a parenting time order. Where a request is denied, it must be done on the record and only be if the judge finds the request to be arbitrary or capricious.

During the risk assessment, a court can either suspend visitation or order supervised visitation with the child.[430] The *Prevention of Domestic Violence Act of 1990* provides in pertinent part: "The Court shall consider suspension of the visitation order and hold an emergent hearing upon an application made by the plaintiff certifying under oath that the defendant's access to the child pursuant to the visitation order has threatened the safety and well-being of the child. *L. 1991 c. 261 s.* 13(b)(3)(b)."

Suspension of visitation occurs only in the "most extreme situations where the mere presence of the parent would visit physical or emotional harm upon the child." In all other cases suspension of visitation is improper, and supervised visitation should be ordered. While suspension or supervised visitation may be deemed to infringe upon the freedom of a parent and child to maintain, cultivate, and mold their ongoing relationship, it has been deemed permissible, since the state has compelling interest in protecting the welfare of the subject child(ren).[431]

The statute does not limit risk assessment requests to initial orders. Risk assessment may also be requested in an application to modify a final restraining order that already provides for parenting time, granted there has been a change in circumstance.

A requested risk assessment should be ordered where requested, unless the defendant can show by a preponderance of the evidence that the request is arbitrary and capricious. The defendant thus has the burden of proof. This is due to the following facts: the primary concern in custody and visitation determinations is the well being of the child; policy findings show a "positive correlation between spousal abuse and child abuse; and that children, even when they are not themselves physically assaulted, suffer deep and lasting emotional effects from

---

[429] *Comas v. Comas,* 257 N.J. Super. 585, 608 A.2d at 100 (Ch. Div. 1992).
[430] *Cosme v. Figueroa,* 258 N.J. Super. 333, 609 A.2d 523 (Ch. Div. 1992).
[431] *Ibid.*

exposure to domestic violence;" and because risk assessment does not unduly prejudice the interests of either party and may be an extremely helpful tool in determining visitation disputes.[432]

Arbitrary and capricious means having no rational basis. It can also be defined as willful and unreasoning action, without consideration and in disregard of the circumstances. "Where there is room for two opinions, action is not arbitrary or capricious when exercised honestly and upon due consideration, even though it may be believed that an erroneous conclusion has been reached."[433]

In a case on the issue, the court held that a request for risk assessment could not be deemed arbitrary or capricious since plaintiff cited prescription and non-prescription drug use, excessive video game playing, as well as an injury that occurred to the child while in defendant's care. When making its determinations, the court is required to exercise its discretion in the best interest of the child, and must also be protective of the domestic violence victim.[434]

(4) MONETARY COMPENSATION- COMPENSATORY AND PUNITIVE DAMAGES.

The victim may be awarded monetary support, which comes in many forms. First, the victim may be compensated for losses suffered as a direct result of the act of domestic violence. This includes, but is not limited to:

- Loss of earnings or other support, including child or spousal support;
- Out-of-pocket losses for injuries sustained (includes medical or dental bills, hospital bills, prescription drugs bills, and other out of pocket expenses for injuries sustained);
- Cost of repair or replacement of real or personal property damaged or destroyed or taken by the defendant;
- Cost of counseling for the victim;
- Moving or other travel expenses,
- Reasonable attorney's fees;
- Court costs; and

---

[432] *Cosme v. Figueroa*, 258 *N.J. Super.* 333, 339, 609 *A.2d* 523 (Ch. Div. 1992).

[433] *Bayshore Sew Co. v. Department of Env.*, N.J., 122 *N.J. Super.* 184, 299 *A.2d* 751 (Ch. Div. 1973), *aff'd*, 131 *N.J. Super.* 37 A.2d 246 (App. Div. 1974) (*citing Bicknell v. United States*, 422 *Fed.* 1055, 1057 (5th. Cir. 1970)).

[434] *Lavine v. Lanza*, 429 *N.J. Super.* 164, 57 *A.3d* 62 (Ch. Div. 2012).

- Compensation for pain and suffering.

The order may require the defendant to pay the victim directly, to reimburse the Victim of Crime Compensation Agency for any and all compensation paid by the Victim of Crime Compensation Agency directly to, or on behalf of the victim, and require that the defendant reimburse any parties that may have compensated the victim, as the court may determine.

Each county shall establish procedures for collecting/distributing emergent monetary relief, ordered by the Superior Court or Municipal Court, to ensure special care is taken not to have any contact between the victim and the defendant.

Emergent monetary support may be ordered in an FRO under *N.J.S.A.* 2C:25-29(b) (4) and (10). This includes emergency child support and compensatory losses for child or spousal support. An order for emergency monetary relief or child support or spousal support may be entered without prejudice to a pending dissolution case. Monetary compensation in the form of ongoing support utilizing the child support guidelines, should be issued at the final hearing if the court is able to consider testimony. All child support must be paid via income withholding from any source of funds or income.

Plaintiff brought an action in the law division for damages sustained in a domestic violence case. The Appellate Court ruled that the defendant was not collaterally estopped from challenging the claims in the Law Division, because defendant should have been permitted to defend against plaintiff's allegations.[435]

In the event that the plaintiff has incurred any moving or travel expenses after having fled the residence, in order to protect themselves or their children, these expenses are also to be reimbursed by the defendant.

The Act also provides for payment of attorneys' fees and costs if it can be established that the fees were incurred as a direct result of the domestic violence (*N.J.S.A.* 2C:25-29(b)(4)); the fees are reasonable; and the fees are presented by affidavit pursuant to *N.J. Ct. R.* 4:42-9(b). Since they are viewed as compensatory damages, attorney's fees are not subject to the traditional analysis contained in statute or law.[436-437]

---

[435] *L.T. v. F.M.*, 438 *N.J. Super.* 76, 102 *A.3d* 398 (App. Div. 2014).
[436] *Schmidt v. Schmidt*, 262 *N.J. Super.* 451, 620 A.2d 1388 (Ch. Div. 1992).
[437] *N.J. Ct. R.* 4:42-9 (b); *N.J.S.A.* 2A:34-23; *Williams v. Williams*, 59 *N.J.* 299, 281 *A.2d* 273 (1971); and *N.J. RPC* 1.5 for reasonableness; *Grandovic v. Labrie*, 348 *N.J. Super.* 193, 791 A.2d 1038 (App. Div. 2002).

The reasonableness of attorney's fees is determined by considering several factors. The factors include:

> 1. The time and labor required, the novelty and difficulty of the questions involved, and the skill requisite to perform the legal service properly;
> 2. The likelihood, if apparent to the client, that the acceptance of the particular employment will preclude other employment by the lawyer;
> 3. The fee customarily charged in the locality for similar legal services;
> 4. The amount involved and the results obtained;
> 5. The time limitations imposed by the client or by the circumstances;
> 6. The nature and length of the professional relationship with the client;
> 7. The experience, reputation, and ability of the lawyer performing the services;
> 8. Whether the fee is fixed or contingent.[438]

If the court finds a party filed a domestic violence complaint in bad faith, based on his or her own perjured testimony or suborned perjured testimony, *N.J.S.A.* 2A:15-59.1 (Frivolous Litigation Statute), permits the award of counsel fees in order to punish the filing party and deter the improper conduct of litigation in the future.[439]

An award of counsel fees cannot be made for municipal court actions related to domestic violence, since there is no authority for an award of fees to a complaining witness in a municipal court action. That court also noted that since attorney's fees are expressly included in the Act as compensatory damages, the considerations which apply to an award of counsel's fees in a matrimonial action are inapplicable.[440]

"What factors should be used to make the threshold determination as to whether an attorney's fee should be awarded under the Act? Without holding that *N.J. Ct. R.* 5:3-5 applies to the Act (there are conflicting appellate court holdings), it is interesting to note that the

---

[438] *Schmidt v. Schmidt*, 262 *N. J. Super.* 451, 454-55, 620 A.2d 1388 (Ch. Div. 1992); *see also Grandovic v. Labrie*, 348 *N.J. Super.* 193, 196, 791 *A.2d* 1038 (App. Div. 2002).
[439] *M.W. v. R.L.*, 286 *N.J. Super.* 408, 412, 669 *A.2d* 817 (App. Div. 1999).
[440] *Wine v. Quezada*, 379 *NJ Super.* 287, 877 A.2d 377 (Ch. Div 2005)

aforesaid rule, entitled "Attorney Fees and Retainer Agreements in Civil Family Actions; Withdrawal" allows in subpart (c) for "the court in its discretion" to award attorney's fees *pendente lite* and on final determination.

If discretion is exercised, taking *N.J. Ct. R.* 5:3-5 (c) into account when determining the amount of the fee award, the court will consider the following factors, in addition to the information required to be submitted pursuant to *N.J. Ct. R.* 4:42-9:

> (1) the financial circumstances of the parties; (2) the ability of the parties to pay their own fees or to contribute to the fees of the other party; (3) the reasonableness and good faith of the positions advanced by the parties both during and prior to trial; (4) the extent of the fees incurred by both parties; (5) any fees previously awarded; (6) the amount of fees previously paid to counsel by each party; (7) the results obtained; (8) the degree to which fees were incurred to enforce existing orders or to compel discovery; and (9) any other factor bearing on the fairness of an award.

According to one court, The first three enumerated factors in *N.J. Ct. R.* 5:3-5(c) seek out the information that is necessary for the threshold determination as to whether discretion should be exercised or not in favor of a fee award under *N.J.S.A.* 2C:25-29(b); that is to say, the plaintiff's need, ability to pay, and the good faith of parties in advancing positions should be the cornerstone. If the trial court, in weighing those factors, determines that an award of fees would be appropriate, then attention should be turned to reasonableness of the fee award under *N.J. Ct. R.* 4:42-9(b) and *N.J. R. Prof. Conduct* 1.5(a). Considering the above factors, and finding that the defendant acted in bad faith during the proceedings leading up to and subsequent to the Final Restraining Order being entered (defendant necessitated additional court appearances, caused by the significant delay in the proceedings), the court ordered attorneys fees in favor of the Plaintiff.[441]

Other Appellate courts have disagreed with the approach used in *Pullen*, specifically, Pamula and McGowan, which state that an award of attorneys' fees in a domestic violence matter is governed solely by the factors enumerated in *N.J. Ct. R.* 4:42-9(b) and not by those set forth in *N.J. Ct. R.* 5:3-5(c).[442]

Due process does not require the appointment of counsel for indigents "presenting or defending a private party's civil domestic violence action."[443] Compare this with another case where the court appointed an attorney to represent the plaintiff interest in a domestic violence

---

[441] *Pullen v. Pullen*, 365 *N.J. Super.* 623, 839 *A.2d* 1006 (App. Div. 2003).

[442] *McGowan v. O'Rourke*, 391 *N.J. Super.* 502, 918 *A.2d* 716 (App. Div. 2007)

[443] *D.N. v. K.M.*, 216 *N.J.* 587, 83 *A.3d* 825 (App. Div. 2014).

matter.[444]

PUNITIVE DAMAGES:

The Domestic Violence Act provides that where appropriate, punitive damages may be awarded in addition to compensatory damages. Whether or not an award for punitive damages is appropriate lies within the discretion of the judge.[445]

In order to warrant an award of punitive damages, the defendant's conduct must have been wantonly reckless or malicious. There must be intentional wrongdoing in the sense of an "evil-minded act," or an act that is accompanied by a wanton and willful disregard of the rights of another. Moreover:

> The prerequisite for punitive damages may be satisfied upon a showing that there has been a deliberate act or omission with knowledge of a high degree of probability of harm and reckless indifference to consequences. The requirement is defined as not only ill will, or some wrongful motive, implying a willingness or intent to injure but also such a want of feeling as to impute a bad motive. Something more than the mere commission of an intentional tort is required. The key to the right to punitive damages is the wrongfulness of the intentional act. The right to award exemplary damages primarily rests upon the single ground-wrongful motive.[446]

The purpose of punitive damages is to punish a defendant for wrongful, malicious or particularly egregious conduct," to deter such conduct in the future," and to vindicate the rights of a party.[447]

It has been established that punitive damages may be assessed regardless of whether or not compensatory damages are awarded. Thus, if there are no actual damages, and nominal damages are awarded, punitive damages can be used to compensate the plaintiff and punish the defendant.[448]

---

[444] *J.L. v. G.D.*, 422 *N.J. Super.* 487, 29 *A.3d* 752 (Ch. Div. 2010).

[445] *Reeves v. Reeves*, 265 *N.J. Super.* 126, 625 *A.2d* 589 (App. Div. 1993).

[446] *Sielski v. Sielski*, 254 *N.J. Super.* 686, 604 *A.2d* 206 (Ch. Div. 1992).

[447] *Belinski v. Goodman*, 139 *N.J. Super.* 351, 359, 354 A.2d 92 (App. Div. 1976); *Winkler v. Hartford Acc. And Ind. Co.*, 66 *N.J. Super.* 22, 29, 168 *A.2d* 418 (App. Div. 1961).

[448] *Nappe v. Anschelewitz, Barr, Ansell & Bonello*, 97 *N.J.* 37, 477 A.2d 1224 (1984).

The more egregious conduct is, even where it only generates minimal compensatory damages, can result in the award of higher punitive damages, in comparison to cases where substantial compensatory damages are awarded.[449]

In determining the amount of punitive damages, the defendant's finances are important (discovery at the proper time can be made of their finances), so the judge can determine whether this award will serve as a punishment and a deterrent for the defendant.[450]

There are no steadfast rules of thumb, charts or calculations that can be easily followed in order to assess the amount of a punitive damages award. Despite the lack of any clear standard, cases have held that the amount must have some reasonable relation to the injury suffered. A sprained finger would not result in a million dollars worth of punitive damages, but wiretapping of the spouse's phone, and the dissemination of the information contained therein, although perhaps only resulting in nominal damages to the plaintiff, could result in $100,000 worth of punitive damages.[451]

In the *Sileski* case, the Court awarded punitive damages in the amount of $5,000, emphasizing that the brutality of the assault and the torture committed by the defendant deserved significant punitive damages, so as to deter this defendant from repeating such violent behavior.

In this case, the defendant entered Plaintiff's home without her permission, proceeded to her bedroom where plaintiff was in bed, and pulled the plaintiff out of her bed by her hair, punching her about her head. The defendant then ripped plaintiff's clothes off and pulled her to the bathroom where he unsuccessfully attempted to push her head in the toilet. Defendant next filled a waste basket with water and threw the water in plaintiff's face. Subsequent to leaving the bathroom, the defendant started to torture plaintiff by grabbing her pubic hair and twisting/pulling at that area. Defendant then grabbed a lamp and threw it. Lastly, the defendant pulled the wire out of the phone so that plaintiff could not call the police.

The court found:

> The Defendant committed these acts without a legal provocation
> or justification; his only conceivable purpose was to intentionally

---

[449] *Fischer v. Johns-Manville Corp.*, 103 N.J. 643, 512 A.2d 466 (1986).
[450] *Fischer v. Johns-Manville Corp.*, 103 N.J. 643, 669, 512 A.2d 466 (1986).
[451] *Fischer v. Johns-Manville Corp.*, 103 N.J. 643, 673, 512 A.2d 466 (1986).

and maliciously torture plaintiff; the defendant's actions satisfy the requirements for the imposition of punitive damages under all the relevant cases; his actions were done with the knowledge of, and indifference to the harmful consequences, reflected " such a want of feeling so as to impute a bad motive, and clearly represent a wrongful intentional act; and his conduct clearly represented a wrongful intentional act.[452]

In another case, the Appellate court mandated the trial court to reconsider the punitive damages award because separate amounts were assessed against defendant for each of the many acts of domestic violence, all but one of which took place before the effective date of the amendment. The court stated that on remand, the judge may award punitive damages only with respect to the August 31, 1994 act of domestic violence. The trial judge was not bound by his prior itemization but could increase the punitive damages award for the post amendment incidents to reflect the history of domestic violence between the parties providing that the aggregate of the award did not exceed the original award of $5,875.00.[453]

Failure to set forth a domestic tort claims (monetary damage for injuries) at domestic violence trial does not bar plaintiff from bringing a later action in the matrimonial case. The claim that would be made in the matrimonial proceeding is commonly known as a *Tevis* claim.[454]

The Court refused to narrowly apply the Entire Controversy Doctrine which requires that the adjudication of a legal controversy should occur in one litigation in only one court; accordingly, all parties involved in a litigation should at the very least present in that proceeding all of their claims and defenses that are related to the underlying controversy. *See* Comment, *The Entire Controversy Doctrine: A Novel Approach to Judicial Efficiency,* 12 *Seton Hall L.Rev.* 260 (1982) to preclude the later bringing of the Act and noted:

> To construe the Act any other way would be to frustrate the Legislature's purpose of providing emergent but comprehensive relief. The words of the statute must be considered in the context of the entire Act and given a common sense meaning which advances the Legislative purpose.[455]

---

[452] *Sielski v. Sielski,* 254 *N.J. Super.* 686, 604 *A.2d* 206 (Ch. Div. 1992).

[453]*D.C. v. F.R.,* 286 *N.J. Super.* 502, 608, 670 *A.2d* 51 (App. Div. 1996).

[454]*Tevis v. Tevis,* 79 *N.J.* 422, 400 *A.2d* 1189 (1979).

[455]*Lickfield v. Lickfield,* 260 *N.J. Super.* 21, 24, 614 *A.2d* 1365 (Ch. Div. 1992).

(5) PROFESSIONAL DOMESTIC VIOLENCE COUNSELING

Under the act, the defendant may be ordered to undergo professional domestic violence counseling from either a private or court appointed source. Where so ordered, the court has the discretion to require the defendant to provide the court with documentation of attendance. The defendant is responsible with paying for the professional counseling specified herein. [*N.J.S.A.* 2C:25-29(b)(5).]

(6) RESTRAINTS FROM SPECIFIED LOCATIONS

The defendant may be restrained from entering the residence, property, school, or place of employment of the victim, or any of the victim's family or household member(s). A restraining Order may also require the defendant to stay away from any specified place that is named in the order and is frequented regularly by the victim or other family or household members. [*N.J.S.A.* 2C:25-29(b)(6).]

The restraining Order should include (where appropriate) specific names and addresses of the locations from which the defendant is barred and the people that the defendant is restrained from contacting, communicating with, harassing, or stalking.

Note: A victim is not required to disclose their address or place of employment nor shall the court require such disclosure on the record.

The Court cannot banish the abuser from the State of New Jersey.[456]

In a case where the defendant and plaintiff were divorced, the plaintiff/ mother refused to give defendant the address and/or telephone number to where she and the son were staying. The mother subsequently filed a domestic violence complaint which was dismissed, and later applied for entry into the Address Confidentiality Program ("ACP") which was accepted.[457]

The Supreme Court's decision stated, the Address Confidentiality Program ("ACP") is a program that the Legislature provided as an additional measure of protection for abuse victims. A prior domestic violence restraining order is not necessary to qualify for ACP protection. The program can be utilized as a stand-alone remedy" or as a resource in a judicial proceeding

---

[456] *State v. J.F.*, 262 *N.J. Super.* 539, 621 *A.2d* 520 (App. Div. 1993).
[457] *Sacharow v. Sacharow*, 177 *N.J.* 62, 826 *A.2d* 710 (2003).

where address confidentiality is warranted by the conduct of a domestic abuser." Since the ACP does not involve notice, a hearing, or a merits determination, courts are not bound by ACP action. In each case court are free to decide whether or not it is necessary for the address to remain confidential, based on the record before it and on any binding prior adjudications on the subject. When child custody and visitation are in issue, the best interests of the child are always the primary focus of the inquiry.

(7) RESTRAINTS FROM CONTACT

Restraints can be put in place against the defendant, restraining them from making contact with the plaintiff or others. This includes an order forbidding the defendant from personally or through an agent, initiating any communication likely to cause annoyance or alarm including, but not limited to, personal, written, or telephone contact with the victim or additional family members, their employers, employees, co-workers, or additional persons with whom communication would likely to cause annoyance or alarm to the victim. [*N.J.S.A.* 2C:25-29(b)(7).]

If a restraining order does not specifically prohibit a defendant from being in the same public place at the same time as a plaintiff, then such conduct is not prohibited.[458]

> The court concluded the existing provisions of the parties' restraining order preclude the simultaneous presence of Finamore and Aronson at the child's school or activities. In fact it does not. The restraining order in this case prohibits contact and communication by Finamore with Aronson at all times; however, the trial court's presumption that the restraints in the domestic violence order restricted Finamore from any area Aronson might be, is error.[459]

In another case, the court held it cannot prohibit the defendant's parents from having contact with the plaintiff or her family, even though they were embroiled in the dispute, so long as there was no complaint filed against them. The parents were not a party to the suit and had no opportunity to file answering pleadings, present witnesses on their behalf, cross examine plaintiff's witnesses or enjoy separate legal representation; thus no orders may be directed to the parents. The Court believed that the plaintiff was sufficiently protected by an order "forbidding the defendant from personally or through an agent initiating any communication

---

[458] *Finamore v. Aronson*, 382 *N.J. Super.* 514, 516, 889 *A.2d* 1114 (App. Div. 2006).
[459] *Ibid.*

likely to cause annoyance or alarm...,"[460] and such indirect restraint also comports with *N.J. Ct. R.* 4:52-4 which provides that restraints are binding not only upon parties to the action but also upon "such of their officers, agents, employees, attorneys, and upon such persons in act of concert or participation with them as to receive actual notice of the order by personal service or otherwise."[461]

After a stalking and harassment conviction, the defendant was ordered to move out of his house, which was in the same neighborhood as plaintiff's, based upon the finding that his purpose in moving there was to continue his conduct of harassment. The court stated that the remedies under the Act are liberally construed for the protection and safety of the victims and the public at large. The court further stated that it could look beyond the four walls of a victim's residence. Referencing other cases, the court pointed out that where parties lived in different houses in the same neighborhood or separate apartments in the same apartment complex, they were deemed as part of the same household for purposes of The Act.[462]

In *N.G. v. J.P,* the Defendant was found guilty of domestic violence and an FRO was issued, prohibiting him from living in the same township as the Plaintiff. Defendant appealed and the Appellate Court affirmed the issuance of the ban, preventing the defendant from, entering the town; however, the court remanded the case to the Family Part for the purpose of "entertaining defendant's request for a narrowing of the ban on his entry into the confines of the township."[463]

(8) RENT OR MORTGAGE PAYMENTS

The court can order the defendant to pay the victim monies that are necessary to make rent or mortgage payments, either at the residence they are presently occupying or for another residence to which they have to move. This requirement is only imposed if the defendant already had a duty to support the victim, and where the issue has not been resolved or is not being litigated between the parties in another action. [*N.J.S.A.* 2C:25-29(b)(8).] Thus, if the parties were not married, and there was a different relationship between them other than husband and wife, and this issue is not being litigated or resolved, this remedy could not be ordered.

---

[460] *N.J.S.A.* 2C:25-29(b)(7).

[461] *D.C. v. F.R.*, 286 *N.J. Super.* 502, 609, 670 *A.2d* 51 (App. Div. 1996).

[462] *Zappaunbulso v. Zappaunbulso,* 367 *N.J. Super.* 216, 842 *A.2d* 300 (App Div 2004)(*citing Storch v. Sauerhoff*, 334 *N.J. Super.* 226, 230, 757 *A.2d* 836 (Ch. Div. 2000); *South v. North*, 304 *N.J. Super.* 104, 114, 698 *A.2d* 553 (Ch. Div. 1997).

[463] *N.G. v. J.P.*, 426 *N.J. Super.* 398, 45 *A.3d* 371 (App. Div. 2012).

(9) POSSESSION OF PERSONAL PROPERTY

When victims are forced to flee the marital home, they leave behind most of their personal belongings, leaving the defendant to take control of same. In other instances, where the defendant leaves the home, they will often take personal property because they realize they may not have access to same. Due to the likely scenarios, the Act provides that Orders may be allowed, granting either party temporary possession of specified property, such as an automobile, checkbook, documentation of health insurance, an identification document, a key, and other personal effects.

(10) SUPPORT FOR VICTIM AND MINOR CHILDREN

An order may also be granted, providing emergency monetary relief, including emergency support for the children, the victim, and other dependents, if any. Any ongoing obligation of support will be determined at a later date under the applicable law. [*N.J.S.A. 2C:25-29(b)(10)*.]

The granting of the relief to a victim is meant to be only temporary because the Court does not have before it all the requisite information it would need, including Case Information Statements of parties, sworn certifications, income tax returns, and other financial documentation that would normally be produced in a matrimonial proceeding.

Economic dependence on a domestic violence perpetrator is one of the single most important reasons why victims stay is volatile households. The Legislature did not intend victims of domestic violence to be discouraged from making complaints, where there is such a threat of financial distress. Therefore they provided that financial assistance must be readily available so the abused woman has the option to leave.[464]

This support order is only intended to bridge the emergent situation, and not to be a substitute for more orderly procedures for support.[465] If the parties were married there will be either reconciliation of the parties, disposing of financial distribution issues, or the filing for divorce, wherein the matter could be litigated properly. If in fact the parties were not married, either a child support application (if applicable) could be applied for, or in rare instances, a palimony suit in which temporary support would be sought.

---

[464] *New Jersey Advisory Committee to the United States Commission on Civil Rights, Battered Women in New Jersey*, 26 (1981) (a report employed by the Legislature in drafting *N.J.S.A.* 2C:25-13(b); *see Senate Judiciary Committee of New Jersey, Statement to Senate Committee Substitute for S. No.* 3127 (1981)).

[465] *Mugan v. Mugan*, 231 *N.J. Super.* 31, 555 *A.2d* 2 (App. Div. 1989).

A domestic violence proceeding does not create support obligations which did not exist beforehand. Thus if a person is not entitled to specific support under existing law, the act does not create a new category of support.[466]

Where the parties were not married, just cohabitants, a court held that they "were not entitled to alimony or equitable distribution," and any support orders must be temporary.[467] Contrast this with the wording of the Statute which refers not to "spousal support", but to support of the victim or "other dependants", which might open up other claims.

A spousal support order entered in an emergent situation without detailed evaluation of the financial resources or circumstances of the parties remains in full force and effect unless vacated or amended. Such an Order is not automatically canceled after a period of time. "It is incumbent upon a party against whom an order is entered to take some affirmative step to deal with it, either by discharging the obligation or by moving for relief from the order. The initiative must be taken by the party against whom the order runs." Delay in enforcement does not constitute a waiver of the right to enforce even 6 years later. The support order will continue even if not enforced, or not paid, unless the defendant moves for affirmative relief dissolving the order.[468]

It is better practice to file a separate child support application under the "FD" or "FM" docket in light of the fact that the domestic violence orders are temporary orders, which do not fully consider and explore all of the relevant factors. These orders are expected to change by virtue of the parties' acts, ie., reconciliation. A decision of the Domestic Violence Court as to support is not *res judicata* on subsequent awards.[469]

A judge in a domestic violence case is not limited to awarding future support, but could make the award retroactive.[470]

(11) TEMPORARY CUSTODY OF A MINOR CHILD

Temporary custody can be awarded to either party, but the Legislature has made it clear

---

[466] *Maksuta v. Higson*, 242 *N.J. Super.* 452, 577 *A.2d* 185 (App. Div. 1990); see also *Mugan v. Mugan*, 231 *N.J. Super.* 31, 555 *A.2d* 2 App. Div. 1989).

[467] *Ibid.*

[468] *Federow v. Federow*, 256 *N.J. Super.* 75, 606 *A.2d* 415 (App. Div. 1992), *reversing, Hayes v. Hayes*, 251 *N.J. Super.* 160, 597 *A.2d* 567 (Ch. Div. 1991).

[469] *Hayes v. Hayes*, 251 *N.J. Super.* 160, 163, 597 *A.2d* 567 (Ch. Div. 1991).

[470] *Brazzel v. Brazzel*, 345 *N.J. Super.* 19, 783 *A.2d* 257 (App. Div. 2001).

in one of the preambles to this Act that they believe that the best interest of the child(ren) are served by an award of custody to the non-abusive parent. [*N.J.S.A.* 2C:25-29(b)(11).]

(12) POLICE TO ACCOMPANY REMOVAL OF PERSONALITY

In the event that the defendant is found guilty of domestic violence and removed from the home, or the plaintiff has fled the home and does not intend to return, the Act requires that the police accompany either party to the residence, or to any shared business premise, to supervise the removal of personal belongings, in order to ensure the personal safety of the plaintiff when a restraining order has been issued. This order shall be restricted in duration. [*N.J.S.A.* 2C:25-29(b)(12).]

The police departments loathe this duty and are usually not the most cooperative in effectuating this provision. The Act itself provides that this duty on the part of the police officer is restricted in duration, accordingly, the police will not wait for long periods, or go back more than once.

If you represent the client who maintains the residence, it is good practice for you to communicate to them ahead of time, which items the other party is requesting; and have your client <u>neatly</u> pack the specified items. This will lessen the amount of time that the other party must spend in the home. The more time the other party spends in the home, they will be more inclined to remember other items they would like to take.

Personal items which are encompassed by this section include things such as clothing, personal jewelry, and other items that the removed party needs in order to function outside of the marital home. Not included are items such as television sets, DVD players or bedroom sets, which can only be taken with the express consent of the remaining party. The latter items are part of equitable distribution (if the parties are married), and their final disposition will be decided pending the adjudication of the matrimonial case, if same exists.

(13) MISCELLANEOUS RELIEF, INCLUDING MONITORING OF ORDERED RELIEF

The plaintiff and any dependent children may be granted miscellaneous relief, whether or not it was requested at the time of the granting of the initial emergency Order, as long as the plaintiff consents to such relief, including relief requested by the plaintiff at the final hearing. [*N.J.S.A.* 2C:25-29(b)(14).] The Plaintiff should not be denied any relief on the ground that it was not requested at the emergent hearing.

The court has the ability to order the sale and equal division of the party's home.[471]

The court can also order the defendant to report to the intake unit of the Family Division of the Chancery Division of the Superior Court for monitoring to ensure compliance with the provisions of the Order. [N.J.S.A.2C:25-29(b)(15).] Thus, if they are ordered to counseling, substance abuse centers, and/or take drug tests, the Probation Department can monitor these provisions in any order(s).

(14) PSYCHIATRIC EVALUATION OF DEFENDANT

An order may be granted requiring the defendant to undergo a psychiatric evaluation. [N.J.S.A. 2C:25-29(b)(18).]

(15) PROHIBITION AGAINST WEAPONS

In addition to the order prohibiting the defendant from possessing any firearm, the court may also issue an order prohibiting the defendant from possessing any other weapon specified in subsection r of *N.J.S.A.* 2C:39-1. It may also provide for the search for and seizure of any firearm or other weapon at any location where the judge has reasonable cause to believe the weapon is located, provided the judge states with specificity the reasons for and scope of the search and seizure authorized by the order [*N.J.S.A.* 2C:25-29(b)(16).] The court must make findings on the record and state with specificity the reasons for its decision and the scope of the search. (*See also Section on Weapons.*)

A specific description of the weapon and its location should be provided by the client, giving as much detail as possible.

(16) PROHIBITION AGAINST FIREARMS

The Order can of course bar the defendant from purchasing, owning, possessing or controlling a firearm, receiving or retaining a firearms purchaser identification card, or permit to purchase a handgun under *N.J.S.A.* 2C:58-3. This restriction remains in effect during the period in which the restraining order is in effect, or two years whichever is greater. This provision does not apply to any law enforcement officer while actually on duty, or to any member of the Armed Forces of the United States or member of the National Guard while actually on duty or traveling to or from an authorized place of duty. [*N.J.S.A.* 2C:25-29(b), effective January 14, 2004.]

---

[471] *Mitchell v. Oksienik*, 380 *N.J. Super* 119, 880 *A.2d* 1194 (App Div 2005).

(17) PROHIBITION AGAINST DEFENDANT STALKING

An order can be instated, prohibiting the defendant from stalking or following, or threatening to harm, to stalk or to follow the victim or any other person specified, in a manner that would put the complainant in reasonable fear that the defendant would cause the death or injury of the victim or any other person, taken in the context of the defendant's past actions. Prohibited behavior includes but it not limited to those specified under *N.J.S.A.* 2C:12-10. [*N.J.S.A.* 2C:25-29(b)(17).]

(18) "INDEFINITE" TEMPORARY RESTRAINING ORDER

A new phenomenon was created by the courts, which is neither a temporary restraining order (T.R.O.) nor a final restraining order (F.R.O.) but is instead labeled an "Indefinite Temporary Restraining Order." In *Shah*, the court kept the TRO ongoing where the Defendant could have "easily rid himself of the temporary restraining order by coming into New Jersey and substantively defending against the domestic violence complaint," or he could have requested that both matters be heard in Illinois. The court found it was necessary to keep the restraints in place to protect the victim, where there was no personal jurisdiction over the defendant, until so ordered by the court.[472]

(See also Relief Under the Act Chapter 2.6 and Chapter 9)

---

[472] *Shah v. Shah*, 184 *N.J.* 125, 128, 875 *A.2d* 931 (2005).

10.8   CONDITIONS OF SENTENCE

After an FRO has been entered, upon a finding the defendant has committed domestic violence, the court will oftentimes impose conditions on sentencing, which include the following:

1.   Restricting the Defendant from committing further acts of domestic violence against the victim.

2.   Requiring that the defendant undergo professional domestic violence counseling. This includes provisions for monitoring or periodic court review.

3.   Requiring each county to develop and implement procedures to monitor compliance with court ordered provisions, including counseling and evaluation.

If the FRO includes provisions for emergent monetary relief, monetary compensation, including child support or spousal support, custody, visitation, counseling, any evaluations, or where the order includes third parties for whom addresses and other information are needed, or when intake monitoring is ordered, each party shall be referred to the Family staff, who will conduct separate post-court interviews. The staff is to ensure that the parties have no contact during the interview process.

Ongoing support Orders for monetary compensation in a FRO pursuant to *N.J.S.A.* 2C:25-29(b)(4) are to be made payable to the New Jersey Family Support Payment Center (P.O. Box 4880, Trenton, NJ 08625-4880), and said order shall be enforced by the Probation Division in the county in which the order was entered.

Failure to abide by any of these conditions would subject the defendant to contempt of court provisions for violation of a restraining order under *N.J.S.A.* 2C:25-30, or the imposition of further sanctions.

Some courts have tried to get inventive by creating new conditions of parole, which are not authorized by statute. However, a sentencing judge cannot impose conditions of parole on the defendant in the absence of legislative authorization.

In one case, a court imposed a condition of parole, which stated that the defendant could not reside in the State of New Jersey. The provision was invalidated since it was not a remedy authorized by the Domestic Violence Act.[473]

---

[473] *State v. J.F.*, 262 *N.J. Super.* 539, 543, 621 *A.2d* 520, 524 (App. Div. 1993).

In another case, the judge's "conditions" included that the defendant was not permitted to come within a five mile radius of his wife's home, nor into the Township of Fairfield where she lived. On appeal, the court reversed and held that the sentencing judge was without authority to impose conditions of parole, and that such provisions should instead be considered as recommendations and not mandates.[474]

---

[474] *State v. Beauchamp*, 262 N.J. Super. 532, 621 A.2d 516 (App. Div. 1993).

CHAPTER ELEVEN

DISSOLUTION, MODIFICATION AND DISMISSAL OF RESTRAINING ORDERS [475]

In domestic violence cases the facts and circumstances change. This can result in the victim seeking a modification, which involves adding to or changing the provisions of an existing Order; or where the parties reconcile, a dismissal/withdrawal of any existing Orders. When the victim seeks to have the defendant comply with an existing Order, they are looking to enforce the TRO or FRO.

Enforcement of Orders is governed by *N.J.S.A.* 2C:25-30 and 2C:29-9(b), depending on the conduct and the provision violated. The relief contained in Part I of the restraining order can be enforced by instituting criminal or civil remedies. All relief contained in Part II must be enforced by civil remedies, which includes filing an application with the Superior Court, Family Division.

Withdrawals of the TRO

When a victim seeks to withdraw a TRO, after a TRO has been entered, but before the entry of a final order, the victim must do so in person and before a judge. This can be done on a walk-in basis or on the scheduled final hearing date. Victims do not need to wait until the final hearing to request a dismissal.

A victim advocate shall speak to the plaintiff, however where this is not possible, the staff should make the plaintiff aware of the existence of an advocate along with a name and telephone number, preferably in writing.

A professional staff person must meet with the victim to determine the following:

> A. The victim has read and understood "What Dissolving a Restraining Order Means"
> B. The victim has not been coerced or placed under duress to withdraw the Complaint/TRO;
> C. The victim understands the cycle of domestic violence and its probable recurrence;
> D. The victim is aware of the protective resources available through the court and the local domestic violence program,

---

[475] *State of New Jersey Domestic Violence Procedure Manual*, p. IV-9 *et seq.*

especially with regard to housing and court-ordered emergency custody and support;

E. The victim clearly understands that withdrawal of the Complaint/TRO and dismissal of the TRO will eliminate the protections that had been issued;

F. The victim is aware that such withdrawals, while they should not be done without careful thought, are not prejudicial if [s]he should need to seek protection in the future; and

G. The victim is informed that any parallel criminal matters are separate and distinct and must be addressed in a separate venue. Victims are advised to discuss the matter with the appropriate prosecutor.

Once the victim has been counseled in regard to the above, and where they still wish to pursue withdrawal, (s)he must fill out a Certification to Dismiss Complaint/ TRO. Once completed, the victim will be sent before the judge who entered the order, or any available judge who has the complete court file. The judge will complete a review of the file and certification, and question the victim on the record, using the same procedure as a request for dismissal of a final order. The judge will then review the facts with the victim on the record. If the judge finds that the request for withdrawal is informed and not made under duress, the withdrawal will be granted.

The requirement that the judge, deciding the matter, be the original judge who issued the restraining order, or one who is made familiar with the original facts and circumstances through a review of the complete record, assures that the judge is familiar with the case, and has a complete record of the hearing from which the restraining Order was issued.[476] This insures the judge can make an informed decision as to modification or dissolution, and alleviates the potential problem of a wrong decision, which could possibly place the victim in harm's way. In one instance where the judge was not familiar with the case, and did not check the Defendant's prior record, the judge granted the dissolution of a restraining order, at which time the defendant went back and killed the victim.

Under circumstances where a defendant accused of domestic violence seeks an immediate appeal hearing to dismiss the temporary restraining order (TRO), or significantly modify the restraints contained therein, the court may consider granting said relief pursuant to *N.J.S.A.* 2C:25-28(i). However, the plaintiff must be given reasonable advance notice of the defendant's request for an immediate appeal hearing, and that notice must specify the type of

---

[476] The complete record for a victim is the domestic violence complaint, the affidavit filed with the complaint, the affidavit of dismissal and the testimony of the plaintiff. Unlike the defendant, under these circumstances, any family court judge may dismiss a restraining order; *I.J. v. I.S.* 328 *N.J. Super.* 166, 744 *A.2d* 1246 (Ch. Div. 1999)

relief that defendant will be seeking at that hearing. The appeal hearing should then be limited to issues encompassed by the requested relief.[477] Furthermore, if a victim is not provided notice of said appeal and does not appear at the hearing, a court will not vacate the TRO, but instead the matter will be rescheduled. (In comparison, if the victim is provided notice and does not appear, a dismissal of the TRO may be entered by the court).

In one case the court denied a victim's telephonic request to dismiss a most recent TRO, where said victim had a past history of obtaining eight TROs against the boyfriend in a five year period. All of the previous TROs were dismissed prior to a final restraining order (FRO) hearing, usually based upon plaintiff's failure to appear for the hearing to determine whether a final restraining order (FRO) should be issued. In addition to the nine TROs, Plaintiff had also filed six prior contempt charges filed against the boyfriend based upon the victim's allegation of violations of those TROs (all of which were likewise dismissed prior to an adjudication). The court held that the denial of the victims request to dismiss the TRO was justified and issued an indefinite TRO, based on the history of the case, mainly plaintiff's repeated dismissals and re-filings, which constituted a waste of judicial resource.

"There were too many substantial and significant domestic violence matters requiring the urgent attention of the court system to squander judicial and prosecutorial resources on patently unmeritorious litigation."[478]

Dismissal of FRO at the Request of the Plaintiff

Upon good cause shown, any final order may be dissolved or modified upon application to the Family Division of the Chancery Division of the Superior Court, but only if the judge who dissolves or modifies the order is the same judge who entered the order, or the judge dissolving the order has available a complete record of the hearing or hearings on which the order was based. [*N.J.S.A.* 2C:25-29(d).]

Where a victim seeks to dismiss a FRO, the dismissal should be handled in the same manner as a request for withdrawal of a Complaint/TRO. The dismissal must be requested in person, and before the judge who entered the order or a judge who has available the complete court file, only after the victim has been informed of her/his rights and the consequences of a dismissal. Where there is an order for child support, custody and/or visitation entered as part of the FRO, the judge is to question whether the victim wants the relief to continue. If so, these provisions will be made part of an FD order, then and there.

Dissolution of a final restraining order at the request of plaintiff is not mandatory. Rather, dissolution in such cases is at the court's discretion, and should depend upon a showing

---

[477] *Vendetti v. Meltz,* 359 *N.J. Super.* 63, 69, 818 *A.2d* 357 (Ch. Div 2002)
[478] *Kelleher v. Galindo,* 350 *N.J. Super.* 570, 796 *A.2d* 306 (Ch. Div. 2002).

of good cause, with an independent finding by the court based upon the facts presented in each case.[479]

In *Stevenson*, the court found that even where there has been reconciliation, the court must make an independent finding that continued protection is unnecessary prior to vacating a restraining order. The court reasoned that under the domestic violence act, *it is the responsibility of the courts to protect victims of domestic violence* by ordering those remedies and sanctions that are *available to assure the safety of the victims* and the public, even where the victim's actions threaten their own safety. The court noted that phase three of "the battered woman's syndrome" consists of a period of loving behavior by the batterer, wherein they plea for forgiveness and promises to change. This will eventually fade, and phases one and two, the "tension-building" phase and the "acute battering incident" phase, will start anew.

The court went on to say that when considering a victim's application to dissolve, and whether there is good cause to do so, a court must determine whether objective fear "can be said to continue to exist, and also whether there is a real danger of domestic violence recurring, in the event the restraining order is dissolved."

In *Stevenson*, the court denied the dissolution of the Order, given the uncontroverted evidence of defendant's brutality against his wife, his history of violence both within and without the domestic arena, his alcohol abuse and uncontrolled assaultive behavior when under the influence, and the reports of experts before the court. The court held that a reasonable, objective and independent examination of the facts, leads to the inescapable conclusion that there is a real threat domestic violence committed by the defendant upon his battered wife will exist, if the Final Restraining Order is dissolved.

In *N.B. v. S.K.*, a domestic violence victim agreed to vacate a domestic violence FRO, and replace it with restraints in the divorce action. Thereafter, the marital restraints proved ineffectual, and the plaintiff filed a domestic violence action, which the trial court dismissed. Plaintiff then filed a motion to vacate the prior dismissal of the FRO, which had been the basis for the entry of the marital restraints. The Appellate Division reversed the dismissal of the new domestic violence action and remanded for a new trial, holding that the trial judge mistakenly failed to give sufficient consideration to defendant's past and present violations of the matrimonial restraints. The Appellate Court also affirmed the denial of the motion to vacate the prior order which vacated the prior FRO, on the sole basis that plaintiff filed to seek that relief within a reasonable period of time.[480]

In its decision, the Appellate Division addressed the issue of the significance of a

---

[479] *Stevenson v. Stevenson,* 314 *N.J. Super.* 350, 353, 714 A.2d 986 (Ch. Div. 1998).
[480] *N.B. v. S.K,* 435 *N.J. Super.* 298, 305-308, *88 A.3d 937* (App. Div. 2014).

238

defendant's violation of a matrimonial restraining order in a domestic violence action.[481] The court recognized that violations of matrimonial restraints are not per se "acts of domestic violence," rather they support the claim that defendant engaged in acts of harassment by making communications "with purpose to alarm or seriously annoy." Such evidence puts into context why the recipient would be alarmed or seriously annoyed by the communications.[482]

The Court stated:

> To put this discussion in perspective, however, we observe that plaintiff did not argue in the trial court that she had a right to a FRO because defendant violated the matrimonial restraints contained in the PSA or in later orders. To the contrary, plaintiff alleged that defendant engaged in an act, or acts, of harassment by leaving five voice messages on a telephone he was ordered not to call. And, as evidence of her claim that these messages were "alarm[ing] or seriously annoy[ing]," and made with the purpose to harass, plaintiff sought admission of the prior orders and evidence of prior violations of those orders as a means of demonstrating how alarming or annoying these telephone calls were to her. We agree with plaintiff that this evidence was relevant to whether defendant engaged in harassing conduct on June 24, 2012, and that the trial judge erred in excluding this evidence.

> The greatest difficulties encountered with the day-to-day application of the PDVA in our trial courts have been with claims of domestic violence based on alleged acts of harassment. In determining the extent of the authority granted by the PDVA for courts to intervene in such disputes, the many decisions of our jurisprudence reveals the importance of the context or setting in which the act or acts of harassment occurred.[483]

Dismissal of an FRO at the request of the Defendant

Pursuant to *N.J.S.A.* 2C:25-29(d), an FRO may be dissolved upon "good cause shown. A dismissal request by the defendant must be initiated by the filing of a Notice of Motion, accompanying certification and brief. Service of said documents must be made upon the plaintiff, and shall be done through the Family Division (not served directly by the defendant.

---

[481] *Ibid.*

[482] *N.B. v. S.K,* 435 *N.J. Super.* 298, 305-308, *88 A.3d 937* (App. Div. 2014).

[483] *Ibid.*

The court cannot hold a hearing on this application unless the plaintiff is given notice and an opportunity to be heard.

The motion is to be heard by the judge who entered the FRO if that judge, or by another judge who shall read and consider the complete record. The court is to consider the following factors in determining whether the defendant has established good cause to dissolve the FRO:

A.   As required by *N.J.S.A.* 2C:25-29(b)(5), determine whether the defendant attended and completed all court ordered counseling. If not, the motion must be denied.

B.   Past history of domestic violence. If no findings were made by the court at a final hearing regarding any past history of domestic violence, the record may be supplemented with regard to such past history.

C.   Any other factors the court deems appropriate to assess whether the defendant has shown good cause that the FRO should be modified or dissolved.

D.   To protect the victim, courts should consider a number of factors when determining whether good cause has been shown that the FRO should be dissolved upon request of the defendant, including:

(1) Whether the victim consented to dismiss the restraining order;
(2) Whether the victim fears the defendant;
(3) The nature of the relationship between the parties today;
(4) The number of times that the defendant has been convicted of contempt for violating the order;
(5) Whether the defendant has a continuing involvement with drug or alcohol abuse;
(6) Whether the defendant has been involved in other violent acts with other persons;
(7) Whether the defendant has engaged in counseling;
(8) The age and health of the defendant;
(9) Whether the victim is acting in good faith when opposing the defendant's request;
(10) Whether another jurisdiction has entered a restraining order protecting the victim from the defendant; and,
(11) Any other factors deemed relevant by the court. (eleven factors also cited in *Carafagno*)

The 11 factors to consider in determining whether good cause has been shown that the FRO should be dissolved are to be weighed qualitatively not quantitatively. [484] Thus, even if ten factors are present, but one is overriding, the court can deny the dismissal of the restraining Order.

"Subjective fear is the fear produced within the mind of the victim as the victim understands and communicates it. Objective fear is that fear which a reasonable victim similarly situated would have under the circumstances." The court in *Carafagno* held that courts should focus on objective fear.[485] Compare this to the standard of fear in *State v. Hoffman and*[486] *See also Stevenson v Stevenson*.[487]

In the case of *Kanaszka*, the court adopted the eleven *Carfagno* factors trial courts should consider in determining whether good cause has been shown. [488] The court then went on to say: When confronted with an application to dissolve a final restraining order, the court should carefully consider the particular facts and circumstances of the case within the context of the intent of the legislature to protect victims. "The previous history of domestic violence between the parties must be fully explored and considered to understand the totality of the circumstances of the relationship and to fully evaluate the reasonableness of the victim's continued fear of the perpetrator."[489] The "inquiry into the history of the relationship and prior acts of domestic violence become important considerations in evaluating the necessity for continued protection."[490] This may include exploration of incidents that were not testified to at the final hearing.[491] However, "the linchpin in any motion addressed to dismissal of an [FRO] should be whether there have been substantial changed circumstances since its entry that constitute good cause for consideration of dismissal."[492]

As a tool to accomplish this, the complete record of the case is necessary. The "complete record" requirement of the statute includes, at a minimum, all pleadings and orders, the court file, and a complete transcript of the final restraining order hearing. The better practice is for a transcript to accompany the motion for dissolution of a final restraining order to enable the motion judge to fully understand the totality of the circumstances and dynamics of the relationship and the application.

---

[484] *Stevenson v. Stevenson*, 314 *N.J. Super.* 350, 353, 714 *A.2d* 986 (Ch. Div. 1998).

[485] *Carfagno v, Carfagno*, 288 *N.J. Super.* 424, 437, 672 *A.2d* 751 (Ch. Div. 1995) (Plaintiff victim still feared defendant).

[486] *State v. Hoffman*, 149 *N.J.* 564, 575, 695 *A.2d* 236 (1997).

[487] *State v. Hoffman*, 149 *N.J.* 564, 575, 695 *A.2d* 236 (1997).

[488] *Kanaszka v. Kunen*, 313 *N.J. Super.* 600, 713 *A.2d* 565 (App. Div. 1998).

[489] *Kanaszka v. Kunen*, 313 *N.J. Super.* 600, 607, 713 *A.2d* 565 (App. Div. 1998).

[490] *Kanaszka v. Kunen*, 313 *N.J. Super.* 600, 609, 713 *A.2d* 565 (App. Div. 1998).

[491] *Kanaszka v. Kunen*, 313 *N.J. Super.* 600, 607, 713 *A.2d* 565 (App. Div. 1998).

[492] *Kanaszka v. Kunen*, 313 *N.J. Super.* 600, 609, 713 *A.2d* 565 (App. Div. 1998).

Note: even where the matter is heard by the judge presiding over the case when the previous Order was entered, it is beneficial to present the complete record here as well as they may not remember all of the facts of the case.

As to procedure, the court in *Kanaszka* stated that a plenary hearing is not required in every motion for dissolution of a restraining Order. The moving party has the burden to make a prima facie showing good cause exists for dissolution of the restraining order prior to the judge fully considering the request for dismissal. If the burden is met, the court should next determine whether there are facts in dispute, which are material to the resolution of the motion before ordering a plenary hearing. Only where the answer to this is affirmative should the court conduct a plenary hearing.

In *Sweeney,* a Plaintiff obtained a domestic violence restraining order against defendant/appellant, following the end of a brief romance.[493] The defendant requested dissolution of the FRO after 6 months and the trial court denied appellant's motion, despite plaintiff's testimony that she no longer desired to have the order in place. The Appellate court reversed and ordered the restraining order dissolved. The Appellate Court held that the conduct involved was, in terms of domestic violence, marginal at best, as there was no evidence of physical or verbal abuse by the defendant.

The *Sweeney court* stated the factors to be considered when determining whether good cause exist to dissolve an order include: the consent of the victim to the dissolution of the order, the victim's continued fear of defendant, the nature of the parties' present relationship, whether there have been any contempt convictions against defendant, whether defendant has been involved in alcohol or drug use or other violent acts, whether defendant has engaged in counseling, defendant's age and health, the victim's good faith in opposing the dissolution, and whether restraining orders have been entered in any other jurisdiction. The court held that in considering these factors, all the factors weighed in appellant's favor and supported the relief sought. The court stated:

> This was [merely] a brief dating relationship, which plaintiff broke
> off and defendant hoped to revive during the course of exactly
> one week by telephone calls and visits in which plaintiff
> participated.

While the Defendant's actions were unwelcome, the court didn't think they constituted domestic violence, since they lacked purpose to achieve that result or a course of alarming conduct and stated: "Surely the law must have some tolerance for a disappointed suitor trying

---

[493] *Sweeney v. Honachefsky*, 313 *N.J. Super* 443, 447-448, 712 *A.2d* 1274 (App. Div. 1998).

to repair a romantic relationship when his conduct is not violent or abusive or threatening but merely importuning."[494]

The court noted that defendant attended counseling, did not initiate contact with the Plaintiff or the roommate, Plaintiff consented to the dissolution, Plaintiff did not fear Defendant, etc, and concluded that there was nothing in the record that suggested that respondent would be at any risk if the motion were granted, but that its denial severely prejudiced appellant because the order interfered with his employment plans.

Reconciliation

Does the reconciliation of the parties, subsequent to entry of a domestic violence order constitute "good cause" for dissolution of the prior restraints? One court that addressed this issue was *AB v. LM*.[495] In that case, the court held that a final restraining order should not be set aside based upon the parties' reconciliation or mutual violation without careful consideration by the court of the need for continued protection.

The rationale for this is guided by the complexity of relationships, along with the strong public policy to protect victims of domestic violence. As the court noted:

> [A]pparent reconciliation between people with a long history of domestic violence seldom marks the end of the difficulties.. It would be unwise and improper to automatically vacate an order issued on a domestic violence complaint upon reconciliation or mutual violations without further analysis...
>
> Victims come from a variety of circumstances but the optimism that often underlies their forgiveness of their abusers should not deny them the protection of the law. When confronted with a party's request to vacate a domestic violence order on the grounds of reconciliation, the Court should closely scrutinize the record to determine whether there is a likelihood that the violent conduct would be repeated...and consider the factors set forth in *N.J.S.A.* 2C:25-29 (a) before removing the shield of protection afforded by the restraining order.[496]

Similarly in *Torres,* the court held that no order should be vacated upon a reconciliation

---

[494] *Ibid.*

[495] *A.B. v. L.M.,* 289 *N.J. Super.* 125, 672 *A.2d* 1296 (App. Div. 1996).

[496] *A.B. v. L.M.,* 289 *N.J. Super.* 125, 131, 672 *A.2d* 1296 (App. Div. 1996); *see also* .

or mutual violation without an analysis of the necessity for continued protection and restraints. The court went on to say, that upon a reconciliation or mutual violation by the parties, courts should consider the previous history of domestic violence between the plaintiff and defendant; the existence of immediate danger to person or property; the financial circumstances of the plaintiff and defendant; the best interests of the victim and any child; in determining custody and visitation the protection of the victim's safety; and the existence of a verifiable order of protection from another jurisdiction, as well as any proof of changed circumstances since the entry of the prior order. The court went on to find that where a true reconciliation has occurred and the need for protection is no longer present, the order can be vacated.[497] However, where the reconciliation consists of an isolated sexual encounter or an attempted reconciliation of short duration that has failed the order can remain in effect to protect the victim.[498]

Compare the above cases to *Mohamed v. Mohamed*,[499] which held that an intervening reconciliation of the parties requires Orders previously entered to be dismissed. Thus a defendant could not be held in contempt for violation of restraining order where there was reconciliation with the plaintiff. This is not longer the case, and many contempt proceedings are brought by the state for violations of protective orders, even where there has been reconciliation between the parties. (*See contempt section for more information*)

Time between Entry of the FRO or TRO and the Request for dissolution

Courts have held that a final restraining order should be in effect for a reasonable amount of time before the courts may consider a request for dissolution. This ensures that the domestic violence victim is maximally protected, and preserves the victim's right to depend on the protection and finality of a judgment.[500]

In *MV v. JRG,* the Defendant, a Hudson County Sheriff's Officer, requested the dissolution of a restraining Order 8 months after it was issued. The facts of the case are as follows. Plaintiff and defendant were in a dating relationship that ended. Thereafter, the plaintiff filed a domestic violence complaint against defendant, resulting in the entry of a TRO. As part of the order, defendant was prohibited from possessing all firearms except for his service revolver while on duty. In fact however, defendant was not permitted to retain his service revolver, as the Hudson County Sheriff's Department policy requires officers to carry their weapons at all times. Thereafter, defendant was placed on restricted duty. The final hearing resulted in a finding of an act of domestic violence, and an FRO was issued, prohibiting the defendant from future contact with plaintiff. It was also determined that defendant did not pose a danger in his possession of firearms. Thereafter, the defendant sought dissolution,

---

[497] *Torres v. Lancellotti, 257 N.J. Super.* 126, 130-131, 607 *A.2d* 1375 (App. Div. 1992).

[498] *Ibid.*

[499] *Mohamed v. Mohamed, 232 N.J. Super.* 474, 477, 557 *A.2d* 696 (App. Div. 1989).

[500] *M.V. v. J.R.G., 312 N.J. Super.* 597, 711 *A.2d* 1379 (Ch. Div. 1997).

which the court denied.

The court noted that final restraints granted under the Act do not have a statutorily imposed expiration date. *See N.J.S.A.* 2C:25-29. After an FRO has been entered, it is appropriate that such an order be in effect for a reasonable time before the "criteria cited as reasons for dissolution should be examined to determine their permanency and viability." Lastly, the court found that one year must expire from the date of the entry of the FRO before a defendant may make an application to dissolve an FRO under *N.J.S.A.* 2C:25-29(d), absent other exigent circumstances particular to that application.

The amount of time courts consider "reasonable" may vary. In one case, the Defendant, an aspiring law enforcement officer, sought to dissolve an FRO entered against him approximately 6 months after its entry. The trial court denied this request, even though Plaintiff consented to the dissolution, and the Appellate Court reversed, granting the dismissal. [501]

In another case, the Defendant appealed from an amended FRO that denied his request for joint legal custody of the party's son three years. The court acknowledged that under New Jersey law "joint legal custody" is favored while joint physical custody is rare.[502] However, the court also noted that where there has been a finding of domestic violence, a presumption arises, favoring an award in custody (both legal and physical) to "the non-abusive spouse," pursuant to *N.J.S.A.* 2C:25-29(b)(11). The presumption weakens as time passes without any conduct which can be said to jeopardize the "non-abusive spouse" or the child. [503] At the conclusion of this case, the Appellate Court affirmed the denial of Defendant's motion, despite the passage of three years and the fact that defendant was seeking to merely modify rather than dissolve the FRO.

Conditions Set by the Parties to Dismiss an Order- Conditional Dismissal by the Court Improper

While a dismissal order or restraining order may be voluntary, it can still be based on conditions. The court should examine the victim to see if there are conditions, and indicate the conditions on the dismissal order. If conditions of dismissal are not kept, the Order can be reinstated. (*See* section on civil restraints.)

In one case, a Plaintiff obtained a restraining order against the defendant, and subsequently applied to dismiss the restraining order on condition that defendant attend counseling. The parties agreed that the restraining order would be reinstated upon the failure of the condition. The defendant failed to attend counseling and plaintiff sought to reinstate the

---

[501] *Sweeney v. Honachefsky,* 313 *N.J. Super.* 443, 446, 712 *A.2d* 1274 (App. Div. 1998).
[502] *Grover v. Terlaje,* 379 *N.J. Super* 400, 879 *A.2d* 138 (App. Div 2005).
[503] *Grover v. Terlaje,* 379 *N.J. Super* 400, 407, 879 *A.2d* 138 (App. Div 2005).

restraining order. At the hearing, the defendant admitted he failed to attend counseling, and the court vacated its dismissal order, reinstating the restraining order. The court held that it had authority to reinstate the restraining order without evidence of additional acts of violence because *N.J.S.A.* 4:37-1(b) required that the dismissed restraining order be vacated when defendant breached the condition to attend counseling and because *N.J.S.A.* 2C:25-29(d) of the Domestic Violence Act permitted dissolution or modification of a restraining order upon good cause.[504]

The CO decision was subsequently overruled in *T.M. v. J.C.,* which held:

"A conditional dismissal of a domestic violence complaint is improper as not being authorized either by statute or rule. Each domestic violence complaint represents a separate action in which the court must determine whether the temporary restraining order (TRO) will be converted into a final restraining order (FRO). Hence, if a domestic violence complaint is designated as "dismissed," the court loses jurisdiction to adjudicate whether an FRO should be entered. A conditional dismissal cannot be reconciled with the purpose of the Domestic Violence Act of 1990, *N.J.S.A.* 2C:25-17 to -33, which is to afford relief to persons who are at risk of domestic violence. Such a person is either at risk or not at risk. If the court finds the person is at risk, then the TRO must remain in place; if the court finds that the person is not at risk, then the restraints must be dissolved and the complaint dismissed.[505]

Dismissal based on Non-Service

In *State v. Mernar*, the court dismissed the criminal complaint against defendant for violating a domestic violence temporary restraining order (TRO), *N.J.S.A.* 2C:29-9(b), finding that the TRO was not properly served on defendant by a law enforcement officer. The State appealed. The Appellate Division stated in regard to notice:

> It is a matter of no consequence how the fact of the issuing of the
> injunction is brought to the knowledge or notice of a defendant. If
> he has notice or knowledge of it, his conscience is bound, and he
> is liable to the consequences of its breach to the same extent as if
> it had been actually served upon him in writing.

The Appellate Court held that the question of actual notice should have been further explored before determining whether the complaint was to be dismissed, where defendant claimed he never received a TRO. The trial court's focus should have been on the conflicting facts concerning whether defendant actually received the TRO. In addition, the defendant's admitted alcoholism and his possible state of inebriation when he was allegedly handed the

---

[504] *C.O. v. J.O.,* 292 *N.J. Super.* 219, 678 *A.2d* 748 (Ch. Div. 1996).
[505] *T.M. v. J.C.,* 348 *N.J. Super.* 101, 791 *A.2d* 300 (App. Div. 2002).

TRO, raised the question of whether he comprehended any order that he may have received. In conclusion the Appellate court reinstated the Order and the matter was remanded.[506]

Result of Non Appearance

A court found that a simple failure to appear at a routine status conference will not dismiss a complaint because the state, and not the victim, was the party in interest. Proceedings in which defendant had been charged with contempt for violating Domestic Violence restraining orders entered by the Superior Court "have two objectives: protection of the victim and vindication of the authority of the court."[507]

Because the state has an interest in a Domestic Violence case, the non-appearance of plaintiff is not enough to dismiss the case. In this particular case, three matters were decided based on identical facts. The arraignment order stated that the order would be dismissed if plaintiff failed to appear. The court held that they have "no authority to condition the prosecution of these matters on the willingness or ability of the complaining party to appear for routine status conferences."[508]

---

[506] *State v. Mernar*, 345 N.J. Super. 591, 786 A.2d 141 (App. Div. 2001).
[507] *State v. Brito*, 345 N.J. Super. 228, 231, 784 A.2d 746 (App. Div. 2001).
[508] *State v. Brito*, 345 N.J. Super. 228, 230, 784 A.2d 746 (App. Div. 2001).

CHAPTER TWELVE

CONTEMPT

12.1   CONTEMPT [509]

Under the Act, there are several sections dealing with contempt proceedings and violations of orders. Any violation of an order issued pursuant to the Domestic Violence Act, by a defendant can constitute an offense subject to contempt proceedings under the Act.

N.J.S.A. 2C:29-9 states:

> a. A person is guilty of a crime of the fourth degree if he purposely or knowingly disobeys a judicial order or protective order, pursuant to section 1 of *P.L.*1985, *c.*250 (*C.*2C:28-5.1), or hinders, obstructs or impedes the effectuation of a judicial order or the exercise of jurisdiction over any person, thing or controversy by a court, administrative body or investigative entity.

> b. Except as provided below, a person is guilty of a crime of the fourth degree if that person purposely or knowingly violates any provision in an order entered under the provisions of the "Prevention of Domestic Violence Act of 1991," or an order entered under the provisions of a substantially similar statute under the laws of another state or the United States when the conduct which constitutes the violation could also constitute a crime or a disorderly persons offense. In all other cases a person is guilty of a disorderly person's offense if that person knowingly violates an order entered under the provisions of this act or an order entered under the provisions of a substantially similar statute under the laws of another state or the United States. Orders entered pursuant to paragraphs (3), (4), (5), (8) and (9) of subsection b. of section 13 of or substantially similar orders entered under the laws of another state or the United States shall be excluded from the provisions of this subsection.

---

[509] *N.J. S.A.* 2C:25-30; *N.J.S.A.* 2C:25-31; *N.J.S.A.* 2C:25-32.

As used in this subsection, "state" means a state of the United States, the District of Columbia, Puerto Rico, the United States Virgin Islands, or any territory or insular possession subject to the jurisdiction of the United States. The term includes an Indian tribe or band, or Alaskan native village, which is recognized by a federal law or formally acknowledged by a state.

If the violation of restraining order took place in the State of New Jersey, the violation is handled in the county in which the restraining order was issued. If the violation occurred outside the State of New Jersey, but the parties reside in New Jersey or the victim has sought refuge in New Jersey, the court still has jurisdiction over the matter, although it may not have *in personam* jurisdiction over the individual.[510] The Order and any subsequent violation could also be enforced in the state where the violation occurred.[511]

Contempt for violating a domestic violence restraining order may be either a fourth-degree offense or a disorderly person's offense. *N.J.S.A.* 2C:29-9(a). It is a fourth-degree offense if the conduct constituting the violation of the court order could itself also constitute a crime or a disorderly person's offense. *N.J.S.A.* 2C:29-9(b). In all other cases, a contempt based on a violation of a domestic violence restraining order is a disorderly person's offense unless the conduct is expressly exempt by statute.[512] If the contempt charge is a disorderly persons offense, the violation of the restraining order is heard exclusively in the Family Part, Chancery Division of the Superior Court, and not in the Municipal Court or in the Criminal Part, Law Division. If the contempt charge is an indictable fourth degree offense under *N.J.S.A.* 2C:25-28(a), the violation of the restraining order is heard in the Criminal Part, law Division of the Superior Court.[513]

The action of contempt can either be brought by the victim through the County Prosecutor's Office, or by a law enforcement officer. When a law enforcement officer is involved, they may arrest the defendant and transport them to the police station and do the following:

1. Sign a complaint concerning the incident which gave rise to the contempt charge;

2. Telephone or in otherwise communicate with the judge and request bail to be set on a contempt charge during regular court hours. The defendant has bail set by the Superior Court judge that day. On weekends, holidays, and other times when the court is closed, the officer can have a municipal court judge set the bail;

---

[510] *J.N. v. D.S.,* 300 *N.J. Super.* 647, 651, 693 *A.2d* 571 (Ch. Div. 1996).
[511] 18 *U.S.C.A.* 2262 to -2265.
[512] *State v. Hoffman,* 149 *N.J.* 564, 589; 695 *A.2d* 236, 261 (1997).
[513] *N.J.S.A.* 2C:29-9; *N.J.S.A.* 2C:25-28(a).

3. If the defendant is unable to meet bail, take the necessary steps to be sure that the defendant be incarcerated;

The Act also gives police officers discretion not to arrest an individual, even if the victim claims that they have committed an act of contempt. In that instance, if the police officer believes there is not probable cause sufficient to arrest the defendant, he is to advise the complainant of the procedure for completing and signing a criminal complaint. The victim then, during regular court hours, can have the assistance of the Clerk of the Chancery Division of the Superior Court, and the victim can institute other criminal actions against the defendant.[514]

The Courts are instructed under the Act not to delay disposition of a case because there is a concurrent dissolution of marriage case at the time a violation is charged.[515] Other circumstances may exist where a contempt proceeding is delayed as explained *infra*.

In *State v. Nelson*, a Defendant violated a TRO entered against him, preventing him from contacting the victim, by allegedly attempting to murder the victim. While in jail defendant wrote several letters to the victim, which resulted in the victim filing a complaint for contempt and harassment. The trial for the contempt/harassment charges was set before the trial for attempted murder. The Defendant filed a motion to adjourn the contempt/harassment trial until after the murder trial based upon the rationale that his right against self-incrimination would be violated if he were required to defend himself in the contempt/harassment matter prior to the murder trial. The court granted the adjournment and held that defendant's rights might be prejudiced by trying the contempt/harassment case first. The court weighed the respective prejudice that would inure to each party and concluded that there was more prejudice to defendant in denying the motion than there was to the state in granting it. If the defendant testified in his own defense during the contempt/harassment matter, his statements could then be used against him in his murder trial. Since there was no prejudice to the state, the adjournment was granted.[516]

Judges are instructed that if the victim fails to appear at the contempt proceeding, that they should not immediately dismiss the contempt charge. This is because oftentimes the lack of appearance is the result of other factors, such as coercion, fear or duress.[517] Rather, if the victim does not appear, an attempt should be made to reach them by phone. If no contact is made, the matter should be rescheduled. The court may then direct that the matter be heard at a specific return date and that personal service be made on the victim and defendant. On this

---

[514] *N.J.S.A.* 2C:25-32.

[515] *N.J.S.A.* 2C:25-25.

[516] *State v. Nelson*, 255 *N.J. Super.* 270, 604 *A.2d* 999 (Law Div. 1992).

[517] *State of New Jersey Domestic Violence Procedural Manual*, p. IV-10.

date, the court may dismiss the matter.[518]

Once the matter is dismissed, unless a witness was sworn and double jeopardy would attach, the dismissal is without prejudice. This gives a victim of domestic violence an opportunity to file a second criminal complaint for violation of the restraining order.

An order of the court must be obeyed unless and until a court acts to change or rescind it. In order for there to be contempt, it only needs to be proven that the order was in existence at the time of the alleged contempt. Thus, where a violation occurs, it is irrelevant that the TRO and domestic violence case were subsequently dismissed.[519]

Where there is an alleged violation of a restraining order, the question becomes whether the party accused of violating the order had actual notice, as opposed to the manner of service that was utilized.[520]

In order to prove contempt, it must be shown that defendant knowingly violated the restraining order. Where defendant had no knowledge that attending his children's soccer game where his ex-wife was also attending at an outdoor athletic field was prohibited, he could not be convicted of contempt. In addition, the court held that the provision in the restraining order that barred defendant from any other place where the ex-wife was located was an invalid provision.[521]

In one case (not a domestic violence matter), the Defendant was tried and found guilty of breaking and entering and larceny. He lied about his age and was tried as an adult. Defendant subsequently jumped bail. The Appellate Court found that the trial court had jurisdiction over the appellant's contempt charge for jumping bail, even though at the time of the original criminal charges, the appellant was a juvenile and the court lacked jurisdiction over the criminal charges. The court ultimately held that he jurisdictional basis for criminal contempt was independent of the basis for jurisdiction over defendant's initially charged offenses.[522]

A. CRIMINAL VS CIVIL CONTEMPT

Under the Criminal Code, the purposeful or knowing violation of any judicial order or protective order (restraining order) is a crime of the fourth degree,[523] as "The primary purpose for tying the contempt conviction to criminal conduct is to elevate the seriousness of the

---

[518] See N.J. Ct. R. 7:8-5 (applying same for municipal courts).
[519] State v. Sanders, 327 N.J. 385, 743 A.2d 385 (App. Div. 2000).
[520] State v. Mernar, 345 N.J. Super 591, 786 A.2d 141 (App. Div. 2001).
[521] State v. S.K., 423 N.J. Super 540, 33 A.3d 1255 (App. Div. 2012).
[522] State v. Roberts, 212 N.J. Super 476, 515 A.2d 799 (App. Div. 1986).
[523] N.J.S.A. 2C:29-9(a).

contempt from a disorderly persons offense to a fourth-degree crime."[524]

On the other hand, if the conduct constituting the violation involves the defendant merely contacting the victim, problems with visitation, attendance at counseling, or making payments as ordered, this would be a disorderly person's offense and not a violation of the criminal contempt statute.[525]

In trials for criminal contempt of court, pursuant to *N.J.S.A.* 2C:29-9(b)(violation of domestic relations order as a fourth degree offense), the Superior Court retains the same plenary power to enter appropriate remedial orders against a defendant as are authorized by the Domestic Violence Act and customarily entered in the Family Part.[526]

Note: Regardless of whether or not a violation of a restraining order constitutes contempt, the plaintiff may also pursue an enforcement proceeding by filing a motion under N.J. Ct. R. 1:10-3.

In *Von Pein*, the Appellate Division found that a trial judge has the discretion to refuse to institute criminal contempt proceedings if they find that the Act did not rise to the level of contempt. A judge refusing to do so does not bar either party from filing a complaint with the appropriate law enforcement agency.[527] Similarly, in a domestic violence matter the court may elect not to to entertain a contempt action, which it deems no encompassed by the domestic violence restraining order, ie failure to pay support.

B. CONTEMPT WHERE THE PARTIES HAVE RECONCILED

In the prior section, dealing with dismissal and modification of Orders, we mentioned in the cases of *Mohamed* and *Torres*. The Court in *Mohamed* held that an intervening reconciliation of the parties requires Orders previously entered to be dismissed. Thus theoretically, a contempt charge for a violation of said Order could not ensue.[528] The law as to this issue is no longer accurate.

In the subsequent case of *Torres*, the court held that no order should be vacated upon a reconciliation or mutual violation without an analysis of the necessity for continued protection and restraints. The court went on to say, that upon a reconciliation or mutual violation by the

---

[524] *State v. Hoffman*, 149 *N.J.* 564, 590, 695 *A.2d* 236, 262 (1997).

[525] This provision eliminates relief under *N.J.S.A.* 2C:29-9(b) for violations of *N.J.S.A.* 2C:25-29(b)(3), (4), (5), (8), and (9).

[526] *State v. Beauchamp*, 262 *N.J. Super.* 532, 621 *A.2d* 516 (App. Div. 1993).

[527] *Von Pein v. Von Pein*, 268 *N.J. Super.* 7, 632 *A.2d* 830 (App. Div. 1993)(failing to report husbands fraud to prosecutor for prosecution in a matrimonial matter).

[528] *See Mohamed v. Mohamed*, 232 *N.J. Super.* 474, 557 *A.2d* 696 (App. Div. 1989); *see also A.B. v. L.M.*, 289 *N.J. Super.*, 125, 672 *A.2d*. 1296 (App. Div. 1996); *Hayes v. Hayes*, 251 *N.J. Super.* 160, 597 *A.2d*. 567 (Ch. Div. 1991)

parties, courts should consider the previous history of domestic violence between the plaintiff and defendant; the existence of immediate danger to person or property; the financial circumstances of the plaintiff and defendant; the best interests of the victim and any child; in determining custody and visitation the protection of the victim's safety; and the existence of a verifiable order of protection from another jurisdiction, as well as any proof of changed circumstances since the entry of the prior order. The court went on to find that where a true reconciliation has occurred and the need for protection is no longer present, the order can be vacated. However, where the reconciliation consists of an isolated sexual encounter or an attempted reconciliation of short duration that has failed the order can remain in effect to protect the victim.[529]

The previous courts, however, never specifically addressed the issue of whether the reconciliation between the parties vitiates the Restraining Order so as to serve as a defense to a charge of contempt. This was answered in the case of *State v. Washington*. In its decision, the court stated that when confronted with a party's request to vacate a domestic violence order on the ground of reconciliation, the court should closely scrutinize the record to determine whether there is a likelihood that violent conduct will be repeated, based upon a careful consideration of the factors set forth in *N.J.S.A.* 2C:25-29(a). After this has occurred, the court can decide whether or not to remove the shield of protection afforded by the restraining order.[530]

Notably and specifically in regard to contempt, the court went on to hold:

> While, reconciliation may very well serve as a ground to dismiss a restraining order. The conduct of the parties to a domestic violence order cannot serve as a defense to a contempt charge. Courts must control the operation of their own orders. An order of a court must be obeyed unless and until a court acts to change or rescind it. In contempt proceedings, the primary consideration is vindication of the authority of the court. For the continuation of our society in its present form court orders must be obeyed. Therefore the paramount purposes in sentencing for contempt of court are retribution and deterrence.[531]

Therefore, in both a criminal and quasi criminal action for contempt, the reconciliation of parties is not a defense to a contempt charge.

---

[529] *Torres v. Lancellotti*, 257 N.J. Super. 126, 131, 607 A.2d 1375 (App. Div. 1992).
[530] *State v. Washington*, 319 N.J. Super, 681, 686, 726 A.2d 326 (Law Div. 1998).
[531] *Ibid.*

C. BIFURCATION

Where a defendant was charged with contempt, trial counsel was not ineffective for failing to move for a separate trial on the charge of violating the restraining order. [532]

The court in *Silver* held that a bifurcated proceeding, separating a burglary and aggravated assault charges from the contempt charge, were necessary to avoid the potential for prejudice, however the state was not precluding from introducing evidence attesting that the defendant was not licensed or privileged to enter the structure in order to prove burglary. [533]

Where a defendant repeatedly stabbed and clubbed a man at close range until he died, there was no issue with respect to his state of mind-he intended to kill. Therefore, the trial courts error in failing to sever a charge of contempt of a domestic violence restraining order the victim's girlfriend had obtained against the defendant, was harmless (and not of such a nature as to have been clearly capable of producing an unjust result) with respect to the murder conviction because that evidence only went to defendant's state of mind, which was plain and undeniable. [534] However, a domestic violence order is unduly prejudicial evidence in a trial of the underlying crime. [535]

A defendant's prior felony convictions may be admitted, but must be limited to the degree of the offence and cannot reference the nature of the offense. The Appellate Division has held in a defendant's trial for fourth degree criminal contempt in violation of *N.J.S.A* 2C:29-9(b), that the trial court impermissibly allowed the nature of the offense to be raised despite defendant's objection. This was error as conceded by the state as there was a substantial danger the defendant's prior firearms offense would buttress the victim's testimony and thus the prior firearms conviction constituted a prior similar conviction and same should have been sanitized prior to its submission to the trier or fact. [536]

---

[532] *State v. Keys,* 331 *N.J. Super.* 480, 752 *A.2d* 368 (App. Div. 1998).

[533] *State v. Silva,* 378 *N.J. Super.* 321, 875 *A.2d* 1005 (App. Div. 2005).

[534] *State v. Lewis,* 389 *N.J. Super.* 409, 913 *A.2d* 157 (App. Div. 2007).

[535] *State v. Lewis,* 389 *N.J. Super.* 409, 913 *A.2d* 157 (App. Div. 2007).

[536] *State v. Chenique-Puey,* 145 *N.J. Super.* 334, 678 *A.2d* 334 (App. Div. 1996).

12.2 SUFFICIENCY OF EVIDENCE

In one case the Appellate Division found that a father is not guilty of contempt, where he violated a final restraining order, prohibiting him from contacting the defendant. During a pickup/drop off of the child, the defendant uttered the words, "Am I going to get to see her tomorrow?" in a gruff voice. This was the extent of the conduct in question. The court concluded this was not a violation subject to a prosecution for criminal contempt, as it was a trivial and non actionable event. (*Note: the parties had a child and the FRO required the defendant's mother and the victim to communicate regarding visitation of the child etc. The Defendant and victim subsequently started communicating directly as to same, without amending the Order to reflect this change. The calls were also initiated by the victim)*[537]

The Appellate Court also noted that the prosecutor has the prosecutorial discretion to decide whether or not to prosecute a matter and should not "squander judicial and prosecutorial resources on patently unmeritorious litigation which, moreover, unfairly subjects people to criminal penalties," where the conduct in question is *de minimis*.[538] The court went on to say:

> The Domestic Violence Act affords critically needed protections in
> appropriate situations. It was not intended to attempt to regulate
> and adjudicate every loss of temper, angry word, or quarrel
> between persons connected by a familial relationship.

The Appellate Court reached similar findings in *State v. Krupinski*. Plaintiff received and FRO against Defendant, which ordered, among other things: (1) "Defendant is prohibited against future acts of domestic violence"; (2) "Defendant is barred from the marital residence in Sicklerville; (3) "Defendant is prohibited from having any (oral, written, personal or other) form of contact or communication with victim"; .... (6) "Law enforcement accompaniment of Plaintiff to scene or residence"; (7) "Defendant is prohibited from stalking, following, or threatening to harm, to stalk or to follow victim"; (8) "Defendant may visit Children under the following conditions: Mon--Wed & Thurs & weekends. Defendant may call Plaintiff to set up schedule. Pick up & drop off. Moreover, in a space designed for additional comments, the Family Part judge noted: "Defendant may telephone Plaintiff re picking up personal items from house." The provisions of the restraining order were authorized under *N.J.S.A.* 2C:25-29(b). Defendant, thereafter started a divorce proceeding. A *pendente lite* order defining the rights and obligations of each party was handed down by the family court as a result of the divorce litigation. This Order also consolidated the domestic violence final restraining order with the

---

[537] *State v. Wilmouth,* 302 *N.J. Super.* 20, 22, 694 *A.2d* 584 (App. Div. 1997).
[538] *State v. Wilmouth,* 302 *N.J. Super.* 20, 23, 694 *A.2d* 584 (App. Div. 1997).

divorce dissolution proceeding.[539]

The Plaintiff alleged contempt by the Defendant where he dropped off the children at the front door of her home and requested the lawn mower he was required to fix in accordance with the *pendente lite* Order. The trial court found the defendant guilty of contempt and the Appellate Division reversed. The Appellate Court noted that "To convict a defendant of the . . . crime of contempt of a restraining order issued pursuant to the [PDVA]," the State must establish beyond a reasonable doubt that:(1) a restraining order was issued under the [PDVA]; (2) the defendant's violation of the order; (3) that defendant acted purposely or knowingly; and (4) the conduct that constituted the violation also constituted a crime or disorderly persons offense. The court then concluded that there was insufficient evidence to support a contempt conviction, and that Defendant's conduct in returning the children to the front door, returning a car seat to his wife, and in requesting the lawn mower in an effort to comply with the *pendente lite* order, cumulatively was nevertheless a "trivial, non-actionable event," unless specifically proscribed by a prior court order.

In another case previously mentioned (*Hoffman*), a final restraining order existed, which prohibited Defendant from committing future acts of violence and from having contact with the victim or her children. While in jail for a violation of the Order along with additional aggravating conduct, the Defendant mailed torn-up support order to his former spouse. The victim filed charges for harassment and contempt. Ultimately, while finding that that the requisites for harassment were not met, the court conversely found that defendant did violate the contempt statute by making mailings that contravened his restraining order which barred any contact between former spouses.[540]

In *LC*, a restraining order was in place prohibiting defendant from "having contact" with the victim and "from making harassing communications to victims girlfriend and her children." An FRO was also issued, barring Defendant from having contact with the victim, except in matters related to their children. Defendant was subsequently convicted of violating the temporary restraining order and the final restraining order, after showing up at the Defendant's home and ringing the doorbell 6-10 times. However, she was not charged with harassment for conduct involving screaming at the victim and calling his girlfriend a "whore" and a "slut" in front of a large group of people in a school parking lot. (*Note: girlfriend not present at second incident.*)

In its decision, the court noted that the standard of proof in contempt charges is "beyond a reasonable doubt" rather than the standard of "Preponderance of Evidence" in the

---

[539] *State v. Krupinski,* 321 *N.J. Super.* 34, 728 *A.2d* 247 (App. Div. 1999); *see also State v. S.K.,* 423 *N.J. Super.* 540, 33 *A.2d* 1255 (App. Div. 2012)(stating defendant's alleged violation was too trivial for prosecution.)

[540] *State v. Hoffman,* 149 *N.J.* 564, 695 *A.2d* 236 (1997).

initial domestic violence finding.[541] The Appellate Court found that in order to satisfy a contempt charge, the court must make specific findings that the defendant knowingly and violated the restraining Order. In this case, the record supported the trial court's determination that defendant violated the temporary restraining order by visiting her husband's home and ringing the doorbell several times. The court concluded, however, that defendant did not exhibit the purpose to harass required for the second conviction.

As with the previous cases, state of mind is an essential element of contempt. Thus, a defendant has to knowingly or purposely violate a Restraining Order to be held in contempt. In *Finamore*, the Defendant and his wife entered a settlement agreement, which incorporated a prior restraining order the wife had obtained, but also permitted defendant and his wife to contact each other to arrange child visitation and to discuss other issues involving the parties' child. Defendant thereafter made four telephone calls to the Plaintiff, wherein they argued over the visitation. Stemming from these calls, Defendant was charged with knowingly violating that restraining order. The appellate court held that (1) the scope of the order was unclear, and defendant's actions could not, as a matter of law, be found to constitute a knowing violation of the order; and (2) because the defendant was charged with knowingly violating a restraining order, and not with violating a restraining order that constituted a crime or disorderly persons offense, defendant's state of mind was an element of the offense and the trial judge erred by not making a specific finding that defendant had the requisite state of mind.[542]

In *Castagno*,[543] Defendant, a police chief, appealed the judgment of conviction and sentence that convicted defendant of harassment, and contempt of a judicial order prohibiting him from causing anyone else to make harassing communications. Defendant's conviction resulted from a domestic dispute with his wife. His Wife had obtained a temporary restraining order against him, which included a prohibition against making or causing anyone else to make a harassing communication. Defendant had contacted his wife's uncle, with whom he had a longtime friendship with and to whom he confided about the marital troubles he was experiencing with his wife. Defendant asked the uncle to talk to his wife to stop putting his pension and job at risk. The trial court concluded that, as a matter of law, defendant's communication to the uncle, which was later relayed to defendant's wife, constituted harassment, and as result, contempt of the temporary restraining order as well. Defendant was a police chief and, as part of his judgment of sentence, was ordered to forfeit his office and was barred him from future public employment. The court held that the evidence in the case did not support the essential finding since the uncle was the only witness to the conversation, and he did not conclude that defendant was threatening his wife. Rather, the uncle only concluded that defendant wanted to have a conciliatory message relayed, and therefore the evidence was

---

[541] *State v. L.C.*, 283 *N.J. Super.* 441, 443, 662 *A.2d* 577 (App. Div. 1995).
[542] *State v. Finamore*, 338 *N.J. Super.* 130, 135, 768 *A.2d* 248 (App. Div. 2001).
[543] *State v. Castagno*, 387 *N.J. Super.* 598, 905 *A.2d* 415 (App. Div. 2006).

"not adequate to permit a finding that defendant had a purpose of harassing his wife by causing her uncle to communicate an alarming message."[544]

12.3 ENHANCED PENALTIES

The Act also provides for enhanced penalties for any person convicted of a second or subsequent non-indictable domestic violence contempt offense, and mandates a sentence of no less than thirty days for these violations.[545]

Where a Defendant was charged of violating a restraining order on three separate occasions, in separate complaints, the defendant was found guilty of two of the three charges at the same trial. Based on these facts, the court sought to enhance defendant's sentence under statute, which required that a 30 day imprisonment be imposed for defendants convicted of violating a restraining order on two or more occasions. The court held that the enhanced penalty statute applied only to chronologically sequential convictions and did not apply to simultaneous convictions. The court further held that the imposition of enhanced penalties should only be applied to individuals <u>previously convicted</u> of an offense on the date the subsequent offense was committed.[546]

As a practical matter, the Prosecutor's Office will usually only seek an enhanced penalty for domestic violence violations in the most heinous or egregious instances.

12.4 BAIL; CONTEMPT

Once an individual is arrested, the police officer transports the person to the police station, or such other place deemed proper, and shall: Conduct a search of the domestic violence central registry; and sign a complaint concerning the incident giving rise to the contempt charge.[547]

Thereafter, the police officer is required to contact a judge to have bail set on the contempt charge.[548]

Bail is either set by:
a.   A Superior Court Judge during normal Court hours (8:30 a.m. to 4:00 p.m.);
b.   Emergent Superior Court Judge when courts are closed.
c.   Municipal Court Judge if designated by the Assignment Judge of the Court to set

---

[544] *State v. Castagno*, 387 *N.J. Super.* 598, 608, 905 *A.2d* 415 (App. Div. 2006).

[545] *N.J.S.A.* 2C:25-30.

[546] *State v. Bowser*, 272 *N.J. Super.* 582, 640 *A.2d* 884 (Law Div. 1993).

[547] *State of New Jersey Domestic Violence Procedural Manual*, p. III-13 to -14; *N.J.S.A.* 2C:25-31.

[548] *N.J.S.A.* 2C:25-31(a-d).

bail for a contempt charge where the violation is a petty disorderly offense or if the defendant had disobeyed a "no contact" restraining order.

*A Court administrator cannot set bail.

CHAPTER THIRTEEN

SPECIAL PROBLEMS FOR ATTORNEYS

A special problem exists where attorneys are defendants in domestic violence cases. As a general matter, attorneys are officers of the court and as such are subject to certain ethical obligations. In turn, attorneys are subjected to higher penalties than members of the general public if they are found guilty of domestic violence. Three cases on the topic have defined the enhanced penalties, along with the obligations imposed upon attorneys.

A defendant/attorney was criminally convicted of simple assault (*N.J.S.A.* 2:12-1(a)(1)), against a client he had been having sexual relations with. Said client had been referred to him from a battered women's shelter. Based on the conviction, the Office of Attorney Ethics filed a motion for final discipline before the Disciplinary Review Board (New Jersey), pursuant to *N.J. Ct. R.* 1:20-6(c)(2)(i). The Disciplinary Review Board found that respondent had engaged in unethical conduct and initially recommended a private reprimand. In turn, the Supreme Court was faced with the sole issue of determining the extent of the discipline to be imposed. [549]

> In its decision, the Court stated:

> A criminal conviction is conclusive evidence of guilt in a disciplinary proceeding. Therefore, respondent's conviction of the disorderly persons offense of simple assault is clear and convincing evidence that he has violated [New Jersey] *RPC* 8.4(b) (by committing a criminal act that reflects adversely on his honesty, trustworthiness, or fitness as a lawyer). The sole issue to be determined is the extent of discipline to be imposed. ...In determining appropriate discipline, we consider the interests of the public, the bar, and the respondent.. The primary purpose of discipline is not to punish the attorney but to preserve the confidence of the public in the bar. The appropriate discipline depends on many factors, including the "nature and severity of the crime, whether the crime is related to the practice of law, and any mitigating factors such as respondent's reputation, his prior trustworthy conduct, and general good conduct.

> Furthermore:

> Although the assault itself was not related to respondent's legal

---

[549] *In the Matter of Principato*, 139 *N.J.* 456, 460, 655 *A.2d* 920 (1995).

practice, respondent assaulted his client. An attorney in his relations with a client is bound to the highest degree of fidelity and good faith. To the public he is a lawyer whether he acts in a representative capacity or otherwise.[550]

The Court went on to state:

> To be admitted to the bar, an applicant "must possess a certain set of traits--honesty and truthfulness, trustworthiness and reliability, and a professional commitment to the judicial process and the administration of justice." We described those traits as the fundamental norms that control the professional and personal behavior of attorneys. Acts of domestic violence violate those fundamental norms.[551]

The Supreme Court determined that a public reprimand was appropriate, due to the seriousness of defendant's misconduct, notably because respondent's assault on "a particularly vulnerable client, referred to him by a battered women's shelter, was a serious violation of [*New Jersey Rule of Professional Conduct*] 8.4(b)." In making its determination, the court considered mitigating factors, including: the fact that respondent recognized he used poor judgment in becoming personally involved with a client; his conduct was highly unlikely to recur; and respondent's previous ethics record was untarnished."

Due to the fact that the court had not previously addressed the appropriate discipline to be imposed on a lawyer who was convicted of domestic violence, and that the respondent's offense was an isolated incident and did not present a pattern of abuse, the court in this instance simply ordered that the defendant be: publicly reprimanded; that the entire record of the matter be made a permanent part of defendant's file as an attorney at law of this State; and that defendant reimburse the Disciplinary Oversight Committee for appropriate administrative costs incurred in the prosecution of this matter.[552]

In a case decided on the same day, *In Re Magid*, the court considered same factors utilized in *Principato*, to decide the punishment.[553] Some of the mitigating factors considered by the court were: the fact that Defendant had an unblemished professional record, there was no pattern of abusive behavior, the actual assault lasted for a very short period of time, and

---

[550] *In the Matter of Principato* 139 N.J. 456, 460, 655 A.2d 920 (1995).

[551] *In the Matter of Principato* 139 N.J. 456, 461, 655 A.2d 920 (1995)(citations omitted).

[552] *In the Matter of Principato* 139 N.J. 456, 463, 655 A.2d 920 (1995).

[553] *In the Matter of Magid*, 139 N.J. 449, 454, 655 A.2d 916 (1995).

moreover, the intense negative publicity had drastically affected respondent's career.[554] The court again decided to impose public sanctions, due to the novelty of the issue, but warned that similar future conduct of attorneys would be met with the more severe consequence of suspension:

> But for the fact that we have not previously addressed the appropriate discipline to be imposed on an attorney who is convicted of an act of domestic violence, and that respondent did not engage in a pattern of abusive behavior, respondent's discipline would be greater than the public reprimand we hereby impose. We caution members of the bar, however, that the Court in the future will ordinarily suspend an attorney who is convicted of an act of domestic violence.[555]

In another case, the subject incident occurred 7 months after the Court decided *Magid* and *Principato*. Accordingly, the Court in determining the punishment held that the respondent was or should have been aware of the two prior cases. In addition, the Court found that Respondent had previously engaged in physical violence against his wife on several occasions, and during the subject incident had struck his three year old child. As a result, the court imposed a three month suspension on Respondent.[556]

Lastly, in *In Re Toronto*, Defendant attempted to strangle his ex-wife with a telephone cord, and pleaded guilty to simple assault. Defendant argued that he merely pushed the ex wife and should not be suspended because his prior good behavior. However, at the same time the Office of Attorney Ethics was investigating another complaint against the Defendant involving a former romantic partner. (*As to that investigation, and the Defendant's subsequent misrepresentations about his relationship with the woman, the ethics committee found defendant had violated N.J. R.P.C. 8.4(c), which states that it is professional misconduct for a lawyer to "engage in conduct involving dishonesty, fraud, deceit or misrepresentation"*) Based upon defendant's assault, in addition to his unethical behavior, (i.e. misrepresenting this sexual and employment relations with a complainant) the court imposed a three-month suspension. (*Note: This is prior to the announcement of a new rule based on aggravating factors.*)[557]

---

[554] *Ibid.*
[555] *In the Matter of Magid*, 139 N.J. 449, 455, 655 A.2d 916 (1995).
[556] *In the Matter of Margrabia,* 150 N.J. 198, 695 A.2d 1378 (1997).
[557] *In the Matter of Toronto,* 150 N.J. 191, 695 A.2d 8 (1997).

CHAPTER FOURTEEN

MISCELLANEOUS

14.1   NO MEDIATION

The Domestic Violence Act provides that there is no mediation or negotiation, on the issue of custody or parenting time, where there has been a violation of the Act.[558]

The rationale behind forbidding mediation is based on to the process itself. Generally, a mediator is supposed to sit with two relatively equal parties, and work on achieving a mutually agreeable settlement. In domestic violence situations, one party has battered the other party and/or attempted to control them. Where such a dynamic exists, the stronger party is more likely to manipulate their partner during mediation, to achieve their individual goals, rather than trying to achieve what is beneficial to both parties.

In addition, the mediation process itself could be physically and emotionally harmful to the victim of domestic violence, since they would be forced to communicate repeatedly with their abuser during the mediation session. These sessions would present the abuser with an opportunity to assault, threaten, or emotionally coerce the victim. Furthermore, the victims would be unable to express their real needs when faced with fear of the abuser and fear of future retribution.

14.2   JUDGES

By advisory letter of the Administrative Conference, dated November 9, 1993, the Supreme Court decided that municipal court judges may represent clients in domestic violence matters in those municipalities where they do not serve or are not cross assigned. Municipal court judges are prohibited from hearing matters in which they have actual and potential jurisdiction.

14.3   PROSECUTION OF THE COMPLAINT

There is a lack of necessary manpower in regard to prosecutors available to institute legal proceedings against defendants in domestic violence matters. As a result, private prosecution in municipal court are permissible, *N.J. Ct. R.* 7:8-7(b), but not a favored practice. The Supreme Court held whenever an attorney for a private party applies for permission to prosecute a criminal complaint in the municipal court, the court should determine whether to allow the complaint under standards of propriety and conflict of interest.   To make this

---

[558] *N.J.S.A.* 2C:25-29(a)

decision, it is necessary to weigh the benefits against the burdens of permitting a private attorney to prosecute.[559]

Following *Storm*, the Appellate Division, in a very recent case which was approved for publication, but not to date reported, held that a defendants conviction for harassment was procedurally defective and cannot stand as matter of law because the requirements set forth in *Storm* and subsequently supplemented and codified in *N.J. Ct. R.* 7:8-7(b) were not followed where he was prosecuted by a private attorney.[560] The municipal court proceedings were presented for *de novo* review to the Law Division and showed that the Secaucus Municipal Court permitted the private attorney retained by the complaining witness to assume the authority ordinarily reserved to duly appointed municipal prosecutors without adhering to the procedural requirements of *N.J. Ct. R. 7:8-7(b)*. The Appellate Division found the Law Division erred by not declaring his conviction in the municipal court void *ab initio*. Specifically, the *New Jersey Court Rule* requires a Court to allows for private prosecution on "cross-complaints" only if the Court has first reviewed the private prosecutor's motion to so appear and accompanying certification submitted on a form approved by the Administrative Director of the Courts, and it is satisfied that a potential for conflict exists for the municipal prosecutor due to the nature of the charges set forth in the cross-complaints. The Court must also put such findings on the record. There were no cross-complaints, and without cross-complaints, the Court held that there "are no legal grounds for the municipal court to permit a private attorney to represent the State . . . because public policy favors that prosecutions be conducted by duly appointed independent prosecutors."[561]

14.4   DOUBLE JEOPARDY

The <u>Double Jeopardy Clause</u> provides that no person shall be subject for the same offence to be twice put in jeopardy of life or limb. *U.S. Const. Amend. V.* This protection applies both to successive punishments and to successive prosecutions for the same criminal offense.

Double jeopardy bars additional punishment and prosecution for an offense unless "each offense contains an element not contained in the other.[562]

In *Morton*, the Defendant was charged with domestic violence by his former girlfriend. At trial, the chancery court, family division found that defendant committed said acts, ordering him to pay the medical costs and pain and suffering damages to the victim. Defendant was then indicted, charged, and convicted with second degree aggravated assault. The defendant appealed the criminal charges based upon double jeopardy. The Appellate Court affirmed,

---

[559] *State v. Storm,* 141 *N.J.* 245, 661 *A.2d* 790 (1995).
[560] *State v. Myerowitz,* ___ *N.J. Super.* ____, ____ *A.3d* ____ (App. Div. 2015).
[561] *Ibid.*
[562] *United States v. Dixon,* 509 *U.S.* 688, 113 *S. Ct.* 2849,125 *L. Ed.* 2d 556 (1993).

finding that double jeopardy did not attach when defendant was both assessed a civil penalty, which was designed to be remedial, and then criminally prosecuted for offenses arising from the same incident. Furthermore, the civil domestic violence proceeding was between the victim and defendant and did not involve the state. The court also found that the sentence was "neither illegal nor excessive when it was within the statutory guidelines and the trial court properly balanced the aggravating factors against the mitigating factors." [563]

The *Morton* Court ultimately held that "Double Jeopardy" clause does not preclude a criminal prosecution for second degree aggravated assault of defendant's girlfriend even though a separate action has taken place in which there is a $250,000.00 judgment entered against defendant in a proceeding under Domestic Violence Act arising out of the same incident that gave rise to criminal indictment. Monetary award for pain and suffering was remedial in nature and prior proceeding between girlfriend and defendant did not involve the State.

14.5   REINSTATEMENT OF ORDER

Conditional dismissal of domestic violence restraining order based on domestic abuser attending counseling was properly reinstated after domestic abuser failed to attend counseling.[564] *See chapter 11 for further information regarding conditional dismissals.*

14.6   EXPUNGEMENT

The expungement of domestic violence charges is not permitted. In one case, the court affirmed the order granting petitioner's application for the expungement of criminal charges, but denied his application for the expungement of domestic violence charges. The court held that the statutory policy of expunging records connected with criminal charges or convictions against petitioner did not extend to non-criminal matters such as domestic violence proceedings or matrimonial actions.[565]

14.7   AMENDMENT OF RESTRAINING ORDER

A restraining order should not be prepared in a format containing substantial interlineations, added paragraphs, and cross-outs. This creates a poor and confusing record for the parties and for the Appellate Court. All restraining orders should be neatly prepared and typed for the sake of the parties, the courts, and the police who may have to enforce a

---

[563] *State v. Morton,* 292 *N.J. Super.* 92, 678 *A.2d* 308 (App. Div. 1996).

[564] *C.O. v. J.O,* 292 *N.J. Super.* 219, 223, 678 *A.2d* 748 (Ch. Div.1996); *See also T.M. v. J.C.,* 348 *N.J. Super.* 101, 791 *A.2d.* 300 (App. Div. 2002)(conditional dismissal of a domestic violence complaint is improper as not being authorized either by statute or rule).

[565] *In re Expungment of the Criminal Record of M.D.Z.,* 286 *N.J. Super.* 82, 668 *A.2d* 423 (App. Div. 1995).

restraining order.[566]

14.8 CHANGE OF NAME

In his counterclaim to plaintiff's domestic violence complaint, the defendant (husband) requested that the court issue an order changing the surname of the couple's minor child to that of defendant. The court denied defendant's application. The court noted that the Prevention of Domestic Violence Act of 1991 sets forth an exhaustive list of remedies available to a judge of the Family Part of the Chancery Division of the Superior Court hearing a complaint, and might entertain the request in different circumstances. Furthermore, the Domestic Violence Act provided that the court could grant "other" appropriate relief for the plaintiff and dependent children "provided that the plaintiff consents to such relief". However, in this particular case, the court had to deny the Defendant's request based on the following reasons: The plaintiff objected to the name change, defendant failed to comply with the requirements of *N.J.S.A.* 2A:52-1, in that the complaint did not contain the necessary elements for a change of name, and the defendant did comply with *N.J. Ct. R.* 4:72-1 and serve a copy of the complaint upon the proper parties.[567]

In another matter, and after the domestic violence, a victim sought to change her name. The court held that requiring publication of the application to change her name would result in an injustice, as publication of the application would provide her abuser with her address and new name. Therefore, there was a compelling interest to waive the publication requirements of *N.J. Ct. R.* 4:72-3 pursuant to *N.J. Ct. R.* 1:1-2, and good cause existed to seal the court record pursuant to *N.J. Ct. R.* 1:2-1 and 1:38(e).[568]

14.9 UNEMPLOYMENT BENEFITS

Appellant, a victim of domestic violence, left her job at a law firm, after obtaining protective orders against her husband, which proved futile. In "fear for her life," she moved to California to be close to her family for protection. Appellant subsequently filed for unemployment benefits and was denied same.

It was determined by the Administrative Agency that the appellant was disqualified from receiving unemployment benefits since she left work "voluntarily without good cause attributable to such work" against the requisites of *N.J.S.A* 43:21-5(a). Appellant sought review of this decision. On review, the Appellate Division found that the appellant left work because of personal reasons, not because of good cause attributable to work, and the decision of the was supported by substantial, credible evidence and was not arbitrary, capricious or unreasonable.

---

[566] *Fillippone v. Lee*, 304 *N.J. Super.* 301, 700 *A.2d* 384 (App. Div. 1997).
[567] *Basile v. Basile*, 255 *N.J. Super.* 181, 604 *A.2d* 693 (Ch. Div. 1992).
[568] *In re: Application of E.F.G.*, 398 *N.J. Super.* 539, 942 A.2d 166 (App. Div. 2008).

The decision was affirmed accordingly.[569]

14.10 INSURANCE

Acts of domestic violence are so reprehensible that public policy dictates that wrongdoers be denied insurance coverage, even when they are found to have possessed only reckless mental state. In the case of Bittner, the defendant alleged that his conduct of punching his girlfriend in the face, was not intentional, and therefore should be covered under the homeowner's insurance policy. The court held that the "public policy of the New Jersey, to provide maximum protection to victims of domestic violence, and to deter acts of domestic violence," precludes the availability of insurance coverage to provide a defense to a domestic violence claim or indemnification for such an award."[570]

In an early case, it was held that homeowners insurance does not provide coverage for harassing phone calls, as they are "intentional acts" and therefore not covered under the homeowner's policy.[571]

In another case, the court held that an insurer was not obligated to defend or indemnify the insured for his acts of abuse against his former wife under a homeowner's policy, which excluded indemnity for injuries expected or intended. On the issue of whether the insured's subjective intent with respect to the consequences of his alleged abusive behavior toward his wife were relevant in determining if coverage existed under his homeowner's policy, the court ruled that an objective approach which focused on the likelihood that injury would result from an actor's behavior was more appropriate, rather than a subjective approach. The court found that spousal abuse was so inherently injurious that it could never be an accident, therefore to expand coverage to include injuries sustained as a result of domestic violence would violate public policy. Lastly, the court commented on recourse available for the abused spouse, where such a *Tevis* claim is denied. "An abused spouse will not be left without a remedy if the abuser's homeowner's insurance is found not to cover *Tevis* claims. In almost all divorce actions, there are equitable assets to distribute. Therefore, as was done in this case, the abused spouse's claims will be compensated by a greater share of the marital assets."[572]

In a later case, the Appellate Court was again confronted with an insurance coverage appeal, which required it to address the scope of its decision in *Merrimack Mutual Fire*

---

[569] *Pagan v. Board of Review*, 296 N.J. Super. 539, 687 A.2d 328 (App. Div. 1997).

[570] *Bittner v. Harleysville Insurance Co.* 338 N.J. Super. 447, 769 A.2d 1085 (App. Div. 2001).

[571] *Mroz v. Smith*, 261 N.J. Super. 133, 617 A.2d 1259 (App. Div. 1992); *see Mazzilli v. Acci. & Casualty Ins. Co.*, 35 N.J. 1, 170 A.2d 80 (1961)(noting controlling language of an insurance policy is subject to multiple interpretations, the interpretation sustaining coverage must be applied and courts are bound to protect insured to extent with interpretation of law).

[572] *Merrimack Mut. Fire v. Coppola*, 299 N.J. Super. 219, 690 A.2d 1059 (App. Div. 1997).

Insurance Co. v. Coppola, and whether it applied where a defendant suggests that his objectively assaultive conduct was not intended to cause injury but was intended to protect a plaintiff from potential harm. The facts in the case consisted on the Defendant grabbing his girlfriend's hair, allegedly meaning to grab her coat, to prevent her from crossing a roadway, while in an inebriated state. The girlfriend suffered injuries initiated by this act, when she thereafter struggled to get free and struck her knee. The girlfriend then filed a tort action against the Defendant, and Defendant sought to have his homeowner's insurance policy defend him in the action. The action was decided in favor of the insurance company, denying Defendant coverage, from which he appealed. The Appellate Court reversed and remanded, finding that a genuine issue of material fact existed, which precluded a determination, as a matter of law, that defendant was not entitled to coverage under his homeowner's policy. The court stated that where a factual inquiry is necessary to determine coverage, that issue should be resolved in a plenary proceeding prior to resolution of the underlying tort action. The matter was remanded for a plenary hearing to resolve the factual dispute and determine whether the acts complained of "fall within the exclusion under the policy." That finding, in essence, requires a determination of whether defendant committed an act of domestic violence, a determination which will test the quality of his acts as well as the intended result."[573]

14.11 BIFURCATION

(Note: See Chapter 12)

14.12 RECENT AMENDMENTS TO THE ACT

- *N.J.S.A.* 2C:25-21(d)(1) was amended to make it mandatory (previously "may"), for police, when investigating a DV incident, to question persons to determine whether weapons are on the premises; to seize any weapons the officer reasonably believes exposes the victim to a risk of serious bodily injury; and to deliver seized weapons to county prosecutor, when the officer has probably cause to believe that an act of DV has been committed.

- *N.J.S.A.* 2C:25-21(d)(3) – the "weapons return" section of PDVA – was amended to provide that if the owner of a weapon is subject to any of the disabilities set forth in *N.J.S.A.* 2C:58-3(c), the firearm shall not be returned to the owner (previous version permitted return if the complaint had been dismissed, if defendant was found not guilty, or if court found the DV situation no longer exists).

---

[573] *Cumberland Mutual Insurance Company v. Beeby*, 327 N.J. Super. 394, 743 A.2d 853 (App. Div. 2000).

- *N.J.S.A.* 2C:25-21(d)(5) was added, stating that "no law enforcement officer or agency shall be held liable in any civil action brought by any person for failing to learn of, locate or seize a weapon pursuant to this act, or for returning a seized weapon to its owner."

- *N.J.S.A.* 2C:58-3(c)(1), as amended, provides that any person who has been convicted of a disorderly persons offense involving an act of DV, whether or not armed with or possessing a weapon at the time cannot purchase a firearm or be issued a firearms purchaser identification card.

- *N.J.S.A.* 2C:58-3(c)(6), as amended, provides that any person who is subject to a DV restraining order is prohibited from possessing any firearm (therefore, every DV restraining order must prohibit defendant from possession of firearms).

- *N.J.S.A.* 2C:58-3(c)(8) was amended to prohibit purchase of firearm or issuance of a firearms purchaser ID card by any person whose firearm has been seized pursuant to the PDVA and whose firearm has not been returned.

ABOUT THE AUTHORS AND THE FIRM

Gourvitz & Gourvitz has a reputation for professionalism and their aggressive representation of clients.

Gourvitz & Gourvitz, LLC. represents individuals in New Jersey, New York and Internationally in the broad spectrum of family legal matters. They appear frequently in State and Federal Courts in cases involving every facet of family law. They are particularly well known for their aggressive representation of clients.

The firm, which specializes in cases involving abduction of children and removal of children, has extensive ability to find and locate the children and have them returned to their rightful parents. The firm has:

Successfully found and located a kidnapped child from Trinidad to the United States and had the Court order her return.

Successfully located a child taken to wilderness of Peru by the mother and returned to the United States where the Court awarded custody to the father.

Successfully prevented a child from being abducted to Japan by obtaining a Koseki from Japan utilizing self-help and meeting at the Japan Consulate to prevent a passport from being issued.

Successfully had the FBI board a plane on the tarmac of Newark Airport to seize a child who was illegally taken to Brazil.

Successfully, through self-help, had a child legally returned to the Netherlands.

Successfully had the Court compel the return of children from Switzerland.

Successfully had the State Court grant the mother's relocation to Italy with her two children.

Successfully had the Court grant a mother's relocation with her children to Russia.

Successfully had the Court prevent a mother from abducting her children to Russia.

Successfully had a Court prevent two children from being returned to Paraguay.

Successfully prevented a child from being returned to Argentina to a pedophile father, only after two trials and a Federal appeal.

Successfully had a Court grant visitation to a father who lives in Malaysia and Singapore.

Successfully compelled, through Court action, support from a father living in Hong Kong.

Successfully returned a child to the mother who was the sole custodian after the child was abducted from Pennsylvania to New Jersey by the maternal grandparents.

Successfully had the interstate removal of a mother and child with new husband move from NJ to Alabama.

ELLIOT H. GOURVITZ, ESQ.

E-mail: ehg@gourvitz.com

Elliot H. Gourvitz is an attorney who has practiced matrimonial and family law for 46+ years and has been certified by the Supreme Court of New Jersey as a specialist in family law (1991-2008). He has successfully argued many State and Federal appellate cases and is the author of _Domestic Torts in New Jersey_, _Domestic Violence Source Book_, and numerous articles. He is a Lecturer and speaker on family law and has been quoted as an authority in many articles. Mr. Gourvitz also serves as an expert witness in international child abduction, Hague Convention, and other cases throughout the Country.

Elliot Gourvitz is an attorney known for his aggressively representing his clients in high profile cases involving substantial assets. He has championed victims of domestic abuse and the recovery of abducted children which has litigated to the far points of the world.

Elliot H. Gourvitz has represented high profile clients in difficult situations.

His charitable works began early with his being Chairman of the Teen United Jewish Appeal of Essex County. He was named man of the year of the United Cerebral Palsy Foundation and served on and was President of the American Academy of Matrimonial Lawyers Foundation for 10 years whose goal is to elevate the burden of divorce and help victims of domestic violence and abuse.

He has served on various New Jersey Supreme Court Committees, New Jersey Bar Association and was head of the Union County Early Settlement Panel for over 20 years.

He was the Chairman of the New Jersey Chapter of the American Academy of Matrimonial Lawyers and a delegate to the National Chapter. He was one of the founding members of the American College of Diplomats which limits its members to 100 throughout the world.

He has lectured at various colleges in the nation including William & Mary College in Virginia and Seton Hall University.

He has appeared on Oprah Winfrey, Geraldo Rivera, Gordon Ethan, Dr. Laura, UCN8 of the Comcast Network, Telemundo and various other news programs which sought his expert advice and input on such matters as domestic violence, wire tapping and the abduction of children and on international law.

He has testified for other attorneys as an expert witness on prenuptial agreements, the Hague Convention and Abduction of Children in many states including Arizona and Florida.

He has been in the forefront of instituting domestic torts in New Jersey and has written the only guide to this in the State. He, along with his partner and son, Ari Gourvitz, Esq. and his daughter-in-law, Melissa Gourvitz, Esq. wrote the seminal book, Domestic Violence Source Book, and have recently updated it.

Court Admissions:

States of New Jersey and New York
United States District Court, District of New Jersey, Southern District of New York, Eastern District of Wisconsin
United States Tax Court, Court of Claims, Court of International Trade
Temporary Emergency Court of Appeals of the United States
United States Court of Appeals of District of Columbia, Second, Third, Fourth, Fifth, Sixth, Seventh, Eighth, Ninth, Tenth and Federal Circuits
United States Supreme Court
Certified as a Civil Trial Attorney by the Supreme Court of New Jersey, 1981; recertified 1989 and 1996
Certified Matrimonial Attorney by the Supreme Court of New Jersey (1991-2008)

Bar Associations:

Member, Supreme Court of New Jersey Family Practice Division Committee, 1992-96
Former Fellow, American Academy of Matrimonial Lawyers (1981-2008); recertified 1991, 1995, and 2000; President of New Jersey Chapter 1992-94; National Delegate 1994-2000.; President of New Jersey Chapter 1992-94; National Delegate 1994-2000
Certified Matrimonial Arbitrator by the American Academy of Matrimonial Lawyers
Certified Matrimonial Mediator by the American Academy of Matrimonial Lawyers
Former Fellow, International Academy of Matrimonial Lawyers (1989-2009)
Former Diplomat, American College of Family Trial Lawyers (1991-2008)
Chair New Jersey State Bar Association Certified Trial Attorneys Section of the New Jersey State Bar Association 1999-2001

Chairman, Union County Matrimonial Early Settlement panel, 1986-2002

Panelist in Early Settlement Program of Essex, Middlesex and Union Counties, 1982-2002

Member of the Executive Committee of the Family Law Section of the New Jersey State Bar Association, 1986-2004

New York State, Federal and American Bar Associations (Member, Mediation and Arbitration Committee)

New Jersey Trial Lawyers' Association

The Association of Trial Lawyers of America (Member of the Board of Governors)

ARI H. GOURVITZ, ESQ.

E-mail: ahg@gourvitz.com

Ari H. Gourvitz, Esq. began his legal career at an early age interning for various well known and respected matrimonial attorneys both in high school and college.

Mr. Gourvitz continued his legal career by first interning and then becoming a law clerk for the Honorable Virginia Long (Ret.), Justice of the New Jersey Supreme Court.

In that capacity, he aided the Justice in researching, writing and developing some of the most important matrimonial decisions and precedents of today's Court.

Mr. Gourvitz served while in law school as an extern to the Honorable Michael Diamond, J.S.C. in Passaic County while involved in the Family Law Clinic at Seton Hall Law School. Mr. Gourvitz then joined the law offices of Elliot H. Gourvitz, Esq. as an associate.

In 2008, he formed Gourvitz & Gourvitz, LLC, and is the managing member of the firm. Mr. Gourvitz has concentrated his entire legal career on divorce and other family law-related matters, but handles other legal matters for existing clients.

Mr. Gourvitz was admitted to the New Jersey Bar and the United States District Court, District of New Jersey, and Third Circuit Court of Appeals in 2004, and to the New York Bar in 2005. Mr. Gourvitz is a member of the New Jersey State Bar Association, a member of the Union County Bar Association and a Barrister in the Justice Virginia A. Long Inns of Court. Mr. Gourvitz zealously represents his clients while paying close attention to each client's individual needs.

He has co-authored the first, second, and third editions of the firm's Domestic Violence Source Book and has been responsible for handling most of the firm's Federal and State practice helping to establish precedent which is not only shaped but changed and defined existing law.

Because of his various successes in litigation in both Federal and State Courts, he has been recognized by his peers as "Rising Star" as published by "Superlawyers" in 2013, 2014 and 2015.

Education:

University of Michigan, B.A.
Seton Hall University School of Law, J.D.

Court Admissions:

States of New Jersey and New York
United States District Court, District of New Jersey
United States Court of Appeals For the Third Circuit

Bar Associations:

New Jersey and New York Bar Associations
Union County Bar Association
The Justice Virginia Long Family Law American Inn of Court

Past Experience:

Judicial Law Clerk to Justice Virginia A. Long of the New Jersey Supreme Court.
Extern to the Honorable Michael Diamond, J.S.C.

Author:

Articles:

Why New Jersey is Correct Forum for Expansion of Gay Marriage," by Elliot H. Gourvitz and Ari H. Gourvitz, New Jersey Law Journal (August 2002).

"Pay or Stay Hearings: Court must assess ability to pay before ordering coercive measures", by Elliot H. Gourvitz and Ari H. Gourvitz, New Jersey Law Journal (August 2004).

"Domestic Violence Update-The Cases Over the Past Couple of Years that Shaped the Current Law," by Elliot H. Gourvitz and Ari H. Gourvitz, New Jersey Lawyer (September 2003).

"Parents Cannot Move Children Intrastate Without Impunity," by Ari H. Gourvitz and Elliot H. Gourvitz, New Jersey Law Journal (August 2003).

"When Enough is Enough Unequal Equitable Distribution in Large Marital Estate Cases," Elliot H. Gourvitz and Ari H. Gourvitz, New Jersey Law Journal (September 2002).

Books:

Domestic Violence Source Book, 2nd Edition, By Elliot H. Gourvitz and Ari H. Gourvitz.
Domestic Violence Source Book, 3rd Edition, By Elliot H. Gourvitz, Ari, H. Gourvitz, and Melissa Gourvitz.*

Lecture(s):

AAML Forum, September 2005, "How To Try a Hague Convention Case."

MELISSA GOURVITZ, ESQ.

E-mail: mp@gourvitz.com

Melissa Gourvitz, Esq. is a native New Yorker. She was born in Brooklyn, New York and later moved with her family to Staten Island, New York where she grew up and is presently living in New York City.

Mrs. Gourvitz graduated from Fordham University in New York City where she earned her Bachelor of Arts (B.A). She attended and graduated Seton Hall University Law School where she received her Juris Doctorate (JD).

Mrs. Gourvitz interned for Michael Diamond, J.S.C. (Ret.), the Presiding Judge of the Passaic County Matrimonial Court.

She handles all phases of matrimonial law, but concentrates on custody, domestic violence and needs of children litigation, as well as Appeals.

Education:

Fordham University, B.A.
Seton Hall University School of Law, J.D.

Court Admissions:

States of New Jersey
United States District Court, District of New Jersey

Bar Associations:

Member of New Jersey Bar Association

Past Experience:

Extern to the Honorable Michael Diamond, J.S.C.

Author:

Domestic Violence Source Book, 3rd Ed., by Elliot H. Gourvitz, Ari H. Gourvitz, and Melissa Gourvitz

TABLE OF APPENDICES

APPENDIX A

Shelters and Help for Battered Women

Atlantic County

Atlantic County Women's Center
Violence Intervention Program (VIP)
1201 New Road, Suite 240
Linwood, NJ 08221
Emergency Shelter
24 Hr. Toll free Hotline: 1-800-286-4184
Phone: (609) 646-6767
TTY: (609) 645-2909
Office: (609) 601-9925
Web: www.acwc.org

Bergen County

Shelter our Sisters
PO Box 217
Hackensack, NJ 07602
Emergency Shelter
24 Hr. Hotline: (201) 944-9600
TTY: (201) 836-3071
Shelter: (201) 836-1075
Fax/Shelter: (201) 836-7029
Administrative Offices:
405 State Street
Hackensack, NJ 07601
Office:(201) 498-9247
Fax/Office: (201) 498-9256
Email: sos@shelteroursisters.org
Web: www.shelteroursisters.org

Alternatives To Domestic Violence
County of Bergen Department of Human Services
One Bergen County Plaza, 2nd Floor
Hackensack, NJ 07601
Non-Residential Services/Outreach/Clinical Counseling/CrisisIntervention/Legal

Advocacy Services
24 Hr. Hotline: (201) 336-7575
TTY: (201) 336-7525
Email: adv@co.bergen.nj.us
Web: www.co.bergen.nj.us/adv/

Burlington County

Providence House Burlington County
PO Box 496
Willingboro, NJ 08046
Emergency Shelter
24 Hr. Hotline: (609) 871-7551
Toll free: 1-877-871-7551
TTY: (609) 871-7551 or 1-877-871-7551
Fax/Office: (856) 824-9340
Web: www.catholiccharitiestrenton.org
Counseling Center
950A Chester Avenue
Delran, NJ 08075
Phone: (856) 824-0599

Camden County

Camden County Women's Center
PO Box 1459
Blackwood, NJ 08021
Emergency Shelter
24 Hr. Hotline: (856) 227-1234
TTY: (856) 227-9264
Office: (856) 227-1800
Outreach Center:
PO Box 1459, Attn: Outreach
Blackwood, NJ 08021
Phone: (856) 963-5668

Cape May County

CARA, Inc. (Coalition Against Rape & Abuse, Inc.)
PO Box 774
Cape May Court House, NJ 08210
Emergency Shelter
24 Hr. Hotline: (609) 522-6489
Toll free: 1-877-294-CARA [2272]
TTY: (609) 463-0818
Office: (609) 522-6489
Email: carasafe1@verizon.net
Web: www.cara-cmc.org

Cumberland County

Center for Family Services
3462 East Landis Avenue
Vineland, NJ 08362
24 Hr. Hotline: 1-800-225-0196
Office: 856-696-2032
Web: www.centerffs.org

Essex County

Babyland Family Violence Program
755 South Orange Avenue
Newark, NJ 07106
Emergency Shelter
24 Hr. Hotline: (862) 438-8045
TTY: (862) 399-3400
Office: (973) 399-3400
Outreach
Family Violence Outreach
755 South Orange Avenue
Newark, NJ 07106
Phone: (973) 399-3400

The Safe House
PO Box 1887
Bloomfield, NJ 07003
Emergency Shelter
24 Hr. Hotline: (973) 759-2154
Office: (973) 759-2378

The Rachel Coalition c/o Jewish Family Service
570 W. Mt. Pleasant Ave, Suite 106
Livingston, NJ 07039
Emergency Safehouse
24 Hr. Emergency Paging Service: (973) 740-1233
Outreach
Office: (973) 740-1233
E-mail: Rachel@jfsmetrowest.org
Web: www.rachelcoalition.org

Linda & Rudy Slucker National Council of Jewish Women (NCJW) Center For Women
70 South Orange Avenue, Suite 120
Livingston, NJ 07039
Outreach/Non-Residential Services
Office: (973) 994-4994
Email: centerforwomen@ncjwessex.org
Web: www.CENTERFORWOMENnj.org

Gloucester County

Center for Family Services - Services Empowering the Rights of Victims (SERV)
PO Box 566
Glassboro, NJ 08028
Emergency Shelter
24 Hr. Hotline: (856) 881-3335
Toll free: 1-866-295-7378
TTY: 856-881-9323
Email: serv@centerffs.org
Web: www.centerffs.org

Hudson County

Womenrising, Inc. (formally the YWCA)
Battered Women's Program
270 Fairmount Avenue
Jersey City, NJ 07306

Emergency Shelter
24 Hr. Hotline: (201) 333-5700 ext. 511
Office: (201) 333-5700 ext. 511
Email: womenrising@aol.com
Web: www.womenrising.org
Outreach
270 Fairmount Avenue
Jersey City, NJ 07306
Phone: (201) 333-5700

Hunterdon County

SAFE in Hunterdon
47 E. Main Street
Flemington, NJ 08822
Emergency Shelter
24 Hr. Toll free Hotline: 1-888-988-4033
TTY: 1-866-954-0100
Office: (908) 806-8605
Email: agency@safeinhunterdon.org
Web: www.safeinhunterdon.org/
Outreach
Phone: (908) 788-7666
TTY: (908) 788-7666

Mercer County

Womanspace, Inc.
1530 Brunswick Avenue
Lawrence, NJ 08648
Emergency Shelter
24-Hr. Hotline: (609) 394-9000
State Hotline: 1-800-572-SAFE [7233]
TTY: 1-888-252-SAFE [7233]
Office: (609) 394-0136
Counseling & Support Office
1530 Brunswick Avenue
Lawrenceville, NJ 08648
Phone: (609) 394-2532

Middlesex County

Women Aware, Inc.
250 Livingston Ave.
New Brunswick, NJ 08901
Emergency Shelter
24-Hr. Hotline: (732) 249-4504
TTY: (732) 249-0600
Office: (732) 249-4900
Email: womenaware@aol.com
Web: www.womenaware.net

Manavi, Inc.*
PO Box 3103
New Brunswick, NJ 08903-3103
Office: 732-435-1414
Email: manavi@manavi.org
Website: http://www.manavi.org/ * A non-profit organization for women who trace their cultural heritage to Bangladesh, India, Nepal, Pakistan, and Sri Lanka.

Monmouth County

180 Turning Lives Around
One Bethany Road, Building 3, Suite 42
Hazlet, NJ 07730
Emergency Shelter
24-Hr. Hotline: (732) 264-4111
Toll free: 1-888-THE-WCMC [843-9262]
TTY: (732) 264-3089
Office: (732) 264-4360
Email: info@180nj.org
Web: www.180nj.org
Outreach
Phone: (732) 264-4111

Morris County

Jersey Battered Women's Services, Inc.
(JBWS)
PO Box 1437
Morristown, NJ 07962

Emergency Shelter
24 Hr. Hotline: (973) 267-4763
TTY: (973) 285-9095
Office: (973) 267-7520

Ocean County

Providence House - Ocean
P.O. Box 414
Whiting, NJ 08759
Emergency Shelter
24 Hr. Hotline: (732) 244-8259
Toll free: 1-800-246-8910 (from the "609"
area code only)
TTY: (732) 244-8259 or 1-800-246-8910
(from the "609" area code only)
Office: (732) 244-8259
Web: www.catholiccharitiestrenton.org
Outreach
88 School House Road
Whiting, NJ 08579
Phone: (732) 350-2120

Passaic County

Passaic County Women's Center - Domestic
Violence Program
PO Box 244
Paterson, NJ 07543
Emergency Shelter
24-Hr. Hotline: (973) 881-1450
Office: (973) 881-1450
Outreach
1027 Madison Avenue
Paterson, NJ 07513
Phone: (973) 881-0725

Project S.A.R.A.H.
199 Scoles Avenue
Clifton, NJ 07012
Helpline: 1-888-883-2323
Phone: (973) 777-7638

E-mail: e.stein@projectsarah.org
Web: www.projectsarah.org

Salem County

Salem County Women's Services
PO Box 125
Salem, NJ 08079-0125
Emergency Shelter
24-Hr. Hotline: (856) 935-6655
Toll free: 1-888-632-9511
TTY: (856) 935-7118
Office: (856) 935-8012

Somerset County

Resource Center of Somerset
427 Homestead Road
Hillsborough, NJ 08844
Emergency Shelter
24 Hr. Toll free: 1-866-685-1122
TTY: (908) 359-8604
Web: www.resourcecenterofsomerset.org
Outreach
Office: (908) 359-0003

Sussex County

Domestic Abuse Services, Inc.
PO Box 805
Newton, NJ 07860
Emergency Shelter
24-Hr. Hotline: (973) 875-1211
TTY: (973) 875-6369
Email: info@dasi.org
Web: www.dasi.org
Outreach
Phone: (973) 579-2386

Union County

Project: Protect

c/o YWCA of Eastern Union County
1131 East Jersey Street
Elizabeth, NJ 07201
Emergency Shelter
24-Hr. Hotline: (908) 355-HELP [4357]
TTY: (908) 355-1023
Email: info@ywcamail.com
Web: www.ywca-euc.org
Counseling Services
Office: (908) 355-1995 (ext. 5) or (908) 355-1996

Warren County

Domestic Abuse & Sexual Assault Crisis Center
PO Box 88
Washington, NJ   07882-0088
Emergency Shelter

24-Hr. Hotline: (908) 453-4181
Toll free: 1-866-6BE-SAFE [623-7233]
TTY: (908) 453-2553
Office: (908) 453-4121
Web: www.besafewc.org/

Statewide Domestic Violence Hotline

(800) 572-7233

NJ Coalition for Batter Women

(609) 584-8107
1670 Whitehorse Hamilton Square Road,
Trenton, NJ 08690

Battered Lesbian Hotline

(800) 224-0211

APPENDIX B

FINANCIAL SUPPORT

- WELFARE
- FOOD STAMPS
- CHILD SUPPORT
- MEDICAL CARE COSTS
- RESTITUTION

LEGAL

- PDV ACT
- PROTECTIVE ORDERS
- CIVIL ACTIONS
- CHILD CUSTODY/VISITATION
- DIVORCE
- EXPERT WITNESSES

HOUSING

- PROTECTIVE SHELTERS
- SAFE HOUSES
- RELATIVES/FRIENDS
- TRANSITIONAL AND AFFORDABLE HOUSING

ADVOCACY

- COURTROOM ACCOMPANIMENT
- WELFARE, FOODSTAMPS AND OTHER SERVICES
- CRIMINAL JUSTICE SYSTEM
- COMMUNITY RESPONSE
- RESTITUTION

NEEDS OF THE BATTERED WOMAN

EMPLOYMENT

- CAREER COUNSELING
- INFORMATION
- TRAINING/EDUCATION
- CHILD CARE
- TRANSPORTATION

COUNSELING

- DOMESTIC VIOLENCE SUPPORT GROUPS
- INFORMATION ABOUT DOMESTIC VIOLENCE
- INFORMATION ABOUT BATTERERS
- INFORMATION ABOUT CHILD EXPOSURE TO DOMESTIC VIOLENCE
- SAFETY PLANNING, SHORT & LONG TERM
- ACTION PLANNING

EDUCATION

- GED
- POST-SECONDARY
- CHILDREN'S SCHOOLING
- TRANSPORTATION

PARENT/CHILD RELATIONSHIP

- SAFETY FOR CHILDREN
- EFFECTS OF DOMESTIC VIOLENCE ON THE RELATIONSHIP
- SPECIALIZED INTERVENTION(S)

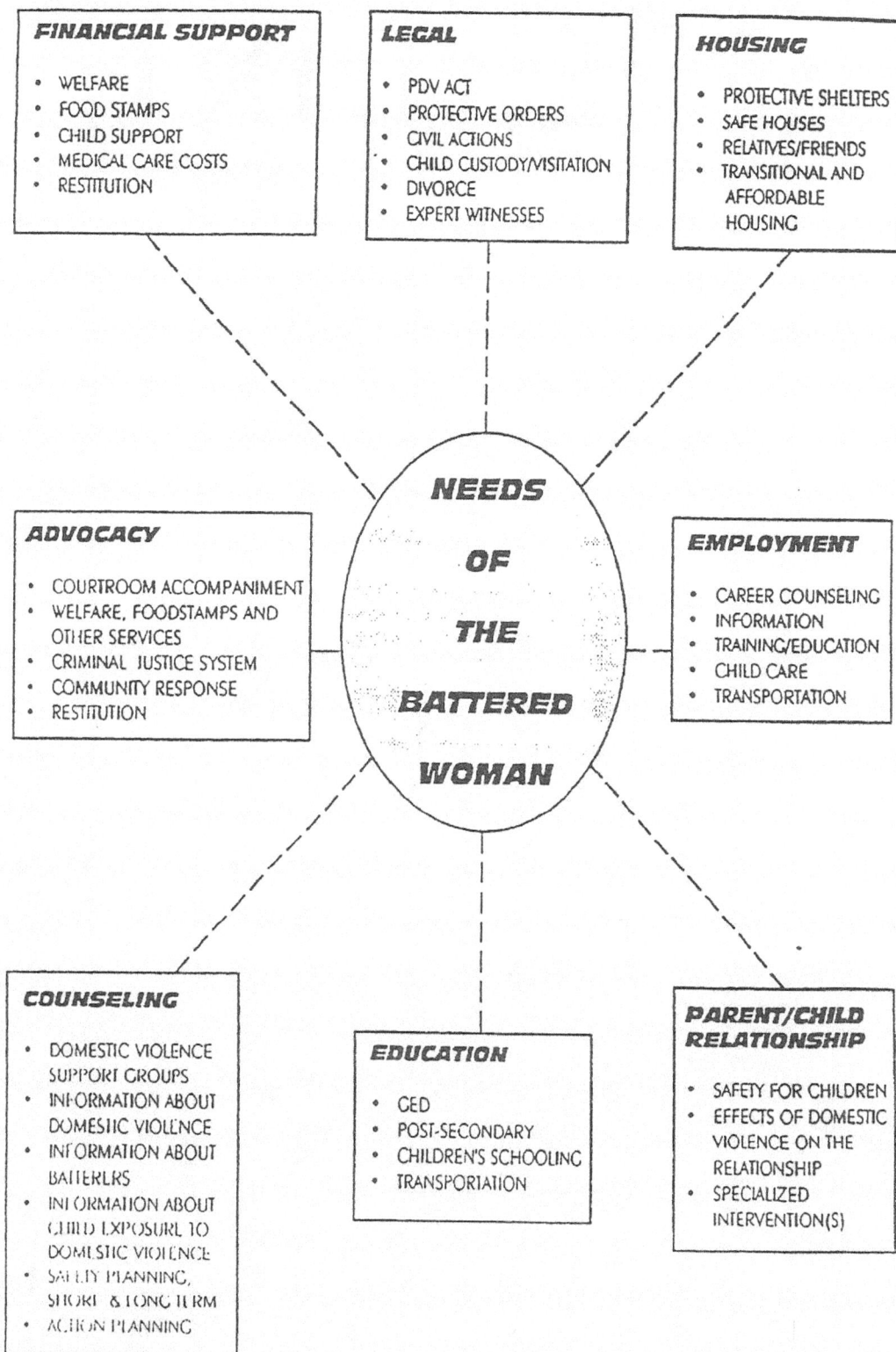

Adapted by NJCBW from Womanspace, Inc., Mercer County

APPENDIX C

CONTINUUM OF FAMILY VIOLENCE

PHYSICAL → Pushing Punching Slapping Kicking Throwing objects Choking Using weapons Homicide/suicide → **DEATH**

VERBAL EMOTIONAL → Name calling Criticizing "You're no good" Ignoring Yelling Isolation Humiliation → **SUICIDE**

SEXUAL → Unwanted touching Sexual name calling Unfaithfulness False accusations Forced sex Hurtful sex → **RAPE**

Without some kind of help, the violence usually gets worse. The end result can be death.

Distributed by the NJ Dept Community Affairs
Division of Women, Domestic Violence Prevention Program

From VILLAGE TO VILLAGE
Alaska Dept of Public Safety

APPENDIX D

Attempts to calm him/her

Nurturing

Silent/Talkative

Stays away from family, friends

Keeps kids quiet

Agrees

Withdraws

Tries to reason

Cooks his/her favorite dinner

General feeling of walking on eggshells

Tension Building

Batterer:

Moody   Nitpicking
Isolates   Withdraws Affection
Put Downs Yelling
Drinking/Drugs Threatens
Destroys Property
Criticizes   Sullen
Crazy-Making

Acute Explosion

Batterer:

Hitting
Choking
Humiliation
Imprisonment
Rape
Use of Weapons
Beating
Imprisonment

Victim Response:

Protects herself anyway she can

Police called by her/him, kids, neighbor

Tries to calm batterer

Tries to Reason with batterer

Leaves

Fights back

Denial

Honeymoon

Batterer:

I'm Sorry... Begs forgiveness... Promises to get counseling... Goes to Church... AA... Sends Flowers... Brings presents... "I'll never do it again..." Wants to make love... Declares love... Enlists family support...

Cries...

Victim Response:

Agrees to stay, returns, or takes batterer back.... Attempts to stop legal proceedings... Sets up for counseling appointments for batterer... Feels Happy, Hopeful

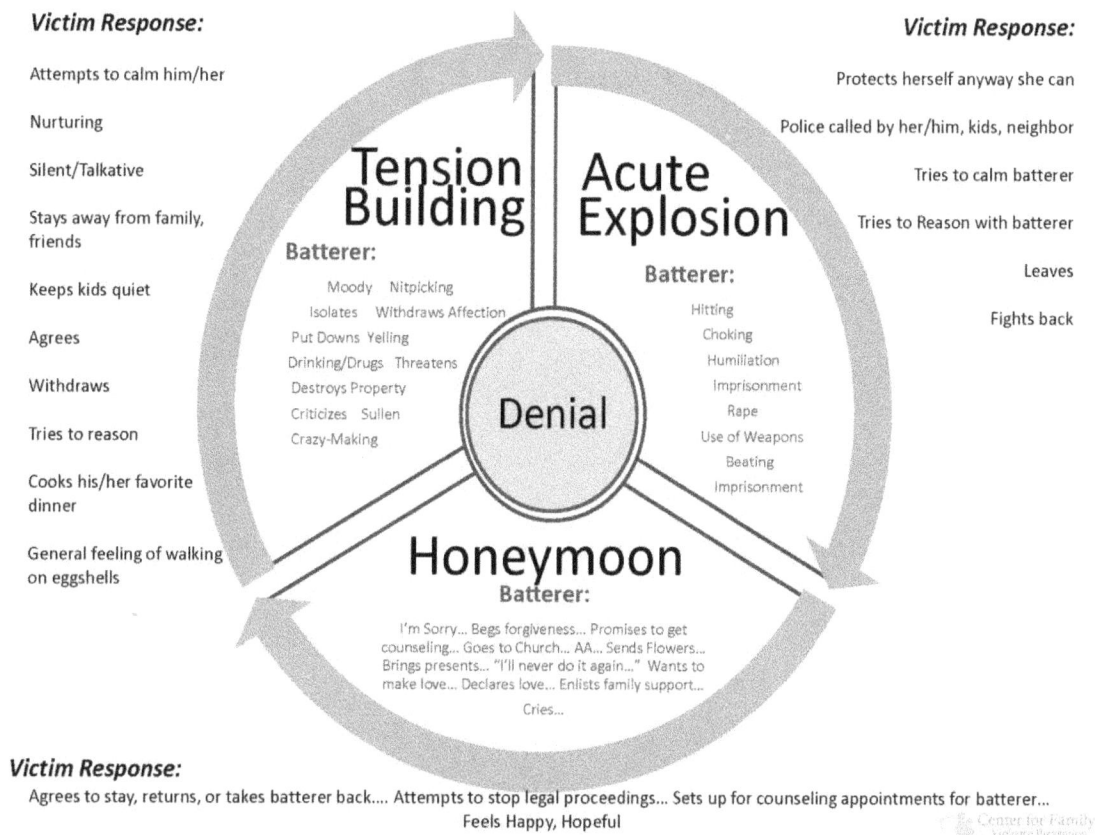

How denial works in each state of the cycle to keep the cycle going. (Only by braking through this denial can the cycle be broken)

Tension Building

She denies its happening, excuses it as some outside stress (work, etc.); blames herself for his behavior, denies that the abuse will worsen. He denies by blaming the tension on her, work, the traffic, anything; by getting drunk he denies his responsibility for his actions.

Explosion

She denies her injuries, only minor ("I bruise easily"), doesn't require police or medical help; blames it on drinking ("He didn't know what he was doing."); does not label it rape because it was her husband.

He blames it on her, stress, etc. ("She had it coming.")

Honeymoon

She minimizes injuries ("It could have been worse."); believes this is the way it will stay, the man of her dreams, believes his promises. He also believes it won't happen again.

APPENDIX E

SERVICES FOR MEN WHO BATTER

Atlantic County

Alternatives to Violence
201 Shore Road
Northfield, NJ 08225
(609) 646-6775

Bergen County

Alternatives to Domestic Violence
1 Bergen County Plaza # 2
Hackensack, NJ 07601
(201) 487-8484

Camden County

Dove Counseling Service
710 West Laurel Road
Stratford, NJ 08084
(856) 435-8505

Cape May County

Men Explore New Directions
(MEND)
PO BOX 774
Cape May Court House, NJ 08210
(609) 522-6489

Cumberland County

A.C.T. (Abuse Ceases Today)
(856) 691-3713

Essex County
Men for Peace
(973) 399-3400

Hunterdon County

Batterer's Services
(908) 788-6401
Mercer County

Family Growth Center
39 N. Clinton Avenue
Trenton, NJ 08607
(609) 394-5157

Middlesex County

Batterers Intervention Program at
Women Aware
(732) 640-2860

Monmouth County

Alternatives to Abuse
1 Bethany Road, Building 3, Suite 42
Hazlet, NJ 07730
(732) 671-6222

Morris County

A.C.T. (Abuse Ceases Today)
PO BOX 1437
Morristown, NJ 07962
(201) 539-7801

Salem County
Alternatives to Violence
PO BOX 125
Salem, NJ 08079
(856) 935-6655

Somerset County

Batterer's Referral Line
1-866-685-1122

Warren County
Batterer Services
(908) 813-8820

APPENDIX F

CHILD SUPPORT GUIDELINES - SOLE PARENTING WORKSHEET			

Case Name:			County:

Plaintiff vs. *Defendant*

Custodial Parent is the: ☒ Plaintiff ☐ Defendant

Docket #:

Number of Children:

All amounts must be weekly		CUSTODIAL	NON-CUSTODIAL	COMBINED
1. Gross Taxable Income				
1a. Mandatory Retirement Contributions (non-taxable)	-			
1b. Alimony Paid (Current and/or Past Relationships)	-			
1c. Alimony Received (Current and/or Past Relationships)	+			
2. Adjusted Gross Taxable Income ((L1-L1a-L1b)+L1c)				
2a. Federal, State and Local Income Tax Withholding	-			
2b. Prior Child Support Orders (Past Relationships)	-			
2c. Mandatory Union Dues	-			
2d. Other Dependent Deduction (from L14 of a separate worksheet)	-			
3. Net Taxable Income (L2-L2a-L2b-L2c-L2d)				
4. Non-Taxable Income (source:)	+			
5. Government (Non-Means Tested) Benefits for the Child	+			
6. Net Income (L3+L4+L5)				
7. Each Parent's Share of Income (L6 Each Parent ÷ L6 Combined)				1.00
8. Basic Child Support Amount (from Appendix IX-F Schedules)				
9. Net Work Related Child Care (from Appendix IX-E Worksheet)	+			
10. Child's Share of Health Insurance Premium	+			
11. Unreimbursed Health Care Expenses over $250 per child per yr.	+			
12. Court-Approved Extraordinary Expenses	+			
13. Total Child Support Amount (L8+L9+L10+L11+L12)				
If line 13 total support amount is zero, STOP – benefit apportionment is substituted for support order.				
14. Each Parent's Share of Support Obligation (L7 x L13)				
15. Government Benefits for the Child Based on Contribution of NCP	-			
16. Net Work-Related Child Care Paid	-			
17. Health Insurance Premium for the Child Paid	-			
18. Unreimbursed Health Care Expenses Paid (>$250/child/year)	-			
19. Court-Approved Extraordinary Expenses Paid	-			
20. Adjustment for Parenting Time Expenses (L8 x L20b for Non-Custodial Parent x 0.37) *Note: Not presumptive in some low income situations (see App IX-A., ¶13)*	-			
20a. Number of Annual Overnights with Each Parent		365	0	365
20b. Each Parent's Share of Overnights with the Child (L20a for Parent ÷ L20a Combined)		1.0000		1.00
21. Net Child Support Obligation (L14-L15-L16-L17-L18-L19-L20)				
Continued on Page 2				

294

CHILD SUPPORT GUIDELINES – SOLE PARENTING WORKSHEET – PAGE 2			
All amounts must be weekly	CUSTODIAL	NON-CUSTODIAL	COMBINED
If neither parent is requesting the other-dependent deduction, go to line 25			
22. Child Support Order WITH Other Dependent Deduction			
23. Child Support Order WITHOUT Other Dependent Deduction			
24. Adjusted Child Support Order ((L22 + L23) ÷ 2)			
25. Self-Support Reserve Test (L6 – L21 or L24 for NCP; L6 - L14 for CP). If L25 for NCP is greater than 105% of the federal poverty guideline for one person (105% value defined as *pg*) or L25 for CP is less than *pg*, enter L21 or L24 amount on L27. If NCP L25 is less than the *pg* and CP L25 is greater than the *pg*, go to L26. (The *pg* for tax year 2014 is 236)			
26. Obligor Parent's Maximum Child Support Obligation. (L6 NCP income – 105% of federal poverty guideline for one person). Enter result here and on Line 27.			
27. Child Support Order			
COMMENTS, REBUTTALS, AND JUSTIFICATION FOR DEVIATIONS			

1. This child support order for this case ☐ was ☐ was not based on the child support guidelines award.

2. If different from the child support guidelines award (Line 27), enter amount ordered:

3. The child support guidelines were not used or the guidelines award was adjusted because:

4. The following court-approved extraordinary expenses were added to the basic support obligation:

5. Custodial Taxes:　　☒ App IX-H　☐ Circ E　☐ Other　　#Allowances: 1　Marital: S

   Non-Custodial Taxes:　☒ App IX-H　☐ Circ E　☐ Other　　#Allowances: 1　Marital: S

Prepared By:　　　　　Title:　　　　　　　Date:

CHILD SUPPORT GUIDELINES - SHARED PARENTING WORKSHEET

Case Name:		County:
vs.		
Plaintiff	*Defendant*	Docket #:
PPR is the: ☒ Plaintiff ☐ Defendant		Number of Children:

All amounts must be weekly		PARENT OF PRIMARY RESIDENCE (PPR)	PARENT OF ALTERNATE RESIDENCE (PAR)	COMBINED
1. Gross Taxable Income				
1a. Mandatory Retirement Contributions (non-taxable)	-			
1b. Alimony Paid (Current and/or Past Relationships)	-			
1c. Alimony Received (Current and/or Past Relationships)	+			
2. Adjusted Gross Taxable Income ((L1-L1a-L1b)+L1c)				
2a. Federal, State and Local Income Tax Withholding	-			
2b. Prior Child Support Orders (Past Relationships)	-			
2c. Mandatory Union Dues	-			
2d. Other Dependent Deduction (from L14 of a separate worksheet)	-			
3. Net Taxable Income (L2-L2a-L2b-L2c-L2d)				
4. Non-Taxable Income (source:)	+			
5. Government (Non-Means Tested) Benefits for the Child	+			
6. Net Income (L3+L4+L5)				
7. Each Parent's Share of Income (L6 Each Parent ÷ L6 Combined)				1.00
8. Basic Child Support Amount (from Appendix IX-F Schedules)				
9. Number of Overnights With Each Parent		365	0	365
10. Each Parent's Share of Overnights with the Child (L9 for Parent ÷ L9 Combined)		1.0000		1.00
If PAR time sharing is less than the equivalent of two overnights per week (28%), use Sole Parenting Worksheet.				
11. PAR Shared Parenting Fixed Expenses (L8xPAR L10x0.38 x2)				
12. Shared Parenting Basic Child Support Amount (L8 + L11)				
13. Each Parent's Share of SP Basic Child Support Amount (L7 x L12)				
14. PAR Shared Parenting Variable Expenses (PAR L10 x L8 x 0.37)				
15. PAR Adjusted SP Basic Child Support Amount (PAR L13 – L11 – L14)				
16. Net Work-Related Child Care (from Appendix IX-E Worksheet)				
17. Child's Share of Health Insurance Premium	+			
18. Unreimbursed Health Care Expenses over $250 per child per yr.	+			
19. Court-Approved Extraordinary Expenses	+			
20. Total Supplemental Expenses (L16+L17+L18+L19)				
21. PAR's Share of Total Supplemental Expenses (PAR L7 x L20)				
22. Government Benefits for the Child Based on Contribution of PAR	-			
23. PAR Net Work-Related Child Care PAID				
Continued on Page 2				

296

CHILD SUPPORT GUIDELINES - SHARED PARENTING WORKSHEET – PAGE 2			
All amounts must be weekly	**PPR**	**PAR**	**COMBINED**
24. PAR Health Insurance Premium for the Child PAID +			
25. PAR Unreimbursed Health Care Expenses (>$250/child/yr) PAID +			
26. PAR Court-Approved Extraordinary Expenses PAID +			
27. PAR Total Supplemental Expenses PAID (L23+L24+L25+L26)			
28. PAR Net Supplemental Expenses (L21 – L27)			
29. PAR Net Child Support Obligation (L15 – L22 + L28)			
If neither parent is requesting the other dependent deduction, go to line 33			
30. Line 29 PAR CS Obligation WITH Other Dependent Deduction			
31. Line 29 PAR CS Obligation WITHOUT Other Dependent Deduction			
32. Adjusted PAR Child Support Obligation ((L30 + L31) ÷ 2)			
33. Self-Support Reserve Test: (L6 – L29 or L32 for PAR; L6 - L13 for PPR) If L33 for PAR is greater than 105% of the federal poverty guideline for one person (105% value defined as *pg*) or L33 for PPR is less than *pg*, enter L29 or L32 amount on PAR L35. If PAR L33 is less than the *pg* and PPR's L33 is greater than the *pg*, go to L34. If L29 or L32 is negative, see App. IX-B for instructions. (The *pg* for tax year 2014 is 236)			
34. Maximum CS Obligation (Obligor Parent's L6 net income – 105% of the poverty guideline for one person). Enter result here and on Line 35.			
35. Child Support Order (negative L29 or L32 denotes PPR Obligation)			
If the PAR is the Obligor, Continue on Line 36			
36. PPR Household Income Test (L6 PPR net income from all sources + net income of other household members + L35 order). If less than the PPR household income threshold (see App. IX-A, ¶14(c)), the SOLE PARENTING WORKSHEET should be used.			

COMMENTS, REBUTTALS, AND JUSTIFICATION FOR DEVIATIONS
1. This child support order for this case ☐ was ☐ was not based on the child support guidelines award.
2. If different from the child support guidelines award (Line 35), enter amount ordered:
3. The child support guidelines were not used or the guidelines award was adjusted because:
4. The following extraordinary expenses were added to the basic support obligation on Line 19:

5. PPR Taxes:	☒ App IX-H	☐ Circ E	☐ Other	#Allowances: 1	Marital: S
PAR Taxes:	☒ App IX-H	☐ Circ E	☐ Other	#Allowances: 1	Marital: S

Prepared By:	Title:	Date:

APPENDIX G

VISITATION RISK ASSESSMENT
INTERVIEW SHEET

TRACKING INFORMATION

PERSON INTERVIEWED			DATE	ASSESSOR
☐ PLAINTIFF ☐ DEFENDANT ☐ CHILD(REN)				

CASE NAME	DOCKET NUMBER	DATE RECEIVED

GENERAL INFORMATION

WHAT ARE PLAINTIFF'S CONCERNS ABOUT VISITATION?

_____

_____

ARE BOTH PARTIES THE BIOLOGICAL PARENTS OF ALL CHILDREN?

☐ YES ☐ NO PLEASE EXPLAIN: _____

_____

AGES AND SEX OF CHILDREN INVOLVED

FIRST CHILD: AGE: _____ SEX: _____ **SECOND** CHILD: AGE: _____ SEX: _____ **THIRD** CHILD: AGE: _____ SEX: _____ **FOURTH** CHILD: AGE: _____ SEX: _____

DO ANY OF THE CHILDREN HAVE PHYSICAL OR MENTAL SPECIAL NEEDS WHICH WOULD IMPACT VISITATION?   ☐ YES ☐ NO   IF YES, WHICH CHILD: _____

DESCRIBE THE SPECIAL NEEDS OF THE CHILD: _____

_____

IS THE DEFENDANT FROM ANOTHER COUNTY? ☐ YES ☐ NO	WHERE?

HOW WOULD CHILDREN BE TRANSPORTED TO THE VISITATION SITE?

DO THE PARTIES HAVE SUGGESTIONS FOR THE FREQUENCY AND STRUCTURE OF VISITATION? (INCLUDE SUGGESTED CONDITIONS OF SUPERVISION, IF ANY)

PLAINTIFF: _____

DEFENDANT: _____

HAS THE CHILD(REN) EXPRESSED ANY FEELINGS CONCERNING VISITATION WITH DEFENDANT?

DESCRIBE: _____

DOMESTIC VIOLENCE

LENGTH AND NATURE OF DOMESTIC VIOLENCE HISTORY

_____

_____

MINOR INJURIES SUSTAINED?

DESCRIBE: _____

_____

MAJOR INJURIES SUSTAINED?

DESCRIBE: _____

_____

SPECIFY OBJECTS OR WEAPONS USED, IF ANY

_____

DOMESTIC VIOLENCE *continued*

HAS ABUSE INCLUDED THREATS TO KILL
OR HARM MORE EXTENSIVELY? ☐ YES ☐ NO

HAS ABUSE INCLUDED SEXUAL ASSUALT/EXPLOITATION?

DESCRIBE: _____

_____

HAS ABUSE INCLUDED DAMAGE TO PLAINTIFF'S POSSESSIONS OR PETS?

DESCRIBE: _____

_____

HAS ABUSE INCLUDED VERBAL/PSYCHOLOGICAL ABUSE?

DESCRIBE: _____

_____

HAS VIOLENCE INCREASED OVER TIME?

☐ YES ☐ NO

DESCRIBE: _____

_____

DOES PHYSICAL/SEXUAL VIOLENCE OCCUR FOUR TIMES A YEAR OR MORE?

☐ YES ☐ NO

DESCRIBE FREQUENCY: _____

AVAILABLE VERIFICATION ☐ RESTRAINING ORDER ☐ COURT ORDERS ☐ MEDICAL REPORTS ☐ POLICE REPORTS

☐ SOCIAL AGENCY REPORTS ☐ PROFESSIONAL REPORTS ☐ OTHER _____

CHILD ABUSE

LENGTH OF CHILD ABUSE HISTORY

☐ ACTIVE DYFS CASE ☐ PREVIOUS DYFS CASE ☐ NO DYFS INVOLVEMENT

DESCRIBE: _____

MINOR INJURIES SUSTAINED?

DESCRIBE: _____

_____

MAJOR INJURIES SUSTAINED?

DESCRIBE: _____

_____

SPECIFY OBJECTS OR WEAPONS USED, IF ANY:

_____

HAS ABUSE INCLUDED THREATS TO KILL OR HARM MORE
EXTENSIVELY?

☐ YES ☐ NO

HAS ABUSE INCLUDED SEXUAL ABUSE/EXPLOITATION?

DESCRIBE: _____

_____

_____

HAS ABUSE INCLUDED DAMAGE TO CHILD'S POSSESSIONS OR PETS?

DESCRIBE: _____

_____

HAS DEFENDANT EXHIBITED INDIFFERENCE OR NEGLECT OF CHILD'S PHYSICAL NEEDS, INCLUDING FOOD, CLOTHING, SAFETY, MEDICAL ATTENTION?

DESCRIBE: _____

_____

_____

CHILD ABUSE *continued*

HAS DEFENDANT THREATENED TO KIDNAP CHILDREN?

☐ YES ☐ NO

HAS DEFENDANT EVER KIDNAPPED CHILDREN?

DESCRIBE: _____

_____

HAS VIOLENCE AGAINST CHILD(REN) INCREASED OVER TIME?

☐ YES ☐ NO

DESCRIBE: _____

_____

HAS ABUSE INCLUDED VERBAL/PSYCHOLOGICAL ABUSE?

☐ YES ☐ NO

DESCRIBE: _____

AVAILABLE VERIFICATION: ☐ DYFS ☐ MEDICAL ☐ POLICE ☐ SCHOOL

☐ SOCIAL AGENCY ☐ PROFESSIONAL ☐ OTHER _____

EXPOSURE TO DOMESTIC VIOLENCE

HAVE CHILDREN WITNESSED OR HEARD EPISODES OF DOMESTIC VIOLENCE EITHER IN THE HOME OR ELSEWHERE?

☐ YES ☐ NO

IF YES, WAS AN OBJECT OR WEAPON USED?

☐ YES ☐ NO

DESCRIBE: _____

_____

HAVE CHILDREN BEEN INJURED DURING A DOMESTIC VIOLENCE EPISODE?

DESCRIBE: _____

_____

HAVE CHILDREN EXHIBITED CONCERN FOR THEIR OWN PERSONAL SAFETY BECAUSE OF THE DOMESTIC VIOLENCE?

☐ YES ☐ NO

DESCRIBE: _____

_____

HAVE CHILDREN WITNESSED OR HEARD PHYSICAL ABUSE OF ANOTHER CHILD OR FAMILY PET?

DESCRIBE: _____

_____

AVAILABLE VERIFICATION

☐ POLICE REPORT ☐ COURT ☐ HOSPITAL ☐ OTHER _____

SUBSTANCE ABUSE

DOES THE DEFENDANT HAVE A DRUG/ALCOHOL PROBLEM?

DESCRIBE: _____

_____

DOES DEFENDANT ABUSE SUBSTANCES IN THE PRESENCE OF THE CHILDREN?

DESCRIBE: _____

_____

IS DEFENDANT USUALLY ABUSING SUBSTANCES WHEN VIOLENT?

☐ YES ☐ NO

IS DEFENDANT CURRENTLY UNDERGOING SUBSTANCE ABUSE TREATMENT?

DESCRIBE (INCLUDING VOLUNTARY OR COURT-ORDERED): _____

_____

_____

_____

SUBSTANCE ABUSE *continued*

DOES DEFENDANT DRIVE WHILE IMPAIRED?

DESCRIBE: _____

_____

HAS DEFENDANT BEEN CONVICTED OF DWI OFFENSES?

☐ YES   ☐ NO

AVAILABLE VERIFICATION: ☐ PROFESSIONAL REPORTS   ☐ DWI ARRESTS/CONVICTIONS   ☐ POSSESSION/INTENT TO DISTRIBUTE ARRESTS/CONVICTIONS

☐ IDRC REPORT   ☐ OTHER _____

CRIMINAL HISTORY

HAS THE DEFENDANT BEEN ARRESTED FOR AN ACT OF DOMESTIC VIOLENCE OR CHILD ABUSE?

WHEN? _____

HAS THE DEFENDANT BEEN CONVICTED OF OTHER CRIMES OF VIOLENCE OR CHILD ABUSE?

WHEN? _____

WHICH CRIMES? _____

HAS THE DEFENDANT EVER VIOLATED A RESTRAINING ORDER?

☐ YES   ☐ NO

WHEN AND HOW: _____

_____

HAS THE DEFENDANT EVER VIOLATED ANY OTHER ORDER INVOLVING OTHER PARENT OR CHILD?

WHEN AND HOW: _____

_____

IS THE DEFENDANT FACING PENDING CRIMINAL CHARGES FOR OTHER CRIMES OF VIOLENCE OR CHILD ABUSE?

☐ YES   ☐ NO

WHICH CRIMES: _____

_____

HAS THE DEFENDANT BEEN CONVICTED OF OTHER CRIMES?

WHEN? _____

WHICH CRIMES? _____

IS THE DEFENDANT FACING PENDING CRIMINAL CHARGES FOR OTHER CRIMES?

☐ YES   ☐ NO

WHICH CRIMES? _____

AVAILABLE VERIFICATION: ☐ CONVICTIONS   ☐ PENDING CHARGES   ☐ POLICE

☐ OTHER _____

PSYCHO-SOCIAL FACTORS

DOES THE DEFENDANT EXHIBIT EXTREME ABERRANT BEHAVIORS DUE TO MENTAL HEALTH PROBLEMS?

DESCRIBE: _____

_____

_____

HAS THE DEFENDANT EVER BEEN TREATED FOR ABOVE PROBLEM?

WHEN: _____

DESCRIBE: _____

IDENTIFY MEDICATIONS, IF ANY: _____

HAS THE DEFENDANT EVER THREATENED OR ATTEMPTED SUICIDE?

WHEN: _____

DESCRIBE: _____

_____

THIS IS SIDE #4

302

PSYCHO-SOCIAL FACTORS *continued*

DOES THE DEFENDANT POSSESS CHILD PORNOGRAPHY?

☐ YES   ☐ NO

AVAILABLE VERIFICATION:

☐ PROFESSIONAL REPORTS   ☐ OTHER _____

PREVIOUS VISITATION EXPERIENCE

HAS THE DEFENDANT EVER KIDNAPPED THE CHILDREN?

WHEN: _____

DESCRIBE: _____

_____

_____

HAS THE DEFENDANT EVER PHYSICALLY ABUSED PARTNER IN THE COURSE OF VISITATION?

WHEN: _____

DESCRIBE: _____

_____

_____

HAS THE DEFENDANT EVER REFUSED TO RETURN THE CHILDREN?

WHEN: _____

DESCRIBE: _____

_____

_____

HAS THE DEFENDANT VIOLATED THE VISITATION ORDER IN OTHER WAYS?

WHEN: _____

DESCRIBE: _____

_____

_____

HAVE THE CHILDREN EVER EXHIBITED SIGNS OF PHYSICAL/SEXUAL ABUSE OR NEGLECT AFTER VISITATION?

WHEN: _____

DESCRIBE: _____

_____

_____

HAS DEFENDANT EVER ABUSED SUBSTANCES DURING VISITATION?

WHEN: _____

DESCRIBE: _____

_____

_____

HAS THE DEFENDANT FAILED TO APPEAR FOR SCHEDULED VISITATION?

WHEN: _____

_____

HAS THE DEFENDANT FAILED TO ATTEND TO THE CHILD'S MEDICAL, SAFETY, PHYSICAL OR EDUCATIONAL NEEDS DURING VISITATION?

EXPLAIN: _____

_____

AVAILABLE VERIFICATION:

☐ COURT REPORT   ☐ POLICE   ☐ ARRESTS/CONVICTIONS

☐ PROFESSIONAL   ☐ SCHOOL   ☐ OTHER _____

PARENTAL CAPACITY/EXPERIENCE

DOES THE DEFENDANT HAVE EXPERIENCE IN CARING FOR CHILDREN ALONE?

☐ YES   ☐ NO

DESCRIBE FREQUENCY OF SOLE CARETAKING: _____

_____

CHECK RELEVANT PARENTING SKILLS, IF ANY, THAT DEFENDANT REPORTEDLY LACKS:

☐ DIAPERCHANGING   ☐ FEEDING   ☐ BATHING   ☐ PLAYING   ☐ DISCIPLINE

☐ TRANSPORTING   ☐ SENSITIVITY   ☐ OTHER _____

PARENTAL CAPACITY/EXPERIENCE *continued*

DOES DEFENDANT HAVE ADEQUATE VISITATION FACILITIES?

☐ YES ☐ NO

DESCRIBE POTENTIAL VISITATION ENVIRONMENT: _____

_____

DOES DEFENDANT DISPLAY ERRATIC OR UNSTABLE TEMPERAMENT TOWARDS CHILDREN?

☐ YES ☐ NO

DESCRIBE: _____

_____

DOES DEFENDANT HAVE A GOOD RELATIONSHIP AND RAPPORT WITH CHILDREN?

☐ YES ☐ NO

DESCRIBE RELATIONSHIP: _____

_____

DOES DEFENDANT HAVE EXPERIENCE OR SKILLS REQUIRED TO CARE FOR SPECIAL PHYSICAL OR MENTAL NEEDS OF ONE OR MORE CHILDREN?

☐ N/A ☐ YES ☐ NO

EXPLAIN: _____

_____

APPENDIX H

EVALUATION OF INTERVIEW

Appearance: (Check all that apply.)

_____ Neat   _____ Well Dressed   _____ Dirty   _____ Clean   _____ Not Well Dressed

_____ Blurry Eyes   _____ Bad Smell   _____ Disorganized   _____ Disheveled

_____ Other_____ Explain:_____

_____

_____

Behavior/Attitude/Mood: (Check all that apply.)

_____ Pleasant   _____ Complaining   _____ Calm   _____ Resentful   _____ Violent

_____ Remorseful   _____ Angry   _____ Cooperative   _____ Distant/Cold

_____ Tearful   _____ Vindictive   _____ Apprehensive   _____ Uncooperative

_____ Focused   _____ Confused   _____ Other_____

Explain:_____

_____

_____

_____

_____

Speech: (Check all that apply.)

_____ Coherent   _____ Incoherent   _____ Clear   _____ Loud   _____ Slurred

_____ Soft   _____ Able to express thoughts   _____ Unable to express thoughts

_____ Other_____ Explain:_____

_____

_____

_____

_____

ADDITIONAL DOMESTIC VIOLENCE INQUIRY FOR VICTIM

What does the other party do when he really wants to hurt you?_____

_____

_____

_____

Were you ever forced to leave your home as a result of an incident between you and the other party?

_____yes _____no Explain:_____

_____

_____

Can you give examples of how you were victimized? (i.e. control, isolation, forced dependency, money)

_____yes _____no Explain:_____

_____

_____

Are verbal threats used? (If yes, describe how often and describe the worst threat ever used.)

_____yes _____no Explain:_____

_____

_____

Has the other party ever threatened you at your job?

_____yes _____no Explain:_____

_____

Has there been any recent change in the other party's use of intimidation or threats?

_____yes _____no Explain:_____

_____

_____

Are there ways the other party scares you?

_____ yes _____ no Explain:_____

_____

_____

Do you have any friends or family you can talk to or with whom you feel safe?

_____ yes _____ no Explain:_____

_____

_____

Does the other party ever pressure you to stop seeing friends or family?

_____ yes _____ no Explain:_____

_____

_____

Has the other party ever threatened to hurt your friends or family?

_____ yes _____ no Explain:_____

_____

_____

Has the other party ever restricted you in other ways, such as going to church, work or school?

_____ yes _____ no Explain:_____

_____

_____

Do you feel free to come and go as you please and to talk to whomever you like?

_____ yes _____ no Explain:_____

_____

Has the other party ever restricted you from seeking help for yourself or your children?

_____ yes _____ no Explain:_____

_____

_____

Does the other party ever act jealous or possessive?

_____yes _____no Explain:_____

_____

_____

Is there any place you feel safe?

_____yes _____no Explain:_____

_____

_____

Have there been periods of time in your relationship with the other party in which you feel things are calm?

_____yes _____no Explain:_____

_____

_____

Has there been any recent change in the other party's abusive behavior?

_____yes _____no Explain:_____

_____

_____

Are there certain things you don't do or say because you are afraid of how the other party will respond?

_____yes _____no Explain:_____

_____

_____

Did you ever feel as though you are walking on eggshells at home?

_____yes _____no Explain:_____

_____

_____

What are your "punishments"?_____

_____

_____

Do you feel as though you have any power in this situation?

_____ yes _____ no Explain:_____

_____

When the other party wants to insult you, what names are you called and how often does this occur?

_____

_____

Does the other party make you feel like you just can't do anything right?

_____ yes _____ no Explain:_____

_____

_____

Does the other party ever play mind games with you (e.g. wake you up at night, refuse to let you sleep, tell you one thing one minute and then change it the next)?

_____ yes _____ no Explain:_____

_____

_____

Has the other party ever made you do humiliating things?

_____ yes _____ no Explain:_____

_____

_____

Does the other party constantly criticize you for little things?

_____ yes _____ no Explain:_____

_____

_____

Do you believe that the other party is capable of severely hurting you or killing you?

_____ yes _____ no Explain:_____

_____

_____

Has the other party ever hurt you so badly, you needed a doctor?

_____yes _____no Explain:_____

_____

Can you think of a time when the other party hurt you during pregnancy?

_____yes _____no Explain:_____

_____

Has the other party ever forced you to have sex when you did not want it?

_____yes _____no Explain:_____

_____

Has the other party ever forced you to have sex with other partners?

_____yes _____no Explain:_____

_____

Has the other party forced you to perform sexual acts?

_____yes _____no Explain:_____

_____

What made you decide to get a restraining order against the other party?_____

_____

Are you afraid of the other party?

_____yes _____no Explain:_____

_____

_____

What scares you the most about the other party?_____

_____

_____

Describe how the violence in your home has affected your child(ren)._____

_____

_____

What was the worst incident of violence you can remember?_____

_____

_____

Who controls the money in your household?_____

Who controls the checkbook?_____

Do you have any money on your own to spend?

_____yes _____no Explain:_____

_____

Has the other party ever controlled or stolen your money?

_____yes _____no Explain:_____

_____

Has the other party ever forced you to account for everything you spend?

_____yes _____no Explain:_____

_____

Has the other party ever prevented you from buying things for yourself or the child(ren)?

_____yes _____no Explain:_____

_____

Has the other party ever used the children against you?

_____yes _____no Explain:_____

_____

_____

Has the other party ever prevented you from using birth control?

_____yes _____no Explain:_____

_____

Has the other party ever listened in on your phone calls or violated your privacy in other ways?

_____yes _____no Explain:_____

_____

Has the other party ever checked up on you frequently during the day?

_____yes _____no Explain:_____

_____

Has the other party ever told you what to wear or stopped you from wearing certain clothes?

_____yes _____no Explain:_____

_____

Has the other party ever tracked all of your time?

_____yes _____no Explain:_____

_____

Has the other party ever made a list of rules for you to follow?

_____yes _____no Explain:_____

_____

Has the other party ever watched you when you were unaware of his presence?

_____yes _____no Explain:_____

_____

Has the other party ever searched for men in the house?

_____yes _____no Explain:_____

_____

Has the other party ever taken your car or denied you transportation?

_____yes _____no Explain:_____

_____

Has the other party ever forbidden you to use the telephone?

_____yes _____no Explain:_____

_____

Has the other party ever prevented you from calling the police?

_____yes _____no Explain:_____

_____

ADDITIONAL INQUIRY

Is the other party from another county?

_____ yes _____ no If yes, what county?_____

_____

If visitation is ordered, do you have a suggestion as to the frequency and structure of visitation? (Include suggested supervised visitation conditions, if any.)_____

_____

_____

_____

If visitation is ordered, where would you like to see visitation take place? (Describe the location.)

_____

_____

_____

Who lives at the above referenced location?_____

_____

_____

_____

Will the child(ren) have his/her own bed?

_____ yes _____ no Explain:_____

_____

_____

Will the child(ren) be permitted open phone contact with the other parent?

_____ yes _____ no Explain:_____

_____

_____

_____

If you are the visiting parent, will you be available during the entire visitation period?

_____yes _____no Explain:_____

_____

_____

If the answer to the above question is no, who will be available for the child(ren) in your absence?

_____

_____

_____

Will the child(ren) have his/her own clothes?

_____yes _____no Explain:_____

_____

_____

Do you have an active, legal driver's license?

_____yes _____no Explain:_____

_____

_____

How would child(ren) be transported to the visitation site?_____

_____

_____

Would you be willing to provide transportation for visitations?

_____yes _____no Explain:_____

_____

_____

If applicable, would you be willing to provide a car seat for visitations?

_____yes _____no Explain:_____

_____

_____

APPENDIX I

New Jersey Judiciary
Confidential Litigant Information Sheet (*R. 5:4-2(g)*)

To assure accuracy of court records - To be filled out by Plaintiff, or Defendant, or Attorney
Collection of the following information is pursuant to *N.J.S.A.* 2A:17-56.60 and *R.* 5:7-4.

Confidentiality of this information must be maintained

Please complete the entire form, leaving no blank spaces. If something does not apply to you, enter "N/A". This form is confidential and will not be shared with the other party.

Docket Number:	CS Number:	Do you have an active Domestic Violence Order with the other party in this case? ☐ Yes ☐ No

Plaintiff	Defendant
Name (last, first, middle initial)	Name (last, first, middle initial)

Plaintiff

Social Security Number	Date of Birth	Place of Birth

Address: Street

City	State	Zip

Plaintiff Telephone Number	Employer Telephone Number

Employer Name (or other income source)

Employer Address: Street

City	State	Zip

Professional, Occupational, Recreational Licenses
(include types and license numbers)

Driver's License Number	State of Issuance

Sex	Race/Ethnicity	Height	Weight	Eyes	Hair

Auto: License Plate	State	Make	Model	Year

Attorney Name

Attorney Address: Street

City	State	Zip

Defendant

Social Security Number	Date of Birth	Place of Birth

Address: Street

City	State	Zip

Defendant Telephone Number	Employer Telephone Number

Employer Name (or other income source)

Employer Address: Street

City	State	Zip

Professional, Occupational, Recreational Licenses
(include types and license numbers)

Driver's License Number	State of Issuance

Sex	Race/Ethnicity	Height	Weight	Eyes	Hair

Auto: License Plate	State	Make	Model	Year

Attorney Name

Attorney Address: Street

City	State	Zip

Children Information

Name (last, first, middle initial)	Date of Birth	Race	Sex	Social Security Number	Place of Birth
1.					
2.					
3.					
4.					

Health Coverage for Children - available through parent filling out this form (☐ Plaintiff / ☐ Defendant)

Health Care Provider:	Policy Number:	Group Number:
Health Care Provider:	Policy Number:	Group Number:
Health Care Provider:	Policy Number:	Group Number:

I certify that the foregoing statements made by me are true to the best of my knowledge. I am aware that if any of the foregoing statements made by me are wilfully false, I am subject to punishment.

Date	Signature

Revised: 10/2012, CN 10486

page 1 of 1

317

APPENDIX J

New Jersey Judiciary
CONFIDENTIAL VICTIM INFORMATION SHEET
(DO NOT GIVE TO DEFENDANT)

Date: _____

Your Information (Party Filing-Plaintiff)	Information of Person you're filing against (Defendant)
Name of Police Department where you reside:	Name of Police Department where defendant resides:
Name Any Prior Names	Name AKA
Street Address	Street Address
City Zip	City Zip
Phone (h) (cell)	Phone (h) (cell)
SS#	SS#
Birth Date	Birth Date
Sex ☐ Male ☐ Female	Sex ☐ Male ☐ Female
Race	Race
Employment Information Employer	Employment Information Employer
Address	Address
Phone	Phone
Days Hours	Days Hours
Emergency Contact Name	Other place(s) defendant may be reached
Phone	

CONFIDENTIAL VICTIM INFORMATION SHEET
(DO NOT GIVE TO DEFENDANT)

Relationship to Defendant	Defendant Identifier's				
☐ Married	Height			Eye Color	
☐ Divorced	Weight			Hair Color	
☐ Never married	Complexion ☐ Light ☐ Medium ☐ Dark				
☐ Currently living together	Scars, Tattoos, Glasses, Facial Hair, Body Piercing				
☐ Previously lived together					
☐ Have child(ren) with defendant	Other				
☐ Expecting child with the defendant	Defendant's vehicle				
☐ Have had a dating relationship	Make	Model	Year	Color	License plate #
☐ Family relationship (specify)					

Do you and the defendant have children together?

	Name	DOB	SS#	Resides with
1.				
2.				
3.				
4.				
5.				
6.				
7.				

Are there any custody/visitation/support orders pending or in effect?

Where   Docket Number

Child Support Case Number

Are you currently asking the court for child support or medical coverage?	☐ Yes ☐ No
Does either party require an interpreter or have other special needs? Describe	☐ Yes ☐ No
Does the defendant have a criminal history?	☐ Yes ☐ No
Do you have a lawyer for this matter? Name Phone	☐ Yes ☐ No

YOU WILL BE ASKED ABOUT THE INCIDENT WHICH BROUGHT YOU HERE TODAY. PLEASE BE PREPARED TO DISCUSS THE INCIDENT, PLUS ANY PRIOR HISTORY, IF APPLICABLE.

APPENDIX K

ABERDEEN TWP MUNICIPAL COURT
1 ABERDEEN SQ
ABERDEEN, NJ, 07747
PHONE: 732-583-4200
OFFICE HOURS: MON – FRI - 8:30 AM - 4:00 PM

ABSECON MUNICIPAL COURT
500 MILL ROAD
ABSECON, NJ, 08201
PHONE: 609-641-0663
OFFICE HOURS: MON – FRI - 8:30 AM - 4:30 PM

ALLAMUCHY TWP MUNICIPAL COURT
BOX A ALPHANO RD
ALLAMUCHY, NJ, 07820
PHONE: 908-852-6667
OFFICE HOURS: MON - THUR 9:00 AM – 2:00 PM

ALLENDALE BORO MUNICIPAL COURT
333 WARREN AVE
HO-HO-KUS, NJ, 07423
PHONE: 201-652-0699
OFFICE HOURS: MON-THUR 9:00 AM - 4:00 PM
CLOSED 1:00 PM – 2:00 PM

ALLENHURST BORO MUNICIPAL COURT
125 CORLIES AVE
ALLENHURST, NJ, 07711
PHONE: 732-531-3217
OFFICE HOURS: MON – FRI - 8:30 AM - 4:30 PM

ALLENTOWN MUNICIPAL COURT
8 NORTH MAIN STREET
ALLENTOWN, NJ, 08501
PHONE: 609-259-9206
OFFICE HOURS: MON – FRI - 9:00 AM - 2:00 PM

ALLOWAY TWP MUNICIPAL COURT
1180 ROUTE 40
PILESGROVE, NJ, 08098
PHONE: 856-769-1275
OFFICE HOURS: MON-THU 8:30-3:00, CLOSED FRI

ALPHA BORO MUNICIPAL COURT
675 CORLISS AVE
PHILLIPSBURG, NJ, 08865
PHONE: 908-454-3211
OFFICE HOURS: MON – FRI - 8:30 - 4:30

ALPINE BORO MUNICIPAL COURT
100 CHURCH ST
ALPINE, NJ, 07620
PHONE: 201-768-6866
OFFICE HOURS: TUES & THURS - 4:30 PM - 6:30 PM

ANDOVER TWP MUNICIPAL COURT
134 NEWTON-SPARTA RD
NEWTON, NJ, 07860
PHONE: 973-383-4280
OFFICE HOURS: MON – FRI - 8:30 AM - 3:30 PM

ASBURY PARK MUNICIPAL COURT
ONE MUNICIPAL PLAZA
ASBURY PARK, NJ, 07712
PHONE: 732-775-1765
OFFICE HOURS: MON – FRI - 8:00 AM - 4:00 PM

ATL HIGHLANDS MUNICIPAL COURT
100 FIRST AVE
ATL HIGHLNDS, NJ, 07716
PHONE: 732-291-3225
OFFICE HOURS: MON – FRI - 8:30 AM - 4:30 PM

ATLANTIC CITY MUNICIPAL COURT
2715 ATLANTIC AVENUE
ATLANTIC CITY, NJ, 08401
PHONE: 609-347-5560
OFFICE HOURS: MON – FRI - 8:30 AM - 7:00 PM

AUDUBON BORO MUNICIPAL COURT
606 W. NICHOLSON RD.
AUDUBON, NJ, 08106
PHONE: 856-547-0712
OFFICE HOURS: MON – FRI - 9:00 AM - 4:00 PM

AUDUBON PARK BORO COURT
135 HADDON AVE
HADDON TWP, NJ, 08108
PHONE: 856-854-1176
OFFICE HOURS: MON – FRI - 8:30 AM - 4:00 PM

AVALON MUNICIPAL COURT
3100 DUNE DRIVE
AVALON, NJ, 08202
PHONE: 609-967-4457
OFFICE HOURS: MON – FRI - 8:30 AM - 4:00 PM

AVON-BY-THE-SEA MUNICIPAL COURT
106 WEST SYLVANIA AV

NEPTUNE CITY, NJ, 07753
PHONE: 732-775-1690
OFFICE HOURS: MON – FRI - 8:30 AM - 4:00 PM
BARNEGAT LIGHT MUNICIPAL COURT
10 WEST 10TH ST
BARNEGAT LIGHT, NJ, 08006
PHONE: 609-494-7336
OFFICE HOURS: MON AND THURS 4:00 PM -6:00 PM

BARNEGAT TOWNSHIP MUNICIPAL CO
900 WEST BAY AVE
BARNEGAT, NJ, 08005
PHONE: 609-698-0080

BARRINGTON MUNICIPAL COURT
500 WHITE HORSE PIKE
OAKLYN, NJ, 08107
PHONE: 856-858-0074
OFFICE HOURS: MON-THUR - 8:00 AM -3:30 PM, FRI
8:00 AM - 11:30 AM

BASS RIVER MUNICIPAL COURT
PO BOX 214
NEW GRETNA, NJ, 08224
PHONE: 609-296-1410
OFFICE HOURS: MON – FRI - 9:00 AM - 4:00 PM

BAY HEAD BORO MUNICIPAL COURT
2233 BRIDGE AVE
PT. PLEASANT, NJ, 08742
PHONE: 732-892-4737
OFFICE HOURS: WED - 4:30 PM - 6:30 PM

BAYONNE CITY MUNICIPAL COURT
630 AVENUE "C"
BAYONNE, NJ, 07002
PHONE: 201-858-6918
OFFICE HOURS: MON – FRI - 8:30 AM - 4:30 PM

BEACH HAVEN BORO MUNICIPAL COURT
420 PELHAM AVE
BEACH HAVEN, NJ, 08008
PHONE: 609-492-0111
OFFICE HOURS: MON, WED, THUR – 9:00 AM -4:00
PM, TUES, FRI – 9:00 AM - 1:30 PM

BEACHWOOD MUNICIPAL COURT
1600 PINEWALD ROAD
BEACHWOOD, NJ, 08722

PHONE: 732-286-6000
OFFICE HOURS: MON – FRI - 9:00 AM - 4:00 PM

BEDMINSTER TWP MUNICIPAL COURT
45 MILLER LANE
BEDMINSTER, NJ, 07921
PHONE: 908-212-7020
OFFICE HOURS: MON – FRI - 9:00 AM - 4:00 PM

BELLEVILLE TWP MUNICIPAL COURT
152 WASHINGTON AVE
BELLEVILLE, NJ, 07109
PHONE: 973-450-3319
OFFICE HOURS: CALL COURT

BELLMAWR MUNICIPAL COURT
21 E. BROWNING RD.
BELLMAWR, NJ, 08099
PHONE: 856-931-1081
OFFICE HOURS: MON – FRI - 8:30 AM - 4:00 PM

BELMAR BORO MUNICIPAL COURT
601 MAIN STREET
BELMAR, NJ, 07719
PHONE: 732-681-3700
OFFICE HOURS: MON – FRI - 9:00 AM - 4:30 PM

BELVIDERE TOWN MUNICIPAL COURT
691 WATER STREET
BELVIDERE, NJ, 07823
PHONE: 908-475-5331
OFFICE HOURS: MON – FRI - 9:00 AM - 4:30 PM

BERGENFIELD MUNICIPAL COURT
198 N WASHINGTON AVE
BERGENFIELD, NJ, 07621
PHONE: 201-387-4055
OFFICE HOURS: MON – FRI - 9:00 AM - 4:00 PM

BERKELEY HEIGHTS COURT
360 ELKWOOD AVENUE
NEW PROVIDENCE, NJ, 07974
PHONE: 908-743-1055
OFFICE HOURS: MON – FRI - 8:30 AM - 4:00 PM

BERKELEY TWP MUNICIPAL COURT
P O BOX B
BAYVILLE, NJ, 08721
PHONE: 732-240-6661

BERLIN BORO MUNICIPAL COURT
59 S WHITEHORSE PIKE
BERLIN, NJ, 08009
PHONE: 856-767-1721
OFFICE HOURS: MON – FRI - 8:00 AM - 4:30 PM

BERLIN TWP MUNICIPAL COURT
135 ROUTE 73 SOUTH
WEST BERLIN, NJ, 08091
PHONE: 856-767-2533
OFFICE HOURS: MON – FRI - 9:00 AM - 4:00 PM

BERNARDS TWP MUNICIPAL COURT
1 COLLYER LANE
BASKING RIDGE, NJ, 07920
PHONE: 908-630-5538
OFFICE HOURS: MON – FRI - 9:00 AM - 4:00 PM

BERNARDSVILLE BORO COURT
166 MINE BROOK RD
BERNARDSVILLE, NJ, 07924
PHONE: 908-766-7348
OFFICE HOURS: MON – FRI - 9:00 AM - 4:00 PM

BETHLEHEM TWP MUNICIPAL COURT
405 MINE RD,
ASBURY, NJ, 08802
PHONE: 908-735-4559
OFFICE HOURS: MON – FRI - 8:30 AM - 3:30 PM

BEVERLY CITY MUNICIPAL COURT
446 BROAD ST
BEVERLY, NJ, 08010
PHONE: 609-387-1881
OFFICE HOURS: MON-FRI - 8:00 AM - 5:00 PM

BLAIRSTOWN TWP MUNICIPAL COURT
407 HOPE/GRT MEADOWS
HOPE, NJ, 07844
PHONE: 908-459-5800
OFFICE HOURS: TUES – THUR - 9:00 AM - 4:00 PM

BLOOMFIELD TWP MUNICIPAL COURT
MUNICIPAL PLAZA
BLOOMFIELD, NJ, 07003
PHONE: 973-680-4078
OFFICE HOURS: MON – FRI - 9:00 AM - 4:00 PM

BLOOMINGDALE MUNICIPAL COURT
101 HAMBURG TPKE
BLOOMINGDALE, NJ, 07403
PHONE: 973-838-0127
OFFICE HOURS: MON-FRI - 8:00 AM - 4:00 PM

BOGOTA BORO MUNICIPAL COURT
215-217 LIBERTY ST
LITTLE FERRY, NJ, 07643
PHONE: 201-440-2111
OFFICE HOURS: MON - THUR 10:00 AM – 3:00 PM;
FRI 10:00 AM - 1:30 PM

BOONTON MUNICIPAL COURT
100 WASHINGTON ST
BOONTON, NJ, 07005
PHONE: 973-402-9410
OFFICE HOURS: MON – FRI - 8:30 AM - 4:00 PM

BOONTON TWP MUNICIPAL COURT
155 POWERVILLE RD
BOONTON TWSP, NJ, 07005
PHONE: 973-402-4006
OFFICE HOURS: TUES – THUR - 2:00 PM-4:30 PM

BORDENTOWN CITY MUNICIPAL COURT
1 MUNICIPAL DRIVE
BORDENTOWN, NJ, 08505
PHONE: 609-298-2800
OFFICE HOURS: MON – FRI - 8:30 AM -4:30 PM

BORDENTOWN TWP MUNICIPAL COURT
1 MUNICIPAL DR.
BORDENTOWN, NJ, 08505
PHONE: 609-298-2802
OFFICE HOURS: MON – FRI - 9:00 AM - 4:30 PM

BORO OF GLEN RIDGE MUNICIPAL COURT
825 BLOOMFIELD AVE.
GLEN RIDGE, NJ, 07028
PHONE: 973-748-8116
OFFICE HOURS: MON – FRI - 9:00 AM - 4:30 PM

BORO OF MILFORD MUNICIPAL COURT
P.O. BOX 199
BAPISTOWN, NJ, 08803
PHONE: 908-996-0799
OFFICE HOURS: TUES AND THURS 9:00 AM - 12:00 NOON

BOROUGH OF ROSELLE MUN COURT
210 CHESTNUT STREET
ROSELLE, NJ, 07203
PHONE: 908-259-3040
OFFICE HOURS: MON - FRI – 9:00 AM – 3:00 PM

BOROUGH OF RUNNEMEDE MUN CT
24 N.BLACK HORSE PKE
RUNNEMEDE, NJ, 08078
PHONE: 856-939-3671
OFFICE HOURS: MON – FRI – 9:00 AM – 4:00 PM

BOUND BROOK MUNICIPAL COURT
230 HAMILTON ST
BOUND BROOK, NJ, 08805
PHONE: 732-356-0833
OFFICE HOURS: MON-FRI - 8:30 AM - 4:30 PM

BRADLEY BEACH BORO COURT
106 W. SYLVANIA AVE
NEPTUNE CITY, NJ, 07753
PHONE: 732-775-1690
OFFICE HOURS: MON – FRI - 8:30 AM - 4:00 PM

BRANCHBURG TWP MUNICIPAL COURT
1077 ROUTE 202 NORTH
BRANCHBURG, NJ, 08876
PHONE: 908-526-1300
OFFICE HOURS: MON – FRI - 8:00 AM - 4:30 PM

BRICK TOWNSHIP MUNICIPAL COURT
401 CHAMBERS BRIDGE
BRICK, NJ, 08723
PHONE: 732-262-1226
OFFICE HOURS: MON – FRI - 9:00 AM - 3:00 PM

BRIDGETON MUNICIPAL COURT
330 FAYETTE ST
BRIDGETON, NJ, 08302
PHONE: 856-451-7565
OFFICE HOURS: MON – FRI - 9:00 AM - 4:00 PM

BRIDGEWATER TWP COURT
100 COMMONS WAY
BRIDGEWATER, NJ, 08807
PHONE: 908-725-6375
OFFICE HOURS: MON – FRI - 8:30 AM - 4:00 PM

BRIELLE BORO MUNICIPAL COURT

201 E. MAIN ST.
MANASQUAN, NJ, 08736
PHONE: 732-223-0600
OFFICE HOURS: MON – FRI - 9:00 AM - 4:00 PM

BRIGANTINE MUNICIPAL COURT
1417 BRIGANTINE AVE
BRIGANTINE, NJ, 08203
PHONE: 609-266-0440
OFFICE HOURS: MON – FRI - 8:00 AM - 4:00 PM

BROOKLAWN MUNICIPAL COURT
BOROUGH HALL
BROOKLAWN, NJ, 08030
PHONE: 856-456-2427
OFFICE HOURS: MON – FRI - 8:30 AM - 5:00 PM

BUENA BORO MUNICIPAL COURT
1571 DELSEA DRIVE
FRANKLINVILLE, NJ, 08322
PHONE: 856-694-1661
OFFICE HOURS: MON- WED AND FRI 8:00 AM -3:00 PM, THUR 8:00 AM-

BUENA VISTA REGIONAL MUN COURT
PO BOX 605
BUENA, NJ, 08310
PHONE: 856-697-3859
OFFICE HOURS: MON – FRI - 9:00 AM - 4:30 PM

BURLINGTON CITY COURT
851 OLD YORK RD
BURLINGTON, NJ, 08016
PHONE: 609-239-5825
OFFICE HOURS: MON – FRI - 9:00 AM - 4:00 PM

BURLINGTON TOWNSHIP M C
851 OLD YORK RD
BURLINGTON, NJ, 08016
PHONE: 609-239-5825
OFFICE HOURS: MON – FRI - 9:00 AM - 4:00 PM

BUTLER BORO MUNICIPAL COURT
1 ACE RD
BUTLER, NJ, 07405
PHONE: 973-838-0559
OFFICE HOURS: MON – FRI - 8:30 AM - 4:30 PM

BYRAM TWP MUNICIPAL COURT
10 MANSFIELD DRIVE

BYRAM, NJ, 07874
PHONE: 973-347-3612
OFFICE HOURS: MON – FRI - 8:30 AM - 4:30 PM

CALDWELL BORO MUNICIPAL COURT
ONE PROVOST SQUARE
CALDWELL, NJ, 07006
PHONE: 973-403-4630
OFFICE HOURS: MON – FRI - 9:00 AM - 4:00 PM

CALIFON BOROUGH MUNICIPAL COURT
43 SCHOOLEYS MTN RD
LONG VALLEY, NJ, 07853
PHONE: 908-876-3852
OFFICE HOURS: MON – FRI - 8:00 AM -4:00 PM

CAMDEN CITY MUNICIPAL COURT
520 MARKET ST
CAMDEN, NJ, 08101
PHONE: 856-757-7000
OFFICE HOURS: MON – FRI - 8:30 AM - 3:00 PM

CAPE MAY CITY MUNICIPAL COURT
643 WASHINGTON ST
CAPE MAY, NJ, 08204
PHONE: 609-884-9550
OFFICE HOURS: MON – FRI - 8:00 AM - 4:00 PM

CAPE MAY POINT MUNICIPAL CT
643 WASHINGTON ST
CAPE MAY, NJ, 08204
PHONE: 609-884-9550
OFFICE HOURS: MON – FRI - 8:00 AM TO 4:00 PM

CARLSTADT BORO MUNICIPAL COURT
500 MADISON ST
CARLSTADT, NJ, 07072
PHONE: 201-438-4306
OFFICE HOURS: MON – FRI - 9:00 AM - 4:00 PM

CARNEYS POINT TWP MUNICIPAL COURT
303 HARDING HIGHWAY
CARNEYS POINT, NJ, 08069
PHONE: 856-299-1013
OFFICE HOURS: MON-FRI - 8:30 AM - 4:00 PM

CARTERET MUNICIPAL COURT
230 ROOSEVELT AVENUE
CARTERET, NJ, 07008

PHONE: 732-541-3900
OFFICE HOURS: MON – FRI - 8:00 AM - 4:00 PM

CEDAR GROVE MUNICIPAL COURT
525 POMPTON AVE
CEDAR GROVE, NJ, 07009
PHONE: 973-239-1410
OFFICE HOURS: MON-FRI - 8:30 AM - 4:30 PM

CENTRAL MUNICIPAL COURT BERGEN COUNTY
71 HUDSON STREET
HACKENSACK, NJ, 07601
PHONE: 201-336-6222
OFFICE HOURS: MON – FRI - 9:00 AM - 4:00 PM

CENTRAL WARREN JOINT COURT
100 PORT MURRAY RD
PORT MURRAY, NJ, 07865
PHONE: 908-689-7066
OFFICE HOURS: MON – FRI - 9:00 AM - 4:00 PM

CHATHAM BORO MUNICIPAL COURT
50 KINGS ROAD
MADISON, NJ, 07940
PHONE: 973-593-3026
OFFICE HOURS: MON – FRI - 8:00 AM - 4:00 PM

CHATHAM TWP MUNICIPAL COURT
50 KINGS ROAD,
MADISON, NJ, 07940
PHONE: 973-593-3026
OFFICE HOURS: MON – FRI - 8:00 AM - 4:00 PM

CHERRY HILL TWP MUNICIPAL COURT
820 MERCER STREET
CHERRY HILL, NJ, 08002
PHONE: 856-488-7850
OFFICE HOURS: MON – FRI - 9:00 AM - 5:00 PM

CHESILHURST MUNICIPAL COURT
201 GRANT AVE
CHESILHURST, NJ, 08089
PHONE: 856-767-1548
OFFICE HOURS: MON – THUR - 9:00 AM - 2:00 PM

CHESTER BORO MUNICIPAL COURT
50 NORTH ROAD
CHESTER, NJ, 07930
PHONE: 908-879-3660

OFFICE HOURS: MON – FRI - 9:00 AM - 4:00 PM

CHESTER TWP MUNICIPAL COURT
1 PARKER RD
CHESTER, NJ, 07930
PHONE: 908-879-5100
OFFICE HOURS: MON – FRI - 9:00 AM - 4:00 PM

CHESTERFIELD MUNICIPAL COURT
41 SCHOOLHOUSE RD
JACOBSTOWN, NJ, 08562
PHONE: 609-758-2522
OFFICE HOURS: MON – FRI - 8:30 AM - 4:30 PM

CINNAMINSON MUNICIPAL COURT
1621 RIVERTON RD
CINNAMINSON, NJ, 08077
PHONE: 856-829-4027
OFFICE HOURS: MON – FRI - 8:30 AM - 4:00 PM

CITY OF ESTELL MANOR MUNI COURT
148 CUMBERLAND AVE
ESTELL MANOR, NJ, 08319
PHONE: 609-476-4338
OFFICE HOURS: WED 6:00 PM – 8:00 PM, FRI 9:00
AM – 1:00 PM

CLARK MUNICIPAL COURT
315 WESTFIELD AVENUE
CLARK, NJ, 07066
PHONE: 732-381-5395
OFFICE HOURS: MON – FRI – 9:00 AM – 4:00 PM

CLAYTON BORO MUNICIPAL COURT
680 WHIG LANE
MONROEVILLE, NJ, 08343
PHONE: 856-881-6631
OFFICE HOURS: MON, TUES, THUR – 9:00 AM -4:00
PM, WED 9:00 AM - 5:30 PM, FRI 9:00 AM -2:30 PM
CLEMENTON MUNICIPAL COURT
101 GIBBSBORO ROAD
CLEMENTON, NJ, 08021
PHONE: 856-783-6464
OFFICE HOURS: MON – FRI 8:30 AM - 4:00 PM

CLIFFSIDE PARK MUNICIPAL COURT
525 PALISADE AVE
CLIFFSIDE PARK, NJ, 07010
PHONE: 201-945-3456
OFFICE HOURS: MON – FRI – 9:00 AM – 4:00 PM

CLIFTON MUNICIPAL COURT
900 CLIFTON AVENUE
CLIFTON, NJ, 07013
PHONE: 973-470-5860
OFFICE HOURS: MON – FRI - 8:30 AM - 4:00 PM

CLINTON TWP MUNICIPAL COURT
1370 ROUTE 31 NORTH
ANNANDALE, NJ, 08801
PHONE: 908-735-3730
OFFICE HOURS: MON - FRI 8:30 AM - 4:00 PM

CLOSTER BORO MUNICIPAL COURT
295 CLOSTER DOCK RD
CLOSTER, NJ, 07624
PHONE: 201-784-0600
OFFICE HOURS: MON – FRI - 9:00 AM - 4:00 PM

COLLINGSWOOD MUNICIPAL COURT
28 W. COLLINGS AVE
COLLINGSWOOD, NJ, 08108
PHONE: 856-854-7535
OFFICE HOURS: MON – FRI - 9:00 AM - 4:00 PM

COLTS NECK TWP MUNICIPAL COURT
124 CEDAR DRIVE
COLTS NECK, NJ, 07722
PHONE: 732-431-1799
OFFICE HOURS: MON – FRI - 9:00 AM - 4:00 PM

COMMERCIAL JOINT MUNICIPAL COURT
1768 MAIN STREET
PORT NORRIS, NJ, 08349
PHONE: 856-785-3100
OFFICE HOURS: MON-FRI 8:00 AM – 12:00 NOON,
1:00 PM – 4:00 PM

CORBIN CITY MUNICIPAL COURT
P.O. BOX 414
TUCKAHOE, NJ, 08250
PHONE: 609-628-2015
OFFICE HOURS: MON – FRI - 8:30 AM - 4:00 PM

CRANBURY TWP MUNICIPAL COURT
641 PLAINSBORO ROAD
PLAINSBORO, NJ, 08536
PHONE: 609-799-0863
OFFICE HOURS: MON – FRI - 8:45 AM - 4:15 PM

CRANFORD MUNICIPAL COURT
8 SPRINGFIELD AVE
CRANFORD, NJ, 07016
PHONE: 908-709-7242
OFFICE HOURS: MON – FRI - 8:30 AM -3:30 PM

CRESSKILL BORO MUNICIPAL COURT
67 UNION AVENUE
CRESSKILL, NJ, 07626
PHONE: 201-569-7636

CUMBERLAND SALEM REGIONAL COURT
1325 HIGHWAY 77
SEABROOK, NJ, 08302
PHONE: 856-455-8722
OFFICE HOURS: MON – FRI - 9:00 AM - 4:00 PM

DEAL BORO MUNICIPAL COURT
190 NORWOOD AVE
DEAL, NJ, 07723
PHONE: 732-531-1343
OFFICE HOURS: MON – FRI - 8:30 AM - 4:30 PM

DEERFIELD TWP MUNICIPAL COURT
1325 HWY 77
SEABROOK, NJ, 08302
PHONE: 856-455-8722
OFFICE HOURS: MON-FRI - 8:00 AM -12:00 NOON

DELANCO TWP MUNICIPAL COURT
770 COOPERTOWN ROAD
DELANCO, NJ, 08075
PHONE: 856-461-0181
OFFICE HOURS: MON – THURS - 9:00 AM - 1:00 PM

DELRAN MUNICIPAL COURT
900 CHESTER AVENUE
DELRAN, NJ, 08075
PHONE: 856-461-3888
OFFICE HOURS: MON – FRI - 9:00 AM - 5:00 PM

DEMAREST BORO MUNICIPAL COURT
118 SERPENTINE RD
DEMAREST, NJ, 07627
PHONE: 201-768-1160

DENNIS TWP MUNICIPAL COURT
P.O. BOX 414
TUCKAHOE, NJ, 08250

PHONE: 609-628-2015
OFFICE HOURS: MON – FRI - 8:30 AM - 4:00 PM

DENVILLE TWP MUNICIPAL COURT
1 SAINT MARY'S PLACE
DENVILLE, NJ, 07834
PHONE: 973-625-8300
OFFICE HOURS: MON – FRI - 9:00 AM - 3:00 PM

DEPTFORD TWP MUNICIPAL COURT
1011 COOPER ST
DEPTFORD, NJ, 08096
PHONE: 856-686-2230
OFFICE HOURS: MON-FRI – 9:00 AM – 4:00 PM

DOWNE TWP MUNICIPAL COURT
1768 MAIN ST
PORT NORRIS, NJ, 08349
PHONE: 856-785-3100
OFFICE HOURS: MON-FRI – 8:00 AM – 12:00 NOON
AND 1:00 PM – 4:00 PM

DUMONT BORO MUNICIPAL COURT
50 WASHINGTON AVE
DUMONT, NJ, 07628
PHONE: 201-387-5032
OFFICE HOURS: MON – FRI - 9:00 AM - 4:30 PM

DUNELLEN BORO MUNICIPAL COURT
355 NORTH AVE,
DUNELLEN, NJ, 08812
PHONE: 732-968-3400
OFFICE HOURS: MON – FRI - 9:00 AM - 4:00 PM

EAGLESWOOD TWP MUNICIPAL COURT
665 RADIO ROAD
LITTLE EGG HARBOR, NJ, 08087
PHONE: 609-296-7241
OFFICE HOURS: MON – FRI - 9:00 AM - 4:00 PM

EAST AMWELL JOINT MUNICIPAL COURT
1070 HGWY 202
RINGOES, NJ, 08551
PHONE: 908-782-6855
OFFICE HOURS: MON – THU - 8:30 AM - 3:00 PM

EAST BRUNSWICK MUNICIPAL COURT
P O BOX 1081
EAST BRUNSWICK, NJ, 08816

PHONE: 732-390-6915
OFFICE HOURS: MON – FRI - 8:00 AM - 4:30 PM

EAST GREENWICH TWP COURT
159 DEMOCRAT RD
MICKLETON, NJ, 08056
PHONE: 856-423-3010
OFFICE HOURS: MON – FRI - 8:30 AM - 4:30 PM

EAST HANOVER MUNICIPAL COURT
1000 RTE #10
WHIPPANY, NJ, 07981
PHONE: 973-428-2519
OFFICE HOURS: MON – FRI - 8:30 AM - 4:30 PM

EAST NEWARK MUNICIPAL COURT
34 SHERMAN AVE
EAST NEWARK, NJ, 07029
PHONE: 973-483-7606
OFFICE HOURS: MON – FRI - 9:00 AM - 4:00 PM

EAST ORANGE MUNICIPAL
221 FREEWAY DR EAST
EAST ORANGE, NJ, 07018
PHONE: 973-266-5300
OFFICE HOURS: MON – FRI - 8:30 AM - 4:00 PM

EAST RUTHERFORD BORO COURT
117 STANLEY ST
EAST RUTHERFORD, NJ, 07073
PHONE: 201-438-0169
OFFICE HOURS: MON – FRI - 9:00 AM - 3:30 PM

EAST WINDSOR MUNICIPAL COURT
80 ONE MILE ROAD
EAST WINDSOR, NJ, 08520
PHONE: 609-448-3228
OFFICE HOURS: MON – FRI - 8:00 AM - 6:00 PM

EASTAMPTON TWP MUNICIPAL COURT
710 RANCOCAS RD
WESTAMPTON, NJ, 08060
PHONE: 609-267-1895
OFFICE HOURS: MON – FRI - 8:00 AM - 3:00 PM

EATONTOWN MUNICIPAL COURT
556 TINTON AVE
TINTON FALLS, NJ, 07724
PHONE: 732-542-3400

OFFICE HOURS: MON, WED, THUR, FRI - 8:30 AM - 4:30 PM, TUES - 8:00 – 4:00

EDGEWATER BORO MUNICIPAL COURT
55 RIVER RD
EDGEWATER, NJ, 07020
PHONE: 201-943-1700
OFFICE HOURS: MON – FRI – 9:00 AM – 5:00 PM

EDGEWATER PARK MUNICIPAL COURT
400 DELANCO RD
EDGEWATER PARK, NJ, 08010
PHONE: 609-877-7645
OFFICE HOURS: MON – FRI - 9:00 AM - 4:30 PM

EDISON TWP MUNICIPAL COURT
100 MUNICIPAL BLVD
EDISON, NJ, 08817
PHONE: 732-248-7328
OFFICE HOURS: MON – FRI - 8:30 AM - 4:30 PM

EGG HARBOR CITY COURT
500 LONDON AVENUE
EGG HARBOR CITY, NJ, 08215
PHONE: 609-965-0700
OFFICE HOURS: MON – FRI - 9:00 AM - 4:00 PM

EGG HARBOR TOWNSHIP COURT
3515 BARGAINTOWN RD
EGG HARBOR TWP, NJ, 08234
PHONE: 609-926-4196
OFFICE HOURS: MON – FRI - 8:30 AM - 4:30 PM

ELIZABETH MUNICIPAL COURT
208 COMMERCE PLACE
ELIZABETH, NJ, 07201
PHONE: 908-558-6800
OFFICE HOURS: MON – FRI - 8:00 AM - 9:30 PM

ELK JOINT MUNICIPAL COURT
680 WHIG LANE
MONROEVILLE, NJ, 08343
PHONE: 856-881-6631
OFFICE HOURS: MON, TUES, THUR – 9:00 AM – 4:00 PM, WED – 9:00 AM - 5:30 PM, FRI – 9:00 AM - 2:30 PM

ELMER BORO MUNICIPAL COURT
25 WEST AVE
WOODSTOWN, NJ, 08098

PHONE: 856-769-2424
OFFICE HOURS: MON, TUES 9:00 AM - 3:30 PM WED,
THUR, FRI – 9:00 AM – 2:00 PM

ELMWOOD PARK BORO MUNICIPAL COURT
182 MARKET STREET
ELMWOOD PARK, NJ, 07407
PHONE: 201-796-1457
OFFICE HOURS: MON – FRI - 8:30 AM - 4:00 PM

EMERSON BORO MUNICIPAL COURT
LINWOOD AVE
EMERSON, NJ, 07630
PHONE: 201-262-6058
OFFICE HOURS: MON-FRI – 9:00 AM – 5:00 PM

ENGLEWOOD CITY MUNICIPAL COURT
73 SO VAN BRUNT ST
ENGLEWOOD, NJ, 07631
PHONE: 201-569-0255
OFFICE HOURS: MON – FRI - 9:00 AM - 4:00 PM

ENGLEWOOD CLIFFS BORO COURT
10 KAHN TERRACE
ENGLEWOOD CLIFF, NJ, 07632
PHONE: 201-568-7860
OFFICE HOURS: MON – FRI – 9:00 AM – 12:00
NOON, 1:00 PM – 4:00 PM

ENGLISHTOWN BORO MUNICIPAL COURT
15 MAIN STREET
ENGLISHTOWN, NJ, 07726
PHONE: 732-446-4457
OFFICE HOURS: MON – FRI - 8:00 AM - 4:00 PM

ESSEX FELLS BORO MUNICIPAL COURT
GOULD AVE, BORO HALL
NORTH CALDWELL, NJ, 07006
PHONE: 973-228-6420
OFFICE HOURS: MON – FRI - 9:00 AM - 4:00 PM

EVESHAM TWP MUNICIPAL COURT
984 TUCKERTON RD
MARLTON, NJ, 08053
PHONE: 856-983-2929
OFFICE HOURS: MON – FRI - 8:30 AM - 4:30 PM

EWING TOWNSHIP MUNICIPAL COURT
2 JAKE GARZIO DRIVE
EWING, NJ, 08628
PHONE: 609-883-2900
OFFICE HOURS: MON – FRI - 9:00 AM - 3:00 PM

FAIR HAVEN BORO MUNICIPAL COURT
748 RIVER RD
FAIR HAVEN, NJ, 07704
PHONE: 732-747-0241
OFFICE HOURS: MON – FRI – 9:00 AM – 4:00 PM

FAIRFIELD MUNICIPAL COURT
P.O. BOX 240
FAIRTON NJ 08320
PHONE: 856-453-3157
OFFICE HOURS: MON – FRI - 8:30 AM - 12:00 NOON

FAIRFIELD TWP MUNICIPAL COURT
230 FAIRFIELD RD
FAIRFIELD, NJ, 07004
PHONE: 973-882-2700
OFFICE HOURS: MON – FRI - 8:30 AM - 4:30 PM

FAIRLAWN MUNICIPAL COURT
8-01 FAIR LAWN AVE
FAIR LAWN, NJ, 07410
PHONE: 201-794-5348
OFFICE HOURS: MON – FRI – 9:00 AM – 4:00 PM

FAIRVIEW BORO MUNICIPAL COURT
59 ANDERSON AVE
FAIRVIEW, NJ, 07022
PHONE: 201-943-4368
OFFICE HOURS: MON-FRI - 8:30 AM - 4:00 PM

FANWOOD BORO MUNICIPAL COURT
75 N MARTINE AVE
FANWOOD, NJ, 07023
PHONE: 908-322-6750
OFFICE HOURS: MON –FRI - 8:30 AM - 4:00 PM

FAR HILLS BORO MUNICIPAL COURT
PO BOX 858
FAR HILLS, NJ, 07931
PHONE: 908-781-1911
OFFICE HOURS: MON, TUES, THUR - 10:00-4:00 PM,
2&4 TUES 10:30 AM

FARMINGDALE BORO MUNICIPAL COURT
11 ASBURY AVE
FARMINGDALE, NJ, 07727
PHONE: 732-938-4080
OFFICE HOURS: MON – FRI - 9:00 AM - 4:00 PM

FIELDSBORO MUNICIPAL COURT
204 WASHINGTON ST
FIELDSBORO, NJ, 08505
PHONE: 609-298-1616

FLEMINGTON BORO MUNICIPAL COURT
2 MUNICIPAL DRIVE
FLEMINGTON, NJ, 08822
PHONE: 908-782-5770
OFFICE HOURS: MON – FRI - 9:00 AM - 4:00 PM

FLORENCE TWP MUNICIPAL COURT
711 BROAD STREET
FLORENCE, NJ, 08518
PHONE: 609-499-2222
OFFICE HOURS: MON – FRI - 10:00 AM – 4:00 PM

FLORHAM PARK MUNICIPAL COURT
111 RIDGEDALE AVE
FLORHAM PARK, NJ, 07932
PHONE: 973-410-5324
OFFICE HOURS: MON-FRI - 9:00 AM - 4:00 PM

FOLSOM BORO MUNICIPAL COURT
1700 12TH STREET
FOLSOM, NJ, 08037
PHONE: 609-561-0711
OFFICE HOURS: MON – FRI - 8:30 AM - 4:00 PM

FORT LEE MUNICIPAL COURT
309 MAIN ST
FORT LEE, NJ, 07024
PHONE: 201-592-3575
OFFICE HOURS: MON-FRI - 8:30 AM – 4:00 PM

FRANKFORD JOINT MUNICIPAL COURT
151 US HIGHWAY 206
AUGUSTA, NJ, 07822
PHONE: 973-948-4045
OFFICE HOURS: MON – FRI - 9:00 AM - 3:30 PM

FRANKLIN BORO MUNICIPAL COURT
46 MAIN STREET

FRANKLIN, NJ, 07416
PHONE: 973-827-9280
OFFICE HOURS: MON – FRI - 8:30 AM - 4:00 PM

FRANKLIN JOINT MUNICIPAL COURT
1571 DELSEA DRIVE
FRANKLINVILLE, NJ, 08322
PHONE: 856-694-1661
OFFICE HOURS: MON, TUES, WED, FRI – 8:00 AM – 3:00 PM, THUR 8:00 AM-

FRANKLIN LAKES BORO COURT
DEKORTE DR
FRANKLIN LAKES, NJ, 07417
PHONE: 201-891-5480
OFFICE HOURS: MON – FRI - 8:30 AM - 4:00 PM
FRANKLIN TWP MUNICIPAL COURT
1070 HGWY #202
RINGOES, NJ, 08551
PHONE: 908-782-6855
OFFICE HOURS: MON – THUR - 8:30 AM - 3:00 PM

FRANKLIN TWP MUNICIPAL COURT
495 DEMOTT LANE
SOMERSET, NJ, 08875
PHONE: 732-873-2500
OFFICE HOURS: MON – FRI - 9:00 AM - 4:00 PM

FRANKLIN TWP MUNICIPAL COURT
628 RTE.#94
COLUMBIA, NJ, 07832
PHONE: 908-496-4131
OFFICE HOURS: MON – FRI - 8:00 AM - 4:00 PM

FREEHOLD BORO MUNICIPAL COURT
38 JACKSON STREET
FREEHOLD, NJ, 07728
PHONE: 732-462-2444
OFFICE HOURS: MON- FRI - 8:30 AM - 4:00 PM

FREEHOLD TWP. MUNICIPAL COURT
ONE MUNICIPAL PLAZA
FREEHOLD, NJ, 07728
PHONE: 732-294-2150
OFFICE HOURS: MON – FRI – 9:00 AM – 4:00 PM

FRELINGHUYSEN TWP MUN COURT
628 RT 94
COLUMBIA, NJ, 07832

PHONE: 908-496-4131
OFFICE HOURS: MON – FRI - 8:00 AM - 4:00 PM

GALLOWAY TOWNSHIP MUNICIPAL COURT
300 E. JIM LEEDS RD
GALLOWAY, NJ, 08205
PHONE: 609-652-3726
OFFICE HOURS: MON-FRI - 8:30 AM - 4:30 PM

GARFIELD CITY MUNICIPAL COURT
111 OUTWATER LANE
GARFIELD NJ 07026
PHONE: 973-340-6119
OFFICE HOURS: MON - FRI 9:00 AM - 4:00 PM

GARWOOD BORO MUNICIPAL COURT
403 SOUTH AVE
GARWOOD, NJ, 07027
PHONE: 908-789-0780
OFFICE HOURS: MON – FRI - 9:00 AM - 3:30 PM

GIBBSBORO BORO MUNICIPAL COURT
49 KIRKWOOD RD
GIBBSBORO, NJ, 08026
PHONE: 856-783-6655
OFFICE HOURS: MON-THUR – 9:00 AM – 4:00 PM,
FRI – 9:00 AM – 12:00 NOON

GLASSBORO MUNICIPAL COURT
1 SOUTH MAIN STREET
GLASSBORO, NJ, 08028
PHONE: 856-881-0383
OFFICE HOURS: MON – FRI - 8:30 AM - 4:30 PM

GLEN GARDNER BORO MUNICIPAL COURT
405 MINE RD
ASBURY, NJ, 08802
PHONE: 908-735-4559
OFFICE HOURS: MON – FRI - 8:30 AM - 3:30 PM

GLEN ROCK MUNICIPAL COURT
HARDING PLAZA
GLEN ROCK, NJ, 07452
PHONE: 201-670-3950
OFFICE HOURS: MON – FRI - 8:30 - 4:30 PM

GLOUCESTER CITY MUNICIPAL COURT
313 MONMOUTH STREET
GLOUCESTER CITY, NJ, 08030
PHONE: 856-456-3958

OFFICE HOURS: MON – WED - 8:00 AM – 5:00 PM,
THUR 10:00 – 7:00, CLOSED FRI

GLOUCESTER TWP MUNICIPAL COURT
PO BOX 8
BLACKWOOD, NJ, 08012
PHONE: 856-228-4000
OFFICE HOURS: MON – FRI - 8:00 AM - 5:45 PM

GREEN JOINT MUNICIPAL COURT
150 KENNEDY ROAD
ANDOVER NJ 07821
PHONE: 908-850-0990
OFFICE HOURS: MON – FRI - 8:30 AM - 2:30 PM

GREENBROOK TWP MUNICIPAL COURT
111 GREENBROOK RD
GREEN BROOK, NJ, 08812
PHONE: 732-968-1110
OFFICE HOURS: MON – FRI - 8:30 AM - 3:30 PM

GREENWICH TWP MUNICIPAL COURT
21 NORTH WALNUT ST
GIBBSTOWN, NJ, 08027
PHONE: 856-423-0113
OFFICE HOURS: MON – FRI - 9:00 AM - 4:00 PM

GREENWICH MUNICIPAL COURT
321 GREENWICH ST
STEWARTSVILLE, NJ, 08886
PHONE: 908-859-0922
OFFICE HOURS: MON – FRI - 9:00 AM - 4:00 PM

GUTTENBERG MUNICIPAL COURT
6808 PARK AVE
GUTTENBERG, NJ, 07093
PHONE: 201-868-2923
OFFICE HOURS: MON – FRI - 9:00 AM - 3:30 PM

HACKENSACK MUNICIPAL COURT
215 STATE STREET
HACKENSACK, NJ, 07601
PHONE: 201-646-3971
OFFICE HOURS: MON – FRI - 9:00 AM - 4:00 PM

HACKETTSTOWN MUNICIPAL COURT
215 STIGER ST
HACKETTSTOWN, NJ, 07840
PHONE: 908-852-0688
OFFICE HOURS: MON – FRI - 9:00 AM - 4:30 PM

HADDON HEIGHTS MUNICIPAL COURT
500 WHITE HORSE PIKE
OAKLYN, NJ, 08107
PHONE: 856-858-0074
OFFICE HOURS: MON-THUR - 8:00 AM -3:30 PM, FRI
- 8:00 AM - 11:30 AM

HADDON TWP MUNICIPAL COURT
135 HADDON AVE
HADDON TWP, NJ, 08108
PHONE: 856-854-1176
OFFICE HOURS: MON – FRI - 8:30 AM - 4:00 PM

HADDONFIELD MUNICIPAL COURT
606 W NICHOLSON RD
AUDUBON, NJ, 08106
PHONE: 856-547-0712
OFFICE HOURS: MON – FRI - 8:30 AM - 4:00 PM

HAINESPORT TWP MUNICIPAL COURT
710 RANCOCAS RD
WESTAMPTON, NJ, 08060
PHONE: 609-267-1895
OFFICE HOURS: MON – FRI - 8:00 AM - 3:00 PM

HALEDON BORO MUNICIPAL COURT
510 BELMONT AVE
HALEDON, NJ, 07508
PHONE: 973-790-0500
OFFICE HOURS: MON – FRI - 9:00 AM - 4:00 PM

HAMBURG MUNICIPAL COURT
11 ORCHARD ST
HAMBURG, NJ, 07419
PHONE: 973-209-4545
OFFICE HOURS: MON – FRI - 8:00 AM - 3:00 PM

HAMILTON TWP (ATL) MUNI COURT
6101 13TH STREET
MAYS LANDING, NJ, 08330
PHONE: 609-625-6621
OFFICE HOURS: MON – FRI - 9:00 AM - 5:00 PM

HAMILTON TWP MUNICIPAL COURT
1270 WHITEHORSE AVE
HAMILTON, NJ, 08619
PHONE: 609-581-4071
OFFICE HOURS: MON – FRI - 8:00 AM -3:30 PM

HAMMONTON MUNICIPAL COURT
100 CENTRAL AVE
HAMMONTON, NJ, 08037
PHONE: 609-567-4322
OFFICE HOURS: MON – FRI - 9:00 AM - 4:30 PM

HAMPTON BORO MUNICIPAL COURT
ONE MUNICIPAL DRIVE
FLEMINGTON, NJ, 08822
PHONE: 908-782-8818
OFFICE HOURS: MON - FRI - 8:30 AM - 4:30 PM

HAMPTON/STILLWATER MUNICIPAL COURT
888 RT. 23
WANTAGE, NJ, 07461
PHONE: 973-875-7310
OFFICE HOURS: MON-FRI - 10:00 AM - 4:30 PM

HANOVER MUNICIPAL COURT
1000 RT #10
WHIPPANY, NJ, 07981
PHONE: 973-428-2519
OFFICE HOURS: MON – FRI - 8:30 AM - 4:30 PM

HARDING TWP MUNICIPAL COURT
50 KINGS ROAD
MADISON, NJ, 07940
PHONE: 973-593-3026
OFFICE HOURS: MON – FRI - 8:00 AM - 4:00 PM

HARDWICK TWP MUNICIPAL COURT
PO BOX 134
HOPE, NJ, 07844
PHONE: 908-459-5800
OFFICE HOURS: TUES-THUR - 9:00 AM - 3:00 PM

HARDYSTON MUNICIPAL COURT
149 WHEATSWORTH RD
HARDYSTON, NJ, 07419
PHONE: 973-823-7038
OFFICE HOURS: MON – FRI - 9:00 AM - 4:00 PM

HARMONY TWP MUNICIPAL COURT
232 S. THIRD STREET
PHILLIPSBURG, NJ, 08865
PHONE: 908-859-3355
OFFICE HOURS: MON – FRI - 8:00 AM – 5:00 PM

HARRINGTON PARK BORO COURT

85 HARRIOT AVE
HARRINGTON PK, NJ, 07640
PHONE: 201-768-0500

HARRISON MUNICIPAL COURT
318 HARRISON AVE
HARRISON, NJ, 07029
OFFICE HOURS: MON- FRI - 9:00 AM – 4:00 PM

HARRISON TWP MUNICIPAL COURT
114 BRIDGETON PIKE
MULLICA HILL NJ 08062
PHONE: 856-478-4049
OFFICE HOURS: MON-FRI - 9:00 AM - 4:00 PM

HARVEY CEDAR BORO MUNICIPAL COURT
76TH & LONG BEACH BL
HARVEY CEDARS, NJ, 08008
PHONE: 609-494-9026
OFFICE HOURS: TUES AND FRI - 2:00 PM – 4:00 PM

HASBROUCK HTS MUNICIPAL COURT
248 HAMILTON AVENUE
HASBROUCK HTS, NJ, 07604
PHONE: 201-288-4004
OFFICE HOURS: MON – FRI - 9:00 AM- 3:00 PM

HAWORTH BORO MUNICIPAL COURT
300 HAWORTH AVE
HAWORTH, NJ, 07641
PHONE: 201-384-4883
OFFICE HOURS: MON – FRI - 9:00 AM - 3:00 PM

HAWTHORNE BORO MUNICIPAL COURT
445 LAFAYETTE AVE
HAWTHORNE, NJ, 07506
PHONE: 973-427-4767
OFFICE HOURS: MON – FRI - 9:00 AM - 4:00 PM

HAZLET/KEYPORT/MATAWAN JOINT
255 MIDDLE ROAD
HAZLET, NJ, 07730
PHONE: 732-264-2231
OFFICE HOURS: MON-FRI - 8:30 AM - 4:30 PM

HELMETTA BORO MUNICIPAL COURT
51 MAIN STREET

HELMETTA, NJ, 08828
PHONE: 732-521-4946
OFFICE HOURS: TUES-THUR - 5:30 PM - 7:30 PM

HI-NELLA BORO MUNICIPAL COURT
100 WYKAGYL RD
HI-NELLA, NJ, 08083
PHONE: 856-782-0860
OFFICE HOURS: MON-THUR – 9:00 AM-2:00 PM,
CLOSED FRI

HIGH BRIDGE MUNICIPAL COURT
1370 ROUTE 31 NORTH
ANNANDALE, NJ, 08801
PHONE: 908-735-3730
OFFICE HOURS: MON-FRI – 9:00 AM - 4:00 PM

HIGHLAND PARK BORO COURT
221 S. FIFTH AVE
HIGHLAND PK, NJ, 08904
PHONE: 732-777-6010
OFFICE HOURS: MON-FRI - 8:00 AM - 4:00 PM

HIGHLANDS BORO MUNICIPAL COURT
100 FIRST AVENUE
ATL HIGHLANDS, NJ, 07716
PHONE: 732-291-3225
OFFICE HOURS: MON – FRI - 8:30 AM - 4:30 PM

HIGHTSTOWN MUNICIPAL COURT
1117 ROUTE 130
ROBBINSVILLE, NJ, 08691
PHONE: 609-259-3522
OFFICE HOURS: MON – FR I - 8:30 AM - 04:30 PM

HILLSBOROUGH TWP MUNICIPAL COURT
379 SOUTH BRANCH RD
HILLSBOROUGH, NJ, 08844
PHONE: 908-369-3532
OFFICE HOURS: MON – FRI - 8:00 AM - 4:00 PM

HILLSDALE BORO MUNICIPAL COURT
380 HILLSDALE AVE
HILLSDALE, NJ, 07642
PHONE: 201-666-4800
OFFICE HOURS: MON – FRI - 8:00 AM - 4:00 PM

HILLSIDE TWP MUNICIPAL COURT
1409 LIBERTY AVENUE
HILLSIDE, NJ, 07205

PHONE: 973-926-1881
OFFICE HOURS: MON – FRI - 8:30 AM - 3:30 PM

HO-HO-KUS BORO MUNICIPAL COURT
333 WARREN AVE
HO-HO-KUS, NJ, 07423
PHONE: 201-652-0699
OFFICE HOURS: MON-THUR - 9:00 AM - 4:00 PM
CLOSED 1:00-2:00 PM

HOBOKEN CITY MUNICIPAL COURT
100 NEWARK STREET
HOBOKEN, NJ, 07030
PHONE: 201-420-2123
OFFICE HOURS: MON – FRI - 9:00 AM-4:00 PM

HOLMDEL TWP MUNICIPAL COURT
4 CRAWFORDS CORNER
HOLMDEL, NJ, 07733
PHONE: 732-946-4713
OFFICE HOURS: MON – FRI - 9:00 AM - 4:30 PM

HOPATCONG BORO MUNICIPAL COURT
111 RIVER STYX RD
HOPATCONG, NJ, 07843
PHONE: 973-770-1200
OFFICE HOURS: MON – FRI - 9:00 AM - 4:00 PM

HOPEWELL BORO MUNICIPAL COURT
88 EAST BROAD ST
HOPEWELL, NJ, 08525
PHONE: 609-466-0968
OFFICE HOURS: THURS 3:30PM - 6:00PM

HOWELL TWP MUNICIPAL COURT
P.O. BOX 580
HOWELL, NJ, 07731
PHONE: 732-938-4848
OFFICE HOURS: MON – FRI - 8:30 AM - 4:30 PM

HUDSON CO DISTRICT COURT
ADMINISTRATION BLDG
JERSEY CITY, NJ, 07306
PHONE: 201-795-6050
OFFICE HOURS: MON – FRI - 8:30 AM - 4:30 PM

INDEPENDENCE MUNICIPAL COURT
292 ALPHANO RD
GREAT MEADOWS, NJ, 07838
PHONE: 908-637-6684

OFFICE HOURS: MON – FRI - 10:00 AM - 2:00 PM

INTERLAKEN BORO MUNICIPAL COURT
100 GRASMERE AVE
INTERLAKEN, NJ, 07712
PHONE: 732-531-3689
OFFICE HOURS: MON – FRI - 9:00 AM- 4:00 PM

INTERMUN (ESTELL MANOR)
148 CUMBERLAND AVE
ESTELL MANOR, NJ, 08319
PHONE: 609-476-4338
OFFICE HOURS: WED – 6:00 PM – 8:00 PM, FRI 9:00
AM – 1:00 PM

IRVINGTON MUNICIPAL COURT
ONE CIVIC SQUARE
IRVINGTON, NJ, 07111
PHONE: 973-399-6671
OFFICE HOURS: MON – FRI - 9:00 AM - 4:00 PM

ISLAND HEIGHTS MUNICIPAL COURT
PO BOX 757
ISLAND HEIGHTS, NJ, 08732
PHONE: 732-270-6161
OFFICE HOURS: MON EVENINGS 6:00 PM – 8:00 PM
ONLY

JACKSON TWP MUNICIPAL COURT
102 JACKSON DRIVE
JACKSON, NJ, 08527
PHONE: 732-928-1205
OFFICE HOURS: MON-FRI - 9:00 AM - 4:00 PM

JAMESBURG BORO MUNICIPAL COURT
131 PERRINEVILLE RD
JAMESBURG, NJ, 08831
PHONE: 732-521-0614
OFFICE HOURS: MON – FRI - 8:30 AM - 4:00 PM

JEFFERSON TWP MUNICIPAL COURT
1033 WELDON RD
LAKE HOPATCONG, NJ, 07849
PHONE: 973-208-6129
OFFICE HOURS: MON-FRI - 9:00 AM - 4:30 PM

JERSEY CITY MUNICIPAL COURT
365 SUMMIT AVENUE
JERSEY CITY, NJ, 07306
PHONE: 201-209-6700

OFFICE HOURS: MON –THUR - 8:30 AM -8:00 PM, FRI
8:30-4:00

JOINT COURT DELAWARE VALLEY
29 CHURCH STREET
KEANSBURG, NJ, 07734
PHONE: 732-787-0215
OFFICE HOURS: MON - FRI 9:00 AM - 4:00 PM

KEARNY MUNICIPAL COURT
404 KEARNY AVENUE
KEARNY, NJ, 07032
PHONE: 201-955-7410
OFFICE HOURS: MON – FRI - 8:30 AM - 5:00 PM

KENILWORTH BOR MUNICIPAL COURT
567 BOULEVARD
KENILWORTH, NJ, 07033
PHONE: 908-276-1104
OFFICE HOURS: MON – FRI - 9:00 AM – 3:00 PM
KEYPORT BORO MUNICIPAL COURT
255 MIDDLE ROAD
HAZLET, NJ, 07730
PHONE: 732-264-2231
OFFICE HOURS: MON-FRI - 8:30 AM - 4:30 PM

KINGWOOD TWP MUNICIPAL COURT
P.O. BOX 199
BAPTISTOWN, NJ, 08803
PHONE: 908-996-0799
OFFICE HOURS: TUES AND THURS - 9:00 AM - 12:00
NOON

KINNELON BORO MUNICIPAL COURT
130 KINNELON RD
KINNELON, NJ, 07405
PHONE: 973-838-7644
OFFICE HOURS: MON – FRI - 8:00 AM - 4:00 PM

KNOWLTON TWP MUNICIPAL COURT
628 RT 94
COLUMBIA, NJ, 07832
PHONE: 908-496-4131
OFFICE HOURS: MON - FRI - 8:00 AM - 4:00 PM

LACEY TOWNSHIP MUNICIPAL COURT
818 WEST LACEY ROAD
FORKED RIVER, NJ, 08731
PHONE: 609-693-1100
OFFICE HOURS: MON – FRI - 8:30 AM - 4:30 PM

LAKE COMO MUNICIPAL COURT
601 MAIN STREET
BELMAR, NJ, 07719
PHONE: 732-681-8864
OFFICE HOURS: MON – FRI - 9:00 AM - 4:30 PM

LAKEHURST BORO MUNICIPAL COURT
5 UNION AVE
LAKEHURST, NJ, 08733
PHONE: 732-657-4151

LAKEWOOD MUNICIPAL COURT
231 THIRD ST
LAKEWOOD, NJ, 08701
PHONE: 732-364-2500
OFFICE HOURS: MON – FRI - 9:00 AM - 4:00 PM

LAMBERTVILLE CITY COURT
25 SOUTH UNION ST
LAMBERTVILLE, NJ, 08530
PHONE: 609-397-1335
OFFICE HOURS: MON – FRI - 10:00 AM – 4:00 PM

LAUREL SPRINGS MUNICIPAL COURT
135 BROADWAY
LAUREL SPRINGS, NJ, 08021
PHONE: 856-784-6688
OFFICE HOURS: MON, WED, THUR - 9:00 AM - 4:00
PM, CLOSED TUE/FRI

LAVALLETTE MUNICIPAL COURT
1306 GRAND CNTRL AVE
LAVALLETTE, NJ, 08735
PHONE: 732-830-1911
OFFICE HOURS: MON – FRI - 9:00 AM – 4:00 PM

LAWNSIDE BORO MUNICIPAL COURT
1325 HWY 77
SEABROOK, NJ, 08302
PHONE: 856-455-8722
OFFICE HOURS: MON-THUR - 9:00 AM – 5:00 PM, FRI
9:00 AM – 2:00 PM

LAWRENCE TWP MUNICIPAL COURT
2211 LAWRENCE RD
LAWRENCEVILLE, NJ, 08648
PHONE: 609-844-7159
OFFICE HOURS: MON – FRI - 8:00 AM - 3:30 PM

LEBANON TWP MUNICIPAL COURT
60 WATER STREET
LEBANON, NJ, 08833
PHONE: 908-832-7684
OFFICE HOURS: TUES - 3:45-6:45, WED – 10:00 AM –
1:00 PM

LEONIA MUNICIPAL COURT
312 BROAD
LEONIA, NJ, 07605
PHONE: 201-592-5780
OFFICE HOURS: MON – FRI - 9:00 AM – 4:00 PM

LINCOLN PARK MUNICIPAL COURT
34 CHAPEL HILL RD
LINCOLN PARK, NJ, 07035
PHONE: 973-694-6100
OFFICE HOURS: MON-FRI - 8:00 AM - 4:00 PM

LINDEN MUNICIPAL COURT
MUNICIPAL BUILDING
LINDEN, NJ, 07036
PHONE: 908-474-8423
OFFICE HOURS: MON – FRI - 9:00 AM – 3:00 PM

LINDENWOLD MUNICIPAL COURT
2001 EGG HARBOR ROAD
LINDENWOLD, NJ, 08021
PHONE: 856-344-5538
OFFICE HOURS: MON – FRI - 9:00 AM - 4:00 PM

LINWOOD MUNICIPAL COURT
400 W POPLAR AVE
LINWOOD, NJ, 08221
PHONE: 609-927-3110
OFFICE HOURS: MON – FRI - 9:00 AM – 4:00 PM

LITTLE EGG HARBOR MUNICIPAL COURT
665 RADIO ROAD
LITTLE EGG HARBOR, NJ, 08087
PHONE: 609-296-7241
OFFICE HOURS: MON – FRI - 8:30 AM - 4:00 PM

LITTLE FALLS MUNICIPAL COURT
225 MAIN STREET
LITTLE FALLS, NJ, 07424
PHONE: 973-256-2400

LITTLE FERRY BORO MUNICIPAL COURT
215-217 LIBERTY ST

LITTLE FERRY, NJ, 07643
PHONE: 201-440-2111
OFFICE HOURS: MON – FRI - 9:00 AM – 4:00 PM

LITTLE SILVER BORO COURT
480 PROSPECT AVE
LITTLE SILVER, NJ, 07739
PHONE: 732-842-3881
OFFICE HOURS: MON – FRI - 8:00 AM - 3:30 PM

LIVINGSTON MUNICIPAL COURT
357 S LIVINGSTON AVE
LIVINGSTON, NJ, 07039
PHONE: 973-535-7970
OFFICE HOURS: MON – FRI - 9:00 AM – 4:00 PM

LODI BORO MUNICIPAL COURT
ONE MEMORIAL DRIVE
LODI, NJ, 07644
PHONE: 973-365-4005
OFFICE HOURS: MON – FRI - 8:30 AM - 3:30 PM

LOGAN TWP MUNICIPAL COURT
125 MAIN STREET
BRIDGEPORT, NJ, 08014
PHONE: 856-467-3425
OFFICE HOURS: MON – FRI - 8:30 AM - 4:00 PM

LONG BEACH TWP MUNICIPAL COURT
6805 LONG BEACH BLVD
BRANT BEACH, NJ, 08008
PHONE: 609-361-1000
OFFICE HOURS: MON – FRI - 9:00 AM – 3:30 PM

LONG BRANCH MUNICIPAL COURT
279 BROADWAY
LONG BRANCH, NJ, 07740
PHONE: 732-571-6500
OFFICE HOURS: MON – FRI - 8:00 AM - 3:00 PM

LONG HILL TWP MUNICIPAL COURT
915 VALLEY RD
GILLETTE, NJ, 07933
PHONE: 908-647-8369
OFFICE HOURS: MON, TUES, THUR - 8:30 AM -4:30
PM, WED – 8:30 AM - 6:30 PM, FRI – 8:30 AM - 2:30
PM

LONGPORT BORO MUNICIPAL COURT

2305 ATLANTIC AVE
PHONE: 609-822-2147
LONGPORT, NJ, 08403
OFFICE HOURS: MON – FRI - 9:00 AM - 4:30 PM

LOPATCONG TWP MUNICIPAL COURT
232 S. THIRD STREET
PHILLIPSBURG, NJ, 08865
PHONE: 908-859-3355
OFFICE HOURS: MON – FRI - 8:30-12:00 NOON, 1:00
PM-5:00 PM

LOWER ALLOWAYS CREEK COURT
PO BOX 188
HANCOCKS BRIDGE, NJ, 08038
PHONE: 856-935-1957
OFFICE HOURS: MON – 8:00 AM – 4:00 PM, TUE AND
WED - 3:30 PM - 6:30 PM

LOWER TWP MUNICIPAL COURT
401 BREAKWATER RD
ERMA, NJ, 08204
PHONE: 609-886-6040
OFFICE HOURS: MON – FRI - 8:30 AM - 4:30 PM

LUMBERTON TWP MUNICIPAL COURT
35 MUNICIPAL DR
LUMBERTON, NJ, 08048
PHONE: 609-267-3389
OFFICE HOURS: MON – FRI - 8:00 AM - 4:00 PM

LYNDHURST TWP MUNICIPAL COURT
MUNICIPAL BUILDING
LYNDHURST, NJ, 07071
PHONE: 201-804-2457
OFFICE HOURS: MON – FRI - 9:00 AM - 4:00 PM

MADISON JOINT MUNICIPAL COURT
50 KINGS ROAD
MADISON, NJ, 07940
PHONE: 973-593-3026
OFFICE HOURS: MON – FRI - 8:00 AM - 4:00 PM

MAGNOLIA BORO MUNICIPAL COURT
438 W EVESHAM AVE
MAGNOLIA, NJ, 08049

PHONE: 856-784-7134
OFFICE HOURS: MON-FRI - 10:00 AM – 4:00 PM

MAHWAH TWP MUNICIPAL COURT
475 CORPORATE DRIVE
MAHWAH, NJ, 07430
PHONE: 201-529-2862
OFFICE HOURS: MON-FRI - 8:00 AM – 4:00 PM

MANALAPAN TWP MUNICIPAL COURT
120 RT 522
MANALAPAN, NJ, 07726
PHONE: 732-446-6656
OFFICE HOURS: MON – FRI - 8:30 AM - 4:00 PM

MANASQUAN BORO MUNICIPAL COURT
201 EAST MAIN ST.
MANASQUAN, NJ, 08736
PHONE: 732-223-0600
OFFICE HOURS: MON – FRI - 8:30 AM - 4:00 PM

MANCHESTER TWP MUNICIPAL COURT
1 COLONIAL DRIVE
MANCHESTER, NJ, 08759
PHONE: 732-657-8121
OFFICE HOURS: MON – FRI - 9:00 AM - 4:00 PM

MANNINGTON TWP MUNICIPAL COURT
25 WEST AVE
WOODSTOWN, NJ, 08098
PHONE: 856-769-2424
OFFICE HOURS: MON AND TUES 9:00 AM – 3:00 PM,
WED – FRI – 9:00 AM – 2:00 PM

MANSFIELD TWP. MUNICIPAL COURT
3135 ROUTE 206 SOUTH
COLUMBUS, NJ, 08022
PHONE: 609-298-0649
OFFICE HOURS: MON – FRI – 9:00 AM – 4:00 PM

MANSFIELD TWP MUNICIPAL COURT
100 PORT MURRAY ROAD
PORT MURRAY NJ 07865
PHONE: 908-689-7066
OFFICE HOURS: MON – FRI - 8:00 AM – 4:00 PM

MANTOLOKING MUNICIPAL COURT
POB 4391,340 DRUM PT
BRICK, NJ, 08723
PHONE: 732-475-7398

OFFICE HOURS: CALL FOR OFFICE HOURS

MANTUA JOINT MUNICIPAL COURT
405 MAIN STREET
MANTUA, NJ, 08051
PHONE: 856-468-3078
OFFICE HOURS: MON-FRI - 8:30 AM - 4:00 PM

MANVILLE BORO MUNICIPAL COURT
325 NO. MAIN ST
MANVILLE, NJ, 08835
PHONE: 908-725-9478

MAPLE SHADE TWP MUNICIPAL COURT
200 STILES AVE
MAPLE SHADE, NJ, 08052
PHONE: 856-779-9610
OFFICE HOURS: MON – FRI - 9:00 AM - 3:00 PM

MAPLEWOOD TWP MUNICIPAL COURT
1618 SPRINGFIELD AVE
MAPLEWOOD, NJ, 07040
PHONE: 973-762-2839
OFFICE HOURS: MON – FRI - 9:00 AM - 3:30 PM

MARGATE MUNICIPAL COURT
9001 WINCHESTER AVE
MARGATE, NJ, 08402
PHONE: 609-822-1998
OFFICE HOURS: MON – FRI - 9:00 AM - 4:00 PM

MARLBORO TWP MUNICIPAL COURT
1979 TOWNSHIP DRIVE
MARLBORO, NJ, 07746
PHONE: 732-536-0300
OFFICE HOURS: MON – FRI - 9:00 AM - 4:00 PM

MATAWAN BORO MUNICIPAL COURT
255 MIDDLE ROAD
HAZLET. NJ, 07730
PHONE: 732-264-2231
OFFICE HOURS: MON-FRI - 8:30 AM - 4:30 PM

MAURICE RIVER MUNICIPAL COURT
PO BOX 218
LEESBURG, NJ, 08327
PHONE: 856-785-1120
OFFICE HOURS: MON – FRI - 9:00 AM - 3:00 PM

MAYWOOD BORO MUNICIPAL COURT
1 JOCKISH SQUARE
PARAMUS, NJ, 07652
PHONE: 201-265-2100
OFFICE HOURS: MON - FRI 9:00 AM - 4:00 PM

MEDFORD LAKES MUNICIPAL COURT
1 CABIN CIRCLE
MEDFORD LAKES, NJ, 08055
PHONE: 609-654-7589
OFFICE HOURS: CALL FOR OFFICE HOURS

MEDFORD TWP MUNICIPAL COURT
91 UNION STREET
MEDFORD, NJ, 08055
PHONE: 609-654-8813
OFFICE HOURS: MON – FRI – 9:00 AM – 4:00 PM

MENDHAM BORO MUNICIPAL COURT
50 NORTH ROAD
CHESTER, NJ, 07930
PHONE: 908-879-3660
OFFICE HOURS: MON – FRI - 8:00 AM - 4:30 PM

MENDHAM TWP MUNICIPAL COURT
2 WEST MAIN STREET
BROOKSIDE, NJ, 07926
PHONE: 973-543-7526
OFFICE HOURS: MON – FRI - 9:00 AM - 4:00 PM

MERCHANTVILLE BORO COURT
1 WEST MAPLE AVE
MERCHANTVILLE, NJ, 08109
PHONE: 856-662-7560
OFFICE HOURS: MON – FRI - 8:30 AM - 3:30 PM

METUCHEN MUNICIPAL COURT
500 MAIN STREET
METUCHEN, NJ, 08840
PHONE: 732-632-8505
OFFICE HOURS: MON – FRI - 8:00 AM - 4:00 PM

MID-SALEM COUNTY MUNICIPAL COURT
25 WEST AVE
WOODSTOWN, NJ, 08098
PHONE: 856-769-2424
OFFICE HOURS: MON, TUES 9:00 AM - 3:30 PM, WED
– FRI – 9:00 AM – 2:00 PM

MIDDLE TWP MUNICIPAL COURT
2 SOUTH BOYD STREET
CAPE MAY CT HSE, NJ, 08210
PHONE: 609-465-8729
OFFICE HOURS: MON - 8:30 AM - 6:00 PM, TUE-FRI -
8:30 AM - 4:00 PM

MIDDLESEX BORO MUNICIPAL COURT
1200 MOUNTAIN AVE
MIDDLESEX, NJ, 08846
PHONE: 732-356-4644
OFFICE HOURS: MON – FRI - 9:00 AM - 4:00 PM

MIDDLETOWN TWP MUNICIPAL COURT
1 KINGS HWY TWP HALL
MIDDLETOWN, NJ, 07748
PHONE: 732-615-2036
OFFICE HOURS: MON – FRI - 8:00 AM - 4:00 PM

MIDLAND PARK BORO MUNICIPAL COURT
280 GODWIN AVE
MIDLAND PARK, NJ, 07432
PHONE: 201-445-3838
OFFICE HOURS: MON – FRI - 12:00 NOON - 4:00 PM

MILLBURN TWP MUNICIPAL COURT
435 ESSEX ST
MILLBURN, NJ, 07041
PHONE: 973-564-7066
OFFICE HOURS: MON – FRI - 9:00 AM - 4:00 PM

MILLSTONE BORO MUNICIPAL COURT
495 DEMOTT LANE
SOMERSET, NJ, 08875
PHONE: 732-873-2500
OFFICE HOURS: MON-FRI - 9:00 AM - 4:00 PM

MILLSTONE TWP MUNICIPAL COURT
215 MILLSTONE RD
MILLSTONE TWP, NJ, 08535
PHONE: 732-446-6219
OFFICE HOURS: MON – FRI - 9:00 AM - 4:00 PM

MILLTOWN BORO MUNICIPAL COURT
39 WASHINGTON AVE
MILLTOWN, NJ, 08850
PHONE: 732-247-3936
OFFICE HOURS: MON – FRI - 8:30 AM - 4:30 PM

MILLVILLE MUNICIPAL COURT

18 S HIGH ST
MILLVILLE, NJ, 08332
PHONE: 856-825-7000
OFFICE HOURS: MON-FR I - 8:30 AM - 4:30 PM

MINE HILL TWP MUNICIPAL COURT
37 N. SUSSEX ST.
DOVER, NJ, 07801
PHONE: 973-366-2200
OFFICE HOURS: CALL COURT

MONMOUTH BEACH MUNICIPAL COURT
556 TINTON AVE
TINTON FALLS, NJ, 07724
PHONE: 732-542-3400
OFFICE HOURS: MON, WED – FRI - 8:30-4:30, TUE –
8:00 AM – 4:00 PM

MONROE TOWNSHIP MUNICIPAL COURT
125 VIRGINIA AVE.
WILLIAMSTOWN, NJ, 08094
PHONE: 856-728-9800
OFFICE HOURS: MON – FRI - 9:00 AM – 4:00 PM

MONROE TWP MUNICIPAL COURT
1 MUNICIPAL PLAZA
MONROE, TWP, NJ 08831
PHONE: 732-521-4020
OFFICE HOURS: MON – FRI - 8:30 AM - 4:30 PM

MONTAGUE TWP MUNICIPAL COURT
151 US HIGHWAY 206
AUGUSTA, NJ, 07822
PHONE: 973-948-4045
OFFICE HOURS: MON – FRI - 9:00 AM - 4:00 PM

MONTCLAIR TWP MUNICIPAL COURT
647 BLOOMFIELD AVE
MONTCLAIR, NJ, 07042
PHONE: 973-509-4774
OFFICE HOURS: MON – FRI - 8:30 AM - 3:30 PM

MONTGOMERY TWP MUNICIPAL COURT
379 SOUTH BRANCH RD
HILLSBOROUGH, NJ, 08844
PHONE: 908-369-3532
OFFICE HOURS: MON – FRI - 8:00 AM - 4:00 PM

MONTVILLE TWP MUNICIPAL COURT
360 ROUTE 202, STE 2

MONTVILLE, NJ, 07045
PHONE: 973-335-1022
OFFICE HOURS: MON – FRI – 9:00 AM – 4:00 PM

MOONACHIE BORO MUNICIPAL COURT
RTE 46-MUNICIPAL BLD
TETERBORO, NJ, 07608
PHONE: 201-641-5589
OFFICE HOURS: TUES-THUR - 8:30 AM - 3:30 PM

MOORESTOWN TWP MUNICIPAL COURT
1245 N.CHURCH ST.
MOORESTOWN, NJ, 08057
PHONE: 856-235-0922
OFFICE HOURS: CRT SESSIONS HELD-CINNAMINSON

MORRIS PLAINS MUNICIPAL COURT
531 SPEEDWELL AVE
MORRIS PLAINS, NJ, 07950
PHONE: 973-538-4019
OFFICE HOURS: MON – FRI - 9:00 AM - 4:00 PM

MORRIS TWP MUNICIPAL COURT
50 KINGS ROAD
MADISON, NJ, 07940
PHONE: 973-593-3026
OFFICE HOURS: MON – FRI – 8:00 AM – 4:00 PM

MORRISTOWN MUNICIPAL COURT
PO BOX 150
MORRISTOWN, NJ, 07963
PHONE: 973-292-6687
OFFICE HOURS: MON – FRI - 8:30 AM - 4:30 PM

MOUNTAIN LAKES MUNICIPAL COURT
1 SAINT MARY'S PLACE
DENVILLE, NJ, 07834
PHONE: 973-625-8300
OFFICE HOURS: MON – FRI - 9:00 AM - 3:00 PM

MOUNTAINSIDE MUNICIPAL COURT
1385 ROUTE 22,EAST
MOUNTAINSIDE, NJ, 07092
PHONE: 908-232-5335
OFFICE HOURS: MON – FRI - 8:30 AM - 4:00 PM

MT ARLINGTON MUNICIPAL COURT
37 N. SUSSEX ST.
DOVER, NJ, 07801
PHONE: 973-366-2200

OFFICE HOURS: CALL COURT

MT EPHRAIM BORO COURT
500 WHITE HORSE PIKE
OAKLYN, NJ, 08107
PHONE: 856-858-0074
OFFICE HOURS: MON - THUR - 8:00 AM - 3:30 PM,
FRI 8:00 AM - 11:30 AM

MT HOLLY MUNICIPAL COURT
23 WASHINGTON STREET
MT HOLLY, NJ, 08060
PHONE: 609-267-0170
OFFICE HOURS: MON - FRI - 9:00 AM - 12:30 PM,
1:30 PM - 3:00 PM

MT LAUREL MUNICIPAL COURT
100 MOUNT LAUREL RD
MT LAUREL, NJ, 08054
PHONE: 856-234-0001
OFFICE HOURS: MON – FRI - 8:00 AM – 3:00 PM

MT OLIVE TWP MUNICIPAL COURT
PO BOX 450
BUDD LAKE, NJ, 07828
PHONE: 973-691-0900
OFFICE HOURS: MON – FRI - 9:00 AM - 4:00 PM

MULLICA TWP MUNICIPAL COURT
PO BOX 316
ELWOOD, NJ, 08217
PHONE: 609-561-6696
OFFICE HOURS: MON – FRI - 9:00 AM - 4:30 PM

MUNICIPAL COURT OF PRINCETON
400 WITHERSPOON ST.
PRINCETON TWP, NJ, 08540
PHONE: 609-924-5042
OFFICE HOURS: MON – FRI - 9:00 AM - 4:00 PM

NATIONAL PARK BORO MUN COURT
114 CROWN POINT RD
WESTVILLE, NJ, 08093
PHONE: 856-456-0066
OFFICE HOURS: MON - FRI - 9:00 AM - 3:00 PM

NEPTUNE CITY MUNICIPAL COURT
106 W SYLVANIA AVE
NEPTUNE, CITY, NJ 07753
PHONE: 732-775-1690

OFFICE HOURS: MON – FRI - 8:30 AM - 4:00 PM

NEPTUNE TWP MUNICIPAL COURT
25 NEPTUNE BLVD
NEPTUNE, NJ, 07753
PHONE: 732-988-5200
OFFICE HOURS: MON – FRI - 9:00 AM - 3:30PM

NETCONG BORO MUNICIPAL COURT
PO BOX 450
BUDD LAKE, NJ, 07828
PHONE: 973-691-0900
OFFICE HOURS: MON – FRI - 8:30 AM - 4:00 PM

NEW BRUNSWICK MUNICIPAL COURT
25 KIRKPATRICK ST
NEW BRUNSWICK, NJ, 08903
PHONE: 732-745-5089
OFFICE HOURS: MON – FRI - 8:30 AM – 4:00 PM

NEW HANOVER TWP MUN COURT
2 HOCKAMICK RD
COOKSTOWN, NJ, 08511
PHONE: 609-758-7172
OFFICE HOURS: MON – FRI - 9:30 AM - 4:00 PM

NEW MILFORD BORO COURT
930 RIVER RD
NEW MILFORD, NJ, 07646
PHONE: 201-967-5646
OFFICE HOURS: MON – FRI - 8:00 AM - 4:00 PM

NEW PROVIDENCE MUNICIPAL COURT
360 ELKWOOD AVENUE
NEW PROVIDENCE, NJ, 07974
PHONE: 908-665-1454
OFFICE HOURS: MON- FRI - 8:30 AM - 3:00 PM

NEWARK MUNICIPAL COURT
31 GREEN STREET
NEWARK, NJ, 07102
PHONE: 973-733-6520
OFFICE HOURS: MON – FRI - 8:30 AM - 4:30 PM

NEWFIELD BORO MUNICIPAL COURT
680 WHIG LANE
MONROEVILLE, NJ, 08343
PHONE: 856-881-6631
OFFICE HOURS: MON, TUES, THUR - 9:00 AM -4:00
PM, WED - 9:00 AM -5:30 PM, FRI 9:00 AM - 2:30 PM

NEWTON TOWN MUNICIPAL COURT
39 TRINITY ST
NEWTON, NJ, 07860
PHONE: 973-383-3521
OFFICE HOURS: MON – FRI - 8:30 AM - 4:30 PM

NORTH ARLINGTON MUNICIPAL COURT
4225 BERGEN TURNPIKE
NORTH BERGEN, NJ, 07047
PHONE: 201-392-2088
OFFICE HOURS: MON – FRI - 9:00 AM - 3:30 PM

NORTH BRUNSWICK COURT
710 HERMANN RD
NORTH BRUNSWICK, NJ, 08902
PHONE: 732-247-0922
OFFICE HOURS: MON – FRI - 8:30 AM - 3:45 PM

NORTH CALDWELL MUNICIPAL COURT
GOULD AVE
NORTH CALDWELL, NJ, 07006
PHONE: 973-228-6420
OFFICE HOURS: MON – FRI - 9:00 AM - 4:00 PM

NORTH HALEDON MUNICIPAL COURT
103 OVERLOOK AVE
NORTH HALEDON, NJ, 07508
PHONE: 973-423-0232
OFFICE HOURS: MON – FRI - 9:00 AM - 3:00 PM

NORTH HANOVER MUNICIPAL COURT
41 SCHOOLHOUSE RD
JACOBSTOWN, NJ, 08562
PHONE: 609-758-2522
OFFICE HOURS: MON – FRI - 8:30 AM - 4:30 PM

NORTH HUNTERDON MUNICIPAL COURT
1370 ROUTE 31 NORTH
ANNANDALE, NJ, 08801
PHONE: 908-735-3730
OFFICE HOURS: MON – FRI - 9:00 AM - 4:00 PM

NORTH PLAINFIELD MUNICIPAL COURT
263 SOMERSET ST
NORTH PLAINFIELD, NJ, 07060
PHONE: 908-769-2265

NORTH WARREN MUNICIPAL COURT
PO BOX 134

HOPE, NJ, 07844
PHONE: 908-459-5800
OFFICE HOURS: TUES – THURS - 9:00 AM – 3:00 PM

NORTH WILDWOOD MUNICIPAL COURT
901 ATLANTIC AVE
NORTH WILDWOOD, NJ, 08260
PHONE: 609-729-3818
OFFICE HOURS: MON – FRI - 09:00 AM - 4:00 PM

NORTHFIELD MUNICIPAL COURT
1600 SHORE ROAD
NORTHFIELD, NJ, 08225
PHONE: 609-641-2832
OFFICE HOURS: MON – FRI - 9:00 AM - 4:00 PM

NORTHVALE BORO MUNICIPAL COURT
116 PARIS AVE
NORTHVALE, NJ, 07647
PHONE: 201-767-6673
OFFICE HOURS: MON-FRI – 10:00 AM – 1:00 PM

NORWOOD BORO MUNICIPAL COURT
455 BROADWAY
NORWOOD, NJ, 07648
PHONE: 201-767-7207
OFFICE HOURS: CALL FOR OFFICE HOURS

NUTLEY TOWN MUNICIPAL COURT
228 CHESTNUT ST
NUTLEY, NJ, 07110
PHONE: 973-284-4945
OFFICE HOURS: MON – FRI - 8:00 AM - 4:00 PM

OAKLAND BORO MUNICIPAL COURT
10 LAWLOR DRIVE
OAKLAND, NJ, 07436
PHONE: 201-337-8140
OFFICE HOURS: MON – FRI - 9:00 AM - 4:00 PM

OAKLYN BOROUGH MUNICIPAL COURT
500 WHITE HORSE PIKE
OAKLYN, NJ, 08107
PHONE: 856-858-0074
OFFICE HOURS: MON-THUR - 8:00 AM - 3:30 PM, FRI
8:00 AM - 11:30 AM

OCEAN CITY MUNICIPAL COURT

821 CENTRAL AVE
OCEAN CITY, NJ, 08226
PHONE: 609-525-9386
OFFICE HOURS: MON – FRI - 8:45 AM - 4:30 PM

OCEAN GATE MUNICIPAL COURT
399 MONMOUTH RD
OAKHURST, NJ, 07755
PHONE: 732-531-5005
OFFICE HOURS: MON – FRI – 8:30 AM – 4:30 PM

OCEAN TWP MUNICIPAL COURT
50 RAILROAD AVENUE
WARETOWN, NJ, 08758
PHONE: 609-693-3332
OFFICE HOURS: MON – FRI - 8:30 AM - 4:30 PM

OCEANPORT BORO MUNICIPAL COURT
315 E. MAIN ST.
OCEANPORT, NJ, 07757
PHONE: 732-222-8222
OFFICE HOURS: MON, WED – FRI - 8:30 AM – 4:30
PM, TUE 8:30 AM – 2:30 PM

OGDENSBURG BORO MUNICIPAL COURT
14 HIGHLAND AVE
OGDENSBURG, NJ, 07439
PHONE: 973-827-3895
OFFICE HOURS: MON – THUR - 9:00 AM - 2:00 PM

OLD BRIDGE TWP MUNICIPAL CT
ONE OLD BRIDGE PLAZA
OLD BRIDGE, NJ, 08857
PHONE: 732-721-5600
OFFICE HOURS: MON – FRI - 8:30 AM - 4:00 PM

OLD TAPPAN BORO MUNICIPAL COURT
227 OLD TAPPAN RD
OLD TAPPAN, NJ, 07675
PHONE: 201-664-1849
OFFICE HOURS: TUES AND WED - 1:00 PM - 4:00 PM

OLDMANS TWP MUNICIPAL COURT
25 WEST AVE
WOODSTOWN, NJ, 08098
PHONE: 856-769-2424
OFFICE HOURS: MON, TUES 9:00 AM - 3:30 PM, WED
– FRI - 9:00 AM – 2:00 PM

ORADELL BORO MUNICIPAL COURT

355 KINDERKAMACK RD
ORADELL, NJ, 07649
PHONE: 201-261-8601
OFFICE HOURS: MON – FRI - 9:00 AM - 4:00 PM
ORANGE CITY MUNICIPAL COURT
29 PARK STREET
ORANGE, NJ, 07050
PHONE: 973-266-4161
OFFICE HOURS: CALL COURT

OXFORD TWP MUNICIPAL COURT
100 PORT MURRAY RD
PORT MURRAY, NJ, 07865
PHONE: 908-689-7066
OFFICE HOURS: MON – FRI - 8:00 AM - 4:00 PM

PALISADES INTERSTATE COURT
ALPINE APPROACH RD
ALPINE, NJ, 07620
PHONE: 201-768-8702
OFFICE HOURS: MON – FRI - 8:30 AM - 4:30 PM

PALISADES PARK MUNICIPAL COURT
275 BROAD AVENUE
PALISADES PARK, NJ, 07650
PHONE: 201-585-4115
OFFICE HOURS: MON – FRI - 9:00 AM - 4:00 PM

PALMYRA BORO MUNICIPAL COURT
20 WEST BROAD
PALMYRA, NJ, 08065
PHONE: 856-829-1763
OFFICE HOURS: MON – FRI - 9:00 AM - 4:00 PM

PARAMUS BORO MUNICIPAL COURT
JOCKISH SQUARE
PARAMUS, NJ, 07652
PHONE: 201-265-2100
OFFICE HOURS: MON – FRI - 9:00 AM - 4:00 PM

PARK RIDGE BORO MUNICIPAL COURT
12 MERCEDES DRIVE
MONTVALE, NJ, 07645
PHONE: 201-391-5701
OFFICE HOURS: MON – FRI - 8:30 AM - 4:30 PM

PARSIPPANY TROY HILLS MUNICIPAL COURT
3333 RT 46
PARSIPPANY, NJ, 07054
PHONE: 973-263-4290

OFFICE HOURS: MON – FRI - 9:00 AM - 4:00 PM

PASCACK JOINT MUNICIPAL COURT
12 MERCEDES DRIVE
MONTVALE, NJ, 07645
PHONE: 201-391-5701
OFFICE HOURS: MON – FRI - 8:30 AM - 4:30 PM

PASSAIC CITY MUNICIPAL COURT
330 PASSAIC ST
PASSAIC, NJ, 07055
PHONE: 973-365-3975
OFFICE HOURS: MON – FRI - 9:00 AM - 3:30 PM

PATERSON MUNICIPAL COURT
111 BROADWAY
PATERSON, NJ, 07505
PHONE: 973-321-1515
OFFICE HOURS: MON – FRI - 8:30 AM - 4:00 PM

PAULSBORO BORO MUNICIPAL COURT
1211 DELAWARE ST
PAULSBORO, NJ, 08066
PHONE: 856-423-3888
OFFICE HOURS: MON – FRI - 9:00 AM - 2:00 PM

PEAPACK GLADSTONE MUNICIPAL COURT
ONE SCHOOL STREET
PEAPACK, NJ, 07977
PHONE: 908-234-2255
OFFICE HOURS: MON – WED - 8:00 AM – 4:30 PM,
THUR - 8:30 AM – 4:30 PM, FRI - 8:30 AM – 12:00
PM

PEMBERTON BORO MUNICIPAL COURT
50 EGBERT STREET
PEMBERTON, NJ, 08068
PHONE: 609-894-9363
OFFICE HOURS: MON – FRI - 8:30 AM - 4:30 PM

PEMBERTON TWP MUNICIPAL COURT
500 PEMBERTON BROWNS
PEMBERTON, NJ, 08068
PHONE: 609-894-3337
OFFICE HOURS: MON – FRI - 8:00 AM - 4:30 PM

PENNINGTON BORO MUNICIPAL COURT
30 NORTH MAIN STREET
PENNINGTON, NJ, 08534

PHONE: 609-737-1016
OFFICE HOURS: TUES – THURS - 5:30 PM - 8:30 PM
PENNS GROVE MUNICIPAL COURT
W MAIN & STATE ST
PENNS GROVE, NJ, 08069
PHONE: 856-299-0911
OFFICE HOURS: MON-FRI - 9:00 AM - 3:00 PM

PENNSAUKEN MUNICIPAL COURT
2400 BETHEL AVE
PENNSAUKEN, NJ, 08109
PHONE: 856-663-1403
OFFICE HOURS: MON – FRI - 9:00 AM - 4:00 PM

PENNSVILLE TWP MUNICIPAL COURT
90 N BROADWAY
PENNSVILLE, NJ, 08070
PHONE: 856-678-8036
OFFICE HOURS: MON – FRI - 9:00 AM - 3:00 PM

PEQUANNOCK TWP MUNICIPAL COURT
530 TPKE
POMPTON, PLAINS, NJ 07444
PHONE: 973-835-5700
OFFICE HOURS: MON – FRI - 8:30 AM - 4:30 PM

PERTH AMBOY MUNICIPAL COURT
365 NEW BRUNSWICK AV
PERTH AMBOY, NJ, 08861
PHONE: 732-442-6011
OFFICE HOURS: MON – FRI - 8:00 AM - 5:00 PM

PHILLIPSBURG MUNICIPAL COURT
675 CORLISS AVE
PHILLIPSBURG, NJ, 08865
PHONE: 908-454-3211
OFFICE HOURS: CALL COURT

PILESGROVE JOINT MUNICIPAL COURT
1180 ROUTE 40
PILESGROVE, NJ, 08098
PHONE: 856-769-1275
OFFICE HOURS: MON - THUR - 8:30 AM - 3:00 PM
CLOSED FRI

PINE BEACH BORO MUNICIPAL COURT
599 PENNSYLVANIA AVE
PINE BEACH, NJ, 08741
PHONE: 732-349-6453
OFFICE HOURS: 1ST WEDNESDAY OF MONTH-3PM

PINE HILL BORO MUNICIPAL COURT
45 W 7TH AVE
PINE HILL, NJ, 08021
PHONE: 856-783-2566
OFFICE HOURS: MON – FRI - 8:30 AM - 2:30 PM

PINE VALLEY MUNICIPAL COURT
1 CLUB ROAD
CLEMENTON, NJ, 08021
PHONE: 609-767-5400
OFFICE HOURS: CALL COURT

PISCATAWAY TWP MUNICIPAL COURT
555 SIDNEY RD
PISCATAWAY, NJ, 08854
PHONE: 732-562-2330
OFFICE HOURS: MON – FRI - 9:00AM - 4:00PM

PITMAN BORO MUNICIPAL COURT
405 MAIN STREET
MANTUA, NJ, 08051
PHONE: 856-468-3078
OFFICE HOURS: MON – FRI - 8:30 AM - 4:00 PM

PITTSGROVE TOWNSHIP MUNICIPAL COURT
1325 HIGHWAY #77
SEABROOK, NJ, 08302
PHONE: 856-455-8722
OFFICE HOURS: MON – FRI - 8:30 AM - 4:00 PM

PLAINFIELD MUNICIPAL COURT
325 WATCHUNG AVE
PLAINFIELD, NJ, 07061
PHONE: 908-753-3064
OFFICE HOURS: MON – FRI - 9:00 AM - 4:00 PM

PLAINSBORO TWP MUNICIPAL COURT
641 PLAINSBORO RD
PLAINSBORO, NJ, 08536
PHONE: 609-799-0863
OFFICE HOURS: MON – FRI - 8:45 AM - 4:15 PM

PLEASANTVILLE MUNICIPAL COURT
18 NORTH FIRST ST
PLEASANTVILLE, NJ, 08232
PHONE: 609-484-3663
OFFICE HOURS: MON – FRI - 8:00 AM - 3:30 PM

PLUMSTED TWP MUNICIPAL COURT
5 UNION AVENUE
LAKEHURST, NJ, 08733
PHONE: 732-657-4151
OFFICE HOURS: COURT-207 CENTER ST-LAKEHURST

POHATCONG TWP MUNICIPAL COURT
50 MUNICIPAL DRIVE
PHILLIPSBURG, NJ, 08865
PHONE: 908-454-6425
OFFICE HOURS: MON – FRI - 9:00 AM - 4:30 PM

POINT PLEASANT BEACH MUNICIPAL COURT
2233 BRIDGE AVE
POINT PLEASANT, NJ, 08742
PHONE: 732-899-1636
OFFICE HOURS: MON – FRI - 9:00 AM - 3:30 PM
POINT PLEASANT BORO MUNICIPAL COURT
PO BOX 25
PT PLEASANT, NJ, 08742
PHONE: 732-899-1636
OFFICE HOURS: MON – FRI - 9:00 AM -3:30 PM

POMPTON LAKES MUNICIPAL COURT
25 LENOX AVE
POMPTON LAKES, NJ, 07442
PHONE: 973-616-5908
OFFICE HOURS: MON - FRI - 9:00 AM - 4:00 PM

PORT REPUBLIC MUNICIPAL COURT
143 MAIN ST
PORT REPUBLIC, NJ, 08241
PHONE: 609-652-9321
OFFICE HOURS: MON - 4:00 PM – 6:00 PM, WED
3:30 PM – 6:00 PM

PRINCETON BORO MUNICIPAL COURT
400 WITHERSPOON ST
PRINCETON, NJ, 08540
PHONE: 609-924-5042
OFFICE HOURS: MON – FRI – 9:00 AM - 4:00 PM

PROSPECT PARK MUNICIPAL COURT

106 BROWN AVE
PROSPECT PARK, NJ, 07508
PHONE: 973-790-7902
OFFICE HOURS: MON - FRI - 8:00 AM - 3:00 PM

QUINTON TWP MUNICIPAL COURT
25 WEST AVENUE
WOODSTOWN, NJ, 08098
PHONE: 856-769-2424
OFFICE HOURS: MON, TUES 9:00 AM - 3:30 PM, WED
– FRI - 9:00 AM – 2:00 PM

RAHWAY MUNICIPAL COURT
CITY HALL PLAZA
RAHWAY, NJ, 07065
PHONE: 732-827-2039
OFFICE HOURS: MON – FRI - 9:00 AM - 4:00 PM

RAMSEY BORO MUNICIPAL COURT
33 N. CENTRAL AVE
RAMSEY, NJ, 07446
PHONE: 201-825-0988
OFFICE HOURS: MON – FRI – 9:00 AM – 4:00 PM

RANDOLPH TWP MUNICIPAL COURT
502 MILLBROOK AVE
RANDOLPH, NJ 07869
PHONE: 973-989-7055
OFFICE HOURS: MON – FRI – 8:30 AM – 4:30 PM

RARITAN BORO MUNICIPAL COURT
22 FIRST ST
RARITAN, NJ, 08869
PHONE: 908-231-1303
OFFICE HOURS: MON – FRI - 8:30 AM - 4:00 PM

RARITAN TWP MUNICIPAL COURT
ONE MUNICIPAL DRIVE
FLEMINGTON, NJ, 08822
PHONE: 908-782-8818
OFFICE HOURS: MON-FRI - 8:30 AM - 4:30 PM

READINGTON TWP MUNICIPAL COURT
509 RT 523
WHITEHOUSE ST, NJ, 08889
PHONE: 908-534-2414
OFFICE HOURS: MON - FRI - 8:30 AM - 4:30 PM

RED BANK BORO MUNICIPAL COURT
90 MONMOUTH STREET

RED BANK, NJ, 07701
PHONE: 732-530-2716
OFFICE HOURS: MON – FRI - 8:00 AM - 4:00 PM

RIDGEFIELD BORO MUNICIPAL COURT
604 BROAD AVE
RIDGEFIELD BORO, NJ, 07657
PHONE: 201-943-7155
OFFICE HOURS: MON-FRI - 8:00 AM - 3:30 PM

RIDGEFIELD PK VILLAGE
234 MAIN STREET
RIDGEFIELD PK, NJ, 07660
PHONE: 201-641-6403
OFFICE HOURS: MON – FRI - 9:00 AM - 4:30 PM

RIDGEWOOD VILLAGE MUNICIPAL COURT
131 N MAPLE AVE
RIDGEWOOD, NJ, 07451
PHONE: 201-670-5544
OFFICE HOURS: MON AND THURS 8:30 AM - 1:00
PM, TUES, WED, AND FRI 8:30 AM - 4:00 PM

RINGWOOD BORO MUNICIPAL COURT
60 MARGARET KING AVE
RINGWOOD, NJ, 07456
PHONE: 973-962-6146
OFFICE HOURS: MON-FRI - 9:00 AM - 4:00 PM

RIVER EDGE BORO MUNICIPAL COURT
705 KINDERKAMACK RD
RIVER EDGE, NJ, 07661
PHONE: 201-599-6310
OFFICE HOURS: MON-FRI - 9:00 AM – 3:00 PM

RIVER VALE TWP MUNICIPAL COURT
406 RIVERVALE RD
RIVER VALE, NJ, 07675
PHONE: 201-664-2346
OFFICE HOURS: MON – FRI – 9:00 AM - 4:30 PM

RIVERDALE BORO MUNICIPAL COURT
SCOTT ST/PAVILION AVENUE
RIVERSIDE, NJ, 08075
PHONE: 856-461-8820
OFFICE HOURS: MON – FRI - 9:00 AM - 3:00 PM

RIVERTON BORO MUNICIPAL COURT
1621 RIVERTON RD
CINNAMINSON, NJ, 08077

PHONE: 856-829-4027
OFFICE HOURS: MON – FRI - 8:30 AM - 4:00 PM

ROBBINSVILLE TWP MUNICIPAL COURT
1117 RTE 130
ROBBINSVILLE, NJ, 08691
PHONE: 609-259-3522
OFFICE HOURS: MON - FRI 8:30 AM-4:30 PM

ROCHELLE PARK MUNICIPAL COURT
151 W PASSAIC ST
ROCHELLE PARK, NJ, 07662
PHONE: 201-556-1053
OFFICE HOURS: MON – FRI - 9:00 AM - 4:00 PM

ROCKAWAY BORO MUNICIPAL COURT
37 N. SUSSEX ST.
DOVER, NJ, 07801
PHONE: 973-366-2200
OFFICE HOURS: CALL COURT

ROCKAWAY TWP MUNICIPAL COURT
65 MT HOPE RD
ROCKAWAY, NJ, 07866
PHONE: 973-627-9000
OFFICE HOURS: MON – FRI - 8:30 AM - 4:30 PM

ROCKLEIGH BORO MUNICIPAL COURT
116 PARIS AVENUE
NORTHVALE, NJ, 07647
PHONE: 201-767-6673
OFFICE HOURS: MON – FRI – 10:00 AM – 1:00 PM

ROCKY HILL BORO MUNICIPAL COURT
PO BOX 212
ROCKY HILL, NJ, 08553
PHONE: 609-924-7943
OFFICE HOURS: WED 3:30-6:00, COURT 4TH THURS.

ROOSEVELT BORO MUNICIPAL COURT
215 MILLSTONE RD
MILLSTONE TWP, NJ, 08535
PHONE: 732-446-6219
OFFICE HOURS: MON – FRI - 8:30 AM - 4:00 PM

ROSELAND BORO MUNICIPAL COURT
19 HARRISON AVE
ROSELAND, NJ, 07068
PHONE: 973-226-0641

OFFICE HOURS: MON – FRI - 9:00 AM - 4:00 PM

ROSELLE PARK BORO MUNICIPAL COURT
110 E WESTFIELD AVE
ROSELLE PARK, NJ, 07204
PHONE: 908-241-4631
OFFICE HOURS: MON – FRI – 9:30 AM - 3:00 PM

ROXBURY TWP MUNICIPAL COURT
1715 ROUTE 46W
LEDGEWOOD, NJ, 07852
PHONE: 973-448-2034
OFFICE HOURS: MON – FRI – 9:00 AM – 4:00PM

RUMSON BORO MUNICIPAL COURT
MEMORIAL BORO HALL
RUMSON, NJ, 07760
PHONE: 732-530-7131
OFFICE HOURS: MON – FRI - 8:30 AM - 4:30 PM

RUTHERFORD MUNICIPAL COURT
176 PARK AVE
RUTHERFORD, NJ, 07070
PHONE: 201-460-3030
OFFICE HOURS: MON – FRI - 8:30 AM - 4:30 PM

SADDLE BROOK TWP COURT
63 MARKET STREET
SADDLE BROOK, NJ, 07663
PHONE: 201-843-7642
OFFICE HOURS: CALL COURT

SADDLE RIVER MUNICIPAL COURT
100 E. ALLENDALE RD
SADDLE RIVER, NJ, 07458
PHONE: 201-327-2132
OFFICE HOURS: MON – FRI - 8:00 AM - 3:30 PM

SALEM CITY MUNICIPAL COURT
129 WEST BROADWAY
SALEM, NJ, 08079
PHONE: 856-935-1734
OFFICE HOURS: MON-THUR - 9:00 AM -4:00 PM,
CLOSED FRI

SANDYSTON TWP MUNICIPAL COURT
RTE 560 - BOX 21
LAYTON, NJ, 07851
PHONE: 201-948-4089
OFFICE HOURS: MON – FRI - 3:00 PM - 6:00 PM

SAYREVILLE MUNICIPAL COURT
1000 MAIN STREET
SAYREVILLE, NJ, 08872
PHONE: 732-525-5446
OFFICE HOURS: MON – FRI - 8:00 AM - 4:00 PM

SCOTCH PLAINS TWP COURT
430 PARK AVE
SCOTCH PLAINS, NJ, 07076
PHONE: 908-322-6700
OFFICE HOURS: MON – FRI - 8:30 AM - 3:00 PM

SEA BRIGHT BORO MUNICIPAL COURT
315 E. MAIN ST.
OCEANPORT, NJ, 07757
PHONE: 732-222-6517
OFFICE HOURS: MON – FRI - 8:30 AM - 4:30 PM

SEA GIRT BORO MUNICIPAL COURT
2700 ALLAIRE RD
WALL, NJ, 07719
PHONE: 732-449-4666
OFFICE HOURS: MON – FRI - 9:00 AM - 4:30 PM

SEA ISLE CITY MUNICIPAL COURT
POB 132,4501 PARK RD
SEA ISLE CITY, NJ, 08243
PHONE: 609-263-6101
OFFICE HOURS: MON – FRI - 9:00 AM – 4:00 PM

SEASIDE HGTS MUNICIPAL COURT
116 SHERMAN AVE
SEASIDE HEIGHTS, NJ, 08751
PHONE: 732-830-2202
OFFICE HOURS: MON – FRI - 8:30 AM - 4:30 PM

SEASIDE PARK BORO MUNICIPAL COURT
1 MUNICIPAL PLAZA
SEASIDE PARK, NJ, 08752
PHONE: 732-793-5116
OFFICE HOURS: MON- FR I - 8:00 AM - 4:00 PM

SECAUCUS TOWN MUNICIPAL COURT
1203 PATERSON PLANK
SECAUCUS, NJ, 07094
PHONE: 201-330-2056
OFFICE HOURS: MON – FRI - 9:00 AM - 4:00 PM

SHAMONG TWP MUNICIPAL COURT
5 RETREAT ROAD
SOUTHAMPTON, NJ, 08088
PHONE: 609-859-2747
OFFICE HOURS: MON – FRI - 8:30 AM - 4:00 PM

SHILOH TOWNSHIP COURT
1325 HIGHWAY 77
SEABROOK, NJ, 08302
PHONE: 856-455-8722
OFFICE HOURS: MON- FRI - 8:30 AM - 4:00 PM

SHIP BOTTOM MUNICIPAL COURT
1621 LONG BEACH BL
SHIP BOTTOM, NJ, 08008
PHONE: 609-494-2171
OFFICE HOURS: MON – FRI - 9:00 AM - 4:00 PM

SHREWSBURY BORO MUNICIPAL COURT
PO BOX 7420
SHREWSBURY, NJ, 07702
PHONE: 732-842-2868
OFFICE HOURS: MON – FRI - 8:00 AM - 4:00 PM

SHREWSBURY TWP MUNICIPAL COURT
90 MONMOUTH ST
RED BANK, NJ, 07701
PHONE: 732-530-2716
OFFICE HOURS: MON-THURS - 8:00 AM - 6:00 PM

SOMERDALE BORO MUNICIPAL COURT
105 KENNEDY BLVD
SOMERDALE, NJ, 08083
PHONE: 856-783-0958
OFFICE HOURS: MON – FRI - 8:30 AM - 4:30 PM

SOMERS POINT CITY MUNICIPAL COURT
1 W NEW JERSEY AVE
SOMERS POINT, NJ, 08244
PHONE: 609-927-9088
OFFICE HOURS: MON – FRI - 9:00 AM - 5:00 PM

SOMERVILLE MUNICIPAL COURT
100 COMMONS WAY
BRIDGEWATER, NJ, 08807
PHONE: 908-725-6375
OFFICE HOURS: MON – FRI - 8:30 AM - 4:00 PM

SOUTH AMBOY MUNICIPAL COURT

140 NORTH BROADWAY
SOUTH AMBOY, NJ, 08879
PHONE: 732-525-5929
OFFICE HOURS: MON – FRI - 8:00 AM - 4:00 PM

SOUTH BOUND BROOK MUNICIPAL COURT
12 MAIN ST
S BOUND BROOK, NJ, 08880
PHONE: 732-356-0258
OFFICE HOURS: COURT HELD-230 HAMILTON-BND-
BRK

SOUTH BRUNSWICK TWP COURT
PO BOX 190
MONMOUTH JCT, NJ, 08852
PHONE: 732-823-3963
OFFICE HOURS: MON – FRI - 9:00 AM - 4:00 PM

SOUTH HACKENSACK MUNICIPAL COURT
227 PHILLIPS AVE
SO HACKENSACK, NJ, 07606
PHONE: 201-440-1844
OFFICE HOURS: MON – FRI - 9:00 AM - 4:00 PM

SOUTH HARRISON MUNICIPAL COURT
114 BRIDGETON PIKE
MULLICA HILL, NJ, 08062
PHONE: 856-478-4049
OFFICE HOURS: MON – FRI - 9:00 AM - 4:00 PM

SOUTH ORANGE MUNICIPAL COURT
1618 SPRINGFIELD AVE
MAPLEWOOD, NJ, 07040
PHONE: 973-762-2839
OFFICE HOURS: MON – FRI - 9:00 AM - 4:00 PM

SOUTH PLAINFIELD MUNICIPAL COURT
2480 PLAINFIELD AVE
SOUTH PLAINFIELD, NJ, 07080
PHONE: 908-226-7651
OFFICE HOURS: MON – FRI - 8:00 AM - 4:00 PM

SOUTH RIVER MUNICIPAL COURT
61 MAIN ST
SOUTH RIVER, NJ, 08882
PHONE: 732-257-1233
OFFICE HOURS: MON - FRI 8:00 AM – 4:00 PM
SOUTH TOMS RIVER MUNICIPAL COURT
144 MILL STREET
SOUTH TOMS RIVER NJ 08757

PHONE: 732-349-1141
OFFICE HOURS: MON – FRI - 9:00 AM - 4:00 PM

SOUTHAMPTON MUNICIPAL COURT
5 RETREAT ROAD
SOUTHAMPTON, NJ, 08088
PHONE: 609-859-2747
OFFICE HOURS: MON – FRI - 8:30 AM - 4:00 PM

SPARTA TWP MUNICIPAL COURT
65 MAIN ST
SPARTA, NJ, 07871
PHONE: 973-729-3501
OFFICE HOURS: MON – FRI - 8:30 AM - 4:30 PM

SPOTSWOOD BORO MUNICIPAL COURT
77 SUMMERHILL ROAD
SPOTSWOOD, NJ, 08884
PHONE: 732-251-0700
OFFICE HOURS: MON – FRI - 9:00 AM - 4:30 PM

SPRING LAKE HEIGHTS COURT
2700 ALLAIRE RD
WALL TWP, NJ, 07719
PHONE: 732-449-4666
OFFICE HOURS: MON – FRI - 8:00 AM – 5:00 PM

SPRING LAKE MUNICIPAL COURT
601 MAIN ST
BELMAR, NJ, 07719
PHONE: 732-681-3700
OFFICE HOURS: MON – FRI - 9:00 AM - 4:30 PM

SPRINGFIELD TWP COURT (BURLINGTON COUNTY)
3135 ROUTE 206 SOUTH
COLUMBUS, NJ, 08022
PHONE: 609-298-0649
OFFICE HOURS: MON – FRI - 9:00 AM - 4:00 PM

SPRINGFIELD TWP COURT (UNION COUNTY)
100 MOUNTAIN AVE
SPRINGFIELD, NJ, 07081
PHONE: 973-912-2213
OFFICE HOURS: MON – FRI - 8:00 AM - 4:00 PM

STAFFORD TOWNSHIP MUNICIPAL COURT
260 AST BAY AVENUE
MANAHAWKIN, NJ, 08050

PHONE: 609-597-1000
OFFICE HOURS: MON – FRI - 8:30 AM - 4:30 PM

STANHOPE MUNICIPAL COURT
111 RIVER STYX RD
HOPATCONG, NJ, 07843
PHONE: 973-770-1200
OFFICE HOURS: MON – FRI - 9:00 AM - 4:00 PM

STILLWATER TWP MUNICIPAL COURT
888 ROUTE 23
WANTAGE, NJ, 07461
PHONE: 973-875-7310
OFFICE HOURS: MON - FRI - 10:00 AM - 4:30 PM

STOCKTON MUNICIPAL COURT
1070 HIWY 202
RINGOES, NJ, 08551
PHONE: 908-782-6855
OFFICE HOURS: MON-THURS - 8:30 AM – 3:00 PM

STONE HARBOR MUNICIPAL COURT
9508 2ND AVENUE
STONE HARBOR, NJ, 08247
PHONE: 609-368-2411
OFFICE HOURS: MON – FRI - 9:00 AM - 4:00 PM

STOW CREEK TWP MUNICIPAL COURT
1325 HWY 77
SEABROOK, NJ, 08302
PHONE: 856-455-8722
OFFICE HOURS: TUES, WED, AND FRI - 9:00 AM –
1:00 PM

STRATFORD BORO MUNICIPAL COURT
315 UNION AVE
STRATFORD, NJ, 08084
PHONE: 856-783-1093
OFFICE HOURS: MON – THU – 9:00 AM – 5:00 PM FRI
– 9:00 AM – 4:00 PM
SUMMIT MUNICIPAL COURT
512 SPRINGFIELD AVE
SUMMIT, NJ, 07901
PHONE: 908-273-6112
OFFICE HOURS: MON – FRI – 9:00 AM – 4:00 PM

SURF CITY BORO MUNICIPAL COURT
813 LONG BEACH BLVD
SURF CITY, NJ, 08008
PHONE: 609-494-3984

OFFICE HOURS: MON – FRI - 9:00 AM - 1:00 PM 2:00 PM – 4:00PM

SUSSEX BORO MUNICIPAL COURT
888 ROUTE 23
WANTAGE, NJ, 07461
PHONE: 973-875-7310
OFFICE HOURS: MON – THU – 10:00 AM - 4:00 PM

SWEDESBORO MUNICIPAL COURT
120 VILLAGE GREEN DR
WOOLWICH TWP, NJ, 08085
PHONE: 856-467-1555
OFFICE HOURS: MON – FRI - 8:30 AM - 4:30 PM

TABERNACLE TWP MUNICIPAL COURT
163 CARRANZA RD
TABERNACLE, NJ, 08088
PHONE: 609-268-0363
OFFICE HOURS: MON, WED, FRI - 8:00 AM – 3:00 PM, TUES, THUR 1:00 PM – 3:00 PM

TEANECK TWP MUNICIPAL COURT
TEANECK RD/CEDAR LN
TEANECK, NJ, 07666
PHONE: 201-837-1600
OFFICE HOURS: CALL COURT FOR COURT HOURS

TENAFLY BORO MUNICIPAL COURT
100 RIVEREDGE RD
TENAFLY, NJ, 07670
PHONE: 201-568-6100
OFFICE HOURS: MON – FRI – 9:00 AM – 4:00 PM

TETERBORO BORO MUNICIPAL COURT
RT 46
TETERBORO, NJ, 07608
PHONE: 201-288-6215
OFFICE HOURS: MON – FRI - 9:00 AM - 3:00 PM
TEWKSBURY MUNICIPAL COURT
60 WATER STREET
LEBANON, NJ, 08833
PHONE: 908-832-7684
OFFICE HOURS: TUES 3:45 PM - 6:45 PM, WED 10:00 AM – 1:00 PM

TINTON FALLS MUNICIPAL COURT
556 TINTON AVE
TINTON FALLS, NJ, 07724
PHONE: 732-542-3400

OFFICE HOURS: MON, WED - FRI 8:30 AM - 4:30 PM, TUE - 8:00 AM – 4:00 PM

TOMS RIVER MUNICIPAL COURT
255 OAK AVENUE
TOMS RIVER, NJ, 08753
PHONE: 732-797-3914
OFFICE HOURS: MON – FRI - 9:00 AM - 4:00 PM

TOTOWA BORO MUNICIPAL COURT
537 TOTOWA ROAD
TOTOWA, NJ, 07512
PHONE: 973-956-1006
OFFICE HOURS: MON – FRI - 9:00 AM - 4:00 PM

TOWN OF CLINTON MUNICIPAL COURT
1370 ROUTE 31 NORTH
ANNANDALE, NJ, 08801
PHONE: 908-735-3730
OFFICE HOURS: MON – FRI - 9:00 AM - 4:00 PM

TOWN OF DOVER JOINT COURT
37 N. SUSSEX ST.
DOVER, NJ, 07801
PHONE: 973-366-2200
OFFICE HOURS: MON – FRI - 8:30 AM - 4:00 PM

TOWNSHIP OF HOPEWELL MUNICIPAL COURT
201 WASHINGTON CRSG
TITUSVILLE, NJ, 08560
PHONE: 609-737-1035
OFFICE HOURS: MON – FRI - 9:00 AM - 4:00 PM

TOWNSHIP OF WASHINGTON MUN COURT
350 HUDSON AVENUE
WASHINGTON TWP, NJ, 07676
PHONE: 201-664-2488
OFFICE HOURS: MON – FRI - 8:30 AM - 4:30 PM
TRENTON MUNICIPAL COURT
225 N CLINTON AVE
TRENTON, NJ, 08607
PHONE: 609-989-3700
OFFICE HOURS: MON – FRI - 8:45 AM - 4:45 PM

TUCKERTON BORO MUNICIPAL COURT
420 E MAIN ST
TUCKERTON, NJ, 08087
PHONE: 609-296-2036

UNION BEACH MUNICIPAL COURT

650 POOLE AVE
UNION BEACH, NJ, 07735
PHONE: 732-264-9098
OFFICE HOURS: MON – FRI - 9:00 AM - 4:30 PM

UNION CITY MUNICIPAL COURT
3715 PALISADES AVE
UNION CITY, NJ, 07087
PHONE: 201-392-3663
OFFICE HOURS: MON – FRI – 9:00 AM - 3:30 PM

UNION TWP MUNICIPAL COURT (HUNTERDON COUNTY)
1370 RTE 31 NORTH
ANNANDALE, NJ, 08801
PHONE: 908-735-3730
OFFICE HOURS: MON – FRI - 9:00 AM - 4:00 PM

UNION TWP MUNICIPAL COURT (UNION COUNTY)
981 CALDWELL AV
UNION, NJ, 07083
PHONE: 908-851-5400
OFFICE HOURS: MON – FRI – 8:00 AM – 3:00 PM
UPPER FREEHOLD MUNICIPAL COURT
314 RTE 539
CREAM RIDGE, NJ, 08514
PHONE: 609-758-0262
OFFICE HOURS: MON - THURS 8:30 AM - 3:30 PM

UPPER SADDLE RIVER MUN COURT
376 W SADDLE RIVER
UPPER SADDLE RIVER, NJ, 07458
PHONE: 201-934-3972
OFFICE HOURS: MON – FRI - 8:30 AM - 4:00 PM

VENTNOR CITY MUNICIPAL COURT
6201 ATLANTIC AVENUE
VENTNOR, NJ, 08406
PHONE: 609-823-7906
OFFICE HOURS: MON – FRI - 8:30 AM - 4:00 PM

VERNON TWP MUNICIPAL COURT
21 CHURCH STREET
VERNON, NJ, 07462
PHONE: 973-764-4737 OFFICE HOURS: MON – FRI - 8:30 AM - 4:00 PM

VERONA TWP MUNICIPAL COURT

600 BLOOMFIELD AVE
VERONA, NJ, 07044
PHONE: 973-857-4774
OFFICE HOURS: MON – FRI - 8:30 AM - 4:00 PM

VINELAND CITY MUNICIPAL COURT
736 E. LANDIS AVE.
VINELAND CITY, NJ, 08362
PHONE: 856-794-4214
OFFICE HOURS: MON – FRI - 8:30 AM – 12: 00 PM

VOORHEES TWP MUNICIPAL COURT
2400 VOORHEES CENTER
VOORHEES, NJ, 08043
PHONE: 856-429-0770
OFFICE HOURS: MON – FRI – 8:00 AM – 5:00 PM

WALDWICK BORO MUNICIPAL COURT
63 FRANKLIN TURNPIKE
WALDWICK, NJ, 07463
PHONE: 201-652-5300
OFFICE HOURS: MON - FRI 8:00 AM - 11:30 AM

WALL TOWNSHIP MUNICIPAL COURT
2700 ALLAIRE RD
WALL, NJ, 07719
PHONE: 732-449-4666
OFFICE HOURS: MON – FRI - 9:00 AM - 4:00 PM

WALLINGTON BORO MUNICIPAL COURT
54 UNION BLVD
WALLINGTON, NJ, 07057
PHONE: 973-777-0318
OFFICE HOURS: MON – FRI - 9:00 AM - 3:30 PM

WANAQUE BORO MUNICIPAL COURT
579 RINGWOOD AVE
WANAQUE, NJ, 07465
PHONE: 973-839-3000
OFFICE HOURS: MON - FRI - 9:00 AM - 4:00 PM

WANTAGE/SUSSEX/STILLWATER COURTS
888 ROUTE 23
WANTAGE, NJ, 07461
PHONE: 973-875-7310
OFFICE HOURS: MON - FRI - 10:00 AM - 4:30 PM

WARREN TWP MUNICIPAL COURT
44 MOUNTAIN BLVD

WARREN, NJ, 07059
PHONE: 908-753-1225
OFFICE HOURS: MON – FRI - 8:30 AM - 4:00 PM

WASHINGTON TWP MUNICIPAL COURT
(GLOUCESTER COUNTY)
1 MCCLURE DRIVE
SEWELL, NJ, 08080
PHONE: 856-589-0546
OFFICE HOURS: MON – THUR - 8:00 AM -4:30 PM,
CLOSED FRI

WASHINGTON COURT (WARREN COUNTY)
100 PORT MURRAY RD
PORT MURRAY NJ 07865
PHONE: 908-689-7066
OFFICE HOURS: MON – FRI - 8:00 AM – 4:00 PM

WASHINGTON TWP MUNICIPAL COURT
(BURLINGTON COUNTY)
PO BOX 214
NEW GRETNA, NJ, 08224
PHONE: 609-296-1410
OFFICE HOURS: MON - FRI – 9:00 AM- 3:00 PM

WASHINGTON TWP MUNICIPAL COURT (MORRIS
COUNTY)
43 SCHOOLEYS MTN RD.
LONG VALLEY, NJ, 07853
PHONE: 908-876-3852
OFFICE HOURS: MON – FRI - 8:00 AM - 4:00 PM

WATCHUNG BORO MUNICIPAL COURT
263 SOMERSET ST
NO. PLAINFIELD, NJ, 07060
PHONE: 908-769-2265

WATERFORD TWP MUNICIPAL COURT
2131 AUBURN AVENUE
ATCO, NJ, 08004
PHONE: 856-768-2300
OFFICE HOURS: MON – FRI - 8:30 AM - 4:30 PM

WAYNE TWP MUNICIPAL COURT
475 VALLEY ROAD
WAYNE, NJ, 07470
PHONE: 973-694-1800

OFFICE HOURS: MON – FRI - 8:30 AM - 4:30 PM

WEEHAWKEN TWP MUNICIPAL COURT
400 PARK AVE
WEEHAWKEN, NJ, 07086
PHONE: 201-319-6028
OFFICE HOURS: MON – FRI - 9:00 AM - 4:00 PM

WENONAH BORO MUNICIPAL COURT
1 SOUTH WEST AVE
WENONAH, NJ, 08090
PHONE: 856-468-0242
OFFICE HOURS: MON-FRI – 9:00 AM – 2:00 PM

WEST AMWELL MUNICIPAL COURT
150 ROCKTOWN
LAMBERTVILLE, NJ, 08530
PHONE: 609-397-2027
OFFICE HOURS: MON – FRI - 9:00 AM - 3:00 PM

WEST CALDWELL MUNICIPAL COURT
21 CLINTON RD
WEST CALDWELL, NJ, 07006
PHONE: 973-226-3373
OFFICE HOURS: MON – FRI - 8:30 AM - 4:30 PM

WEST CAPE MAY MUNICIPAL COURT
732 BROADWAY
WEST CAPE MAY, NJ, 08204
PHONE: 609-884-1005
OFFICE HOURS: MON – FRI - 8:00 AM - 3:00 PM

WEST DEPTFORD TOWNSHIP MUNICIP
400 CROWN PT RD
THOROFARE, NJ, 08086
PHONE: 856-845-4004
OFFICE HOURS: MON – FRI - 8:30 AM - 4:00 PM

WEST LONG BRANCH MUNICIPAL COURT
399 MONMOUTH ROAD
OAKHURST, NJ, 07755
PHONE: 732-531-5005
OFFICE HOURS: MON - FRI - 8:30 AM - 4:30 PM

WEST MILFORD TWP COURT
1480 UNION VALLEY RD
WEST MILFORD, NJ, 07480
PHONE: 973-728-2750

OFFICE HOURS: MON – FRI - 8:30 AM - 4:30 PM

WEST NEW YORK MUNICIPAL COURT
428-60 STREET
WEST NEW YORK, NJ, 07093
PHONE: 201-295-5195
OFFICE HOURS: MON, WED, THUR, FRI 9:00 AM -
4:30 PM, TUE 9:00 AM – 7:00 PM

WEST ORANGE MUNICIPAL COURT
60 MAIN STREET
WEST ORANGE, NJ, 07052
PHONE: 973-325-4080
OFFICE HOURS: MON – FRI - 9:00 AM - 4:00 PM

WEST WILDWOOD BORO MUN. COURT
115 WEST DAVIS AVE
WILDWOOD, NJ, 08260
PHONE: 609-522-4924
OFFICE HOURS: MON – FRI - 8:30 AM - 4:30 PM

WEST WINDSOR MUNICIPAL COURT
271 CLARKSVILLE RD
WEST WINDSOR, NJ, 08550
PHONE: 609-799-0915
OFFICE HOURS: MON – FRI - 9:00 AM 4:00 PM

WESTAMPTON TWP MUNICIPAL COURT
710 RANCOCAS RD
WESTAMPTON, NJ, 08060
PHONE: 609-267-1895
OFFICE HOURS: MON – FRI - 8:00 AM - 3:00 PM

WESTFIELD TOWN MUNICIPAL COURT
425 E. BROAD ST
WESTFIELD, NJ, 07090
PHONE: 908-789-4060
OFFICE HOURS: MON – FRI - 9:00 AM - 3:30 PM

WESTVILLE NATIONAL PK MUNICIPAL COURT
165 BROADWAY
WESTVILLE, NJ, 08093
PHONE: 856-456-0066
OFFICE HOURS: MON – FRI - 9:00 AM - 3:00 PM

WESTWOOD BORO MUNICIPAL COURT
101 WASHINGTON AVE
WESTWOOD, NJ, 07675
PHONE: 201-666-8510
OFFICE HOURS: MON – FRI - 8:30 AM - 3:00 PM

WHITE TWP MUNICIPAL COURT
555 CR 519
BELVIDERE, NJ, 07823
PHONE: 908-475-4827
OFFICE HOURS: TUES 5:00 PM – 8:00 PM, THURS -
4:30 PM - 8:30 PM

WILDWOOD CITY MUNICIPAL COURT
115 WEST DAVIS AVE
WILDWOOD, NJ, 08260
PHONE: 609-522-4924
OFFICE HOURS: MON – FRI - 8:30 AM - 4:30 PM

WILDWOOD CREST MUNICIPAL COURT
6101 PACIFIC AVE
WILDWOOD CREST, NJ, 08260
PHONE: 609-522-1352
OFFICE HOURS: MON - FRI – 9:00 AM – 4:00 PM

WILLINGBORO TWP COURT
1 REV.DR M.L.KING DR
WILLINGBORO, NJ, 08046
PHONE: 609-877-2200
OFFICE HOURS: MON-FRI - 9:00 AM - 4:00 PM

WINFIELD TWP MUNICIPAL COURT
12 GULFSTREAM AVE
WINFIELD, NJ, 07036
PHONE: 908-925-3937
OFFICE HOURS: MON – FRI - 9:00 AM - 4:00 PM

WINSLOW TOWNSHIP MUNICIPAL COURT
125 SO RT 73
BRADDOCK, NJ, 08037
PHONE: 609-567-0700
OFFICE HOURS: MON – FRI - 8:30 AM - 4:30 PM

WOOD-RIDGE BORO MUNICIPAL COURT (BERGEN
COUNTY)
85 HUMBOLDT ST
WOOD-RIDGE, NJ, 07075
PHONE: 201-933-1414
OFFICE HOURS: MON – FRI - 8:00 AM-1:00 PM, 2:00
PM – 3:00 PM

WOODBRIDGE MUNICIPAL COURT
(MIDDLESEX COUNTY)
1 MAIN STREET
WOODBRIDGE, NJ, 07095

PHONE: 732-636-6430
OFFICE HOURS: MON – FRI - 9:00 AM- 4:00 PM

WOODBURY CITY MUNICIPAL COURT
200 N BROAD STREET
WOODBURY, NJ, 08096
PHONE: 856-845-0691
OFFICE HOURS: MON – THUR - 8:30 AM - 4:00 PM,
CLOSED FRI

WOODBURY HTS MUNICIPAL COURT
500 ELM AVE
WOODBURY HTS, NJ, 08097
PHONE: 856-848-3256
OFFICE HOURS: MON-FRI - 9:00 AM - 3:30 PM

WOODCLIFF LAKE MUNICIPAL COURT
12 MERCEDES DRIVE
MONTVALE, NJ, 07645
PHONE: 201-391-5701
OFFICE HOURS: MON – FRI - 8:30 AM - 4:30 PM

WOODLAND PARK MUNICIPAL COURT
#5 BROPHY LANE
WOODLAND PARK, NJ, 07424
PHONE: 973-345-8100
OFFICE HOURS: MON – FRI - 8:30 AM - 3:30 PM -
COURT TUES 4:00 PM

WOODLAND TWP MUNICIPAL COURT
PO BOX 214
NEW GRETNA, NJ, 08224
PHONE: 609-296-1410
OFFICE HOURS: MON - FRI - 9:00 AM - 4:00 PM

WOODLYNNE BORO MUNICIPAL COURT
200 COOPER AVE
WOODLYNNE, NJ, 08107
PHONE: 856-962-8300
OFFICE HOURS: MON – FRI - 8:00 AM - 4:00 PM

WOOLWICH JOINT MUNICIPAL COURT
120 VILLAGE GREEN DR
WOOLWICH TWP, NJ, 08085
PHONE: 856-467-1555
OFFICE HOURS: MON – FRI - 8:30 AM - 4:30 PM

WRIGHTSTOWN BORO MUNICIPAL COURT
41 SCHOOLHOUSE RD
JACOBSTOWN, NJ, 08562
PHONE: 609-758-2522
OFFICE HOURS: MON – FRI - 8:30 AM - 4:30 PM

WYCKOFF TWP MUNICIPAL COURT
SCOTT PLAZA
WYCKOFF, NJ, 07481
PHONE: 201-891-7000
OFFICE HOURS: MON – FRI - 9:00 AM - 4:30 PM

APPENDIX L

☐ Superior Court, Chancery Division, Family Part, _____ County ☐ Municipal Court of _____

DOCKET NUMBER FV -	POLICE CASE #

IN THE MATTER OF PLAINTIFF (VICTIM)	PLAINTIFF'S SEX ☐ MALE ☐ FEMALE	PLAINTIFF'S DATE OF BIRTH

DEFENDANT INFORMATION	LAST NAME	FIRST NAME	INITIAL	DATE OF BIRTH

AKA	DEFENDANT'S SOCIAL SECURITY NUMBER

HOME ADDRESS	CITY	STATE	ZIP	HOME PHONE NUMBER ( )	WORK PHONE NUMBER ( )

EMPLOYER	WORK ADDRESS	DEFENDANT'S SEX ☐ MALE ☐ FEMALE

HAIR COLOR	EYE COLOR	HEIGHT	WEIGHT	RACE	SCARS, FACIAL HAIR, TATTOO(S), ETC.

The undersigned complains that said defendant did endanger plaintiff's life, health or well being (give specific facts regarding acts or threats of abuse and the date(s) and time(s) they occurred; specify any weapons):

ON	AT		BY	

which constitute(s) the following criminal offenses(s): (Check all applicable boxes. Law Enforcement Officer: Attach *N.J.S.P.* UCR DV1 offense report(s)):

☐ HOMICIDE	☐ TERRORISTIC THREATS	☐ CRIMINAL RESTRAINT	☐ SEXUAL ASSAULT	☐ LEWDNESS	☐ BURGLARY	☐ HARASSMENT
☐ ASSAULT	☐ KIDNAPPING	☐ FALSE IMPRISONMENT	☐ CRIMINAL SEXUAL CONTACT	☐ CRIMINAL MISCHIEF	☐ CRIMINAL TRESPASS	☐ STALKING

1. ANY PRIOR HISTORY OF DOMESTIC VIOLENCE REPORTED OR UNREPORTED? IF YES, EXPLAIN: ☐ YES ☐ NO

2. DOES DEFENDANT HAVE A CRIMINAL HISTORY? (IF YES, ATTACH CCH SUMMARY) ☐ YES ☐ NO

3. ANY PRIOR OR PENDING COURT PROCEEDINGS INVOLVING PARTIES? (IF YES, ENTER DOCKET NUMBER, COURT, COUNTY, STATE) ☐ YES ☐ NO

4. HAS A CRIMINAL COMPLAINT BEEN FILED IN THIS MATTER? (IF YES, ENTER DATE, DOCKET NUMBER, COURT, COUNTY, STATE) ☐ YES ☐ NO

5. IF LAW ENFORCEMENT OFFICERS RESPONDED TO A DOMESTIC VIOLENCE CALL:
WERE WEAPONS SEIZED? IF YES, DESCRIBE ☐ YES ☐ NO   WAS DEFENDANT ARRESTED? IF YES, DESCRIBE ☐ YES ☐ NO

6. (A) THE PLAINTIFF AND DEFENDANT ARE 18 YEARS OLD OR OLDER OR EMANCIPATED AND ARE ☐ MARRIED ☐ DIVORCED OR
☐ PRESENT HOUSEHOLD MEMBER ☐ FORMER HOUSEHOLD MEMBER   OR
(B) THE DEFENDANT IS 18 YEARS OLD OR OLDER OR EMANCIPATED and PLAINTIFF AND DEFENDANT ARE ☐ UNMARRIED ☐ CO-PARENTS
☐ EXPECTANT PARENTS   OR   ☐ PLAINTIFF AND DEFENDANT HAVE HAD A DATING RELATIONSHIP

7. WHERE APPROPRIATE LIST CHILDREN , IF ANY (INCLUDE NAME, SEX, DATE OF BIRTH, PERSON WITH WHOM CHILD RESIDES)

8. THE PLAINTIFF AND DEFENDANT: ☐ PRESENTLY; ☐ PREVIOUSLY; ☐ NEVER: RESIDED TOGETHER
☐ FAMILY RELATIONSHIP: _____ (SPECIFY)

CERTIFICATION

I certify that the foregoing responses made by me are true. I am aware that if any of the foregoing responses made by me are willfully false, I am subject to punishment.

_____ DATE   _____ SIGNATURE OF PLAINTIFF

NEW JERSEY DOMESTIC VIOLENCE COURT ORDER   CN: 10010-English   (Rev. 2/07)

DOCKET NUMBER	FV -		DEFENDANT'S NAME

PART 1 - RELIEF - Instructions: Relief sought by plaintiff

DEFENDANT:

TRO   FRO   GRANTED

1. ☐   N/A   ☐   You are prohibited from returning to the scene of violence.

2. ☐   ☐   ☐   You are prohibited from future acts of domestic violence.

3. ☐   ☐   ☐   You are barred from the following locations: ☐ RESIDENCE(S) OF PLAINTIFF   ☐ PLACE(S) OF EMPLOYMENT OF PLAINTIFF

☐ OTHER (ONLY LIST ADDRESSES KNOWN TO DEFENDANT): _____

4. ☐   ☐   ☐   You are prohibited from having <u>any</u> oral, written, personal, electronic, or other form of contact or communication with Plaintiff.

☐   ☐   ☐   OTHER(S): _____

5. ☐   ☐   ☐   You are prohibited from making or causing anyone else to make harassing communications to: Plaintiff

☐   ☐   ☐   OTHER(S) - SAME AS ITEM 4 ABOVE OR LIST NAMES: _____

6. ☐   ☐   ☐   You are prohibited from stalking, following or threatening to harm, stalk or follow: Plaintiff

☐   ☐   ☐   OTHER(S) - SAME AS ITEM 4 ABOVE OR LIST NAMES: _____

7.   You must pay emergent monetary relief to (describe amount and method):

☐   ☐   ☐   PLAINTIFF: _____

☐   ☐   ☐   DEPENDANTS: _____

8. ☐   ☐   ☐   You must be subject to intake monitoring of conditions and restraints: _____

☐   ☐   ☐   Other (evaluations or treatment - describe): _____

9. ☐   ☐   ☐   Psychiatric evaluation: _____

10. ☐   ☐   ☐   **Prohibition Against Possession of Weapons:** You are prohibited from possessing **any and all firearms or other weapons** and must immediately surrender these firearms, weapons, permit(s) to carry, application(s) to purchase firearms and firearms purchaser ID card to the officer serving this Court Order: Failure to do so may result in your arrest and incarceration.

PLAINTIFF:

11. ☐   ☐   ☐   You are granted exclusive possession of (list residence or alternate housing only if specifically known to defendant): _____

12. ☐   ☐   ☐   You are granted temporary custody of: _____

13. ☐   ☐   ☐   Other relief for - Plaintiff: _____

☐   ☐   ☐   Other relief for - Children: _____

LAW ENFORCEMENT OFFICER:

You are to accompany to scene, residence, shared place of business, other (indicate address, time, duration and purpose):

☐   ☐   ☐   Plaintiff: _____

☐   ☐   ☐   Defendant: _____

NOTICE TO DEFENDANT: A violation of any of the provisions listed in this order may constitute either civil or criminal contempt pursuant to *N.J.S.A.* 2C:25-30 and may result in your arrest, prosecution, and possible incarceration, as well as an imposition of a fine or jail sentence. **Only a court can modify any of the terms or conditions of this court order.**

DOCKET NUMBER	FV -	DEFENDANT'S NAME

WARRANT TO SEARCH FOR AND TO SEIZE WEAPONS FOR SAFEKEEPING

☐ **To any law enforcement officer having jurisdiction** - this Order shall serve as a warrant to search for and to seize any issued permit to carry a firearm, application to purchase a firearm and firearms purchaser identification card issued to the defendant and the following firearm(s) or other weapon(s): _____

_____

1. **You are hereby commanded** to search for the above described weapons and/or permits to carry a firearm, application to purchase a firearm and firearms purchaser identification card and to serve a copy of this Order upon the person at the premises or location described as: _____

_____

2. **You are hereby ordered** in the event you seize any of the above described weapons, to give a receipt for the property so seized to the person from whom they were taken or in whose possession they were found, or in the absence of such person to have a copy of this Order together with such receipt in or upon the said structure from which the property was taken.

3. **You are authorized** to execute this Order immediately or as soon thereafter as is practicable:

    ☐ ANYTIME   ☐ OTHER: _____

4. **You are further ordered**, after the execution of this Order, to promptly provide the Court with a written inventory of the property seized per this Order.

PART II - RELIEF   DEFENDANT:

TRO	FRO	GRANTED	
1. ☐	☐	☐	No parenting time / visitation until further ordered;
☐	☐	☐	Parenting time / visitation pursuant to F _____ suspended until further order;
☐	☐	☐	Parenting time / visitation permitted as follows: _____
2. ☐	☐	☐	Risk assessment ordered (specify by whom, any requirements, dates): _____

3.   You must provide compensation as follows:

☐	☐	☐	Emergent support for plaintiff: _____
☐	☐	☐	For dependent(s): _____
N/A	☐	☐	Ongoing support for plaintiff: _____
N/A	☐	☐	For dependent(s): _____
☐	☐	☐	Compensatory damages to plaintiff: _____
N/A	☐	☐	Punitive damages to plaintiff: _____
N/A	☐	☐	To Third Party(ies) (describe): _____
☐	☐	☐	Medical coverage for plaintiff: _____
			For dependent(s): _____
☐	☐	☐	☐ Rent ☐ Mortgage payments (specify amount(s) and recipient(s)): _____
☐	☐	☐	You must participate in a batterers intervention program: _____
☐	☐	☐	You are granted temporary possession of the following personal property (describe): _____

PART II - RELIEF   PLAINTIFF:

☐	☐	☐	You are granted temporary possession of the following personal property (describe): _____

COMMENTS:

NOTICE TO DEFENDANT: A violation of any of the provisions listed in this order may constitute either civil or criminal contempt pursuant to *N.J.S.A.* 2C:25-30 and may result in your arrest, prosecution, and possible incarceration, as well as an imposition of a fine or jail sentence. **Only a court can modify any of the terms or conditions of this court order.**

NEW JERSEY DOMESTIC VIOLENCE COURT ORDER   CN: 10010-English   (Rev. 1/07)

DOCKET NUMBER	FV -	DEFENDANT'S NAME

☐ **TRO denied.** Complaint dismissed by Family Part.   ☐ **TRO denied by Municipal Court,** forwarded to Family Part for administrative dismissal, and plaintiff advised of right to file new complaint in Superior Court, Family Division.

☐ **TRO granted.** The Court has established jurisdiction over the subject matter and the parties pursuant to *N.J.S.A.* 2C:25-17 et seq., and has found good cause that a prima facie act of domestic violence has been established; that an immediate danger of domestic violence exists and that plaintiffs life, health and well being are endangered; that an emergency restraining Order is necessary pursuant to *R.* 5:7A(b) and *N.J.S.A.* 2C:25-28 to prevent the occurrence or recurrence of domestic violence and to search for and seize firearms and other weapons as indicated in this order.

_____

DATE / TIME ☐ VIA TELEPHONE   HONORABLE   COURT / COUNTY

ALL LAW ENFORCEMENT OFFICERS WILL SERVE AND FULLY ENFORCE THIS ORDER

This *ex parte* Domestic Violence Complaint and Temporary Restraining Order meets the criteria of the federal Violence Against Women Act for enforcement outside of the State of New Jersey upon verification of service of defendant. 18 *U.S.C.A.* 2265 & 2266

THIS ORDER SHALL REMAIN IN EFFECT UNTIL FURTHER ORDER OF THE COURT AND SERVICE OF SAID ORDER ON THE DEFENDANT

NOTICE TO APPEAR TO PLAINTIFF AND DEFENDANT

1. ☐ Both the plaintiff and defendant are ordered to appear for a final hearing on (date) _____ at (time) _____ at the Superior Court, Chancery Division, Family Part, _____ County, located at (address) _____

Note: You must bring financial information including pay stubs, insurance information, bills and mortgage receipts with you to Court.

2. ☐ The final hearing in this matter shall not be scheduled until: _____

3. ☐ Interpreter needed. Language: _____

Upon satisfaction of the above-noted conditions notify the Court immediately so that a final hearing date may be set.

IMPORTANT: The parties cannot themselves change the terms of this Order on their own. This Order may only be changed or dismissed by the Superior Court. The named defendant cannot have any contact with the plaintiff without permission of the Court.

NOTICE TO DEFENDANT

A violation of any of the provisions listed in this Order or a failure to comply with the directive to surrender all weapons, firearm permits, applications or identification cards may constitute criminal contempt pursuant to *N.J.S.A.* 2C:29-9(b), and may also constitute violations of other state and federal laws which may result in your arrest and/or criminal prosecution. This may result in a jail sentence.

You have the right to immediately file an appeal of this temporary Order before the Superior Court, Chancery Division, Family Part, as indicated above and a hearing may be scheduled.

RETURN OF SERVICE

☐ Plaintiff was given a copy of the Complaint / TRO by:

_____   _____   _____
PRINT NAME   TIME AND DATE   SIGNATURE / BADGE NUMBER / DEPARTMENT

☐ I hereby certify that I served the within Complaint / TRO by delivering a copy to the defendant personally:

_____   _____   _____
PRINT NAME   TIME AND DATE   SIGNATURE / BADGE NUMBER / DEPARTMENT

☐ I hereby certify that I served the within Complaint / TRO by use of substituted service as follows: _____

_____   _____   _____
PRINT NAME   TIME AND DATE   SIGNATURE / BADGE NUMBER / DEPARTMENT

☐ Defendant could not be served (explain): _____

_____   _____   _____
PRINT NAME   TIME AND DATE   SIGNATURE / BADGE NUMBER / DEPARTMENT

DEFENDANT MUST SIGN THIS STATEMENT: I hereby acknowledge the receipt of the restraining Order. I understand that pursuant to this Court Order, I am not to have any contact with the named plaintiff even if the plaintiff agrees to the contact or invites me onto the premises and that I may be arrested and prosecuted if I violate this Order.

_____   _____
SIGNATURE OF DEFENDANT   TIME AND DATE

THE COURTHOUSE IS ACCESSIBLE TO THOSE WITH DISABILITIES. PLEASE NOTIFY THE COURT IF YOU REQUIRE ASSISTANCE.

DISTRIBUTION: FAMILY PART,   PLAINTIFF,   DEFENDANT,   SHERIFF,   OTHER _____

NEW JERSEY DOMESTIC VIOLENCE COURT ORDER   CN: 10010-English   (Rev. 1/07)

APPENDIX M

ORDER OF THE COURT

The Court, having taken notice of Plaintiff's ( ) OR Defendant's ( ) request for an appeal

of a Temporary Restraining Order entered on _____; and

( ) Plaintiff having been advised of this appeal; or

( ) Defendant having been advised of this appeal; or

( ) No notice having been given to the other party; and

IT IS HEREBY ORDERED ON this _____ day of _____,

that the request for Appeal of the Temporary Restraining Order is:

( ) Denied. Final Hearing will proceed as originally scheduled.

( ) GRANTED. A hearing shall be held on _____, 20_____ for the

following:

( ) Final Hearing.

( ) Limited purpose of:

( ) OTHER RELIEF:

( ) THE REASONS FOR ENTRY OF THIS ORDER:

_____
, J.S.C.

RETURN OF SERVICE:

( ) Defendant was given a copy of this Order by:

_____   _____   _____
print name   time and date   signature/ badge number/ dept

( ) Plaintiff was given a copy of this Order by:

_____   _____   _____
print name   time and date   signature/ badge number/ dept

362

APPENDIX N

SUPERIOR COURT OF NEW JERSEY
CHANCERY DIVISION, FAMILY PART
COUNTY OF

DOCKET NO.: FV-___-_____

_____ :
          Plaintiff   :   APPLICATION FOR APPEAL
                             :   AND ORDER
          Vs.   :
                             :
_____ :
          Defendant   :

NAME:
ADDRESS:

PHONE NUMBERS (HOME AND WORK):

DATE OF BIRTH:
SOCIAL SECURITY NUMBER:
EMERGENCY CONTACT (NAME AND PHONE NUMBER):

CERTIFICATION AND REQUEST FOR APPEAL

I am the **Plaintiff( ) or Defendant ( )** in the above captioned matter and make this

request to Appeal the entry of an *ex parte* Temporary Restraining Order entered on

_____ in **Superior Court ( ) OR Municipal Court ( ).**

I am asking for this Appeal for the following reasons (use additional paper if necessary):

I certify that the foregoing statements made by me are true. I am aware that if any of the
foregoing statements made by me are willfully false, I am subject to punishment.

_____   _____
Date   ***Signature***
                                          Name (print):

APPENDIX O

**AFFIDAVIT IN SUPPORT OF A
DOMESTIC VIOLENCE WARRANT FOR
THE SEARCH & SEIZURE OF WEAPONS**

State of New Jersey   :
County of _____ : SS

I, _____, of _____, being
       (Name of Officer)   (Department)
of full age and having been duly sworn upon my oath according to law, depose and say:

1.   On _____ at _____ __.m., I was dispatched to the
following premises:

_____

_____

in response to a domestic violence Incident.

2.   I was told by _____, the victim of the
domestic violence incident, that he or she believes that his or her life, health or
well-being is in imminent danger by the domestic violence assailant,
_____, by one of the weapons listed in paragraph 3. The
victim said:

_____

_____

_____

_____

3.   The victim has described the weapons as follows:

_____

_____

_____

_____

4.   The victim of domestic violence has informed me that the domestic violence assailant has the weapons listed in paragraph 3 at

_____
(Describe Premises in Detail and identify owner of premises if not person listed in Paragraph 1)

_____

_____

_____

5.   Based on the above, I have probable cause to believe that the presence of the weapons described in paragraph 3 exposes the victim to a risk of serious bodily injury.

6.   I want to search the premises described in paragraph 4 for the weapons described in paragraph 3 and to seize any of the above named weapons found at that location for safekeeping purposes. I also want to seize from the defendant any issued permit to carry a firearm, firearms purchaser identification card and any outstanding applications to purchase handguns.

7.   _____
(If Requesting a No Knock Warrant or Entry at Special Hours, Explain Reason here or on Attached Sheet , or enter any additional information here)

_____

_____

_____

_____

_____

_____

_____

_____

_____

_____

_____

_____
(Signature of Affiant)

Sworn and subscribed to before
me this _____ day of
_____ . 20____ .

_____
Judge of the _____ Court of
New Jersey

APPENDIX P

DOMESTIC VIOLENCE WARRANT
FOR THE SEARCH & SEIZURE
OF WEAPONS

TO: ANY LAW ENFORCEMENT OFFICER HAVING JURISDICTION

1.   The Court, having reviewed the affidavit or testimony of

_____
under oath against _____, finds reasonable cause to
believe that the life, health, or well-being of _____ has been and
is endangered by defendant's acts of violence and finds reasonable cause to believe that the defendant
may not be qualified to possess firearms pursuant to *N.J.S.A.* 2C:58-3c(5). The Court finds reasonable
cause to believe that the below listed weapons in defendant's possession may present a risk of serious
bodily injury to plaintiff:

_____
_____
_____
_____
_____

2.   **YOU ARE HEREBY COMMANDED** to search the premises described as_____
_____
_____
_____

for the above described weapons and to serve a copy of this warrant upon the person at that address.

YOU ARE FURTHER COMMANDED to seize from defendant any issued permit to carry a firearm,
firearms purchaser identification card and any outstanding applications to purchase handguns.

3.   **YOU ARE HEREBY ORDERED**, in the event you seize any of the above described weapons and
firearms permits, to give a receipt for the property so seized to the person from whom they were taken
or in whose possession they were found, or in the absence of such person, to leave a copy of this
warrant together with such receipt in or upon the said structure from which the property was taken.

4.   **YOU ARE AUTHORIZED** to execute this warrant within 10 days from the issuance hereof:

☐ Between the hours of _____ m. and _____ m., or

☐ Anytime

After the execution of this warrant, you are ordered to forthwith make prompt return to this Court with a
written inventory of the property seized hereunder.

5.   Given and issued under my hand at _____
at _____ o'clock _____ m. this day of _____, 20 ____.

_____
(Signature)
Judge of the _____ Court of New Jersey

Revised 4/04

369

APPENDIX Q

--:

                              :   SUPERIOR COURT OF NEW JERSEY

                              :   Chancery Division – Family Part

          Plaintiff,   :   County of _____

                              :

     vs.   :   Docket No.:

                              :

                            :   Civil Action

          Defendant.   :   **PROTECTIVE ORDER**

                            :

--:

THIS MATTER being opened to the Court, and it appearing that copies of the following confidential reports are being released to the attorneys and parties or the pro-se litigants:

☐ Home Inspection Report   ☐ Psychiatric Report

☐ Social Investigation Report   ☐ Risk Assessment

☐ Psychological Report   ☐ Other _____

and for good cause shown;

IT IS ON THIS _____ day of _____, 20___;

1) **ORDERED** that copies of these reports shall be released to the attorneys and their clients or self-represented litigants with the understanding that the information contained therein is to be used only for purposes of the pending custody/parenting time matter including distribution to experts and may not be used in any other matter without the express written permission of the Court; and it is further

2) **ORDERED** that this information shall not be disclosed to any other person for any reason, nor may it be disseminated or made public by any means, direct or indirect, without the express written permission of the Court; and it is further

3) **ORDERED** that the use of information contained in the investigation and/or report, or information obtained from the investigation for any purpose other than set forth by the Court, shall be a violation of this Court Order and subject to sanctions; and it is further

4) **ORDERED** that under no circumstances is (are) the report(s) to be discussed, revealed, or disclosed to the child(ren).

                                   _____

                                          J.S.C.

(Revised 3/26/04 AOC)

APPENDIX R

STATE OF NEW JERSEY
PREVENTION OF DOMESTIC VIOLENCE ACT
_____ County, Superior Court, Chancery Division, Family Part

☐ Final Restraining Order (FRO)   ☐ Amended Final Restraining Order

DOCKET NUMBER		
FV -		

IN THE MATTER OF: PLAINTIFF		PLAINTIFF'S DATE OF BIRTH

DEFENDANT	DEFENDANT'S SEX	RACE	DEFENDANT'S DATE OF BIRTH	HT WT	DEFENDANT'S SOCIAL SECURITY NO.

DEFENDANT'S HOME ADDRESS	SCARS, FACIAL HAIR, ETC. HAIR COLOR	DEFENDANT'S HOME TELEPHONE NUMBER
DEFENDANT'S WORK ADDRESS	EYE COLOR	DEFENDANT'S WORK TELEPHONE NUMBER

The Court having considered plaintiff's Complaint dated _____ seeking an ORDER under the Prevention of Domestic Violence Act, having established jurisdiction over the subject matter and the parties pursuant to *N.J.S.A.* 2C:25-17 et seq., and having found that defendant has commited an act of domestic violence, and all other statutory requirements having been satisfied:

It is on this _____ day of _____, 20 _____, ORDERED that:

SOUGHT	GRANTED	PART I RELIEF

DEFENDANT:

1. ☐ ☐ You are prohibited against future acts of domestic violence.

2. ☐ ☐ You are barred from the following locations(s):
     ☐ RESIDENCE(S) OF PLAINTIFF   ☐ PLACE(S) OF EMPLOYMENT OF PLAINTIFF
     Other _____
     _____
     _____

3. You are prohibited from having **any** oral, written, personal, electronic, or other form of contact or communication with:
    ☐ ☐ Plaintiff
    ☐ ☐ Others (List names & relationship to plaintiff): _____
    _____

4. You are prohibited from making or causing anyone else to make harassing communications to:
    ☐ ☐ Plaintiff
    ☐ ☐ Others (Same as above or list names & relationship to plaintiff:): _____
    _____

5. You are prohibited from stalking, following, or threatening to harm, to stalk or to follow:
    ☐ ☐ Plaintiff
    ☐ ☐ Others (Same as above or list names & relationship to plaintiff): _____
    _____

6. You must pay emergent monetary relief (describe amount and method):
    ☐ ☐ Plaintiff: _____
    ☐ ☐ Dependents: _____

7. ☐ ☐ Other appropriate relief:
    Defendant (including substance abuse, mental health or other evaluations and subsequent treatment):
    _____

8. ☐ ☐ Psychiatric evaluation: _____
    _____

9. ☐ ☐ Intake monitoring of conditions and restraints (specify): _____
    _____

NOTICE TO DEFENDANT: A violation of any of the provisions listed in this order may constitute either civil or criminal contempt pursuant to *N.J.S.A.* 2C:25-30 and may result in your arrest, prosecution, and possible incarceration, as well as an imposition of a fine or jail sentence. **Only a court can modify any of the terms or conditions of this court order.**

☐ Final Restraining Order (FRO)   ☐ Amended Final Restraining Order   FV -

SOUGHT	GRANTED	PART I RELIEF continued

DEFENDANT:

10. ☐ ☐ **PROHIBITIONS AGAINST POSSESSION OF WEAPONS:** You are prohibited from possessing **any and all firearms or other weapons** and must immediately surrender these firearms, weapons, permits to carry, applications to purchase firearms and firearms purchaser ID card to the officer serviing this court Order. Failure to do so can result in your arrest and incarceration.
Other Weapon(s) (describe): _____

PLAINTIFF:

11. ☐ ☐ You are granted exclusive possession of (residence or alternate housing, list address only if specifically known to defendant):

_____

_____

12. ☐ ☐ You are granted temporary custody of (specify name(s)): _____

_____

_____

13.   Other appropriate relief:
☐ ☐ Plaintiff (describe): _____

_____

☐ ☐ Child(ren) (describe): _____

_____

LAW ENFORCEMENT OFFICER

You are to accompany to scene, residence, shared place of business, other (indicate address, time, duration & purpose):

☐ ☐ Plaintiff: _____

_____

☐ ☐ Defendant: _____

_____

WARRANT TO SEARCH FOR AND TO SEIZE WEAPONS FOR SAFEKEEPING:

☐ **To any law enforcement officer having jurisdiction** - this Order shall serve as a warrant to search for and seize any issued permit to carry a firearm, application to purchase a firearm and firearms purchaser identification card issued to the defendant and the following firearm(s) or weapon(s): _____

_____

1. **You are hereby commanded to** search the premises for the above described weapons and/or permits to carry a firearm, application to purchase a firearm and firearms purchaser ID card and to serve a copy of this Order upon the person at the premises or location described as: _____

_____

2. **You are hereby ordered** in the event you seize any of the above described weapons, to give a receipt for the property so seized to the person from whom they were taken or in whose possession they were found, or in the absence of such person to have a copy of this Order together with such receipt in or upon the said structure from which the property was taken.

3. **You are authorized** to execute this Order immediately or as soon thereafter as is practicable

   ☐ ANYTIME   ☐ OTHER: _____

4. **You are further ordered,** after the execution of this Order, to promptly provide the Court with a written inventory of the property seized per this Order.

NOTICE TO DEFENDANT: A violation of any of the provisions listed in this order may constitute either civil or criminal contempt pursuant to *N.J.S. A.* 2C:25-30 and may result in your arrest, prosecution, and possible incarceration, as well as an imposition of a fine or jail sentence. **Only a court can modify any of the terms or conditions of this court order.**

☐ Final Restraining Order (FRO)　　☐ Amended Final Restraining Order　　　FV -

SOUGHT	GRANTED	PART II RELIEF

DEFENDANT:

1. ☐ ☐ You acknowledge parentage of: _____

2. ☐ ☐ You must submit to genetic testing: _____

3. ☐ ☐ No parenting time (visitation) until further order: _____

4. ☐ ☐ Parenting time (visitation) pursuant to (prior FV, FM, or FD Order) # _____ is
suspended, a hearing is scheduled for: _____

5. ☐ ☐ Parenting time (visitation) is ordered as follows (specify drop-off and pick-up times and locations, participation of or supervision by designated third party): _____
_____
_____
_____

6. ☐ ☐ Risk assessment ordered (specify by whom): _____
_____ Return Date: _____

7. You must provide compensation as follows: (Appropriate notices have been attached as part of this Order):
　☐ ☐ Emergent support - plaintiff: _____
　☐ ☐ Emergent support - dependent(s): _____
　　 ☐ Interim support - plaintiff: _____
　　 ☐ Interim support - dependent(s): _____
　☐ ☐ Ongoing plaintiff support: _____
　　　 Paid via income withholding through the _____ Probation Div. _____
　　　 Other: _____
　☐ ☐ Ongoing child support: _____
　　　 Paid via income withholding through the _____ Probation Div. _____
　　　 Other: _____

8. ☐ ☐ Medical coverage for plaintiff: _____
9. ☐ ☐ Medical coverage for dependent(s): _____
10. ☐ ☐ Compensatory damages to plaintiff: _____
11. ☐ ☐ Punitive damages (describe): _____
12. ☐ ☐ You must pay compensation to (specify third party and/or VCCA, and describe): _____
_____

13. ☐ ☐ You must participate in a batterers' intervention program (specify): _____
_____

14. ☐ ☐ You must make ☐ rent ☐ mortgage payments (specify amount(s), due date(s) and payment manner): _____
_____

15. ☐ ☐ Defendant is granted temporary possession of the following personal property (describe): _____
_____
_____

☐ You must pay a civil penalty of $ _____ ($50.00 to $500.00 per N.J.S.A. 2C:25-29) to:_____
_____ within _____ days. You will be charged a $2.00 transaction fee for each payment or partial payment that you make.
☐ Waived due to extreme financial hardship because: _____

SOUGHT	GRANTED	

PLAINTIFF:

16. ☐ ☐ Plaintiff is granted temporary possession of the following personal property (describe) _____
_____
_____
_____

NOTICE TO DEFENDANT: A violation of any of the provisions listed in this order may constitute either civil or criminal contempt pursuant to N.J.S.A. 2C:25-30 and may result in your arrest, prosecution, and possible incarceration, as well as an imposition of a fine or jail sentence. Only a court can modify any of the terms or conditions of this court order.

☐ Final Restraining Order (FRO)   ☐ Amended Final Restraining Order   FV -

COMMENTS: _____

_____

_____

_____

This Order is to become effective immediately and shall remain in effect until further Order of the Superior Court, Chancery Division, Family Part.

_____   _____

DATE   HONORABLE

ALL LAW ENFORCEMENT OFFICERS WILL SERVE AND FULLY ENFORCE THIS ORDER.

THE PLAINTIFF SHALL NOT BE ARRESTED FOR A VIOLATION OF THIS RESTRAINING ORDER.

- ■ THIS FINAL RESTRAINING ORDER WAS ISSUED AFTER DEFENDANT WAS PROVIDED WITH NOTICE AND THE OPPORTUNITY TO BE HEARD AND SHOULD BE GIVEN FULL FAITH AND CREDIT PURSUANT TO THE VIOLENCE AGAINST WOMEN ACT OF 1991, SEC. 40221, CODIFIED AT 18 U.S.C.A. S2265(A) AND S2266.
- ■ IF ORDERED, SUFFICIENT GROUNDS HAVE BEEN FOUND BY THIS COURT FOR THE SEARCH AND SEIZURE OF FIREARMS AND OTHER WEAPONS AS INDICATED IN THIS COURT ORDER.
- ■ DEFENDANT SHALL NOT BE PERMITTED TO POSSESS ANY WEAPON, ID CARD OR PURCHASE PERMIT WHILE THIS ORDER IS IN EFFECT, OR FOR TWO YEARS, WHICHEVER IS GREATER.

NOTICE TO PLAINTIFF AND DEFENDANT

> **IMPORTANT:** The parties cannot themselves change the terms of this Order on their own. This Order may only be changed or dismissed by the Family Court. The named defendant **cannot** have any contact with the plaintiff without permission of the court. If you wish to change the terms of this Order and/or you resume living together, you **must** appear before this court for a rehearing.

NOTICE TO DEFENDANT

> A violation of any of the provisions listed in this Order or a failure to comply with the directive to surrender all weapons, firearm permits, application or identification cards may constitute criminal contempt pursuant to *N.J.S.A.* 2C:29-9(b), and may also constitute violations of other state and federal laws which can result in your arrest and/or criminal prosecution. This may result in a jail sentence.

RETURN OF SERVICE

☐ Plaintiff was given a copy of the Order by:

_____   _____   _____
PRINT NAME   TIME AND DATE   SIGNATURE / BADGE NO. / DEPT.

☐ I hereby certify that I served the within Order by delivering a copy to the defendant personally:

_____   _____   _____
PRINT NAME   TIME AND DATE   SIGNATURE / BADGE NO. / DEPT.

☐ I hereby certify that I served the within Order by use of substituted service as follows:

_____   _____   _____
PRINT NAME   TIME AND DATE   SIGNATURE / BADGE NO. / DEPT.

☐ Defendant could not be served (explain): _____

_____

_____

_____   _____   _____
PRINT NAME   TIME AND DATE   SIGNATURE / BADGE NO. / DEPT.

Defendant hereby acknowledges receipt of the Restraining Order. I understand that pursuant to this court Order, I am not to have any contact with the named plaintiff even if plaintiff agrees to the contact or invites me onto the premises and that I can be arrested and prosecuted if I violate this Order. I understand that pursuant to *N.J.S.A.* 53:1-15 any person against whom a Final Restraining Order in a domestic violence matter has been entered shall submit to fingerprinting and other identification procedures as required by law and **I HAVE BEEN ADVISED THAT I MUST SUBMIT TO FINGERPRINTING AND OTHER IDENTIFICATION PROCEDURES.**

SIGNATURE: _____   TIME / DATE: _____

The courthouse is accessible to those with disabilities. Please notify the court if you will require assistance.

DISTRIBUTION: FAMILY PART,   PLAINTIFF,   DEFENDANT,   SHERIFF,   OTHER _____   AOC 7/04

APPENDIX S

POWER AND CONTROL

PHYSICAL **V I O L E N C E** **SEXUAL**

USE COERCION AND THREATS
- make threats to hurt her
- make her drop charges
- make her do illegal things • threaten to leave her, to commit suicide, to report her to welfare

USE INTIMIDATION
- make her afraid
- smash things
- display weapons
- destroy property
- abuse pets

USE EMOTIONAL ABUSE
- put her down • make her feel bad and guilty • call her names • humiliate her
- make her think she is crazy
- play mind games

USE ECONOMIC ABUSE
- prevent her from a job • make her ask for money • give her an allowance • not let her know about or have access to family income • take her money

USE ISOLATION
- control what she does, who she sees and talks to, what she reads, where she goes
- limits her outside involvement • use jealousy to justify actions

USE MALE PRIVILEGE
- be the one to define men's and women's roles • make all the big decisions • treat her like a servant • act like the master of the castle

USE CHILDREN
- make her feel guilty about the children • use the children to relay messages • use visitation to harass her • threaten to take the children away

DENY, BLAME & MINIMIZE
- make light of the abuse • not take her concerns seriously • say the abuse didn't happen
- shift the responsibility
- say she caused it

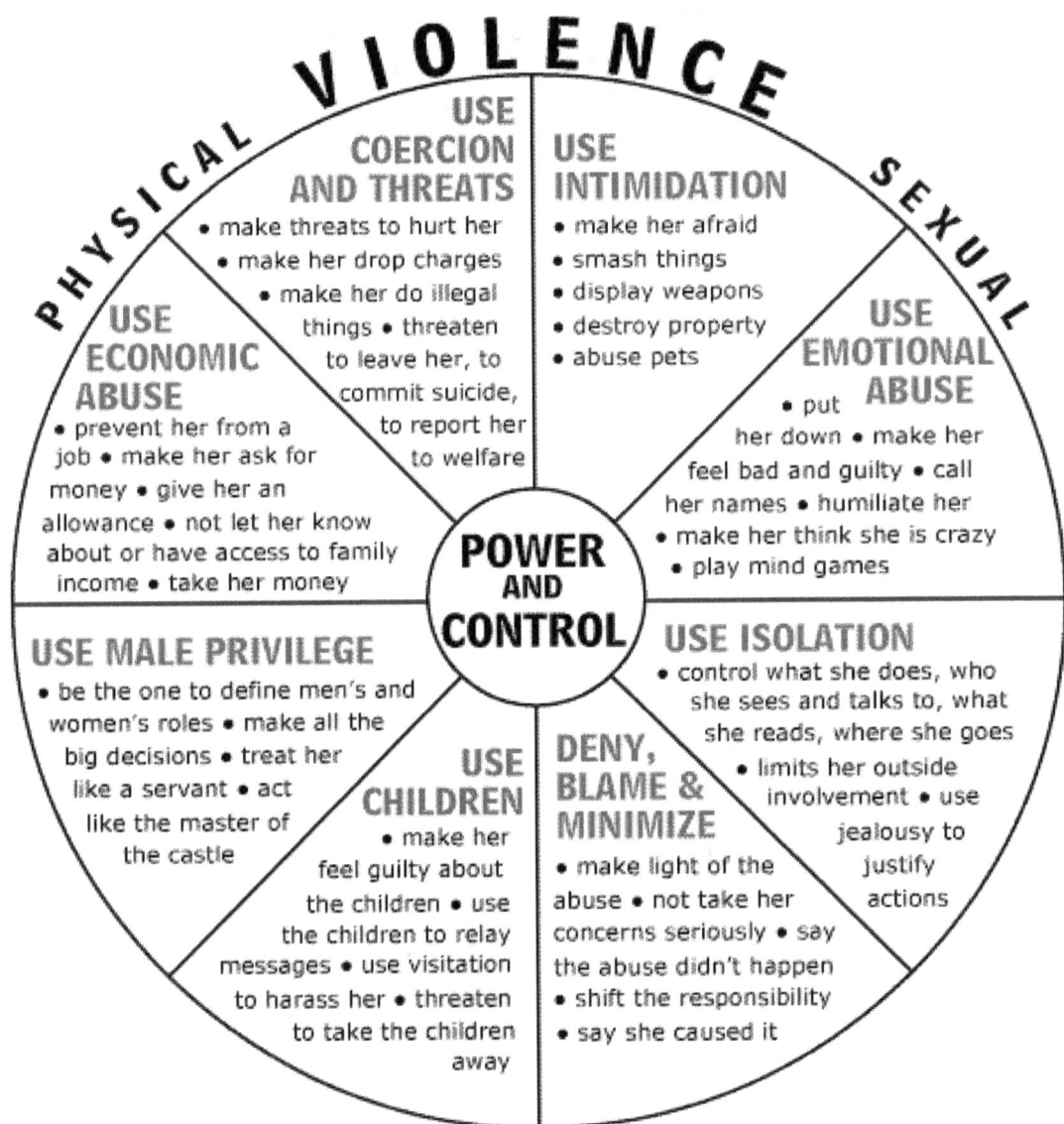

Adapted from
Domestic Abuse Intervention Project
206 West Fourth Street
Duluth, MN 55806

APPENDIX T

PROFILE OF MEN WHO BATTER

Listening to victims of domestic violence, I became aware that there was a great deal of similarity in the experiences that they relate. Yet each woman believed she was the only person to experience such atrocities. As certain elements were repeated over and over, the following profile emerged:

1. <u>Jealousy of Partner</u>. Men who batter almost routinely accuse their partners of having other sexual relationships. Slight evidence is sufficient to fire their imaginations. A van parked across the street was proof enough for one client's partner. Another accused his wife of fellatio with another whenever she suffered influenza symptoms. Such intensely irrational jealousy may arise from the man's own insecurities and projecting. He may be having sexual liaisons outside their primary bond himself. Objectification of women is a third contributing factor.

2. <u>Control and Isolation of Partner.</u> Perpetrators of domestic violence will go to extreme lengths to isolate and control their partners. One woman was not permitted to go into her back yard because her husband called every hour or two. If she did not answer on the first ring, she might have been beaten. Nor could she talk with anyone else by phone, because her husband could hear a busy signal. This woman, like many others, was not permitted to go anywhere alone. Counselors repeatedly hear about this kind of severe isolation. While the male who batters tends to be a loner, he enjoys the company of his own friends and family: Neither is permitted to her.

3. <u>Jekyll and Hyde Personalities</u>. Men who have a problem with violence exhibit drastic personality changes. Much of the time they are gentle and loving husbands and fathers. This is the personality with which the women fell in love originally and continues to love. Periodically, sometimes in rather predictable cycles, he seems to metamorphize into an ogre. Some men display their Dr. Jekyll side to the public consistently. Mr. Hyde only emerges at home. This is doubly treacherous to the partner because others do not believe her when she speaks of his monstrous acts.

4. <u>Explosive Temper.</u> A most trivial happening such as failure to balance a checkbook or burning the toast can trigger a beating. In other cases there is no apparent precipitating event. Many women have been pulled from bed while sleeping soundly and beaten. A frequent response of the victim is to attempt to be the perfect wife and mother.

5.   Legal Problems. The Illinois Coalition Against Domestic Violence explored the circumstances of abusers whose victims took refuse in shelters in July and August of 1981. Fifty-six percent have been involved with the law because of their violent behaviors. Arrest records from other areas of their lives are not uncommon (Safman, 1982). This high percentage may represent a shelter bias.

6.   Projection. A man who batters is a master at blaming other people and external events for his own behavior. A lifelong partner of avoiding the consequences for his behavior effectively limits his sense of personal responsibility for his destructiveness as well as suppresses any motivation or change. The partner becomes a surrogate punching bag. Therefore, when a battered woman says, "he needs me," she is right in one sense; if he can project his faults onto her, thereby not having to deal with himself, he is able to perpetuate his own blameless state.

7.   Verbal as well as Physical Abuse. An enormous amount of verbal abuse accompanies physical abuse. A barrage of derogatory labels such as "stupid bitch" - - "ugly slut" - - "cheap whore" are heaped upon the victim. Mind games are rampant. Some verbal abuse is less obvious to the abused party. It can be so subtle in fact that the woman is unable to identify the intent of the words. She accepts this judgment that her housekeeping is so sloppy, her child care lax, and she is a hopelessly, unappealing drudge; her self-esteem slips even lower.

8.   A History of Family Violence. Forty-two percent of the abusers of those victims interviewed by the Illinois Coalition Against Domestic Violence were abused as children. Fifty-three percent had seen violence in their homes. Of those who had witnessed violence, seventy-five percent had seen their fathers beat their mothers. To researchers these findings indicate that battering is a problem both for families and for society generally (Safman, 1982).

9.   More Violent When Partner is Pregnant or Soon After She Gives Birth. More shocking to observers than the other characteristics is the observation that the batterer is more violent when the partner is pregnant or soon after the birth of their child. Men who batter seem to want to impregnate, yet not necessarily to father or nurture their offspring. It is not unusual for them to tamper with their partner's birth control measures; to assert they had vasectomies when they have not. A reoccurring theme is: "If you would have my baby, or one more baby, then our problems would abate." Yet wife beating has been called "the poor

man's abortion." Women have had miscarriages or stillbirths after savage attacks by their mates.

10. Denial. "I didn't hit her" or "I just pushed her a little bit" are almost universally uttered denials. Sometimes awareness of his own behavior is so totally repressed that he will notice his partners injury that he inflicted the previous evening and ask, "What happened to you?" Indeed one of the most crucial aspects of treatment for men who batter is to help them get in touch with their violence. When they acknowledge the truth of their past behavior they may encounter within themselves a backlog of guilt and revulsion of themselves, so overwhelming that they either fall into a depression or regress into deeper denial. (Everette, 1980).

11. Cycle of Violence and Contrition. Often it seems that the male who batters purposely is trying to drive away his partner. When he succeeds, he will go to great lengths to retrieve her. He may abduct the children; cry real tears; plead; bring flowers; promise to go to counseling every day ("if that is what it takes"); vow to stop drinking; and tell her that he needs her and cannot survive without her. These actions are very convincing. Each time she leaves, then returns, the cycle can escalate. The violence can become more severe; the contrition state can become craftier or disappear. She, sadly, reinforces his behavior by believing him and attempting to resume her life with him.

> This is an excerpt from Wetzel, Laura and Ross, Mary Anne, "Psychological and Social Ramifications of Battering; Observations Leading to a Counseling Methodology for Victims of Domestic Violence, "from Personnel & Guidance Journal, V61 N7, P423-28, March 1983.

APPENDIX U

GENDER MOTIVATED STATUTES.

In August 1994, Congress passed the Violent Crime Control and Law Enforcement act of 1994.[574] Title IV of the Act is entitled the Violence Against Women[575], which contains Subtitle B, Safe Homes for Women576, focuses on crimes of domestic violence. The Act supports the State laws and provides further protections for victims of domestic violence. A few of the pertinent portions of the Act are outlined below.577

42 *U.S.C.* 40221 INTERSTATE ENFORCEMENT (Public Law 103-322, Title IV, 40221 (a) (Amends Part 1 of 18 USC 110)

"Chapter 110A-Domestic Violence"

(a) OFFENSES

(1) CROSSING A STATE LINE. -A person who travels across a State line or enters or leave Indian Country with the intent to injure, harass, or intimidate that person's spouse or intimate partner, and who, in the course of or as a result of such travel, intentionally commits a crime of violence and thereby causes bodily injury to such spouse or intimate partner, shall be punished as provided in subsection (b).

(2) CAUSING THE CROSSING OF A STATE LINE. A person who causes a spouse or intimate partner to cross a State line or to enter or leave Indian County by force, coercion, duress, or fraud and, in the course or as a result of that conduct, intentional commits a crime of violence and thereby causes bodily injury to the person's spouse or intimate partner, shall be punished as provided in subsection (b).

(b) PENALTIES. A person who violates this section shall be fined under this title, imprisoned.

(1) for life or any term of years, if death of the offender's spouse or intimate partner results;

(2) for not more than 20 years if permanent disfigurement or life threatening bodily

---

[574] 42 *U.S.C.* 13701.
[575] 42 *U.S.C.* 40101.
[576] 42 *U.S.C.* 40201.
[577] 42 *U.S.C.* 40221 INTERSTATE ENFORCEMENT (Public Law 103-322, Title IV, 40221 (a) (Amends Part 1 of 18 USC 110).

injury to the offenders spouse or intimate partner results;

(3) for not more than 10 years, if serious bodily injury to the offender's spouse or intimate partner results or if the offender uses a dangerous weapon during the offense;

(4) as provided for the applicable conduct under chapter 109A if the offense would constitute an offense under chapter 109A (without regard to whether the offense was committed in the special maritime and territorial jurisdiction of the United States or in a Federal prison); and

(5) for not more than 5 years, in any other case, or both fined and imprisoned.

Sec. 2262. Interstate Violation of Protection Order

(a) Offenses.-

(1) CROSSING A STATE LINE.-A person who travels across a State line or enters or leaves Indian country with the intent to engage in conduct that-

(A) (i) violates the portion of a protection order that involves protection against credible threats of violence, repeated harassment, or bodily injury to the person or persons for whom the protection order was issued; or

(ii) would violate subparagraph (A) if the conduct occurred in the jurisdiction in which the order was issued; and

(B) Subsequently engages in such conduct, shall be punished as provided in subsection (b).

(2) CAUSING THE CROSSING OF A STATE LINE.-A person who causes a spouse or intimate partner to cross a State line or to enter or leave Indian country by force, coercion, duress, or fraud, and, in the course or as a result of that conduct, intentionally commits an act that injures the person's spouse or intimate partner in violation of a valid protection order issued by a State shall be punished as provided in subsection (b).

(b) PENALTIES.-A person who violates this section shall be fined under this title, imprisoned-

(1) for life or any term of years, if death of the offender's spouse or intimate partner

results;

(2) for not more than 20 years if permanent disfigurement or life threatening bodily injury to the offender's spouse or intimate partner results;

(3) for not more than 10 years, if serious bodily injury to the offender's spouse or intimate partner results or if the offender uses a dangerous weapon during the offense;

(4) as provided for the applicable conduct under chapter 109A if the offense would constitute an offense under chapter 109A (without regard to whether the offense was committed in the special maritime and territorial jurisdiction of the United States or in a Federal prison); and

(5) for not more than 5 years, in any other case, or both fined and imprisoned.

Sec. 2263. PRETRIAL RELEASE OF DEFENDANT

In any proceeding pursuant to section 3142 for the purpose of determining whether a defendant charged under the chapter shall be released pending trial, or for the purpose of determining conditions of such release, the alleged victim shall be given an opportunity to be heard regarding the danger posed by the defendant.

Sec. 2264 RESTITUTION

(a) IN GENERAL.- Notwithstanding section 3663, and in addition to any other civil or criminal penalty authorized by law, the court shall order restitution for any offense under the chapter.

(b) SCOPE AND NATURE OF ORDER.-

(1) Directionality order of restitution under this section shall direct that-

(A) the defendant pay to the victim (through the appropriate court mechanism) the full amount of the victim's losses as determined by the court, pursuant to paragraph (3); and

(B) the United States Attorney enforce the restitution order by all available and reasonable means.

(2) ENFORCEMENT BY VICTIM.-An order of restitution also may be enforced by a victim

named in the order to receive the restitution in the same manner as a judgment in a civil action.

(3) DEFINITION.-For purposes of this subsection, the term "full amount of the victim's losses' includes any costs incurred by the victim for-

(A) medical services relating to physical, psychiatric, or psychological care;

(B) physical and occupational therapy or rehabilitation;

(C) necessary transportation, temporary housing, and child care expenses;

(D) lost income;

(E) attorneys' fees, plus any costs incurred in obtaining a civil protection order; and

(F) any other losses suffered by the victim as a proximate result of the offense.

(4) ORDER MANDATORY.-

(A) The issuance of a restitution order under this section is mandatory.

(B) A court may not decline to issue an order under this section because of-

(i) the economic circumstances of the defendant; or

(ii) the fact that a victim has, or is entitled to, receive compensation for his or her injuries from the proceeds or insurance or any other source.

(i) Notwithstanding subparagraph (A), the court may take into account the economic circumstances of the defendant in determining the manner in which and the schedule according to which the restitution is to be paid.

(ii) For the purposes of this subparagraph, the term "economic circumstances" includes-

(I) the financial resources and other assets of the defendant;

(II) projected earnings, earning capacity, and other income of the defendant; and

(III) any financial obligations of the defendant, including obligations to dependents.

(D) Subparagraph (A) does not apply if-

(i) the court finds on the record that the economic circumstances of the defendant do not allow for the payment of any amount of a restitution order, and do not allow for the payment of any or some portion of the amount of a restitution order in the foreseeable future (under any reasonable schedule of payments); and

(ii) the court enters in its order the amount of the victim's losses, and provides a nominal restitution award.

(5) MORE THAN 1 OFFENDER.-When the court finds that more than 1 offender has contributed to the loss of a victim, the court may make each offender liable for payment of the full amount of restitution or may apportion liability amount the offender liable for payment of the full amount of restitution or may apportion liability amount the offenders to reflect the level of contribution and economic circumstance of each offender.

(6) MORE THAN 1 VICTIM.-When the court finds that more than 1 victim has sustained a loss requiring restitution by an offender, the court shall order full restitution of each victim but may provide for different payment schedules to reflect the economic circumstances of each victim.

(7) PAYMENT SCHEDULE. An order under this section may direct the defendant to make a single lump-sum payment or partial payments at specified intervals.

(8) SETOFF.-Any amount paid to a victim under this section shall be set off against any amount later recovered as compensatory damages by the victim from the defendant in-

(A) any Federal civil proceeding; and

(B) any State civil proceeding, to the extent provided by the law of the State.

(9) EFFECT ON OTHER SOURCES OF COMPENSATION.-The issuance of a restitution order shall not affect the entitlement of a victim to receive compensation with respect to a loss from insurance or any other source until the payments actually received by the victim under the restitution order fully compensate the victim for the loss.

(10) CONDITION OF PROBATION OR SUPERVISED RELEASE.-Compliance with a restitution order issued under the section shall be a condition of any probation or SUPERVISED

release of a defendant. If an offender fails to comply with a restitution order, the court may, after a hearing, revoke probation or a term of SUPERVISED release, modify the terms or conditions of probation or a term of SUPERVISED release, or hold the defendant in contempt pursuant to section 3583 (e). In determining whether to revoke probation or a term of supervised release, modify the terms or conditions of a probation or supervised release or hold a defendant serving a term of supervised release in contempt, the court shall consider the defendant's employment status, earning ability and financial resources, the willfulness of the defendant's failure to comply, and any other circumstances that may have a bearing on the defendant's ability to comply.

(c) **AFFIDAVIT**.-Within 60 days after conviction and, in any event, not later than 10 days before sentencing, the United States Attorney (or such Attorney delegate), after consulting with the victim, shall prepare the file an affidavit with the court listing the amounts subject to restitution under this section. The affidavit shall be signed by the United States Attorney (or other delegate) and the victim. Should the victim object to any of the information included in the affidavit, the United States Attorney (or the delegate) shall advise the victim that the victim may file a separate affidavit and assist the victim in the preparation of the affidavit.

(d) **OBJECTION**.-If, after the defendant has been notified of the affidavit, no objection is raised by the defendant, the amounts attested to in the affidavit filed pursuant to subsection (a) shall be entered in the court's restitution order. If objection is raised, the court may require the victim or the United States Attorney (or the United States Attorney's delegate) to submit further affidavits or other supporting documents, demonstrating the victim's losses.

(e) **ADDITIONAL DOCUMENTATION AND TESTIMONY**.-If the court concludes, after reviewing the supporting documentation and considering the defendant's objections, that there is a substantial reason for doubting the authenticity or veracity of the records submitted, the court may require additional documentation or hear testimony on those questions. The privacy of any records filed, or testimony heard, pursuant to this section, shall be maintained to the greatest extent possible, and such records may be filed or testimony herd in camera.

(f) **FINAL DETERMINATION OF LOSSES**.-If the victim's losses are not ascertainable 10 days before sentencing as provided in subsection_, the United States Attorney (or the United States Attorney delegate) shall so inform the court, and the court shall set a date for the final determination of the victim's losses, not to exceed 90 days after sentencing. If the victim subsequently discovers further losses, the victim shall have 90 days after discovery of those losses in which to petition the court for an amended restitution order. Such order may be granted only upon a showing of good cause for the failure to include such losses in the initial claim for restitutionary relief.

(g) **RESTITUTION IN ADDITION TO PUNISHMENT**.-An award of restitution to the victim of an offense under this chapter is not a substitute for imposition of punishment under this chapter.

Sec.2265. FULL FAITH AND CREDIT GIVEN TO PROTECTION ORDERS

(a) **FULL FAITH AND CREDIT**.-Any protection order issued that is consistent with subsection (9b) of this section by the court of one Sate or Indian tribe (the issuing State or Indian tribe) shall be accorded full faith and credit by the court of another State or Indian tribe (the enforcing State or Indian tribe) and enforced as if it were the order of the enforcing State or tribe.

(b) **PROTECTION ORDER**.-A protection order issued by a State or tribal court is consistent with this subsection if-

(1) such court has jurisdiction over the parties and matter under the law of such State or Indian tribe; and

(2) reasonable notice and opportunity to be heard is given to the person against whom the order is sought sufficient to protect that person's right to due process. In the case of ex parte orders, notice and opportunity to be heard must be provided within the time required by State or tribal law, and in any event within a reasonable time after the order is issued, sufficient to protect the respondent's due process rights.

(c) **CROSS OR COUNTER PETITION**.-A protection order issued by a State or tribal court against one who has petitioned, filed a complaint, or otherwise filed a written pleading for protection against abuse by a spouse or intimate partner is not entitled to full faith and credit if-

(1) no cross or counter petition, complaint, or other written pleading was filed seeking such a protection order; or

(2) a cross or counter petition has been filed and the court did not make specific findings that each party was entitled to such an order.

Sec. 2266. DEFINITIONS

In this chapter-

"Bodily injury means any act, except one done in self defense, that results in physical injury or sexual abuse.

"Indian country' has the meaning stated in section 1151.

"protection order' includes any injunction or other order issued for the purpose of preventing violent or threatening acts or harassment against, or contact or communication with or physical proximity to, another person, including temporary and final orders issued by civil and criminal courts (other than support or child custody orders) whether obtained by filing an independent action or as a pendente lite order in another proceeding so long as any civil order was issued in response to a complaint, petition or motion filed by or on behalf of a person seeking protection."

"Spouse or intimate partner' includes-

(A)   a spouse, a former spouse, a person who shares a child in common with the abuser, and a person who cohabits or has cohabited with the abuser as a spouse; and

(B)   any other person similarly situated to a spouse who is protected by the domestic or family violence laws of the State n which the injury occurred or where the victim resides.

"State' includes a State of the United States, the District of Columbia, a commonwealth, territory, or possession of the United States.

"Travel across State lines' does not include travel across State lines by an individual who is a member or an Indian tribe of which the individual is a member."

42 U.S.C. 13951 CONFIDENTIALITY FOR ABUSED PERSONS

The United States Postal Service is mandated under this section to promulgate regulations to secure the confidentiality of domestic violence shelters and abused persons addresses. This will be accomplished by the individual by the presentation of a valid protection order to the post office. For the domestic violence shelters proof must be submitted to the postal authority from a State domestic violence coalition that meets the requirements of section 311 of the Family Violence Prevention and Services Act (42 USC 10410) verifying that the organization is a domestic violence shelter.

This does not prohibit the disclosure of addresses to State or Federal agencies for legitimate law enforcement or other governmental purposes.

See also: 18 U.S.C. 921 which prohibits any person who is subject to a domestic violence protection order to "...ship or transport in interstate or foreign commerce or possess in or affecting commerce, any firearm or ammunition which has been transported in interstate or foreign commerce."

Also, see: 18 U.S.C. 922(d)(8) which makes it unlawful for any person to sell or otherwise dispose of any firearm or ammunition to any person who the know or have reasonable cause to believe is subject to a domestic violence protection order.

TABLE OF CASES-ALPHABETICAL

ASSAULT

BIFURCATION

BURDEN OF PROOF

BURGLARY

COMPLAINT

CONDITIONS OF SENTENCE

CONFIDENTIALITY

CONSOLIDATION

CONSTITUTIONALITY

CONSTRUCTION

CONTEMPT

CONTINUATION OF ORDER

COUNSEL FEES

COUNTERCLAIM

CRIMINAL RECORD

CRIMINAL RESTRAINT

DOUBLE JEOPARDY

EARLY HEARING

ENFORCEMENT

EXPUNGEMENT

HARASSMENT

HEARING

HOMICIDE

HOUSEHOLD MEMBER & VICTIM

IMMUNITY AND IMMUNITY FROM SUIT

IMPEACHMENT

INDEFINITE TEMPORARY RESTRAINING ORDER

INSURANCE

INTEREST OR BIAS

JURISDICTIONAL DETERMINATION

KIDNAPPING

PURPOSE OF ACT

RECONCILIATION

RES JUDICATA

RESTRAINTS FROM CONTACT

RESTRAINTS FROM RESIDENCE

RESTRAINTS FROM SPECIFIED LOCATION

RETURN OF WEAPONS

SEIZURE OF MARIJUANA

SENTENCING

SEVERANCE OF CLAIMS

SEXUAL ASSAULT

SHELTERED IN STATE

SUPERVISED VISITATION

SUPPORT

TORT CLAIM

TORT IMMUNITY

TIMELINESS OF PROCEEDINGS

UNEMANCIPATED MINOR

UNEMPLOYMENT BENEFITS-DENIED

VACATION OF ORDER

VICTIM OF DOMESTIC VIOLENCE

VISITATION RIGHTS

WEAPONS

www.ingramcontent.com/pod-product-compliance
Lightning Source LLC
Chambersburg PA
CBHW080242030426
42334CB00023BA/2666